Television as a Social Issue

Applied
Social Psychology
Annual
Volume 8

Editorial Advisory Board and Special Reviewers

Andrew Baum, Uniformed Services University of the Health Sciences
Leonard Bickman, Vanderbilt University
Robert B. Cialdini, Arizona State University
Norman T. Feather, Flinders University, South Australia
Joel Goldstein, National Institute of Mental Health
Hilde T. Himmelweit, London School of Economics and Political Science
Lois W. Hoffman, University of Michigan
Arthur J. Kendall, U.S. General Accounting Office
Charles A. Kiesler, Vanderbilt University
Gerardo Marin, University of San Francisco
Stephan Mayer, Oberlin College
John McConahay, Duke University
Serge Moscovici, École des Hautes Études en Sciences Sociales, Paris
Stephen D. Nelson, American Association for the Advancement of Science
Daniel Perlman, University of British Columbia
Judith Rodin, Yale University
Jeffrey Z. Rubin, Tufts University
Leonard Saxe, Boston University
M. Brewster Smith, University of California, Santa Cruz
Daniel Stokols, University of California, Irvine
Sandra S. Tangri, Howard University
Jacobo A. Varela, Montevideo, Uruguay
Lawrence S. Wrightsman, University of Kansas

Publication of the APPLIED SOCIAL PSYCHOLOGY ANNUAL is sponsored by the SOCIETY FOR THE PSYCHOLOGICAL STUDY OF SOCIAL ISSUES (SPSSI), Division 9 of the American Psychological Association. Founded in 1936, SPSSI established as its goal the application of behavioral science research to major social problems of the time. Drawing upon the intellectual traditions of Kurt Lewin, his colleagues, and his successors, SPSSI has consistently sought to promote research that is socially useful and theoretically meaningful. Following these aims, SPSSI has undertaken the editorial responsibility for this annual series—focusing on the broad area where social psychological research interfaces with social issues and problems.

Indiana
Purdue
Library
Fort Wayne

HM
251
.A66
v. 8
C.2

Television as a Social Issue

Applied Social Psychology Annual 8

STUART OSKAMP, EDITOR
Claremont Graduate School

Sponsored by the Society for the
Psychological Study of Social Issues (SPSSI)

SAGE PUBLICATIONS
The Publishers of Professional Social Science
Newbury Park   Beverly Hills   London   New Delhi

Copyright © 1988 by Society for the Psychological Study of Social Issues, Inc.

All rights reserved. No part of this book may be reproduced or utilized in any form or by any means, electronic or mechanical, including photocopying, recording, or by any information storage and retrieval system, without permission in writing from the publisher.

For information address:

SAGE Publications, Inc.
2111 West Hillcrest Drive
Newbury Park, California 91320

SAGE Publications Inc.
275 South Beverly Drive
Beverly Hills
California 90212

SAGE Publications Ltd.
28 Banner Street
London EC1Y 8QE
England

SAGE PUBLICATIONS India Pvt. Ltd.
M-32 Market
Greater Kailash I
New Delhi 110 048 India

Printed in the United States of America

Library of Congress Cataloging-in-Publication Data

International Standard Book Number 0-8039-3069-0
International Standard Book Number 0-8039-3070-4 (pbk.)
International Standard Series Number 0196-4151

FIRST PRINTING

CONTENTS

PHYLLIS A. KATZ

FOREWORD

Most of the chapters in this volume were initially presented, in a briefer form, at a conference on "Television as a Social Issue" sponsored by the Society for the Psychological Study of Social Issues (SPSSI) as part of the celebration of its fiftieth anniversary. As President-Elect of SPSSI for 1985-1986, I organized the conference, and in this foreword I will briefly describe the background both of SPSSI and of the conference.

SPSSI is one of the divisions of the American Psychological Association, but is also an incorporated, nonprofit association whose membership is interdisciplinary and includes not only psychologists but also anthropologists, sociologists, social workers, and educators. When SPSSI was founded in 1936, it started with several objectives, including encouragement of research on social issues, application of this knowledge to the solution of social problems, and defense of research on controversial topics. Additionally, its founders viewed SPSSI as a social conscience for the American Psychological Association, which needed one badly at that time (and perhaps still does). The objectives are as relevant 50 years later as they were then, and the organization has not changed its goals.

Throughout its 50 years the society has been in the forefront of social action research in varying political climates. At its inception SPSSI was concerned with the depression, with labor conflicts, and with the prospect of war. Apropos of our present topic, there was also some attention directed to the effects of media. In an early newsletter, a member suggested that radio listeners' responses to propaganda be investigated. Concern was also expressed about the then growing popularity of occult radio programs—programs that confused psychology with clairvoyance.

SPSSI's major concerns in 1937 and 1938 were about war, however, and its first two published volumes were on the psychology of war and peace. On Armistice Day of 1937, SPSSI published a statement protesting the belief that war was inevitable and focusing on the negative postwar psychological effects on soldiers who had been given license to kill. Although written in 1937, this statement would have been equally relevant after the Vietnam war. In 1938, SPSSI protested the holding of the International Congress of Psychology in Vienna, which had recently been taken over by Hitler. These actions illustrate SPSSI's focus on the interface between social science and societal behavior.

The specific nature of current social issues clearly changes with the times, but over its 50 years SPSSI has often emphasized the "three Ps": peace, prejudice, and poverty. Since these problems have not yet been solved, we all still have something to work for.

Let me mention several other SPSSI accomplishments in these areas. In 1951 SPSSI organized a Committee on Intergroup Relations, which brought together a group of social scientists who reviewed research and wrote a summary statement for the Supreme Court in the *Brown v. Board of Education* decision. This was the landmark decision that legally abolished the so-called separate but equal school systems. Following this, SPSSI pressured foundations and government agencies to support research on desegregation. During the McCarthy era, SPSSI spoke out loudly for academic freedom, supported professors who were dismissed for political causes, and studied the growing anti-intellectualism of that period. In 1963 it contributed from its budget to support an Office of Equal Opportunity within the American Psychological Association. In 1964 the organization corresponded with Martin Luther King, Jr., in attempting to establish a network of social science support. In the late 1960s and 1970s SPSSI was in the forefront of the American Psychological Association in supporting previously disenfranchised groups including blacks, Hispanics, women, and gay psychologists. It gave financial and other support to these organizations and in 1972 voted to finance minority representative attendance at that year's annual convention. Many of the things that SPSSI has worked for within the American Psychological Association have become accepted practice, and our current members can be proud that SPSSI spearheaded these efforts.

Turning to the topic of this volume, television is related to social issues in at least two ways. First, the content of television influences public perception of what constitutes a social issue and what solutions are possible (the "agenda-setting" function of media). Second, many people feel that the power of the television industry to influence public behavior is itself a social issue. Among social scientists, opinions about the effects of television range from emphatically negative to ones that stress its positive benefits. There is also a small group who argue that television has had much less effect than is generally believed.

The negative effect of television most prominently discussed is the impact of frequently portrayed violence, particularly on children. In addition, both researchers and lay people have criticized the distorted view of reality that television presents, the decreased attention spans it may be causing in both children and adults, the materialistic values it presents, its perpetuation of stereotypes, and its possible relationship to the decline in children's reading scores. Other less frequently mentioned potential negative effects include an increase in adolescent eating disorders (because of unrealistic goals of slimness), decreased interest in school, increases in public fearfulness about crime, and encouragement of poor eating and health habits.

On the positive side of television's ledger, a frequently mentioned effect is increased awareness of and accessibility to world events. We have become more of a global village by instantaneously sharing important events such as the NASA Challenger tragedy or the Chernobyl disaster. Some people believe that both the civil rights movement and the women's movement were positively affected by television in its presentation of varying life-styles, which were previously unobservable to most Americans. It has also been argued that television may prevent formation of stereotypes by showing individualized portrayals of people. Many social scientists agree that television can promote social values, though the issue of how much it has done so remains an open question.

In discussing issues such as these, the perspectives of three groups are of particular interest: social scientists, the television industry, and the general public. On many controversial issues the views of these groups differ. Therefore, in this volume we have included papers not only by social science researchers, but also by television industry representatives, media critics, and public officials. Among the issues discussed here are the social functions of television, how it portrays various societal groups, how these portrayals affect behavior, what children learn from television, what holds people's attention, and how family interactions and political choices are affected by television.

Discussion of such issues raises questions that extend beyond social science into the realm of public policy. To take one example, should television networks devote more time than they now do to specific educational television for children? It has been estimated that in the United States about 1% of all commercial television viewing could be categorized as distinctly educational. In contrast, the figure is closer to 15% in Sweden and Great Britain and even higher in Japan. Would an increase to such a figure in the United States, if made involuntarily due to pressure or edict, conflict with other American values regarding regulation and censorship? Would it conflict with other beliefs we have about free enterprise? In essence, how free or regulated should television be? This volume does not finally resolve such questions, but it does raise and examine many of them with the goal of fostering fuller information and better public understanding of the issues and the answers that have been proposed.

Acknowledgments

For all of their help in organizing our conference on "Television as a Social Issue" I would like to acknowledge, with gratitude, Carol Leimas, our New York-based coordinator; Lynda Fuerstnau and Cathy Donahue from the SPSSI Central Office; Susie Siders from my office; Barbara Lee and Philip Harding of CBS for funding and assistance; the SPSSI Conference Committee (Barbara Wallston, Leonard Bickman, Dalmas Taylor, Pam Reid); and our illustrious speakers and panelists.

PART I

The Context of Television

INTRODUCTION
Stuart Oskamp

This volume is unique in several ways. First, it focuses on the social issues related to television, asking important questions about public policy regarding broadcasting. Second, it combines the views of several different interest groups: media researchers, television industry representatives, media critics, and public officials involved in regulation of public communication. Third, it focuses on a mix of topic areas. It begins with consideration of the environmental context of television, including the technological, economic, and organizational constraints under which the industry operates, the views of critics and of the public, and public policy considerations involved in regulation of the industry. Next it takes up the issue of television's portrayal of various social subgroups, such as women and ethnic minorities, and how the industry monitors such role portrayals and other program content. Then it turns to the controversial issue of violence on TV and assesses the evidence concerning its effects on viewers. The following topic presents the other side of the coin: television's potential for promoting prosocial values, and how that potential can be actualized. Finally, the volume discusses social science research on television and speculates about the future of television in terms of viewers' attitudes and behavior, technological changes, and developments in theoretical views about media effects.

With this mix of topics and authors, this volume supplements other recent sources on mass communication. For instance, there have been recent volumes on theories of mass communication (De Fleur & Ball-

Rokeach, 1982) and reviews of theories and research in the field (Comstock, 1986; McQuail, 1985). Many books have concentrated on a single topic: for example, research on what people learn from TV news (Robinson & Levy, 1986) or from television in general (Howe, 1983), public attitudes toward television (Bower, 1985), the initial impact of television when it first arrives in a community (Williams, 1986), organizational aspects of mass media (Gurevitch, Bennett, Curran, & Woollacott, 1982), and how children use and learn from television (Bryant & Anderson, 1983; Dorr, 1986). There are other volumes that deal with various aspects of social issues in the media (e.g., Howitt, 1982). Some of these aspects include the following: whether mass media lead social change or retard it (Katz & Szecsko, 1981), problems and procedures in TV advertising (Geis, 1982), the role of minorities in the media and socialization effects of the media on minorities (Berry & Mitchell-Kernan, 1982; Wilson & Gutierrez, 1985), and the effects of television depiction of pornography and aggression (Malamuth & Donnerstein, 1984; Milavsky, Stipp, Kessler, & Rubens, 1982).

The first section of the present volume contains a wealth of background information about both the external societal factors and the internal technical factors that operate to shape the television industry and the programs we see on the air. Each section of the volume contains chapters by social science researchers who have studied the media as well as by officials of the television networks who can present an informed, practical, inside view of how and why the industry operates as it does. In addition, this section includes papers by public officials and outside critics who have given much thought to possible improvements in our television communication system.

Brief biographies of the authors appear at the end of this volume. The authors in this section have widely varied backgrounds and credentials that are relevant to the issue of television's place in society. Gloria Steinem is noted as a magazine editor, feminist speaker and activist, and social critic. Forrest Sawyer is a well-known television news reporter who, at the time of his presentation, was co-anchor for the "CBS Morning News." Ira Glasser is the Executive Director of the American Civil Liberties Union and has been a magazine editor and political and legal analyst. Donald D. Wear, an attorney, is Vice President for Policy of the CBS Broadcast Group and has had many other posts in the television industry, government, and business. Ellen Wartella is a communications researcher and professor with particular interests in children's television issues. Timothy E. Wirth is a six-term member of Congress and now U.S. Senator from Colorado, with much experience in economic and communication issues. Thomas S. Rogers served as Senior Counsel of the House of Representatives Subcommittee on Telecommunications.

Themes

A number of themes and issues appear in several of the chapters in this section. A major one is whether television's character as a mass medium necessarily requires it to seek a common denominator in programming that will attract the largest possible audiences. This mass audience goal is often criticized as producing the lowest possible denominator, ensuring mediocrity of taste and program content—a view that recalls former FCC Chairman Newton Minow's characterization of television as a "vast wasteland." Network television officials such as Wear tend to feel that serving that largest possible public is necessary and to point to ratings as the best measure of their success in pleasing the public. In contrast, students and critics of television such as Steinem, Glasser, Wartella, and Wirth decry the stereotyped content and lack of diversity in programming that this approach entails.

A central question in all of these discussions concerns television's role in society. Almost every commentator agrees that it should have a public trusteeship role, but what that means is interpreted quite differently by different individuals. Industry officials tend to view this role as giving the public what it wants, whereas critics often interpret it as giving the public what is "good for it"—such as more varied content, educational and cultural programs, and presentation of key public issues. This debate in turn raises the issue of who is to decide on television schedule content and how that decision is to be made. Can it be done through some kind of democratic process, or is it necessarily an arbitrary dictatorial procedure?

A major factor in such questions is the economic one, which frequently limits what networks and stations can or will attempt. Though the public thinks of the television industry as engaged in providing entertainment and information, an economic analysis shows that commercial television is mainly in the business of delivering audiences to advertisers. But that constraint is open to challenge also—should the bottom line necessarily rule decisions? To loosen that constraint, many suggestions have been made for innovative ways of providing and funding higher quality programming, some of which are described in the chapters by Wirth, Rogers, and Wartella.

Another constraint on the television industry is government regulation, and the desirable amount of such regulation is a highly controversial topic. Industry representatives such as Wear complain of an oppressive amount of precise and petty regulations that unnecessarily restrict their freedom of action, whereas regulators such as Rogers claim that very few restrictions at all remain in this era of deregulation. One well-known government rule, called the Fairness Doctrine, requires the broadcast media (unlike the print media) to discuss two or more sides of controversial issues that they present on the air. However, even this well-established rule is controversial and under attack, as described in the chapters by Steinem and Rogers.

Another constraint on television that is often unrecognized is that imposed by the technology of the industry, which limits some types of programs and facilitates others. Some of these considerations are graphically described in Sawyer's chapter, which presents a firsthand account of what life is like at the production end of network news programs. In addition to the technological factors, he describes how television content and procedures are limited by the contractual arrangements between the networks, affiliated stations, advertisers, and program production companies.

As a result of all of these constraints, the important question arises as to whether television correctly displays or seriously distorts the reality of our society. Various aspects of this issue are discussed in the first three chapters by Steinem, Sawyer, and Glasser. Those who believe that it does distort viewers' perception of the world around them tend to hold television at least partly responsible for some of the social ills of our society, and by the same token, to hope that it might be harnessed for beneficial ends to combat some of these problems. However, industry officials such as Wear are generally skeptical of claimed negative effects of television and also more doubtful of its hoped-for potential in remedying social ills.

Three of the major social issues involved in television programming are discussed at length in the following three sections of this volume: the prevalence of violent content on TV and its potential effects, the stereotyped role portrayals of various social groups, and the possibilities for planned prosocial programs. In addition to touching on some of these same issues, this section discusses a number of other important social issues: the low quality and lack of diversity of children's TV, and prospects for its improvement (see Wartella and Wirth); the "agenda-setting" power of television to determine what the public will think and talk about (see Steinem); its frequent overemphasis on extreme and sensationalized individual cases, and its lack of attention to overall social trends that are not sensational or "newsworthy" (see Steinem and Sawyer); its poor coverage of the issues in national elections, and its detrimental election-day emphasis on projections of election results (see Steinem and Wirth); and the need for public activism to try to combat some of these undesirable tendencies (see Steinem, Wear, Wartella, and Wirth). These and other issues are also raised in the edited excerpts from audience question-and-answer sessions that follow several of the chapters.

REFERENCES

Berry, G. L., & Mitchell-Kernan, C. (Eds.). (1982). *Television and the socialization of the minority child.* New York: Academic Press.

Bower, R. T. (1985). *The changing television audience in America.* New York: Columbia University Press.

Bryant, J., & Anderson, D. R. (Eds.). (1983). *Children's understanding of television: Research on attention and comprehension.* New York: Academic Press.

Comstock, G. (Ed.). (1986). *Public communication and behavior* (Vol. 1). New York: Academic Press.

De Fleur, M. L., & Ball-Rokeach, S. (1982). *Theories of mass communication.* New York: Longman.

Dorr, A. (1986). *Television and children: A special medium for a special audience.* Newbury Park, CA: Sage.

Geis, M. L. (1982). *The language of television advertising.* New York: Academic Press.

Gurevitch, M., Bennett, T., Curran, J., & Woollacott, J. (Eds.). (1982). *Culture, society and the media.* London, England: Methuen.

Howe, M.J.A. (1983). *Learning from television: Psychological and educational research.* New York: Academic Press.

Howitt, D. (1982). *Mass media and social change.* Oxford, England: Pergamon.

Katz, E., & Szecsko, T. (Eds.). (1981). *Mass media and social change.* Newbury Park, CA: Sage.

Malamuth, N. M., & Donnerstein, E. (Eds.). (1984). *Pornography and sexual aggression.* New York: Academic Press.

McQuail, D. (1985). Sociology of mass communication. *Annual Review of Sociology, 11,* 93-111.

Milavsky, J. R., Stipp, H. H., Kessler, R. C., & Rubens, W. S. (1982). *Television and aggression: A panel study.* New York: Academic Press.

Robinson, J. P., & Levy, M. (1986). *The main source: Learning from television news.* Newbury Park, CA: Sage.

Williams, T. M. (Ed.). (1986). *The impact of television: A natural experiment in three communities.* New York: Academic Press.

Wilson, C. C., II, & Gutierrez, F. (1985). *Minorities and media: Diversity and the end of mass communication.* Newbury Park, CA: Sage.

GLORIA STEINEM

1

SIX GREAT IDEAS THAT
TELEVISION IS MISSING

My goal in this chapter is not just to criticize television, but to suggest ways to improve it. Fortunately, that's not hard. I'll start out by briefly listing many of the problems of current television content. Then I'll give an example of how television programming can be influenced and suggest six ways in which various aspects of TV could be improved.

The question is often asked, "Should television reflect reality or lead reality?" I think that question is academic, because television is still behind reality. For instance:

- There are still about three times more men on television than women—hardly like life.
- A high proportion of victims of violence on television are women, and women are about 90% of the victims of sadistic violence—usually young, independent, sexual, or achieving women. What are we being told here?
- Even TV violence itself doesn't reflect the fact that, in real life, the most dangerous place for a female, statistically speaking, is not in the street but in her own home. She's most likely to be attacked—and if she's a child, most likely to be sexually attacked—by a male in her family or one who is accepted in her household.
- There are a few shows about black families now, and that's progress—up from invisibility—but they're all comedies, and about the poor or the middle class. Within this convention, Bill Cosby has worked a creative miracle, but his show is still a comedy. Meanwhile, the big shows about white families are melodramas about the very rich ("Dallas," "Dynasty," and so on). What's the political message here? That being rich means a lot of suffering, we wouldn't want to try it, but it's a lot of laughs to live in the ghetto?
- Needless to say, there's also a great deal about sex on television, and almost nothing about contraception. We're one of the very few industrialized democracies that advertises almost everything except contraception. Planned Parenthood, the National Organization for Women, the American College of OB-GYN, and a few others are doing their best to persuade networks to change that policy. But meanwhile, our teenagers are no more sexually active than their European counterparts, yet they have a much higher pregnancy rate.

- When it comes to TV news, more than 20 years of the civil rights movement and 15 years or so of feminism have changed some of the faces, but women of any race and men of color are still disproportionately likely to be doing soft news or sports. As for international news, it is still overwhelmingly white and male. From watching our foreign correspondents, you could go snow blind.
- Being snow blind wouldn't be a great loss for female viewers who are interested in male form over male substance. The average age of an on-camera male is still higher than that of an on-camera female, and even the rare exception, like Barbara Walters, is treated differently. She is seen as a miracle of longevity, while Dan Rather, who is the same age, is an upstart young replacement for Walter Cronkite.
- We've come a long way from the early 1970s, when hard news was not supposed to be credible if read in a female voice, but still the more authoritative the position, the fewer women. Even women doing the weather have diminished as a more scientific, meteorological style has come in.
- As for TV commercials, we hardly ever see men with any relationship to children. It's still only *women* who care about our spouses' breakfast food or our family's bathrooms. Since far more women are now in the paid labor force, this has created superwoman (not a feminist creation but an antifeminist phenomenon). Yes, some of us women are becoming the *men* we wanted to marry. The problem is that too few men are becoming the *women* they wanted to marry, and so we still have the double-role problem. There are still millions of viewers watching the ring-around-the-collar commercial, waiting for the woman to turn to her husband and say, "Why don't you wash your neck?" (Actually, I realized the other day that that was the reformist solution. The radical solution is "Why don't you wash your own shirt?" Political analysis can always go deeper!)
- In the new areas of media innovation, like rock video, so many of the groups seem to be singing along with sadism. Both cable and cassettes are bringing hardcore sadistic pornography into our living rooms, with good production values and living color. I'm grateful for the diversity of cable, but when I see valuable and frank demonstrations of breast examination, and not one prostate exam, I begin to wonder about the motives involved.

TV's Virtues—and How to Strengthen Them

I couldn't resist that little litany of problems. But in truth, I am not someone who disdains television, and I think very few people are. I watch it. I value it. I not only have great faith in its potential, I have some faith in its actuality.

- It brings us together across regionalisms and across national boundaries.

It reduces divisions based on unequal access to information, and gives us shared references.
- From the Kennedys and Martin Luther King to the space shuttle, it has saved our sanity by giving us a national ritual of mourning.
- It can expose the character of our politicians in a way print media cannot.
- It shows us the reality of war, in a way that generals and Hollywood rarely do.
- It shows the poor how the wealthy live—and vice versa—thus making the rich cautious and the poor rebellious. This is all to the good. When viewed from the ghetto, where the depression has never ended, "Lifestyles of the Rich and Famous" may be more powerful than Karl Marx.

I also have faith in the ability of citizens to make television more accurate and more helpful. It can be a much wider window on the world, and more nurturing of our hopes for what that world could be. For instance, if you're feeling powerless to affect the one-eyed monster, let me give you one small concrete example.

Three years ago, Suzanne Levine, the Managing Editor of *Ms.*, heard at a dinner party about a script called "Cagney and Lacey." Though the two women who wrote it had spent 6 years trying to get it on the air, it was just then about to become a minor TV movie. It featured two very different women, leading very different lives, but they were both detectives in New York City and they worked together as partners and friends. This was a minor revolution. There had been television stories about one woman token. There had been stories about two women fighting with each other. But there had never been two women who—like Redford and Newman—were partners and friends.

We screened the movie for real women detectives at the NYPD. They liked it, so we set up an interview with them and the *New York Times*. We talked about it on "Donahue." Most important, we wrote a *Ms.* cover story about the making of this movie and suggested that readers, if they liked it, should write and tell CBS so. It wasn't even in the right slot to become a series, but why not suggest it?

Well, the ratings were pretty good. The letters were very good, so it became a series. But, TV being what it is, "Cagney and Lacey" was put against "9 to 5," one of the few other shows about real women. Furthermore, "Cagney and Lacey" was controversial—too strong. The TV trade press and some executives insinuated that the principals might be lesbians. The show got cancelled.

The letters poured in. It was put back. It was cancelled again. The letters poured in again. The series came back. It since has won many prizes and finally been recognized as a success.

I'm told that "Cagney and Lacey" got more letters when it was canceled than either "Star Trek" or "Lou Grant." And though you still don't see too many women who are friends and colleagues on TV, there are now a few—even domestic partners, such as "Kate and Allie."

So letters work. Activism works. And so do new ideas. From the all-black "Roots" to the all-news "Sixty Minutes," ideas that were supposed to be commercial death have worked anyway. But we need pressure from the public. We need enthusiasm. And we need not just criticism, but concrete ideas for improving television—probably six of them for every one that gets carried through. So here are six ideas as a starter.

Proposals for Improving TV

(1) Presidential debates. On one side of this issue is the current discontent with the manipulation of political commercials, and the supposed bias of TV news departments. On the other side is television's great and almost untapped ability to be a national town meeting, and to expose character. After all, issues represent what a candidate is saying today, but character tells us what he or she will do tomorrow.

The League of Women Voters has done its best, but we're ready for something more; 1988 is an opportunity. For the first time since 1960 and the Kennedy-Nixon Debate and 1968 after Johnson's withdrawal, we won't have an incumbent in the White House to dictate the rules and run from the bunker. So why not ask the three networks to make an offer that sets a new framework?

For instance, three or four sessions, each with two hours of television time for the candidates, European style, with no panel of reporters to chop up the time so that a candidate may never need to go beyond his memorized issue-card. If Reagan had been locked up with his opponent for two hours with no script, would the outcome have been the same? It's a fascinating question. And this more in-depth style could sift down to other political contests.

(2) Beyond the Fairness Doctrine. There's life and a lot of good stories that are being missed beyond the Fairness Doctrine. Its principle, that there are two sides to every question, and that they both should be given attention, was a step—but not enough. It's also a gross distortion of most reality, for most questions don't have just two sides— they may have five, or ten.

The Fairness Doctrine, or the excuse of the Fairness Doctrine, has encouraged the "prize-fight school of journalism"—debates that yield heat but no light. Confrontation may sometimes make exciting television, but it often discourages honest inquiry. In general, viewers are starving for information.

Moreover, the two-sides theory has excused lazy journalism. For instance, in the nine years that the Equal Rights Amendment was debated, there was not one independent TV or major newspaper report on what it would and would not do. Such a report would not have been difficult to do. There was plenty of legislative history on congressional intent. There were even states such as Pennsylvania, where the same ERA had existed for more than a decade *without* integrating bathrooms, and *with* a strengthening of the rights of homemakers.

Yet every TV show I'm aware of was content to present one pro-ERA advocate for every anti-ERA advocate—and that was about all. CBS used to call me up and say, "Bring an anti with you." (They didn't even know one.) Only about 5% of the coverage of the ERA ever even gave the wording of the ERA. (It was simply "Equality of rights under the law not be denied or abridged by the United States or by any state on account of sex." That's all! Nothing about bathrooms, nothing about marriage, and so on.) The result of this "the sky is green" versus "the sky is blue" coverage was that, as the polls showed, news coverage of the ERA actually *increased* confusion instead of helping us to make an informed judgment. That the majority of Americans *did*—and still *do*—support the Equal Rights Amendment was due more to the massive efforts of women's groups than to the mass media.

With the issue of abortion, the problem is getting worse. On November 9, 1985, *TV Guide* published the result of a 2-year study of network evening news. It was titled "Abortion Bias: How Network Coverage Has Tilted to the Pro-Lifers" and subtitled "Even the Anti-Abortionists Acknowledge That the Nightly News Is Paying More Attention to Their Side of This Explosive Issue."

Since more than 70% of Americans do not think abortion should be criminalized, as the right-to-lifers advocate, even the 50-50 coverage of the past was a gross distortion of how we really feel. Now, apparently out of fear of a right wing that has entered the White House—or because of such regulatory anomalies as allowing dead fetuses to be shown on camera, while prohibiting autopsy shots of dead women—pro-choice *majority* views are not even getting equal time.

We need more White Papers, more independent reports—not just on foreign policy, but also on the daily issues of our lives. We are starving for information, and starving for sources we can trust.

(3) We're also starving for activism. Very few television shows display names of groups you can turn to in order to have an impact on

the issue you've just seen on the screen, or tell about books and other sources of information. Thus most shows create frustration. Selling transcripts of the show itself is all very well, but not enough.

Indeed, the video cassette boom might allow local stations to expand the impact of worthwhile shows by offering them for rental. The sponsors should also benefit from some added life for the shows—and thus for their commercials.

It's true that television is the plug-in drug. But the passivity of its form also creates a hunger for action. With some simple changes TV could help to satisfy that hunger.

(4) The power to define. The birth and change of words and phrases is both news in itself, and it defines the news. Why not an occasional TV special, a series, or a feature on our news shows that acknowledges this fact?

For instance, I think we've figured out that one person's terrorist is another person's freedom fighter, but what *is* the definition of terrorism that we're using? Violent action outside of a war zone and against noncombatants? I would agree with that, but if so, it should include firebombings of abortion clinics.

What about history? A TV special might explain that "Near" and "Far" East were near and far from what? Why, England, of course: the center of the Empire. And was this country really "discovered" when the first white man set foot on it?

Then there are daily assumptions. The term "working women" excludes homemakers, but even the Department of Labor admits they work longer hours for less pay than any other class of worker—and with more likelihood of being replaced by a *younger* worker! How about saying "salaried women" or "women who work outside the home," and "women who work at home"? Never again, if we can avoid it, should we use the term "working women."

Why not report the rise of phrases such as "battered women," "displaced homemaker," "sexual harassment"? After all, they're news. A few years ago, those things were just called "life."

Why not discuss the Orwellian potential of referring to the U.S. military budget as the "defense budget"? Why do women and people of color require journalistic adjectives while white men do not?

And how do we know, so mysteriously, that a spokes*person* is always a woman? Women have become "persons," but men are still men.

When we say "the American family" instead of "American families," don't we give the idea that there's only one form that's acceptable? In fact, there have always been many different kinds of families—rural extended families, families where grandparents raise the children—many kinds. The nuclear variety we think of, the Dick and Jane type, is mainly a function of industrialization, which took women off the farm and made them dependent on their husband's salaries. Certainly that form is in the minority now, but we still use the singular form and conjure up that image.

(5) *The other half of the news: seeing the world whole.* Men, as well as women, are asking the question, "How can I combine career and family?" But we don't hear that reported on. Fatherlessness is not just a problem of poor and disproportionately black families in this country—there is global fatherlessness. About one-third of the world's children are being raised without fathers, mainly due to economic dislocation. If we reported the connections, we might not have to "reinvent the wheel" to find solutions.

People used to say to me, "Feminism is the cause of divorce." I said, "No, marriage is the cause of divorce," and I joined in the predictions that the divorce rate would go down once we stopped making everybody feel crazy and alone if they didn't get married. Well, the divorce rate has been down for at least two years now—where are the stories about that?

I'm glad we're reporting that many Jews are unable to leave the Soviet Union, but how about the women of the Middle East who can't leave the country—and sometimes not even their houses—without patriarchal permission? And if freedom of speech is a human right, why isn't reproductive freedom a human right too? Why is what happens to men "politics," while what happens to women is "culture"?

Then there are all those series about "children of divorce." How about "children of marriage"? How can we reach valid conclusions, if we don't make essential comparisons?

Also, a little historical context would be helpful. We might understand the current wave of fundamentalism better, for instance, if we studied the similar wave that took place when our agricultural economy gave way to an industrial one.

(6) *Alternatives to violence.* Television has done a *good* job of turning us off to the romanticism of war. But it's done a *bad* job of reporting alternatives to war. Except for the people in the streets of the Philippines, and a PBS series on how the British left India, I've never seen programs that emphasized the avoidance of violence and how it was avoided—certainly no programs that explored this idea in a

systematic way that we might learn from.

Most of all, television doesn't challenge the idea that violence is inevitable, and it doesn't connect it to root causes. In fact, domestic and international violence are connected. One correlates with the other. When anthropologists study the few societies that *don't* have institutionalized violence—that don't have armies, or go to war for territory—their one shared characteristic seems to be this: sex roles are not polarized—little boys are *not* taught they must be dominant in order to be masculine, and little girls are *not* taught they must be dominated in order to be feminine. Such lessons may be the paradigm for much of the world's violence.

Olaf Palme, the world statesman we recently lost so tragically, is the only chief of state I know of who said that humanizing and depolarizing the sex roles was the deepest responsibility of every country in this delicately balanced nuclear age.

Arms control and moratoriums are vital, but we will go right on killing each other with something—chemical warfare, space stations, climate control, changing the molecular structure of crops in order to starve our enemies into submission—*something*—until we begin to pull out the roots of violence. Violence, domestic or international, is neither an inevitable nor a natural way of solving conflict. We have to have the courage to say that and to challenge the idea that it is inevitable and natural. And no TV analysis or course on foreign policy can be complete unless it includes the so-called machismo factor or "hairy-chested syndrome" (as they say in the State Department) that rewards individuals in policy meetings who offer the most aggressive solution, even when it's wrong, and penalizes those who offer the most cooperative solution, even when it's right.

So when we try to make television a *real* window on the world of possibilities—when we take off our blinders and see the world whole—we women and men of every race not only have our whole selves, our whole human possibilities, to gain. We may also have a key to survival on this fragile spaceship earth that we love so much.

QUESTIONS AND ANSWERS

Q: I would like to see more on television about the distribution of work in America, and what it means on families when people don't have work, and what we could do to redistribute work in such a way that a person working full-time has enough money to support themself and some children.

A: It's true, I think, that we have not yet even caught up with the definition of full employment that Franklin Roosevelt put forward, which was a decent job for everyone who is able to work and wants to work. We're still following the psychology of the Nixon era. You recall that President Nixon used to look only at the unemployment rate of white, married, heads of household. I guess he thought all those minority kids were not going to work anyway, and young men should be at Harvard, and never mind about women. We still rarely see in our news coverage the subgroup rates, nor do we define a living wage in terms of supporting children. Certainly the major difference between single mothers who are in poverty and women who are raising children by themselves because their husbands are working for corporations is not the presence of fathers, it's the presence of money.

Q: Since the creation of *Ms.* magazine brought a feminist magazine into American publishing, I'm curious why, in your discussion of six great ideas for television, you didn't propose a feminist channel on cable or a feminist TV news magazine?

A: It's an interesting fact that, in most countries that I have been in, new ideas and especially feminist ideas come into the culture through magazines—that's true in Japan, in Ghana, in Brazil. It seems that in democratic countries the broadcast media are too expensive, and in nondemocratic countries they're too controlled. In the U.S. I think we have not quite had the *chutzpah* to think in terms of a feminist channel, but instead we are trying to infiltrate. Perhaps you're right about the need for feminist broadcast media. Women's programming on cable now is a myth. Daytime programming has some financial advice, it has horoscopes, it has food—it can't decide what direction to take.

Lack of media access is a problem, whatever the cause may be. When the First Amendment was written in 1789, the average press was like the Guttenberg press. It could produce no more than 300 newspapers a day. So there were thousands and thousands of people who had access to presses, and you could literally have your own press and your own newspaper. Then it got to be, with technology, that only rich individuals could have them. Then, with television and newspaper chains, mostly only corporations could have access. So we lost an access that our founding fathers (indeed) thought we should have, and we have to find other means to spread our views.

Q: TV is a prime reality for many people. Do you think that there is a conspiracy or a plan, or why is television not giving fair representation to many groups of people?

A: It's not a conspiracy unless perhaps in the sense of an unconscious cultural conspiracy. It has a large economic component. It is based in cautiousness, in fear, in avoidance of controversy. For instance, until the early 1970s, divorce was represented on television as widowhood. There were shows about men and women who had been widowed, and they were supposed to represent the divorced constituency because divorce was too controversial to put on the air.

Q: Who's afraid to do things like that?

A: Television executives, and sponsors. We can tell about the case histories that we've experienced. For instance, with "Free To Be You and Me," the television show for kids, we could not get sponsors for it because it had a song called "William Wants a Doll." It took about a year, and we were turned down by General Foods and many other sponsors simply because of that song. But we didn't give up, and finally we found a sponsor.

Q: I'm puzzled by your comments on the Fairness Doctrine, since you are one who's been trying to preserve it as one of the few bits of leverage that the public has on television content.

A: I am trying to preserve it, at least until we have a better safeguard for divergent views. I just want to go beyond it.

Pornography—Regulation Versus Education

Q: Have you changed your position, or how are you reconciling the question of regulation versus education in regard to television issues such as showing extreme violence against women, or sexual use of women?

A: Mainly we have tried to educate rather than to censor, because first, we're well aware that most of the current censorship efforts are directed against us. Sex education books, feminist books, books by black authors, and so on—those are the ones that are being put out of the libraries. And second, we oppose censorship because we don't believe in prior restraint. What we're trying to do is raise the level of awareness of violence against women and pornography to at least the level of awareness of racist and Ku Klux Klan literature. It's a very activist educational effort. We're picketing, we're saying, "Don't buy from this newsstand dealer; throw these magazines out of your house; don't feel that you have to be nice to people who buy this stuff."

However, we haven't turned to legislation except in three cases that I know of. One was to try to get cable regulated when it was being treated as a privileged communication like a telephone call, and as a result you could turn on your cable set and see, as I did, a nude woman sitting in a chair with pins being put into her nipple by a man—that was in your living room! So the New York State Legislature was asked to regulate cable, that is, make it conform to the same standards as other media. The second kind of legislation was regulations against public nuisances—for instance, that you can't display sexually violent material out in the street where people can't avoid it. And the third kind of legislation was a Minneapolis ordinance, which has now been struck down. The Minneapolis ordinance did not use restraint. It did not suggest that anything could not be published; it protected the right of everything and anything to be published. It only said that, after the publication of a particular representation, if you could demonstrate that that had deprived you of your civil rights in a particular way, and prove it to a jury, you might get damages. That was all. So it seemed to me an imaginative ordinance, but it may have been poorly drawn, and in any case it has been struck down.

In dealing with sadistic pornography, we're trying to point out that not all sex and nudity is pornographic. There's pornography, and there's erotica. "Porne" means female slavery; pornography means writing about violence against women. By contrast, "eros" means love, which carries the idea of free choice and mutual pleasure. It helps if we get a grip on this difference, I think. Meanwhile the right wing, of course, is trying to get rid of *all* sex and nudity—they're censoring from their own point of view.

As another aspect of education, there is an effort to try to get some word about contraception and family planning on television—to try to publicize the problem of teenage male fatherhood as has been done for smoking—to do *something*. The American College of OB-GYN went to the networks with very discreet and good public service announcements, which were shown on the "Phil Donahue Show," but which were turned down by both ABC and CBS. And they didn't get much of a response from NBC. So they were shown on cable, and they got such a good response that NBC came back to them and paid for the development of new public service spots, which are now going to go on.

Proposed Legislation

Q: I'd like your viewpoint about the proposed Children's Television Education Act, and the possibility that it may offer more diversity in programs for children. The act requires that each television station provide 7 hours a week of educational programming for young people to make up for the decided lack of such programming now. According to a congressional hearing, there are only about 61 minutes a week now. Of the 7 required hours a week on every station, 5 hours would be on weekdays. The content of those hours would be determined by the stations.

A: My understanding is that this is constructive and desirable legislation.

Q: Would you agree with the view that commercial advertising sponsorship of television, particularly of the news, necessarily exerts a distorting, conservative effect on information on television? And what are your views on publicly supported broadcasting (not the sort of pledge-and-bake-sponsored PBS public broadcasting we see now, but something more akin to the British system of state-sponsored television)? The argument against that always is that we can't afford state-sponsored television, but that ignores the fact that we all pay, every time we buy goods and services, for commercially sponsored television.

A: I agree that commercial sponsorship has some inhibiting effect, although in a very diverse way, not necessarily conspiratorially, but in a gross glacial way. However, if the state is a sponsor, there are even greater problems of potential control. So I would not favor state-sponsored television unless we have both commercial and state-sponsored forms.

2

REALITIES OF TELEVISION
NEWS PROGRAMMING

In this chapter I want to tell you what life is like for the people who actually put on programs in television and get bloodied in the arena. I'll focus on some of the problems that we have in trying to get the news on the air.

Television news is what I do for a living. I'm a journalist by trade, and television is a craft in which I practice that training. Generally speaking, print reporters and television reporters despise one another. Print reporters look down on television reporters because they ask questions such as "How did you feel when the building fell down on you?" What print reporters don't tell you is that they ask those same things—but they don't print the questions. In television you've got the same difficulties a print reporter has in getting information, but in addition you've got a caravan that travels along with you—the cameras, the lights, and all the equipment for actually getting on the screen. You're also faced with other difficulties, because you have a particular amount of time and a particular format in which to present your material, even though the world out there doesn't come so neatly packaged.

A central fact about television is that, except for public broadcasting, which exists through charitable contributions, television is a money-making business. This is a fact with which we have to live. Television is a profit center, and it is shaped by the bottom line. Within the world of profit-making, we strive to put on journalism that is fair and accurate and has some semblance of truth. Sometimes that's hard to do.

Historically, television news was once a loss leader. It was the crown jewel that allowed the networks and television stations to put on entertainment programs and say, "Yes, we do present entertainment and, yes, we do carry away money in buckets. But look, our news operation serves the public good." In those days the news operations lost a lot of money. But through the grace and wisdom of such people as CBS's William Paley, quality news programming was put on despite the financial loss.

However, the television business has changed tremendously. Television news has now become a profit center, in fact the most significant profit center for local television stations, where it often brings in 40% of their profit. In addition, particularly in the past two years, the news business and the television business have gone through a revolution, with buy-outs and takeovers all around. CBS fought one off, ABC was taken over by Capital Cities Corp. Most of these takeovers are done with highly leveraged buy-outs. That is to say, a lot of money is borrowed. When a lot of money is borrowed, there is a lot of interest to pay, and you have to pay back the loan. You pay that back by improving your bottom line. You cut back and you cut back and you cut back. One place where you could cut back is the money that you spend to make the product that goes on the air, and that happens with television news as well as entertainment. CBS News has had many people laid off, and so has ABC News. The entire industry is going through a "streamlining." (That's the word they use. Other people call it butchering.) It's a difficult time, with a lot of people who are simply out of work. The field expanded and now it's collapsing a bit, and those are just the vagaries of the marketplace. Such changes are a given for those of us in the industry. There's nothing we can do about them except try to survive as best we can.

The fact that television news makes so much money has also caused it to change considerably. It used to be that network affiliates and the networks owned what they were putting on the air, lock, stock, and barrel. There was no alternative source, but now there is cable. On cable there is a sports channel, and the Cable News Network, and other potential cable news operations. NBC considered cable news for awhile. The satellite news channel tried for awhile before it turned belly up. Also there are a number of independent television stations that put on their own news operation, so there's a lot of news available. Only about 5 years ago people thought, "This is going to be a wonderful expansion. We are going to see broadcasting turn into narrowcasting. If you're into fishing, you'll have a fishing news channel. If you're into golf, you'll have a golf news channel." This has happened a little, but not nearly so much as expected. There's a lot of financial news on the news channels because most people seem interested in money. But for the most part, television news still exists in its current form for one reason—because of ratings.

The current news form is what you see on the evening news, what you see on cable news—the 20-30 minute window in which the news is assembled. Pieces run anywhere from 60 seconds to 4 minutes. There is research that shows that after awhile people begin to nod off, and so, following that research, television creates the sort of programs that may contribute to people having that short attention span.

The Life of a Newscaster

Let me tell you how it is when you're a working journalist and you exist in that world that I've described. Start with the evening news. Evening news, though the networks would like it to be longer, has a half hour. That's it—to tell what happened in the world that day! It actually is only about 22 minutes because of the ubiquitous commercials. The commercials come in breaks at the top and end, and three in the middle. That's the way it is on all the networks.

To plan the 22 minutes, the producer, as he sits at the center of things, says, "Well, I've got the Philippines, I've got Haiti, I've got South Africa, I've got President Reagan's fight over the defense budget, and I've got a tornado in Kansas City and Omaha. What do I do?" He says, "Well, I'll put the Philippines on first. There are two aspects to it, and I'll give this report arbitrarily a minute and a half. You've got a minute and a half, John. This other report is going to get a minute 15. You've got a minute 15 to fill a sidebar on the Philippines. Gentlemen, that's it. Go for it, and do good!"

Now, if you're a journalist out in the field, the word comes down from on high: "You've got a minute 30." If you say, "I cannot do it in a minute 30; you're a jerk!" then you're fired; you lose. So you have a minute 30 for your report. You say, "Aye, aye, aye! I've got the opposition lady. I've got Marcos screaming and yelling. I've got what the Ambassador to the United States is saying. I've got terrific sound. And I've got lots of facts. All right. I'll include them all because they're important. I can cut this Aquino sound bite. If I take the top end off, we can shorten it a little bit, and if I take the back end off, I can put it in 18 seconds. Look, what if we chopped out that middle?—we've got 16 seconds." You do this with all the sound bites. That leaves you 30 or 40 seconds for the "why" information in the story. You struggle, you labor, you cut down *single words*, until finally you have something that eases into that awful package of a minute 30, and you send it off, cussing all the way.

What you have done, despite your best efforts, is put it in such broad strokes that the subtlety is largely washed out in the glare of the floodlight. You necessarily, by honing that sound bite, have taken the sharpest and most symbolic representation of a position. You look for the greatest clarity in the two positions, and by doing that you lay them against each other in greater combat than may actually be the case. And you look for the sharpest, clearest pictures that illustrate what you have to say. In other words, everything comes out more black-and-white than the world actually is. That is caused by the fact that you don't have enough time, and you don't have enough time because of the economic structure of the entire industry. It finally comes down to the single journalist, who must struggle to try to tell the truth about what's going on out there. But to understand his or her actions and how his or her decisions are made, you have to see them against the ground of the entire industry—and that's a difficult thing to do. If we're biased toward the simplistic, if we're biased toward very short sound bites, that's because we're trying to squeeze the news into too little time.

The Results of Time Constraints

Then what happens? After awhile this format becomes a shorthand in which messages are passed—the drum beats of television. Politicians are savvy creatures. They quickly realize the best thing they can do is talk very rapidly, precisely, and to the point. You will find that the most highly trained, skilled, and schooled politicians—schooled because they sometimes go to coaches who tell them how to get publicity—when television reporters are talking to them, they know they can talk for just about 20 seconds. It's awful to talk to a politician like that! I usually carry a small cattle prod and zap him one as he gets warmed up, in order to get the real news. They've simply got their 20-second sound bites, and they give them to you that way because they've got a message that they want to put across. As a result, I think, the whole process causes people to think in those kinds of short, often simplistic, ways. It's a major problem. We need more time in television news, but right now it doesn't look like we're going to get it.

Now what about morning television? First, we've got more time, we've got two hours. It sounds like a lot of time, but in fact it's not when it comes to what I do, which is interviews. First we do a news block at the beginning of the show because people like to wake up in the morning and hear what's going on in the world. So we present the news in short, concise blocks because that's all the time that we have. We deliver our commercials, and when it finally comes down to the interview time that we have, the longest period is 5 minutes. Now when all hell is breaking loose in the Philippines, you can imagine that it's very difficult to pack all that into 5 minutes, especially when it's live and I'm not able to edit it down to 18-second sound bites. Five minutes is a long time on the evening news, but it's a painfully short time in an unedited discussion format. So we again face the terrible constraints of time, and you will find all of us are racing to get as much information in as we can.

Effects of Competition

There is another key element in television, and that is competition. I'm always amused by those people who feel that there is some sort of conspiracy among the members of the media. The truth is, we are a vile pack of rabble who will do anything, almost, to beat the opposition. We go to great lengths in competition, partly because it's fun and partly because we live in fear that the other guy is going to get a piece of information that we don't have. It's a competitive business. That's healthy in the sense that it causes people to spend more in order to give you better technological coverage, and it causes people to be better at what they do. But it is also dangerous when it leads to excess.

Here's a story that happened to me, which illustrates the terrible ironies under which we live. For two years I covered the Atlanta child murder stories. On many Friday afternoons for two years a Code 100 would sound in the station. Somebody would come in and say it very quietly; that meant a body had been found. For some reason, it was usually found around 5 o'clock in the afternoon. Our program went on at 6 o'clock, so we would go rushing over to cover it. One day I was dispatched to a place called Red Wine Road, where there were two sections of road with the same name. We took a gamble on which way to go. Only one camera crew was sent—I asked for another camera crew, but I didn't get it. We picked the wrong entrance, so I said, "Stop the truck and I'll ask directions." I'd already given the camera crew instructions to set up the live shot and be ready to go on the air because it was very close to 6 o'clock. After I asked directions to the other spot, I turned around and the truck was gone. They were busily setting up the live shot 150 yards down the way. I began screaming, "Come back, come back!" So we started running desperately, we got in the truck, and we went hauling over to the other part of Red Wine Road, where everybody else was already set up—cable was there and the other networks, but we were a long way from ready. They got on the air on the hour at 6 o'clock; we got on the air at 6:23—it's embedded in my memory! Of course I felt it was the fault of only having one camera crew, but I was told very clearly that it was my fault. Even if they send you out with just a super 8mm camera, you should still beat the competition.

Then there came another occasion, when the announcement of the identity of a young murder victim was to be made. I said, "I need two camera crews. If you don't give me two camera crews, we will lose, and it will be your fault." I got two camera crews, so I positioned one below and one above. When the announcement was made, I left as soon as the name was given, went downstairs, and was on the air live first.

Now, that was a small victory, which has no basic importance. Its only significance is in showing that this is a competitive business, where we want to defeat our neighbor psychologically. We're playing war. And we're often playing war at the same time that a terrible tragedy is taking place in front of our cameras. In cases like that we lose our perspective.

We're even more lost when people don't know their business, and I'll tell you about a young man who didn't. He probably shouldn't still be working in the business, but he is. An announcement was made to members of the media about the name of a young man whose body had been found. His parents didn't know about it yet. The police always went to tell them, which is a hard thing to do, as you can imagine. But this young reporter arrived at the house before the police did. He walked up and knocked on the door of the old gentleman who was the victim's grandfather. He opened the door and said, "What do you have to say about the fact that your grandson's body has been found?" The grandfather reeled back in horror. Now if you had any sense, of course you would go away. You would apologize profusely and feel revulsion at what your job had caused you to do. But this young man thought he had a scoop. So he said, "I'll tell you what. Why don't we go inside, and we'll watch the news together?" And he filmed the grandfather watching the newscast. That is excess in competition!

I have seen, in the FBI building in Atlanta, a hostage being wheeled out who had been shot by a man who was holed up in there and a reporter lurching forward with a microphone saying, "Please, can you tell me what happened in there?" And of course, "How do you feel?" That's the excess of competition!

Other Pressures on Television News

You often hear the phrase "agony quotient." If you're going to put something on the air, you want people to watch. And if it doesn't have a sufficient emotional agony quotient, they aren't going to watch. For instance, the advance of high tech in our country is a great story, but you won't see it covered to the same extent as other kinds of issues that are more compelling emotionally. People seem to be drawn toward more human events, and those are the ones that we cover more.

Money is a major pressure. Prime-time documentaries have faded, in large measure because they don't draw nearly as high ratings. The news divisions of all three networks are experimenting with ways that they can hold their costs under their income based on the ratings, so that they can survive in what is a desperately competitive entertainment world.

Because of all these pressures, I think that sometimes television news coverage tends to be too crisis oriented. We heard too little about what was happening in the Philippines leading up to the revolution, quite a bit about what happened during the revolution, and not very much about what happened after the revolution—again, a function of time and of the fact that we cover only the events that are breaking.

I'm not sure in what direction the evolution of television is carrying us. I can tell you that there are good spirited people, highly skilled people, people who care a great deal, who are trying desperately to wrestle with the contradictions of all this. But that's an almost impossible job.

When you look at the television screen and you assess what is in one program or in one reporter's piece, I would ask that you have a certain amount of compassion, because behind that report there is probably a very well-trained person doing the best that he or she can under some very difficult circumstances.

QUESTIONS AND ANSWERS

Q: To me, it's a sad tale that you tell. You pointed out that the financial structure of the whole industry militates against an individual journalist trying to do a good job. You referred to the role of profit-making in television, but said that within the world of profit-making people want to make good TV. By contrast, I would like to emphasize that, historically and legally, television operates in this country as a public trusteeship, and it should make money primarily in order to sustain good programming. Or, stated differently, a television station manager is both a public trustee and a businessman. Do you think that may be a conflict of interest?

A: If I weight the scales more heavily on either side, I don't mean to. I don't quarrel with the idea of television being a profit-making center. The fact that it is, and the fact that it has been so successful, allows me to exist, and it sustains the quality of television news coverage, which I think is extremely high. I'm very proud of it. The fact that it's a profit-making operation is, in the long run, good because it pays for what is an enormously expensive endeavor.

Now you want to say, "It makes money so that you can produce good TV. That money should be funneled back into it." And in a large measure it is. We are a capital-intensive business, and the money keeps rolling over. There are things called KU-band trucks that are coming in now, trucks that travel around and send a beam up to a satellite and back down again, so you can go live from virtually anywhere. The technology of the business is changing incredibly rapidly. We are in ¾-inch tape now. We will soon be in ½-inch tape with high resolution. That's very, very expensive.

I'm not sure that there is a conflict of interest between public trusteeship and making money. If you argue that there is a conflict of interest that should not be allowed to exist, then everything in television should be public. Now if everything were public—and I have seen public television stations and in fact worked in one—I can tell you, you wouldn't have the quality in television that you have right now. So if this is a conflict of interest that we can't endure, then we're in big trouble. If there is merely a tension and a potential contradiction, which I accept, I would argue that that's only one of many tensions that exist in a very volatile industry. One of the reasons that so many contradictions exist from moment to moment is that this industry changes so rapidly. Historically, I think people who work in the industry have taken its public trusteeship very seriously, but to the extent that some operations do not, I agree that there can be a serious problem.

How Should the News Be Structured?

Q: About the problems that you see in putting together the evening news: Do those problems apply to the "MacNeil-Lehrer Report"? If not why not, and why aren't their practices, their approach in gathering and reporting the news, adopted in commercial programming?

A: The reason that they're not adopted in commercial television is that not very many people watch that program. That doesn't mean that it isn't an excellent program. I think it is. However, its audience is minuscule in comparison to the audience that Dan Rather has (about 3 million compared with about 30 million). Furthermore, they have a longer period of time to explore a few issues. That's their choice. By the same token, "Nightline" with Ted Koppel chooses to explore one or two issues. In fact, *that* has very low rating (perhaps 3-5 million viewers). The mandate for the evening news is to be a headline service, to give you the broadest possible picture of the world. We fail *every* single night, but we try to give a sense of it. We start by saying "Is the world safe?" We give the most compelling stories—maybe the Philippines and maybe South Africa and maybe Washington. We then march down from there, and when we run out of time, we cut off at the bottom.

Q: I gathered from your remarks that, as a professional journalist, you would prefer to give a good news program as MacNeil-Lehrer do? I suspect that overconcern with profits keeps people from asking how the quality could change and still allow the profits.

A: I would prefer to have more time. I would prefer to have an hour for the evening news. I think that would be wonderful. But you will find that it's the local affiliates, those stations who are working in partnership with the network, that say we can't have that half hour. So we're stuck. I would love to be able to have 2½, 3, or 4 minutes to report a major story. I'd like to have as much time as the story requires. But we're not going to get it under the current structure.

Your question is sort of basing everything on the MacNeil-Lehrer format, as if that's the "good." However, I'm impressed by a number of other television programs. Given its mandate and what it's trying to do, I'm impressed by the "CBS Evening News." I'm impressed by "Nightline." What my group tries to do in the morning is a rather different sort of thing. The form depends upon the part of day in which you exist, and upon the kind of approach that you're trying to take. I just used the evening news as an example, and I said it's very probable you could do a better job if you had an hour. I think everybody would say that.

Q: You've done a good job of making it clear how very complex the whole thing is, and how it's rooted in the very structure of the country, the way we work economically. Within that context, are there any things that could be done, for example about the agony quotient? Is there a way that the major networks could get together and say, "There are certain things that are in the public interest, and none of us will exploit violence and disasters because we're beginning to understand that we're having a profound effect upon the way our children are thinking and feeling"?

A: When I say that there's an agony quotient, that's shorthand. What it means in practice is that we've got 8-10 hours a year of documentary time available. Given that limit, we know we've got to get pretty good ratings; we have to have enough people watching to show that the public is interested in what we're saying. It's the same way with the newspapers—they're worried about their circulation. So where the agony quotient comes in is that, in choosing a topic for a documentary, we're going to choose one where people are in greater stress than somewhere else. Consequently we're more likely to look at South Africa, for instance, than at the success story of Argentina, which has come back from great problems. People are going to be more interested in the first than in the second. So the term "agony quotient" is just a shorthand for a factor that we are compelled to consider.

Q: Why does violence keep getting broadcast?

A: There are two answers. First, violence is a part of the reporting in the most responsible broadcasts. This is because the world is a violent place. When there is no more terrorism or war or murder, violence won't be such a part of the news. Second, however, some local broadcasts have overemphasized violence in their communities in the perhaps mistaken belief that this will draw more viewers. This trend appears to be waning, probably because it hasn't worked.

Q: Why are specific cases (that is, individual people's actions and problems) emphasized in news stories, so much so that generalized statistical information is overlooked?

A: You are describing a phenomenon found in some local broadcasts. They report the evening's murder or robbing without putting it in perspective. On network news, individual cases are used primarily as ways of *illustrating* general trends. Statistics are often cited to give the proper context. The problem you describe is just sloppy reporting.

Market Influences and the News

Q: Suppose that in a particular city the network evening news is followed by "The Wheel of Fortune," which obviously is another good moneymaker. Just suppose, the bottom line being the dollar, that in fact "The Wheel of Fortune" really made a lot more money, and if you ran two shows like that back to back, there would be a higher profit than in running the network evening news. Could the networks abandon the news? And if not, why not? Are we dependent on their good will? Are we simply fortunate that those 22 minutes get a pretty good market and make a lot of money?

A: A lot of independent stations do run game shows, which are very popular, opposite the evening news programs. I'll start with the networks. Would the networks do that? The answer is no, unequivocally, absolutely no. First, because all the people that I know who work for CBS News and the CBS Network do take their public trusteeship very seriously. They are very proud of the news division, and they feel that, in knocking themselves out for it every day, they are trying to do some good for the world.

Further, news is what makes the identity of the network. Without the news division, CBS would be a program delivery system. And there are a lot of those—a lot of independents, a lot of syndicates that can deliver programs. When you think of CBS, I believe you think of Dan Rather and the CBS News operation. When you think of ABC, I believe you think of Peter Jennings as representative of ABC's approach. And the same with NBC and Tom Brokaw. The news operations make the identity of the networks. So in their own self-interest, they want the news operations to flourish.

And finally, it comes down to, what is the affiliate going to do? The affiliate has local news as its profit center, and it must exist in partnership with the network news. That affiliate would not remain an affiliate very long if it even considered cutting the news back. And for its own self-interest, it would not. So in the desire to serve the public good and the desire to serve self-interest there can be a marriage.

Q: Are we fortunate then that there's a market for 22 minutes, but there just doesn't happen to be one for an hour, or 44 minutes?

A: That's not the point. I believe that there would very much be a market for it. But the local affiliate has that as its own time. They will say, "We depend on that time for our income. You network people have from 8 o'clock until 11 o'clock. If you want to, go ahead and put on another half hour of news there—that'll be fine." That struggle has gone on back and forth for decades. It's just another one of those tensions that exists, and I don't have an answer to it. The network side is, they'd *like* that half hour, and the local side is, they've *got* that half hour.

That is the local access period. In New York it's from 7:30 to 8:00, and that's when "Wheel of Fortune" is often seen, or "The Price Is Right," or whatever. Since that's owned by the local affiliate, all of the commercial time is theirs. If it were the network's programming, then the network would get to put on some of their commercials, and that revenue would simply be lost to the local station. They buy that game show at a certain rate, and their return is tremendous if it's their time period, but much less if it's network time. The reason that many stations don't want to give up the time is because they make so much more revenue. At other stations they feel that their programming is superior for their audience—for instance, high quality local news—and they may be right.

Q: What I object to in what you say is the notion that the present structure and organization of television are cast in stone. I just want to say that they're not. And the continued excesses and outrages will finally bring about a public reaction. So I think the television industry better be wary.

If we believe that a lot of things on television are bad for people, and if television's bottom line is the dollar, why aren't we boycotting it? I already do boycott it. Since I work with children, I suggest that all the time. And particularly with the VCR and home video, which put power in the hands of parents, I recommend very strongly that they strictly control what their children watch.

A: What programs do you want to boycott? Programs of violence—do you want to keep children away from those? If you're going to call for a boycott of any kind of programming, I suggest that you should name those programs you want to boycott *and* have research or evidence to show the harm that they do.

Criteria for Program Content

Q: Concerning the constraints under which you operate, I'm curious about the criteria for making journalistic decisions or editorial decisions about what goes on the program. As an illustration, take the promos for the 11 o'clock news. If you were sitting there in a group of people and deciding between two 5-second headlines, one being "Ivy League Hookers at 11:00," and the other being "Sandinistas Agree to Come to the Table at 11:00"—what would be some of the criteria for decision?

A: That's a good question, because what we *can* control in news programming is the nature of what we cover—not only what we promote, but what's in those 22 minutes. And the fact is, many television stations might want to fill those 22 minutes with a lot of robberies, or with more dead bodies than you've ever seen. That is an enormous problem in television. But I'm happy to say that at my network I don't even feel that problem, because we always begin by saying "What's the news?" I'll take any program that comes on our morning news or the evening news or the documentaries that we produce, and I'll defend our decisions as being based on news value. But even CBS News has wrestled with the blurring of news and entertainment. The news division elected to relinquish a portion of the time devoted to the "CBS Morning News" rather than embark on programming that was clearly entertainment oriented.

But I've also worked in local television, and though I always pushed for coverage of the biggest story, I can tell you that there are people who work in the news business who will say, "Well, we've got to promote things to get the ratings." There are people who are fix-it doctors, who come in to a local station that is losing ground and try to get something in there that's *hot.* "Hot" may be murder, or it may be something that will stimulate fear, because people watch that. Some local broadcasts have become notorious for emphasizing sensational stories or glib conversation between their anchors. Some news directors have hired anchors for cosmetic reasons and not for their journalistic skills. News consultants regularly offer advice to news directors on how to alter their newscasts to increase ratings, and sometimes that advice extends to editorial content. In my view this trend must be resisted, but I think that ultimately viewers get more and more sophisticated about these sorts of things, and they see that kind of hype for what it is.

Where I stand on this issue is: You've got to present the news the best way you can, make the best decisions you can, let the chips fall where they may, and try to sleep at night. News broadcasts are not entertainment. News values should determine what is included in our broadcasts. Once we begin trying to curry favor in the hope of increasing ratings, we have sacrificed both our credibility and integrity. But there are other people who don't feel that way, and they're the ones you've got to watch out for.

Q: What can the public do to help solve all these contradictions?

A: As always, an informed public can have an extraordinary impact. In fact, individuals can affect the thinking of a news department more than they realize. If you see a report that you believe is unfair or inaccurate, don't hesitate to let the news director know what you think. If you're a member of an interest group, ask your local reporters and/or news director to join a public discussion about their work. It will make them pay more attention and it will educate you.

Q: I'm thoroughly disgusted with watching the 5-minute news blocks on the late-night movies. Usually, for a week or two at a time, those 5-minute blocks will be about various aspects of one certain topic. Is that unusual?

A: What you describe is often done in local news, and again it's controversial in the industry. There are periods of the year called sweep periods or rating periods, and a lot of stations load those periods with specials or programs that have been highly publicized, which they hope will draw viewers during that period, and thereby boost their ratings. They do that because those ratings determine their future charges for commercial time. It is a form of promotion or hype. The benefit in that process for a journalist is that he gets to put a little something extra into covering a story. When I worked in local television, I usually used the opportunity to surface an investigative report that I had done and had spent a lot more time and money on than we normally would in another time period. So you can turn the system to your advantage. But I've seen series like "Dumb Dog: How Smart Is Your Pet?" and topics like sexual impotence that try to be flashy. I think it's good that longer news forms are sometimes used, and I don't mind if they're used in sweeps. The key journalistic question is what the subject matter is.

Q: In a major city, how much is one percentage point in the ratings worth in ad revenue, and how much is it worth nationally to a network?

A: I don't know. I don't think about that, honestly, and I don't want to know. It's millions and millions of dollars—big bucks. One rating point is a lot.

Q: There have been a lot of comments about quality versus profit. I want to suggest that quality versus profit is actually a false dichotomy.

I'm thinking about the view that quality is what they do on PBS, whereas what you do at CBS is simply make a profit. One could say that ratings and profits reflect what people actually like to see on TV. People don't watch MacNeil-Lehrer more because they don't like its quality. And this all bears on one aspect of the issue of television's public trust—that is, it should present programs that people like to watch.

A: I don't think that I would hold either position. If the first position is that quality is what exists on public broadcasting, because it's very serious and thoughtful about what it does, whereas what we do on the networks is not quality because it's faster paced and so on—I wouldn't agree with that at all. If, on the other hand, the position is that more people watch one and therefore it's better—I wouldn't agree with that either. The fact that 3 million or more people watch MacNeil-Lehrer tells me that it is a program that provides a powerful service. I watch it and I enjoy it. But I also watch the "CBS Evening News" and draw different sorts of information from it.

My whole point is that we should have a kind of television garden where there are a lot of different program forms that are allowed to grow. We want to have as wide a variety as possible and to have them cross-fertilize one another. It should be a marketplace of ideas, and an exciting and thrilling place to work because it is the nexus into which all of society's ideas and events come and are reflected back out again.

IRA GLASSER

3

TELEVISION AND
THE CONSTRUCTION
OF REALITY

I spend a lot of time at the American Civil Liberties Union (ACLU) dealing, among other things, with the First Amendment and issues of free speech. At the heart of much legal analysis concerning the First Amendment is the notion of the free marketplace of ideas. The media are normally thought of as the marketplace, where people come to exchange information and ideas. While that notion may work for legal analysis, it has always seemed to me that it is insufficient as a way of understanding the role of television in *constructing* reality as well as *mediating* it. I am not an expert on this, but I will give you my impressions as a social activist concerning the impact of television on public policy.

When I was growing up in the 1950s, Newton Minow was my first introduction to television criticism when he called TV "a vast wasteland." Television then was something one watched occasionally, like going to the movies. Young people today wouldn't know what to do without television, and many adults wake up and turn on the television the same way they turn on the coffee, to get them started in the morning. Clearly, the popularity of morning shows such as "Good Morning, America," which have vast audiences, indicates that they have supplemented, and in many cases replaced, the morning newspaper. Indeed, in order to compete, newspapers are beginning to look like television. *USA Today* is designed as the first television newspaper in the country. Basically, it's a headline service. It comes at you in short pulses, the way television does, and not the way print media have traditionally communicated.

The Newton Minow speech launched a whole generation of people, I among them, who focused critically on television's content. We didn't pay a whole lot of attention to the impact of the medium itself. We just treated it as a street on which information flowed—just another format, like radio, or newspapers, or magazines, or books. On television there was entertainment, to which we paid relatively little attention (because it was not focused on "serious" issues of public policy); there were commercials, to which we paid even less attention (for the same reason); and then there was the serious stuff, talk shows, where real issues were discussed. Many critics evaluated television, at least with respect to social issues, by the amount of time it gave to those kinds of "serious" shows and by their content.

I have come to think that that way of evaluating the impact of television on public policy underestimates the degree to which television *as a medium* is influential. There is something unique about television, it seems to me, that transcends its content. Here are some personal impressions related to that point.

The Power of Television

I go to sporting events quite often, and I have been struck by the number of people who now carry portable televisions with them to a game. And watch them! It's as if what they experience isn't real to them unless they're looking at it on a cathode ray tube. What's going on down on the field is just fodder for the reality, which comes through the tube. While I'm looking at the field, other people sit there and point at the screen and say, "Look what happened."

Some stadiums have put up giant television screens in place of scoreboards. They started it first in Los Angeles—where else? And now they're in Queens and other places. They're called Diamond Vision, and basically they are huge television screens that can show replays and things like that. Frequently, you're sitting at a baseball game and a batter comes up to the plate, going through all his motions such as knocking the dirt out of his spikes. You're watching it, and some guy next to you is watching the television screen, and he says, "Oh, there's Tom Seaver." "No, no, no," you say, pointing to the field, "*There's* Tom Seaver." Apparently the television screen has a sort of transcendent reality. It's almost as if you don't know what really happened unless you've seen the replay; you've got to see the replay because you cannot trust your eyes. This tendency has even overcome radio broadcasters, some of whom seem to report what they see on their television monitors, and prefer looking at them instead of the field. It is as if the television screen were more reliable, more true, more real than the field itself.

I do not think that this phenomenon is limited to sports. There's a quality to television that makes it, for many people, more real than the reality it is supposed to be mediating or bringing to us. I appear on television a fair amount, and I notice this phenomenon by the way people react to seeing me on the tube. I am hardly the West Side's answer to Robert Redford, but if I appear on the "Donahue" show in the morning, that night when I go home or the next day I'll be in the elevator of my apartment building, and people who see me every day in various states of dishevelment will get into the elevator and their eyes will widen and they will take a step back and say, "I saw you on television." I think to myself, "You saw me in the street too—more often." But they never mention that. They never say, "Gee, I was riding in a cab the other day and I saw you in the street." Now, since they saw me on television, it appears there's something really special about me; now they really have to listen to what I say. Before, if we got into a conversation in the elevator, well that was just a neighbor talking. Even if a letter to the editor is published in the *New York Times*, it's just a neighbor talking. But now that I was on television, my words have meaning and portent like an oracle who must be respected.

There's a magic to television. There's a magic to people who appear on television. And it's a magic that turns television, I think, from being a mediator of reality into a mechanism that constructs reality. It is *not* a neutral mechanism like a newspaper through which ideas flow, a street along which information passes from a source to a receiver. It is that, but it is something more. And the consequences of that are that the perception of what is real, particularly concerning social issues, is determined more and more by what people see on television—and not only on the news shows. It's a much more powerful force; it's a kind of charismatic force in itself, in the strict sociological sense of that term. Television has a magical capacity to wield influence so that, if the very same idea or words come through a different medium, they are not received or perceived in the same way.

How Television Constructs
the Public Perception of Crime
and Law Enforcement

The perception of reality is fascinating. Take an issue such as crime. Everybody talks about the epidemic of crime, and it seems to be a *fact* for everybody. It's hammered at us all day long that crime is on the rise. Not only on the television news shows, not only in the sensationalism of the stories that the 11 o'clock news chooses to give us, but also in the plethora of shows such as "Miami Vice" that are aired day after day. A member of the audience on a recent "Donahue" show gave as an example of a point he was making something that he saw on television in an entertainment show. The show was purely fiction, but for him the example was real. He was telling it as you might describe a case history. He even said "I saw this on television," and then told it as a fact from which he drew conclusions. I do not think he would have similarly cited as fact something he read in a novel.

In a survey published some time ago there was a striking example of this concerning the perception of crime. The survey asked people in Baltimore three questions: (1) Is crime increasing nationally?—90% said yes. (2) Is crime increasing in Baltimore?—80% said yes. (3) Is crime increasing in your neighborhood?—25% said yes. These are fascinating figures because they did this in a lot of different neighborhoods. They didn't pick a neighborhood where crime wasn't increasing so much, in which case the study wouldn't be interesting at all. They did it in a cross section of neighborhoods, including ones where crime was going up at a higher rate than in Baltimore in general. The true figures are nothing like 80% in Baltimore, nothing like 90% in the country. The truth is that crime statistics have been relatively flat and are even slightly down in the last few years. The big rise took place mostly between the 1960s and early 1970s (Curtis, 1985, p. 23; Walker, 1985, p. 3). But the difference in these percentages is what's interesting to me. Here you had people believing that crime, both nationally and in their city, was rising at a rate that had no relationship to the real rate, but believing it and acting on it and making social policy choices on it, and maybe making political choices and voting decisions on it. And they didn't believe their own experience, because if you focused in and asked them what was happening in their own neighborhood, they didn't think crime was increasing at anything like the rate that they thought it was increasing in the broader society.

Now where do people get their information? Well, in their own neighborhood they mostly get if from their own eyes. They get it from what they see out in the street, from anecdotes, from their own experiences, from the experiences of neighbors. It's anecdotal and impressionistic, but it's direct. Where do ordinary people get information about crime rates in Baltimore or the nation? They don't get it from attending conferences, they don't get it—most of them—by reading studies or subscribing to the victimization reports or the FBI reports. They get it impressionistically, mostly from the news and what they see on television, including the entertainment shows as well as the news shows.

Take another example in the area of crime. In this country it is generally believed that the reason that most criminals get away with crimes is because the courts let them loose or because prison sentences are short. The facts are just the opposite. In most American cities only 15% to 18% of reported felonies ever result in arrests (Silberman, 1978, p. 76; Walker, 1985, pp. 26, 102). Of that number, most people are convicted, and most go away for pretty long periods of time. There are three times as many people in prison today as there were 10 or 12 years ago, and we have the longest prison sentences of any industrialized nation in the Western world. And we've been sending more people away for longer terms in the last 10 years than ever before.

The reason why people are getting away with crimes is because we're not catching them, not because the penalties aren't long enough or the courts aren't tough enough or the conviction rates aren't high. Yet the general perception is exactly the opposite. Why is that? That is a question that one has to ask. In order to answer it, we have to figure out how people are learning these things, where these perceptions are coming from, and what role television has in creating those perceptions—not only through its news shows or talk shows where that information is formally discussed, but also through shows such as "Kojak" and "Miami Vice" and "The Untouchables" and all the other shows that have told us things about crime. In these shows, the police—and the viewers at home—always seem to know who the criminal is; but frequently the criminal justice system hampers the police and makes it difficult to prove. However, in real life, the police often do not know who committed a crime and haven't the faintest idea of where to look. As most people who have been robbed or mugged or burgled know, there are hardly ever any arrests.

Or take the issue of police making illegal searches without warrants. If I speak for the ACLU and argue against permitting illegal searches, the general public—and some politicians who know better—are often unsympathetic. "Those are technicalities; why are you getting in the way? We've got to catch these criminals." Why do people see it that way? When you probe it, you find that we can go on the MacNeil-Lehrer show or on Ted Koppel's "Nightline" and talk very analytically about the Fourth Amendment and the fact that cops shouldn't search you without there being a good reason to believe you're involved in a crime, that they have to get a warrant, and all that; and everybody nods in agreement. But the fact is, there isn't a television crime show in this country, not now, not last year, not in the last 20 years, that doesn't regularly show that the good guys are the ones who break down the door without a warrant and the ones behind the door are the bad guys. So what's the harm? Why does this nut from the ACLU keep talking about cops who make mistakes and innocent people who get their doors broken down and their houses searched?

Moreover, cops never make mistakes on those shows—they always know who's guilty before they catch them. Now of course the reality is exactly the opposite. That's why we have trials. If we knew who was guilty, we wouldn't need trials. And that's why we require search warrants—because often the police don't know who the criminals are and would, if left to their own discretion, break down a lot of wrong doors. This is not fanciful. It happens. Search warrants impel the police to focus on people who are likely suspects by requiring some evidence prior to the search. And as most competent police officials know, search warrants do not hamper effective police work. But that's not the way it's shown on television.

TV crime shows are really like *Alice in Wonderland*. What happens in *Alice in Wonderland*, you remember, is that they identify the criminal first and then they figure out the crime afterward. In television's view of the world, that gets pumped at us all day long. First we see the criminal commit the crime, then we watch the police try to catch him and prove what we already know. We take it as entertainment, but in some subliminal way we absorb that perception, begin to believe it, begin to disbelieve our eyes and disbelieve what we are told if somebody presents us with factual evidence. If someone tells us that most muggers are never identified or caught and that most of those who are caught serve time, we don't believe it. We believe that the police catch the criminals and the courts let them go. We believe that, in part, because that is the message we receive on television crime shows. Factual evidence may be to the contrary, but factual evidence is not as powerful as the force of the messages that are pulsed at us every day.

Television and the Politics of Protest

There are three other pertinent examples of television's power. In my view the civil rights movement in the 1960s was a movement that was fueled and made possible by television. The thing that made the Montgomery bus boycott work, the thing that made the civil rights movement work, the thing that generated the public pressure outside the South to pass civil rights laws in Congress, was television. It was television showing Bull Connor and his cattle prods, showing civil rights demonstrators being smashed with fire hoses in Birmingham. It was television showing the brutality of what happened to the freedom riders on the buses and showing the march over the Selma bridge. You could turn on your television every day, and you could see in stark visible terms something that you couldn't accept. You may have known this was going on, but knowing it intellectually and feeling it in your guts were two different things. It was probably Martin Luther King's chief genius, not enough recognized, that he found a way to dramatize publicly what was a private horror to people living there, to make it real, and to touch others of us who lived elsewhere.

Similarly, the Vietnam war protest was fueled by the fact that for a period of time you could turn television on at 6 o'clock and see war crimes. You could turn it on and see people getting summarily executed or dropped from helicopters. This was astonishing stuff, and to a large extent it was very differently received than if people had just read about it in newspapers.

Finally, I want to mention the current protest movement of Jerry Falwell and the fundamentalist revival in this country, and to suggest that television has something very central to do with that. We have always had communities in this country that are alien to the mainstream culture—the Amish are one of the best examples. The Amish live in a very insular culture, take their kids out of school when they're 14 or 15, don't have electricity, don't have television or telephones, and really try to live a primitive, rural life. And they protect themselves from the rest of society whose values and ways of life they regard as alien. The way they protect themselves is by putting a social tent around themselves. And it is part of our legal system that we allow them to do that.

All over this country in small rural towns there were communities that felt much the same way. Whatever the hell was going on out there—in Times Square and Berkeley and on the two coasts and in the big cities—that was not *their* America. The socializing agents for their children were their families, their churches, and their schools, and they damn well controlled their local schools. Their schools were a reflection of the community that they lived in and of their values. That's the way they brought up their kids.

But television suddenly homogenized everything. It brought MTV into their living room. It brought the West Side of Manhattan into their living room. It brought the mainstream culture into their living room. And it brought these influences in to a degree that they could not control. If you have ever talked to these people about what moves them, you will find that they have a deep rage and fear because they feel assaulted by that mainstream culture and by the fact that they can no longer insulate themselves, because now the communication media have ended all that. Any kid can turn on television and suddenly get all the sexual innuendo, all the steaminess, the political views that they don't like, the relationships that they don't like, and the values that they don't like.

What is their reaction? They can't do what the Amish do. They can't withdraw from television, they can't escape television. So they want to censor it. Understand that the two institutions that the fundamentalists have gone after are television and the schools, and both for the same reason. They regard them as an assault on their values, making it impossible for them to live in their insular world and to transmit their values to their children. Not a small issue! However, their response is impossible for the rest of us to accept, because their response is to censor everybody else, and that's unacceptable in a free society. But if you want to understand the fundamentalist movement, it seems to me you have to begin by understanding television's impact on them.

These examples—from the disparate worlds of sports, criminal justice, the civil rights movement, the antiwar movement, and the fundamentalist revival—demonstrate, I think, the way in which television is much more than just a medium of communication, the way in which it constructs reality, the way in which it imposes reality, the way in which its magical qualities create social reality.

These are just the impressions of someone who is not an expert. But they lead me to suggest that we need to begin to think about, research, and write about television and its effect on us in these ways. Television is, of course, not the only factor that determines social perceptions of reality and the politics that flow from it. But it is a much stronger factor than has generally been recognized, not only because of the content of its talk shows and news shows, but also primarily because of its charismatic ability to construct reality as well as mediate it.

REFERENCES

Curtis, L. A. (Ed.). (1985). *American violence and public policy: An update of the National Commission on the Causes and Prevention of Violence.* New Haven, CT: Yale University Press.
Silberman, C. E. (1978). *Criminal violence, criminal justice.* New York: Random House.
Walker, S. (1985). *Sense and nonsense about crime: A policy guide.* Monterey, CA: Brooks/Cole.

DONALD D. WEAR, Jr.

4

CONSTRAINTS ON
THE TELEVISION INDUSTRY

I will discuss some of the philosophic and public policy constraints under which commercial broadcasters operate. In my view the public context of television is largely determined by two inescapable realities of our business. The first is that we are a mass medium; and the second is that by natural disposition, law, and regulation we are compelled to serve the public interest.

The constraint of being a mass medium requires that the television networks have to try to be a cultural common denominator. We must be a culturally aggregating force rather than a disaggregating force. That means we have to present creative works whose appeal cuts across boundaries of age, sex, education, ethnic origin, and economic station. We serve the viewers' need to belong to a larger cultural whole, rather than serving their need for individualism, which might be reflected in narrow, specialized interests. In the jargon of the industry, we're broadcasters and not "narrowcasters."

This constraint of being a common denominator is sometimes forgotten when expectations for commercial television are stated. Critics often expect things of a mass medium for which it is just not suited. While the television networks try to offer a very diverse menu of program choices, we are by definition unable to serve fully all of the appetites of specialized viewers. Those appetites have to be left to the providers of specialized menus: public broadcasting, cable services, independent television stations, video cassettes, and so on.

The second constraint is that if a mass medium is to succeed in the long term, it must serve the public interest. Otherwise the public simply will not be interested in it, and the medium will atrophy and die. Our government saw the need to confirm this reality first in law and then in regulations. And as years passed, lawmakers, public policymakers, and regulators defined and refined and redefined, with increasingly great detail and precision, their view of what procedures were required in order to serve the public interest. Some very precise constraints were established over broadcasters' discretion in determining what they would broadcast that would serve the public interest.

Our view as broadcasters has generally been that this kind of regulatory detail was unnecessary, and consequently we have supported deregulation. While we have supported efforts to reduce this kind of regulation and constraint, we have never really attacked the fundamental standard of serving the public interest because it is intuitive to our business. Now, how do we determine the public interest, and what is our philosophy in pursuing it? One starting point is a factor that is often spoken of in scathingly derogatory terms: ratings. However, the rationale for ratings is that they are our form of consumer product testing. If a program fails to achieve certain rating levels, our consumers are telling us they don't like the product. If they don't like it, and if we are to serve their interests, we have an obligation to find and schedule a better program, one that more people will watch. Thus we view programming decisions in commercial television as being made through a kind of representative democracy rather than a totalitarian dictatorship.

Our job, we believe, is to entertain and enlighten the American people. We try to determine what *their* interests are, not what our interests are. Before we put a program on the air we test it with normal viewers off the street—Fifth Avenue in Manhattan, Los Angeles, wherever we can find them. That is a very representative cross-section of the American people (since, believe it or not, there are a lot of people from Keokuk, Iowa, walking up and down Fifth Avenue). When a program goes on the air we hold it to program standards, which have been culled over a period of time from our experiences with viewers' tastes, dislikes, needs, and interests. And subsequently we try to measure viewer reactions through ratings, viewer mail, correspondence with our affiliates, telephone calls, conferences—a variety of methods.

People often ask, Isn't it a real shame that some good programs are cancelled because ratings aren't good enough? My response is that, when programs are cancelled, it's not the fault of the ratings concept or of venality on the part of particular program executives. It's the result of television being a mass medium, of our need to search for creative concepts that cut across demographic boundaries. The alternative to this approach is much more of an elitist viewpoint, for it holds that *despite* what the viewing public tells us about their lack of interest in a particular program, we should aggregate to ourselves the arbitrary power to ignore public feelings and to program as we choose—to suit our own tastes, not the public's. We in the television networks don't feel comfortable with that kind of approach.

Someone might say that network executives do exercise complete editorial control over what goes out on the air, so it is a dictatorship. However, I disagree. Yes, we decide what we choose to put on the air. But in doing so we are not asking the question, What do we program executives like? Instead we're asking what viewers will like—what are *their* needs and interests? Of course, we are fallible individuals who are trying to intuit the answer to that question, and as a result the process will be a subjective and imperfect one. But we haven't found a better way to do it.

You might ask, If all you're doing is giving people what they want, how are their cultural and informational horizons going to be expanded? Well, even under the process that I've described, we do try to present some programs that serve narrower audiences and that help to expand the horizons of many of our viewers. We do so because our philosophy is not only to serve a mass audience, but also to provide diversity and texture to our program schedule. But as I mentioned earlier, a mass medium cannot possibly satisfy all the audience's tastes all of the time. In this age of diversity and competition among media, the role of fully satisfying narrower interests must fall mainly to other media.

Finally, you might say, This is a very romantic and appealing notion of your business, but isn't it really advertisers and your commercial goals that you're bound to serve? Yes, that's true, but we can't serve those interests without serving the public's interest first. We can't compel attention; we can't command an audience to sit down in front of the television set and watch a show. We first have to attract them to the screen with something that they find satisfying and that they're interested in watching.

As a final topic, I'd like to comment on the role of technology in determining the public context that affects television. Here I differ with critics such as Ira Glasser, for I believe that there is a tendency to exaggerate television's sociological impact. I think this tendency stems partly from reliance on correlational social science studies and from the absence of valid causal research. I think we need to go beyond the wealth of anecdotes and correlations that we have about the relationship between television and behavior, and really try to establish some definitive, causal conclusions. People's notions about television's impact also stem from their cognitive inclination to estimate a medium's sociological influence by using its technological capability as a base. Thus people seem to conclude that a medium's power per person is greater when it reaches half the people than when it reaches only a tenth or a hundredth of the people. Given that inclination, it's inevitable that a medium with the coverage potential and usage levels of television will be elevated in people's minds to a position of power that transcends almost any other influence in society. But I think that that's a false conclusion, and that it has a number of unfortunate side effects.

Blaming television for troublesome social ills often leads us to let the real causes of those ills go untouched. And at the same time it also raises false hopes of miraculous cures, as though enduring social flaws could be swept out of our nation's life by just sweeping them off of television. Television may be the most popular and pervasive medium we have, but I don't ascribe to it any magical powers to control and determine viewers' thinking and behavior.

QUESTIONS AND ANSWERS

Q: I can accept the importance of ratings as Mr. Wear suggested using them, and I also like the thought that you can't sweep problems out of life by sweeping them off the TV screen. However, CBS at one point produced a program called "Lou Grant," which I thought was excellent both for adults and for adolescents. It had excellent ratings, and it presented realistic problems with an attempt to think about solutions without advocating a particular one. But then the primary actor made a political statement as an individual person, and he disappeared from CBS—swept off the screen. I'd like to hear an explanation of that.

A: The Lou Grant episode was before my time with CBS in my current position, so I can't tell you its history. In general, one of the perspectives that we always try to maintain is that, if we address problems, we want to address a broad spectrum of problems, and we want to discuss them intelligently from a variety of perspectives; but we try to avoid advocacy within the boundaries of the program that would favor any particular viewpoint or issue. That is very difficult to do. Beauty is in the eye of the beholder, and what we think is a balanced discussion of an issue may seem to some people as an advocacy position.

Another important response to your question is that, whatever that show's merits, and whatever the reasons it was taken off the air, "Lou Grant" was not the only program on the CBS schedule that addressed issues and problems in that way. For instance, look at some of the other programs on our contemporary schedule, such as "Cagney and Lacey" or "Kate and Allie." You have to conceive of television as a dynamic and evolutionary medium. Although people may tire of a particular program, as a medium we don't tire of trying to do programs such as "Lou Grant" that are contemporary and discuss issues in a constructive way.

Q: I think that is evading the issue. The "Lou Grant" program still had high ratings, and it took on a whole spectrum of issues without advocacy, allowing open exploration. It had tremendous educational and thought-provoking value, but that was suddenly ignored when somebody upstairs at CBS did not like the fact that the actor as an individual spoke out. What happened to "Lou Grant" had nothing to do with the other programs you mentioned such as "Cagney and Lacey." They are important and welcome programs, but the "Lou Grant" show took up problems across a broader spectrum. The actor, Ed Asner, spoke out on a different issue, unrelated to anything on that program, as a personal private citizen, and he was immediately dropped. I've always held CBS responsible for that, which felt very irresponsible to me.

A: I'm not trying to avoid answering the question, but I can't tell you the specifics of that program decision or why it was made. I can tell you what I know about our current program philosophy, which is that we are quite willing to put programs on the air that are contemporary and issue-oriented so long as we feel that they fairly discuss the issues and don't advocate a particular point of view. We are continually looking for programs of that kind.

One thing that is often overlooked in discussions of network television is that networks are largely passive-reactive participants in the program development process. We have ideas, and we make suggestions to program producers, but CBS itself does not produce very many of its programs. They are produced by outside companies. So in large part we have to look to outsiders for the ideas and the execution of those ideas. We try to stimulate that process as best we can, but we produce our own programs to a very limited extent.

Q [Ira Glasser]: I wrote CBS on Ed Asner's behalf at the time the "Lou Grant" show was dropped because it seemed to me that there was a First Amendment problem involved in the cancellation of the show. In reply, CBS claimed that ratings were the main factor. But I was able to get comparative ratings of other shows that demonstrated that their ratings were not as good, and yet they stayed on.

There wasn't much that anyone could do about the situation. Of course TV networks also have a First Amendment right to do what they want—even if it's the wrong thing. But it was fairly clear as you looked at those comparative ratings, that ratings weren't the whole story—that politics was involved. For anyone who lived through the McCarthy era in the 1950s, you could hardly make a case out, either with respect to television or movies, that ratings were what kept certain people and certain issues off the air in those days.

The problem with appealing to ratings and to the issue of diversity and the spectrum of views presented in the media, is that it implies that there is no politics in the selection of programs, and that ratings are the determining factor. That is definitely not the case. There is a lot of discretion within the ratings game, and how that discretion is exercised is not very much discussed. To a large extent, within the confines of ratings, people in the TV industry have the same discretion that newspaper editors and magazine editors do. They use it, and they frequently use it politically. Syd Schanberg got thrown off the *Times* a couple of months ago for writing something that the publisher didn't like, and Ed Asner got thrown off TV for the same reason. I think those are facts of life that we have to live with, but we should not try to deny them, or to pretend that there is no problem there.

Q: Unlike the initial questioner, I don't really believe your argument. It's quite fallacious to think that a concern for ratings is going to serve the largest public possible. It is fallacious because of the fact that when a network cancels a "low-rated" show, it is often a show that is popular and is *the* most popular show for millions and millions of viewers. You're not talking about depriving a few people, you're talking about depriving millions. So when that is done, the fact is that fewer people are getting what they want. If what you said was true, that your primary concern was the larger public, you wouldn't be concerned with your market share—you'd be concerned with the size of the total audience for all the stations. So I think it's better to call a spade a spade and admit you are concerned with your market share because of the commercial aspect.

A: I accept that view, but let me make one additional comment. When we take a show off the air, for ratings or whatever reasons, we do deprive millions of people of that service. That's an inherent problem with the mass medium that we're dealing with—we're not dealing with hundreds of thousands of homes or people but with millions of people at a time. But, I think, it is still our obligation to do two things: First, to program to that mass audience the very best that we can. And, second, since we don't do that 100% of the time, to keep a number of lower-rated shows on the air because we think there is an additional public purpose in broadcasting them. But you have to bear in mind that there is a limit to how much we can do that and still satisfy our definitional character as a mass medium.

Q: In your comments you have largely equated the public interest with the interest of the public, and I would like you to differentiate the two concepts.

A: I guess I do mean interested public, because you either have to let the public decide what their needs and interests are and the manner in which they should be served, or you let a small group of people do it. As the editors of this broadcast spectrum, we try to exercise that responsibility fairly and responsibly, but we also do it by trying to intuit what are the viewing public's needs and interests.

ELLEN WARTELLA   **5**

THE PUBLIC CONTEXT OF DEBATES ABOUT TELEVISION AND CHILDREN

A front page story in the *New York Times* proclaimed that "scientific answers are now offered" to questions of how the new and radically different mass medium "really affects children and what proportion of the country's youth actually come under its influence." The *Times* story went on to say,

> Children in general are excited far more than adults by what they see, even eight times as much, in some cases; the ideas and action presented are large factors in shaping habits, and judged by numbers, the younger members of the population make up a disproportionately large share of audiences.

The medium being discussed was "movies," specifically thrillers. However it could just as easily have been radio, television, or video. The date was May 28, 1933, but it could be 1986, for concerns about the effects of media on child audiences are recurrent in American history. Moreover, during the twentieth century, many of the issues, actors, and terms of the debate about how media influence children have been repeated since the early days of film's introduction. This chapter discusses the recurring nature of these debates and how they apply to today's issues about television.

With the advent of each of the major electronic technologies of film, radio, and television, their adoption into American society was accompanied by considerable public discussion and debate regarding their likely impact on audiences, particularly on youth. Davis (1965), for instance, in an analysis of popular arguments about the introduction of these three technologies, notes that the media's influence on the *morality* of youth was a recurring theme in popular articles discussing the likely effects of new media on children. When a new medium comes along—film around 1920, or radio in the early 1930s, or television in the late 1940s—proponents point out that these media have a very strong, positive educational benefit for children. Opponents typically point out the potential negative effects of the medium on children; for example, that children spend too much time with the new medium, and that it may have negative effects on the children's behavior. For instance, in 1936 Eisenberg justified his major study of the influence of radio on children as follows:

> The popularity of this new pastime [radio] among children has increased rapidly. This new invader of the privacy of the home has brought many a disturbing influence in its wake. Parents have become aware of a puzzling change in the behavior of their children. They are bewildered by a host of new problems, and find themselves unprepared, frightened, resentful, helpless. (Eisenberg, 1936, pp. 17-18)

A recent article (Wartella & Reeves, 1985) examined the role of public concerns about new media earlier in this century in setting the social science research agenda for studies of media effects on children. The Eisenberg quotation above illustrates this rather well. It seems that the advent of each new medium of film, radio, and television marked the beginning of an epoch of social science research focusing on the dominant medium of the day to the exclusion of studying other media children use. Moreover, the social science research topics from epoch to epoch were highly comparable.

This chapter will examine in greater detail the debates about television's effects and the varying reactions of the television industry to these debates.

EARLY CRITICISM OF TELEVISION (1949-1953)

In a series of newspaper articles in the early 1950s, Shayon referred to television as the "New Pied Piper" (Shayon, 1952). The same concerns were expressed in a variety of popular newspaper and magazine articles about television and youth that began to appear in the late 1940s. A search of the *Reader's Guide to Periodical Literature* for popular articles on television and children shows that until volume 16 (for the period from May 1947 to April 1949) only 14 such articles appeared in popular periodicals indexed in the guide. In contrast, volumes 17 and 18 (covering May 1949 to March 1953) reported 135 such articles. And the number of periodical articles on the topic continued high throughout the 1950s and up to the present.

Perhaps the best early examination of the popular public concerns about television's influence on children appear in an early study conducted at Columbia University's Bureau of Applied Social Research (Klapper, 1953; Levin, 1953; Siepmann, 1953). This inquiry included one of the most systematic and revealing early studies of children and television, a working paper by Joseph Klapper, who later went on to be a major participant in public discussions of TV and social behavior as part of the 1972 Surgeon General's inquiry and through his position in social research for CBS. In the 1953 study, Klapper interviewed 40 opinion leaders (jurists, psychologists, children's TV producers, educators, etc.) about their attitudes toward the social issue of children and television. Moreover, he conducted content analyses of all articles published in the popular magazines between 1949 and 1952 for the themes of the debate regarding television's influence on children. Most striking in this early analysis of public concerns is the extent to which the issues of the debate have changed so little since the introduction of television into American society. For instance, the three major findings of the Klapper analysis were as follows:

(1) The overarching concern about television's short-term impact on children stems from the amount of time children spend with TV and the influence of the violent programming content on children. Klapper refers to this as the "time and crime" problem of TV. Of the popular magazine articles he studied, 40% focused on the time problem and 35% focused on the crime concern. And who was expressing these concerns? Klapper calls them the "PTA groups"—parents, teachers, and professionals associated with adult education. These groups were writing in both women's magazines and general circulation magazines, and their concerns were frequently mirrored in journalists' writing about television and children. These issues also set the agenda for social scientists' early research on children and television (Wartella & Reeves, 1985).

(2) A second theme of the early study was the desire on the part of all of the interviewees for better children's television, in particular educational television; 35% of the magazine articles concerned this issue. Part of the emphasis on educational television could be accounted for by the fact that public television was in its infancy in 1953. In fact, there were no educational television stations on the air until 1954, and during the early 1950s public television was conceived of as an extension of educational institutions, who were the early licensees. Interestingly, when Klapper interviewed the opinion leaders about the kinds of children's television they would like to see on the air, few could offer "meaningful suggestions" beyond wanting "better" programming that served the imagination and that presented the "classics" to children. At that time, commercial television's outstanding example,

which was frequently mentioned as a good show, was "Ding Dong School." This is reminiscent of current arguments for better children's TV which use "Sesame Street" as the model for a programming agenda.

(3) Several of the psychologists, psychiatrists, and educators speculated on the long-term effects of children's watching so much television. Two specific concerns expressed by these interviewees still recur today. First, there was a predecessor to currently popular arguments of Postman (1982) and Meyerowitz (1985) in the 1953 concern that children's viewing of the conflicts of the adult world might have a deleterious effect. The interviewees feared that viewing adult TV shows might accelerate the social impact of the adult world on children and make them either suspicious of the "deceitfulness" of adults or inclined to emulate adults at earlier ages. Second, these concerned professionals worried about the effects of television viewing on "passivity" in children. This fear was based on the notion that children who watch TV are not engaging in more active tasks such as playing outdoors, seeing friends, doing homework, or reading, an argument that recurs in popular criticism today.

I have spent so much time in reviewing the debates of 1949-1953 regarding children and television in order to make several points. First, it is my thesis that the ongoing debates about television's influence on children (and earlier debates about film's and radio's influence) are part of the way that our society negotiates the introduction of communication technologies. Many of the same issues are now being discussed about children's use of video cassettes and of computers. Indeed, debates about the impact of communication media on children may serve to deflect wider public concern about who controls and creates media in the society. When such control issues are not subject to debate—and by 1953, American television was fully entrenched as a large, corporate commercial system—children's issues may be debated instead.

Second, the recurring nature of the topics for discussion—that children spend too much time with media content that is highly violent and of questionable educational character and "quality"—underlines a fact about how media industries have programmed for child audiences. Parents and other child advocates in the society have continually criticized the media industries' view of the child as just another member of the viewing audience. They feel that the special needs of children are not fully met. The economics of commercial television, in particular, are such that instead of any social responsibility standard determining programming for children, the need to deliver an audience to advertisers is the overriding concern.

This leads me to my third point: One salutary effect of the recurring debates about media's influence on children is that when public concern is at its highest point, media industries do respond with greater attempts to meet the needs of child audiences as child advocates would wish. I will examine these last two points in greater detail in the next section on changes in television programming for children since the 1950s.

TELEVISION INDUSTRY RESPONSE
TO PUBLIC DEBATES
ABOUT CHILDREN AND TELEVISION

As suggested above, the worries of parents and educators about the amount of time children spend with TV have been partially provoked by the type of programming available to child audiences. Clearly, programming to children has changed over the years since television's introduction. Although this Chapter will not examine the entire history of television programming for children, two periods are worthy of more detailed examination: the early to mid-1950s, called by one commentator the "halcyon days" of children's television (Melody, 1972); and the early 1970s, when public discussion had heated up concerning the quality of children's television.

Melody's extensive analysis of the first two decades of children's television was published in 1972. In it he argued that, in 1949-1952, network television was in its "promotional period," a time when it was actively seeking to promote the medium and the purchase of television sets. Children's programming during the period also reflected this network desire to attract potential audiences. A considerable amount of diverse programming was directed to children, much of it "sustaining," that is, paid for by the networks without advertiser sponsorship. For instance, 42% of all children's programs on network television in 1949 were sustaining (Melody, 1972, p. 36). An analysis of the genres of programming available to children on network television in the period between 1950 and 1980 by Bence (1985) supports and expands on Melody's point. Bence points out that in 1950 there were 85 children's programs on network television each week, and there was an average of 14 new shows each season until 1956. During 1957 there was a decrease in the number of children's program offerings, reaching a low in 1959 when there were only 25 programs offered by the networks each week.

These programs during the 1950s were diverse both in the genre of programming and the times on the schedule when they could be found. For instance, there were puppet shows like "Kukla, Fran and Ollie" (NBC, 1948) and "Howdy Doody" (NBC, 1947); children's dramas such as "My Friend Flicka" (CBS, 1956), and "Lassie" (CBS, 1954); educational programs such as "Mr. Wizard" (NBC, 1951) and "Ding Dong School" (NBC, 1952); documentaries such as "Watch the World" (NBC, 1950); and variety shows such as "Captain Kangaroo" (CBS, 1955), "Small Fry Club" (Dumont, 1947), and, of course, the best known prime-time variety program for children, "Disneyland" (ABC, 1954). Moreover, these programs could be found throughout the broadcast schedule when children were likely to be in the viewing audience: weekday mornings, late afternoon weekdays, weekend mornings, and even early prime-time evenings.

It would not be correct to argue that it was merely public concern about the likely effects of television on children that made the 1950s the "halcyon days" of copious and diverse programming for children. As Melody points out, up until about 1956, the television industry did all that it could to sell television to the American people. More than trying to deliver an audience to advertisers, the networks needed to develop the market for television, and "specialized children's programming of high quality was viewed as a valuable stimulus to the purchase of television sets" (Melody, 1972, p. 36). Throughout the 1950s public discussion about television's effect on children continued to be frequent in the popular literature: Between March 1953 and February 1961, 261 articles on the topic of children and television appeared in popular periodicals, according to the *Reader's Guide*. Although there was some federal government activity (Senator Kefauver held congressional hearings on juvenile delinquency in 1955 to 1956 that focused somewhat on television's influence), federal investigations into television's influence on children were not particularly prominent during the 1950s. It seems that TV's early children's programming patterns were influenced by the economic needs of the industry coupled with visible public concern. Diverse and frequent children's programming was viewed as a reasonable programming approach for the networks.

TV's Mass Marketing Era

All of this changed, however, with television's conversion to a mass marketing medium, according to Melody (1972). Once the networks had a large enough audience (by 1956, 71.8% of American households had television sets; Sterling & Haight, 1978), they shifted from trying to promote television to selling audiences to advertisers, and the most attractive audiences were adults, preferably women between 18 and 49 years of age. The late 1950s saw the rise of advertisers' interest in mass audiences, and children were not then viewed as a likely target for advertising messages. Consequently, the networks moved children's programming out of the time slots, such as prime time, where mass audiences could be reached and into time slots where "it had an advantage over other kinds of programming as an advertising vehicle" (Melody, 1972, p. 38).

The 1960s continued the trend toward less overall programming for children and a narrowing of diversity in both genres and scheduling times. The rise of Saturday morning as "kidvid" time occurred during the 1960s for a variety of reasons: Children were recognized as a specialized audience for special advertisers such as toy manufacturers and cereal and snack food companies; there was no alternative, more attractive audience watching television on Saturday mornings to be sold to advertisers; and cheap, animated cartoon programming was available through such production companies as Hanna Barbera, which gave Saturday morning a unique character (Melody, 1972). Kidvid in the 1960s featured a Saturday morning schedule on each of the three networks predominantly of animated cartoon shows interspersed with heavy doses of advertising. The percentage of all children's programs available on network television that were scheduled on Saturday or Sunday mornings increased from about one-third in 1960 to a peak of 72% in 1970. Moreover, this period also saw the rise of animated programs on network television. In 1960 there were 8 new or returning network animated shows on each week, compared to 32 animated programs in 1966 and 28 in 1970 (Bence, 1985). The predominance of animated Saturday morning cartoons, many of which were violent, embedded in advertisements for toys and heavily sugared foods was the focus of the next wave of major public debates about children's television in the period between 1970 and 1975.

The Disputes of the 1970s

On February 5, 1970, Action for Children's Television (ACT), a consumer activist group, petitioned the Federal Communications Commission (FCC) with a request that the FCC assume responsibility in the area of children's television. Specifically, ACT recommended that (1) no sponsors or commercials be allowed on children's programs; (2) performers and hosts of programs be forbidden to use or sell products by brand name during children's hours; and (3) each television station be required to provide a minimum of 14 hours per week of "quality" children's programming, divided into age-specific groupings (preschool, primary, and older elementary school ages) as part of its public service presentations (see FCC, 1971). In 1971, the FCC issued a Notice of Rulemaking in the area and started a 4-year investigation into children's programming. In addition to ACT's active lobbying for better children's television, the FCC chairman, Dean Burch, gave major speeches attempting to persuade the networks of his concern that they improve children's television (see *Broadcasting*, September 21, 1970, p. 20; and *Broadcasting*, September 20, 1971, p. 28). During this period, the industry trade journal, *Broadcasting*, disclosed that the FCC had received over 80,000 letters in support of the ACT petition and that Dean Burch had held a "secret meeting" with network executives at which he emphasized the sincerity of his concern for children's programming (*Broadcasting*, July 19, 1971, p. 58).

Over the next few years, public interest was demonstrated at both the federal government level and in the popular press about the issue of children's television. In 1972, the Surgeon General of the United States released a report on *Television and Social Behavior* (Comstock & Rubinstein, 1972), which suggested that there may be a causal relationship between television viewing and aggressive behavior; ACT and other consumer groups such as Robert Choate's Council on Children, Media and Merchandising publicly criticized the content of children's television and advertising; and ACT petitioned the Federal Trade Commission to investigate children's advertising practices.

The networks' response was quick: In early 1971, each network took children's Saturday morning programming decisions out of the hands of daytime programmers and established a separate vice president or senior executive in charge of children's television (*Broadcasting*, March 22, 1971). In January 1972, the National Association of Broadcasters (NAB), an industry self-regulatory group, released a new code for children's television that reduced the allowable non-program time on children's programs from 16 1/2 minutes to first 11, and then 9 1/2 minutes per hour on weekends, and that banned the delivery of commercials in or adjacent to children's shows by hosts or primary cartoon characters, a practice known as host-selling (NAB, 1973).

In addition, programming to children responded to the mounting public pressure. During the 1971-1972 network season, substantial changes in Saturday morning were made: ABC introduced an hour-long, live-action educational program, "Curiosity Shop"; CBS introduced a half-hour adaptation of "You Are There," a look at historical events through old film clips with Walter Cronkite as host, and "In the News," a series of informational "drop-ins" throughout Saturday morning. In addition both ABC and CBS announced showcase-quality children's dramatic programs to be presented throughout the year. NBC brought back "Mr. Wizard" and an hour-long, live-action educational program, "Take a Giant Step." The early 1970s saw further innovations in both educational and dramatic programs: for example, ABC's "Afterschool Specials" were inaugurated, as well as CBS's "Fat Albert," and NBC's "Project Peacock" dramatic programs.

By the close of the 1970s, however, public pressure on the networks and public interest in children's television receded. No new regulations had been enacted, and many of the innovations in children's television had disappeared. By the early 1980s the FCC had made it clear it would not regulate children's television. Ongoing public discussion of the topic ebbs and flows but has not returned to the heated tones of the early 1970s, and the networks are now in competition with first-run syndicators for both child audiences and advertisers interested in reaching children. We have a very different market for children's television today. Yet, many of the same concerns about quality children's programming and the nature of advertising to children are still part of public discussions, as indicated in the proposed Children's Television Education Act, which was considered by Congress in 1986.

My conclusions are that public debates about media's influence on children are recurrent in our nation's history and largely stem from wider concerns about the adoption of new communication technologies into American society. In particular, however, the recurring debates about television's influence on children since the earliest days of the medium emphasize the facts that children are and have been very heavy users of television, and that much or most of what they see does not address the specific needs of the child audience. For the media industry, and specifically television programmers, the child audience is just another audience segment to be delivered to advertisers. Appeals to television's social responsibility, I believe, are only effective when public pressure, best evidence by activity in Washington, is brought to bear on programming policy. Thus I believe that the public context in many ways does set the agenda for initiatives in television programming for children.

REFERENCES

Bence, P. J. (1985, November). *From "Howdy Doody" to the "Smurfs": A critical model for interpreting the history of children's network television.* Paper presented to the conference on Television: Issues for the Industry, Hofstra University.

Comstock, G. A., & Rubinstein, E. A. (Eds.). (1972). *Television and social behavior* (5 vols.). Washington, DC: Government Printing Office.

Davis, R. (1965). *Response to innovation: A study of popular arguments about new mass media.* Unpublished doctoral dissertation, University of Iowa.

Eisenberg, A. L. (1936). *Children and radio programs.* New York: Columbia University Press.

Federal Communications Commission. (1971). *Notice of inquiry and notice of proposed rulemaking.* Docket number 19142.

Klapper, J. (1953). *Children and television: A review of socially prevalent concerns* (Document 3B-0482-2). Unpublished paper, Columbia University, Bureau of Applied Social Research.

Levin, H. J. (1953). *New York State Television Commission: A case study of the use of research by a public commission* (Document B-0482-7). Unpublished paper, Columbia University, Bureau of Applied Social Research.

Melody, W. (1972). *Children and television: The economics of exploitation.* New Haven, CT: Yale University Press.

Meyerowitz, J. (1985). *No sense of place.* New York: Oxford University Press.

National Association of Broadcasters. (1973, June 7). *Statement of principles on children's television advertising.* Washington, DC: Author.

Postman, N. (1982). *The disappearance of childhood.* New York: Delacorte.

Shayon, R. L. (1952). *Television and our children.* New York: Longman.

Siepmann, C. (1953). *Collection and analysis of prevailing criticisms of television programming* (Document B-0482-4). Unpublished paper, Columbia University, Bureau of Applied Social Research.

Sterling, C. H., & Haight, T. R. (1978). *The mass media: Aspen Institute guide to communication industry trends.* New York: Praeger.

Wartella, E., & Reeves, B. (1985). Historical trends in research on children and the media: 1900-1960. *Journal of Communication, 35,* 118-133.

TIMOTHY E. WIRTH **6**

THE TELEVISION ENVIRONMENT:
Cultivating the Wasteland

Television is one part of a vast telecommunications revolution, sweeping the country and the globe. For the last 6 years I've watched this revolution from a special vantage point—the chairmanship of the House Subcommittee on Telecommunications, Consumer Protection and Finance. As earlier legislators oversaw the building of our canals and railroads and superhighways—the opening of America and the connecting of a continent—I have seen our newest infrastructure for commerce and ideas take form.

In telecommunications policy, the challenge of change is equally profound and revolutionary. No longer are we dealing with the rules of the past: scarce spectrum; monopoly; pervasive government regulation; national isolation. Today we are dealing with potential abundance of spectrum; competition and increasing entrepreneurial activity; much less regulation; and an intertwined international economy and communications structure. Public policy cannot remain static, and the challenge that we face is to adapt our policy, laws, and regulations to a rapidly changing environment.

Goals of Telecommunications Policy

To make the necessary changes, we first had to settle on the basic goals that we believed our society's telecommunications policy ought to achieve. Presumably form follows function—but unhappily too little public policy is made with a national set of goals in mind.

In early 1981, we embarked on an extensive set of hearings, designed to solicit views from all quarters on what the goals should be, and then

AUTHOR'S NOTE: This chapter was presented, in slightly longer form, as the 1986 Carlos McClatchy Memorial Lecture at the Department of Communication of Stanford University on February 10, 1986. Permission to print these portions and © copyright by Timothy E. Wirth, 1986.

to try to develop a political consensus around our central goals. The hearings were broadly criticized as being too academic, too abstract, and too comprehensive. But out of them a consensus slowly emerged on what our communications goals ought to be—and I think these goals characterize much of our policy today. Throughout the industry, I think most people are agreed that, first, all citizens of the United States should have *access* to communications at a reasonable price. Second, a *diversity* of information, program, and technology supply should be encouraged. And third, wherever possible, the telecommunications market should be managed by *competition,* not by monopoly and government regulation. Further, these three goals of access, diversity, and competition should be nurtured by government action where necessary.

Now I should not suggest that we reached this consensus and started to act on it without considerable resistance. In this industry, as in others in our national experience, those who become established or entrenched work hard to keep out the newcomers: AM radio broadcasters sought protection against the challenge of FM; VHF television stations lobbied the government not to allocate UHF spectrum; over-the-air broadcasters tried desperately to restrain the cable industry; and now the cable industry is having its problems adjusting to the competitive threat of the backyard satellite dish.

Resisting change brought about by technological developments is nothing new. I recently came across a letter purportedly sent in 1829 by Martin Van Buren, then the Governor of New York, to President Andrew Jackson:

Dear Mr. President:

The canal system of this country is being threatened by the spread of a new form of transportation known as "railroads." The federal government must preserve the canals for the following reasons:
One. If canal boats are supplanted by "railroads" serious unemployment will result. Captains, cooks, drivers, hostlers, repairmen and lock tenders will be left without means of livelihoods, not to mention the numerous farmers now employed in growing hay for horses.

. . .

As you may well know, Mr. President, "railroad" carriages are pulled at the enormous speed of 15 miles per hour by "engines" which, in addition to endangering life and limb of passengers, roar and snort their way through the countryside, setting fire to crops, scaring the livestock and frightening women and children. The Almighty certainly never intended that people should travel at such breakneck speed.

Signed,

Martin Van Buren, Governor of New York

Resistance to change is nothing new. Remarkably, in the field of telecommunications, the industry and public policy underlying it have done a pretty good job of encouraging innovation.

Access to Communications

Concerning access, we have been very successful. Television reaches 98.2% of all U.S. households. More of us own TV sets than have indoor plumbing, telephones, or clothes washers. Indeed, the average American household contains 1.78 televisions. And we have the sets on for an average of seven hours a day—or 2,555 hours a year—25% more than the average American works. We are almost 13 times more likely to be watching the tube than reading a newspaper or a magazine, activities that each take up an average of 200 hours annually. And while Americans in general give only about 10 hours a year to books, our children—by the time they finish high school—have spent more time watching television than in the classroom.

Diversity

Diversity is a second goal—to encourage more video outlets in the marketplace, to bring greater program and viewpoint diversity so that we may have an electronic media market "with many tongues, speaking many voices." That was the marketplace of political ideas envisioned in the Federalist Papers. Government should encourage information to flow from as many sources as possible, carrying many messages and views to animate, to inform, and to engage democracy's decision makers—our citizens. As the Supreme Court, in discussing the First Amendment in its landmark *Red Lion* ruling, clearly stated: "It is the right of the viewers and listeners, not the right of the broadcasters, which is paramount."

Just as government should never determine what information is "good," neither should a handful of *private* entities monopolize such decisions. In our information age, the survival of our democracy depends on an electorate choosing from a broad menu of diverse views.

The Fairness Doctrine ensures that all sides of important public controversies are aired. This Doctrine is not a government regulation to chill or inhibit speech as the Federal Communications Commission (FCC) has suggested in seeking its repeal. It is simply a statement by the government saying let there be more speech—let's make sure that a broadcaster who is licensed to serve the public transmits not only his own views, but other sides as well. And in cable television, the Cable Communications Policy Act requires cable operators to set aside 10-15% of their channels for programming by independent third parties. The public policy goal: More people programming channels bring more diversity of viewpoints.

Competition

We also continue to strive to reach our third goal—to govern through marketplace forces wherever possible.

While the three major networks still dominate the video marketplace, a vast array of outlets now offer viewers choices as never before. Streams of alternative programming flow through electronic media outlets such as cable television, LPTV (low power television), MMDS (multichannel multipoint distribution service), SMATV (satellite master-antenna television), STV (subscription television), ITFS (instructional television fixed service), Videotext, optical discs, DBS (direct broadcast satellites), VCRs (video cassette recorders), and the latest video technology to sweep America, backyard satellite dishes. We now have an all-news channel, a 24-hour public affairs channel, an all-music channel, a financial-news channel, and even an all-weather channel. Programming tastes that traditional broadcasters barely sampled can now be widely satisfied.

The Government's Role

I assumed the Chairmanship of the Telecommunications Subcommittee just as the Reagan administration came to town. To head the regulatory agencies that my subcommittee oversees, the administration appointed officials who felt government should not govern, but should get out of the way. For example, the Chairman of the FCC, Mark Fowler, assumed his position espousing not deregulation, but "unregulation." These consensus goals—access, diversity, and competition—have not been shared by all.

I have no gripe with deregulating markets—but the administration and Chairman Fowler pursue deregulation solely for its own sake.

Deregulation is not a goal. It is a means to an end.

The canals that opened up the way West, and the railroads that Leland Stanford and others built to link the continent, embodied the traditional American partnership of public investment in private vision. The land-grant universities, the G.I. Bill, and the National Defense Education Act committed community resources to developing individual skills. Federal water projects brought electric power and irrigation to desert land; government financing breathed life into public television.

Over and over Americans have seen that such teamwork works. Government serves, as Lincoln imagined it, "to do for a community of people whatever they need to have done, but cannot do at all, or cannot do so well for themselves, in their separate and individual capacities." That definition sets both a positive and a negative agenda for government. It pools our strength to spur progress. And it safeguards our freedoms against the excesses or excessive power of special interests in society. Those are the legitimate purposes of democratic government. They do not assure government a role in every endeavor or make it the answer to every problem. They define its necessary functions and leave each generation of Americans to find the correct balance of power, the right strategy for partnership.

If we have done well in achieving our three goals of access, diversity, and competition; and if most of us agree that government is an important partner in helping to achieve these goals, it then remains to ask the deeper questions: How are we using television's potential for teaching our young, informing our citizens, enriching our lives, and thereby strengthening self-government and democratic society? Twenty-five years ago, Newton Minow, former Chairman of the FCC, described television as a "vast wasteland." Is that description accurate today? And what steps should be taken to cultivate the wasteland? We should take an especially careful look at (1) the impact of television on children, (2) the involvement of television in the political process, and (3) how we might strengthen public television.

Children's Television

Historically, three great institutions have educated and socialized our young—family, church, and school. Now there is a fourth— television—with extraordinary potential.

Unhappily, most of commercial television today treats children—our most precious natural resource—as consumers of products and entertainment, not of useful knowledge. The marketplace provides a special niche for them on Saturday mornings and fills it with such enduring classics as "Snorks," "Gummie Bears," "Smurfs," "Alvin and the Chipmunks," "Kidd Video," "Mr. T.," "Spider Man," "13 Ghosts of Scooby," "The Super Powers Team," and "Hulk Hogan's Rock 'N' Wrestling." The gap between what television could deliver, and what it does provide, is deepest in the field of children's programs.

We have learned what a positive influence educational programming can have on our young. We know that television can teach a wide range of skills and behavior. We know that television can motivate and interest children in what they need to know and learn. We know that TV can simultaneously entertain and educate.

Ignoring these lessons, the FCC has recently lifted the restrictions on commercial minutes allowed, and refused even to consider the issue of increased commercializing of children's programs. The marketplace responded accordingly. It gave us a new phenomenon—the program-length commercial, a vast array of animated shows—not developed to enlighten, teach, or enrich the nation's children, but developed instead to enrich the toy makers who turn their products into cartoon characters.

That, of course, is just what cartoon shows like "G.I. Joe," "He-Man and Masters of the Universe," and "Transformers" now do. They don't advertise toys directly. They just animate them as the centerpieces of the entertainment, but the effect is a protracted, effective sell. If it weren't working, producers would not now be investing $21 million to develop an animated series called "Galaxy Rangers" and planning a line of toys to go on sale when the programs go on the air.

A commercial by any other name is still a commercial.

In contrast, two-thirds of the "Sesame Street" schedule is reruns. The "Electric Company" programs on the air now include no show that is less than 10 years old. And except for 40 half-hours of "3-2-1 Contact" made in 1983, that science series is limited to its original 65 episodes.

In addition, we have explored and documented the effect of televised violence on children. In 1972, the United States Surgeon General issued a report that concluded that there was a short-run causal relationship between viewing of televised violence and aggressive behavior in children. Ten years later, the National Institute of Mental Health released a follow-up study. The conclusion: Televised violence also caused *long-term* aggressive behavior in children, and if you had not already guessed it, you will not be surprised to learn that weekend cartoons have dished up the heaviest frequency of violent acts per hour.

We are aware of what television provides young viewers, and we should also acknowledge what is left out. Why are the comics so accessible, and the classics of children's literature almost impossible to find? With science so vital to our children now and our growth tomorrow, why can children not explore its wonders more fully on television after school? We don't have to teach Latin on television, but we do have to know our history, know the best of our culture—and we *can* teach those lessons on television. We can. But we don't. I would cite here Wirth's paradox: The more we know about the power of television in educating our young, the less we use this powerful medium.

Whether we are parents, educators, public policymakers, or students, we should be fed up with the failure to make television the positive force that it could be for our young. How we have treated children's television in this country is, plain and simple, a national disgrace.

Television and the Political Process

As to TV's influence on the political process, we know that the early projection of election returns by the networks depresses voter turnout. Congress, with the backing of both national political parties and the League of Women Voters, called for voluntary restraint by the networks. We did not want to *mandate* network silence until the polls closed in the West; we simply asked the networks to voluntarily restrain themselves and their desire to be "first" regardless of the consequences. Unfortunately, the response was limited: The network news executives claimed that exit polling results were news, and had to be reported right away. But why don't you exercise judgment, we asked, as you do all the time with news? The networks hold back news shows for three hours every evening between air time on the East and West coasts. Why can't they exercise the same voluntary restraint to protect the most important of all democratic processes, the election of our president?

There is another serious threat to the political process—negative political advertising by independent political action groups with the funds to lay down a barrage of ads against opponents without the resources for adequate response. It creates an imbalance in the political process that gives well- financed special interest groups power beyond their numbers, the power to control political debate. We must ask what these practices are doing to our democratic processes. We can't afford to let the poison spread and seek no antidote.

These problems remain in an industry that has made extraordinary strides, from its introduction of more quality entertainment programming to the stimulating presentation of news and analysis. C-SPAN brings debates live from the House floor and from congressional committees into the voters' living rooms. The legislative process has been put on public display, and we are all the better for it.

It is now time for the legislative and public process to mobilize itself and help to cultivate the wasteland. And I have a number of proposals to share with you. Adlai Stevenson once said, "Your public servants serve you right." So do our public communications. If we don't demand excellence, we won't get it. We will get—we do get—what we appear to want. We must demand excellence in television, just as we pursue it in all our other quests.

Some Proposals

There are some legislative steps that we can take to encourage excellence. For example, to ensure that commercial broadcasters meet the needs of children whom they are licensed to serve, we could require broadcasters to program 1 hour a day intended to enhance the education of children. Until recently, broadcasters were required to pay particular attention to the special population of children, but that preference was dropped by this FCC. I have introduced this legislation for the last 4 years; Senator Lautenberg has introduced identical legislation last session in the Senate. We should open the debate and get going on this legislation.

Turning to commercial TV, how can we treat commercial broadcasting in a deregulatory political climate and simultaneously strengthen public broadcasting. I have proposed the initiation of a "free market" spectrum fee as a way to ensure that the public is compensated for the use the broadcaster gets of a valuable resource. If we treated the airwaves as though they were public lands, we would be charging fees for broadcast licenses as we do for timber, grazing, or mineral rights. The "rents" that would come in from such fees could then be used, instead of general revenues, to underwrite educational, children's, community affairs, and minority programming.

We can exploit the vast number of unused cable access channels to increase public affairs and local programming. I have proposed setting aside a portion of the franchise fee that cable operators pay to the cities where they operate. Rather than putting this money into filling potholes, why not pour a portion of it back into enriching the video marketplace in ways that the market, on its own, will starve?

In the 1950s citizens' groups sprang up all over America to influence neighborhood zoning decisions. In the 1960s, citizens recognized the tremendous problem of air and water pollution and fought it by forming hundreds of environmental groups. In the 1970s came Crime Watch, local citizens' groups to help police their own streets, to make their homes safe. During the rest of this century, why don't we create a new environmental movement—one focused on the television environment? A citizen movement dedicated to establishing grass-roots community organizations to engage in active dialogue with broadcasters, cable operators, and programmers. A citizens' movement overseeing our passive role in our media environment. A citizens' movement serving as a constructive partner with the media in attempting to tackle many of the challenges that regulatory solutions cannot now meet.

The national Parent-Teacher Association (PTA)—with 27,000 local chapters—and the American Academy of Pediatrics have tried to open the dialogue on the impact of children's television. Why not expand their efforts? Broadcasters, cable operators, and programmers should welcome such audience activism and invite criticism, analysis, and questioning.

Recent strides in this area give me hope. For example, when some citizen groups organized to fight drunk driving and alcohol abuse, and called for banning beer and wine advertising on television, broadcasters and community groups got together all across the country. The result has been a veritable blitz of public service TV announcements forcefully making the case against drunk driving and alcohol abuse.

The National Association of Broadcasters (NAB) deserves much credit for helping steer such a constructive course. This broadcast group has undertaken another voluntary initiative—a national telethon or other fund-raising event to support public broadcasting. The NAB is also aggressively pursuing a campaign geared toward making broadcast stations think long and hard before accepting negative political advertising. This is a good beginning—a new beginning—that gives us all hope that a future television environment shaped by a voluntary partnership between mobilized citizens and media managers can be a reality.

No change comes about without leadership. The Carnegie Foundation took the lead 20 years ago, and again in the late 1970s, in laying down a blueprint for what has become the nation's Public Broadcasting System (PBS). Today, public broadcasting is fighting to continue its long-term commitment to excellence. We must do more to encourage this and and other sources of alternative programming, such as cable access channels. Why not call once again on the Carnegie Foundation, for a third Carnegie Commission to study and recommend how we might enhance and enrich programming? We have a multitude of outlets but a poverty of programs—how can we combine resources and better reach the potential of television?

We should stir up trouble over the quality of "kid vid" and the poverty of public TV finances. We should explore the international frontier of telecommunications—TV's role in covering international terrorist incidents, and TV satellites as export earners, carrying our television programming to consumers abroad. Television can bring the peoples of the world closer; it can cut tension and reduce conflict. Telecommunications may even be a major route to economic growth for new generations around the world.

This job of cultivating our electronic resources, however, cannot be left to educational institutions alone. This challenge requires true national leadership at the highest levels. We have held White House conferences on the aging, White House conferences on children, and now it is time for a White House conference on television. Only if we elevate these concerns to such a level of national priority can we realistically expect to raise the public consciousness sufficiently to begin to make our television all it can be.

We must move to make the most of this medium. We must act to get the best of the television environment, the best of ourselves. The wasteland can be cultivated; the spectrum belongs to all of us and we should use it for the excellent, the noble, and the future.

THOMAS S. ROGERS

7

HOW CAN TELEVISION
SERVE THE PUBLIC INTEREST?

As the Senior Counsel of the Telecommunications, Consumer Protection and Finance Subcommittee of the House of Representatives, my basic message might be stated as "all power to the audience." In some ways that is similar to the approach of television industry representatives who stress the importance of ratings in programming decisions. However, I would like to develop that theme by searching for new ways in which the public can shape the media.

The stakes in this area represent a vast public interest issue. Broadcasters are regulated to serve the public interest, but when it comes to many of the critical public policy issues affecting broadcasting, the public is often not very interested. That doesn't mean that the public isn't fascinated and captivated by television. But it does mean that that type of involvement rarely extends to the public policy issues regarding television. We badly need some type of device that is more sophisticated and more constructive than simply turning the dial as a way of affecting some of these policy issues.

In terms of helping us understand the world we live in, our television environment is as important a part of our environment as air and water are in our physical environment. But though we have moved in many ways to protect our natural environment—for example, by working to control toxic waste and acid rain—we have done very little as involved citizens in a concerted effort to try to shape the television environment.

What is the rationale for suggesting that broadcasters ought to be responsive to the public, that they ought to program in the public interest? Well, broadcasters receive a very valuable resource—a broadcast license—a resource that is currently worth astronomical sums of money in the open market. In return for receiving that very

AUTHOR'S NOTE: The following pages contain selected excerpts of my conference presentation that amplify or update the preceding address by Congressman (now Senator) Wirth.

valuable resource, broadcasters should make sure the public gets something back for the use of its airwaves.

However, for the most part the Federal Communications Commission (FCC) has fully deregulated broadcasting, so there are very few requirements left that a broadcaster must live up to as a condition of having a license. About the only meaningful regulation still in place is the Fairness Doctrine, which is intended to encourage a diversity of viewpoints on the air. However, it too is now under severe challenge, for the FCC has recommended its repeal. The Fairness Doctrine is a simple regulation that has minimal impact in terms of what it requires of broadcasters, for it basically just specifies that broadcasters should follow the canons of good journalism in presenting various sides of an issue.

In the view of many public policymakers, there are a number of areas where broadcasters are clearly not living up to what should be their public interest responsibilities. I do not mean to suggest that the government should be dictating program content, for it is extremely important that the government not infringe on the specific editorial decisions of broadcasters. However, if there is going to be some type of meaningful standard for judging how well stations and networks meet their public interest obligations, there will have to be certain broad programming categories for which a broadcaster is held accountable. For instance, the area where the greatest number of public policymakers in Washington agree that broadcasters as a whole have not lived up to their responsibilities is children's television.

Consequently, Congressman Wirth and a number of cosponsors have proposed legislation that would require that programming intended to advance the educational needs of children be aired by all broadcast stations at least 1 hour a day during each week day. It is legislation that has a great deal of support from parents' groups, educators, and the medical establishment. However, I am sorry to say that it is not likely to be enacted in the current environment, given the intensity of the opposition from the broadcast industry, as well as an apparent lack of consensus as to whether that is the best approach for improving children's television.

Another major public policy issue relates to public broadcasting. In trying to obtain sufficient children's television, many have looked to public broadcasting to provide it. Unfortunately, we have twice in the last two years passed legislation to increase the funding for public broadcasting, so that certain needs of children's television could be adequately addressed, and twice the administration has vetoed those bills. You rarely see a political combination with legislators like Tim

Wirth on one hand and Barry Goldwater on the other hand joining forces to pass increased funding for public broadcasting so that the needs and interests of children can be met. However, we have put that political coalition together twice now, but without succeeding in getting public broadcasting legislation enacted. We are currently on the verge of success in a third effort by putting public broadcasting authorizing legislation in a comprehensive budget bill.

In the area of broadcasting early projections of election returns, the Congress has told the networks that they have a public responsibility to make sure that their coverage of elections is not done in a way that depresses voter turnout. However, Congress has realized that to legislate in this area would have huge First Amendment problems, and time and time again it has tried to find some type of cooperative solution with broadcasters. The current situation is that the networks have indicated they will reform their practices if Congress passes some type of uniform poll-closing law, and such legislation is now pending before Congress.

QUESTIONS AND ANSWERS

Q: Mr. Rogers, you said that most of the regulatory avenues that we have been waiting for over the years seem to be kind of hopeless right now. That is discouraging to those of us who have raised our children, waiting for the regulations and the legislation to be passed, and who now have grandchildren. But there is one important thing that legislators could do for us. We are looking toward the new technology to help us. There are many families and schools who are trying to do their own programming by taping with their VCR or picking what's good out of the sky—and believe me, there is plenty if you look for it. Consequently, a crucial issue for the future is keeping these avenues free. So I want to ask you, please don't allow them to scramble it. And don't regulate it out of our lives.

Thomas Rogers: I don't mean to suggest that there is no point in advocating or pushing for children's television legislation any more. I just want to be realistic about its prospects for passage in the current political environment. I hope that citizens and educators will rekindle the interest and support that is necessary in order to counter the very stiff industry opposition to the legislation.

I think we all put a great deal of hope in the new technologies to respond to certain public needs that the larger, least-common-denominator type of mass media have not been able to meet. In areas of new technology, such as cable, we have put out specific proposals as well. For instance, we have suggested that a percentage of the franchise fees already paid by cable operators to a city be put toward educational programming for children, as a way of serving the broader public interest.

Q: What are your views about the legal and regulatory protection of the public interest?

Donald Wear: At the risk of saying something heretical and against self-interest, I do believe there is a role for regulation. I don't believe that the FCC ought to lock its doors and turn off the lights. I believe that there is a need for a "public interest standard" in the communications act. I think the only reservation that I would make is on specific issues and on the degree of regulation. I think there are areas in which the broadcast industry can be trusted, without regulation, to satisfy the public interest. But there ought to be some safety net to ensure that the regulator's or the lawmaker's view of the public interest is served.

Thomas Rogers: I think the way I would come at the question of the public interest compared to the interested public is this: It is very difficult to see how the public is getting anything back for the use of its airwaves, unless a broadcaster is doing something that the marketplace doesn't require. To the extent that broadcasters only do what they would do under marketplace conditions anyway—and responding to the "interest of the public" as shown in the ratings is doing just that— that is *not* responding to the public interest in the way that Congressman Wirth would define it. He would say that the broadcaster should give something that the marketplace doesn't demand, and children's television is the perfect example. There just is *not* a sufficient marketplace demand for quality children's programs. That is the reason that we don't have them. If we are going to have a public interest concept that means anything, it requires programming for those needs that the marketplace does not respond to on its own initiative.

Ellen Wartella: On the children's television issue, I disagree somewhat. I think that there *is* a marketplace demand for quality children's programming, but that there have been a number of historical forces in children's television that have reduced the diversity of children's programming. If you compare the kinds of children's programs that were on the air from the 1950s up to today, you'd see a continued funneling down and reduction of the diversity of programming, so that children's television now means merely Saturday morning animated shows. There's a major problem beyond just the insidiousness of having these stereotyped and violent kinds of programs on the air, and beyond the objection that they're program-length commercials. What has happened is a major change in the economics of children's television, because it's now becoming increasingly difficult to mount children's television shows—even animated shows on Saturday morning, or rerun programs on independent stations sold through syndication—unless you can get backing from a toy company. Children's television is very expensive to produce, considerably more expensive than it was even in the 1970s. So the economics of the marketplace, not the demands or preferences of parents or citizens, are dictating what we see on children's television.

Donald Wear: Let me offer one additional thought and make a plea. All too often in children's television debates, the distinction between network television and independent television is lost. Now, you may not consider the network shows adequate in an ideal sense, but networks subject their children's television programming and children's television advertising to a rigorous set of standards, whereas independent stations do not. We would not accept, and do not accept, many of the shows that are seen on independent stations, and it's killing us economically. Every day we deal with advertisers that come in and say, "Why won't you let us do it?" and we could make lots more money if we went along. So I think parents and interested citizens need to bring pressure on their local independent TV stations to get more quality children's programs and to avoid the ones that you feel are bad.

PART
II
Role Portrayals

This part deals with the important issue of how various social groups, categories of people, and roles are portrayed in television entertainment and news programs. This is a vast topic, and most of the following chapters focus largely on the portrayal of women and of gender roles— the area that has had the most research, and which may serve as an example of the trends that other groups may experience in their changing treatment by television. However, attention is also given to the television portrayals of blacks, Hispanics, the elderly, and handicapped individuals.

Three of the authors in this part, Bradley S. Greenberg, Diana M. Meehan, and Gordon L. Berry, are professors and communication researchers who have written books and articles about the depiction of various social groups in the popular media. The other authors, Alice M. Henderson and Helaine Doktori, are officials of the CBS/Broadcast Group who are responsible for monitoring and approving the content of programs and commercials that are distributed by the CBS Network. They have provided both vivid examples of how women's role portrayals on television have changed over four decades, and detailed information on the program standards enforced by the network in its review of program content. The questions and answers following Chapter 11 also raise other issues about the effects of key television role portrayals, including those of men.

In Chapter 8, Bradley S. Greenberg reviews research findings on how women are depicted on television in many different countries and, more briefly, how blacks, Hispanics, and the elderly are treated by American TV. He then suggests that viewers' images of these groups may be influenced much more by some vivid or crucial programs than by others—the "drench hypothesis," as opposed to the "drip-drip" notion that our social images and stereotypes are built up by gradual accretion from each and every program we see. This intriguing viewpoint has intuitive plausibility, and it challenges researchers to find ways to study it empirically and objectively.

Chapter 9, by Diana M. Meehan, summarizes how various popular media have portrayed one type of female figure, the androgynous heroine who combines both typically masculine and typically feminine valued characteristics. In doing so it shows an overlooked streak of continuity in American media depictions over more than 50 years. It is followed in Chapter 10 by the script of a CBS videotape that demonstrates the other side of the picture—the pronounced changes in television portrayals of American women since World War II.

In Chapter 11, Gordon L. Berry emphasizes that American television is inherently multicultural—that is, it constantly displays one type of societal subgroup to other types—by virtue of the many social groups that it portrays and the diversity of the American viewing audience. After briefly summarizing some of the research showing that television depictions can affect viewers' (particularly children's) images of various social groups, he offers specific guidelines for fair and desirable multicultural portrayals on television. These guidelines deal with six different categories of roles: family roles, cultural and religious groups, racial and ethnic groups, gender roles, age roles, and portrayals of handicapped persons. Though these guidelines seem reasonable and constructive, they raise many questions about how they can be implemented. For instance, do they apply only across a whole period of programming, or can their requirement of balanced treatment of each social category (e.g., the elderly) be implemented within a single program? If so, would all programs about social problems (e.g., the homeless) and all entertainment shows about eccentric characters such as Archie Bunker be forbidden? If not, how would objections to unfair or biased presentations in a single program be reduced? Also there are questions about how "fair" or "even" treatment can be operationalized, and even whether a broad range of role character-izations is desirable for every social group (for instance, should children ever be depicted as the authorities in their family?).

In Chapters 12 and 13, Alice M. Henderson and Helaine Doktori provide detailed information on how one television network attempts to deal with such value questions, by enforcing specific program standards through its review of program content before programs or even commercials are allowed on the air. It appears that these program standards closely approximate the above guidelines suggested by Berry, and yet nevertheless, there is still much public dissatisfaction with TV role portrayals. This raises the possibility that we may be dealing with an insoluble problem, where no matter what course the industry follows, there will always be many criticisms of television content, some of them diametrically opposed. The industry emphasizes that its ultimate standards are imposed by public acceptance based on contemporary norms and mores, and that it changes as society changes, whereas many critics want it to lead society—and frequently in opposite directions. These are among the key issues discussed in Part II.

BRADLEY S. GREENBERG

8

SOME UNCOMMON TELEVISION IMAGES AND THE DRENCH HYPOTHESIS

To prepare this chapter, I began with the television section in my local newspaper. The TV columnist, Mike Hughes, said, "The subject tonight is women. There are angry women, and funny women and passionate women and more" (Hughes, 1986). He was right. On one Monday night, I could watch angry women—"Cagney & Lacey"; I could watch funny women—"Valerie" and "Kate & Allie"; I could watch "Between Two Women" (Colleen Dewhurst and Farah Fawcett); I could watch the final episode of a PBS miniseries about girlhood, "Anne of Green Gables"; I could watch the prevailing television sex expert (Dr. Ruth Westheimer). On an independent TV station, I could watch the first in a series on "Women of the World," seven episodes that showed women doing many things in different parts of the world. In it, there would be found an old Nazi catcher, a debutante devoting her fortune to charity, another who spent 2 years as a geisha, a successful romantic novelist, and a department store magnate. All these I could watch without touching my 30 additional cable channels.

Thus my first question is, Where is the contemporary stereotype of women? Or was it an off night for stereotype hunters? As I will argue, counting heads and averaging across all programs is a limited approach to assessing or cataloging role portrayals. However, the accumulated evidence is that the portrait of women on television is restricted.

This chapter focuses on the television image of women as a prototype, following a structure suggested by Gunter (1986), and it then examines parallel data for some other less common groups, for example, the elderly and ethnic minorities. Following this survey of content analysis findings, some suggestions for pertinent research approaches will be offered.

Images of Women on U.S. Television

First, there has always been and continues to be a substantial *underrepresentation* of women, if one takes 50-50 as a norm. In each of the last four decades, and regardless of whether the focus was adult prime-time programs or Saturday morning cartoons, males have outnumbered females by a ratio of about 3:1 (Signorielli, 1984). Deviations from this figure are found in different program types. The most dominant male province is the action-adventure program, where the ratio is about six males for each female (Miles, 1975). The greatest equivalence is found in the afternoon soaps (1:1 ratio) and in situation comedies (2:1; Barcus, 1983). The television lesson implied by this measure of sheer presence, whether in major, supporting, or minor roles, is that women are a less significant part of the populace. Counting fewer of them suggests that they count less.

Second, there is substantial evidence that women on television are constrained to a much *narrower range of sex roles,* primarily as wives and/or parents (Downing, 1974). Thus marriage (or divorce) and parenthood are of greater significance in the television lives of women than of men. Women's television roles are largely confined to a home life centering on family and personal relationships and interests. Even when seen in out-of-home contexts, the women's expressed concerns more often focus on family and personal matters. For instance, the settings of soaps and situation comedies are primarily domestic and their major activity is conversation—about romance, family matters, and other interpersonal relationships. Similar patterns are also seen in television women's relative lack of employment, their underrepresentation in professional occupations when shown as employed, and their lesser likelihood of combining marriage and any job (McNeil, 1975). Traditional views of the role of women are highlighted in the findings of these studies.

Third, there is a small set of sex traits consistently found among television women in content-analysis studies. One heralded trait is that women on television are more *emotional* and more in need of emotional support than are men, who in turn are more physical and more in need of physical support (Greenberg, Richards, & Henderson, 1980). Another is the *subordination* of women by men in interpersonal relationships. Variously, that has been studied in terms of men's greater competence, authority, order-giving, plan-making, and the eventual greater success that men enjoy in all these acts (Turow, 1974). Filling out this personality syndrome of television women is the finding that they typically appear *less likely to be in control of events* in their lives—that they are more likely to be controlled by forces external to themselves over which they have little if any influence (Hodges, Brandt, & Kline, 1981).

The *employment* status of television women is depicted in both the sex role and sex trait studies. In terms of roles, they are less often employed. In terms of traits, even when employed, they are in lesser occupations, less likely to be married, less likely to be successfully married, and 10 times as likely to be unsuccessful in marriage as housewives (Manes & Melnyk, 1974).

The consistency of this imagery over time is illustrated in one quite specific example. Kalisch, Kalisch, and Scobey (1983) looked at nurses in all U.S. television series and series pilots from the 1950s to 1982. Apart from changing from cotton to synthetic uniforms, the only change noted in 30 years of programming has been the addition of one new stereotype—the sexually promiscuous nurse—to their traditional role as nurturing listener and girlfriend.

These general findings apply to children's television as well as to prime time. In two studies, Barcus (1978, 1983) analyzed approximately 2,000 characters on children's programs and in both studies found that males outnumbered females by a 3:1 ratio. Schechtman (1978) examined occupation portrayals in such children's favorites as "Batman," "The Flintstones," and "Happy Days," and concluded that women were underrepresented as employed, and where employed, were generally portrayed in inferior occupational roles. Women on children's programs were mostly young and attractive, according to Long and Simon (1974).

One-sided pictures of women occur even more intensively in television advertising content than in programming. Knill and colleagues determined that men provided over 90% of the commentary carried with advertisements in the daytime and in prime time, and that 80% of the female product representatives were shown in family or household situations, whereas 70% of the men in commercials were portrayed in upper echelon occupations (Knill, Pesch, Parsey, Giltin, & Perloff, 1981).

Women Elsewhere in the World

All of the above refers to U.S. television. There is, however, more to the world of television than is contained within U.S. borders. In Nairobi, in July 1985, a report was presented to the World Conference to Review and Appraise the Achievements of the United Nations Decade for Women. (I wonder how many knew of this decade?) The report was based on responses from 95 countries, and a portion of it dealt with media images as of 1980 (UNESCO, 1985). In a brief summary, these conclusions were typical regarding the pre-1980 period:

- The media in Turkey tend to portray woman as "mother, wife, sex symbol."
- In Senegal, it is as "mother, wife, agent for development."
- In Korea, in depictions of a working woman, she is "seldom happy."
- Sudanese media find it "incumbent on them to portray women in an optimal image consistent with [Islamic law]."
- The Ivory Coast and the Netherlands note advertising's exploitation of women, who are shown as "charming, beautiful, frivolous, and fragile, or as mothers and housekeepers."
- In Yugoslavia, they report "petty (not pretty) bourgeois images."

This study also asked if there had been any changes in these images of women since 1975, and half the responding countries said there had been changes:

- An increased portrayal of women in professional situations was claimed by Ecuador, Jordan, Madagascar, and Zimbabwe.
- Switzerland said there was greater respect for women.
- Finland said there was greater equality of treatment.
- New Zealand reported that "women are probably being portrayed in a wider variety of roles and occupations in addition to their traditional supportive role, but there is no detailed evidence available to support this statement" (UNESCO, 1985, p. 38). (This leads me to question what detailed evidence was presented to support statements from other countries.)

The conclusion from these pre-1980 studies was similar to those of U.S. research reports:

A consistent picture emerges from these research studies which have investigated the media's portrayal of women. At the very best, that portrayal is narrow, at worst it is unrealistic, demeaning and damaging. There are no notable differences between the mass media in this respect. Some of the recent studies indicate the beginning of changes, which although slight, do provide some evidence that the mass media are not inescapably locked into a particular model of presentation. (UNESCO, 1985, p. 50)

All these findings were obtained from studies 5 years before the 1985 conference. So at the conference, there was an examination of the extent to which the conclusions were the same or different in 1985; studies from areas other than North America and Western Europe were emphasized.

From Niger came an indication of more complex and contradictory images, indicating conflict between traditional and contemporary roles. "Women are sometimes portrayed as strong, productive, individuals who make valuable contributions to their families and the development of their country. At other times, they are portrayed as sex objects . . . [or] convey a traditional image of women who are concerned with their role as mothers, homemakers and wives" (Keita, 1981).

From Sierra Leone, the same dualism—"Women are portrayed as men's equals and as leaders who take the initiative in assuming new responsibilities; some programs tend to emphasize women's traditional roles as housewife and mother" (Anani, 1981).

From Ethiopia and Tanzania came somewhat more qualitative reports indicating the same set of opposing trends (Herouy, 1981; Kundya, 1981).

Women in Egyptian radio, television, and newspapers were portrayed almost exclusively in traditional roles in the home, while the media addressed themselves to young, urban, married, middle-class women and ignored single, professional, and rural women (Rahman, 1981).

From Algeria, a more interesting conclusion: There is the image of the "seductress, whose total life is devoted to beauty questions on the one hand and to love and passion on the other" (Hammouche, 1984).

From Malaysia, Korea, and mainland China, studies of television drama found the conventional image pattern: Women less crucial to plot development, marriage and parenthood more important to women than to men, employed women subordinate to men, and women more passive. In China this represents a change from earlier reviews that emphasized the model revolutionary heroine, toward a pattern of imagery more common in countries with commercial media systems (Siu, 1981).

In India, a trend toward more negative portrayals of women was reported, rather than any improvement. This trend featured increases in violence toward women, in offensive advertising, and in availability of pornography (Agarwal & Bhasin, 1984).

From Canada, a similar refrain to that of India: "Sexism has taken on more subtle forms. Visual and written pornography have become a source of grave concern, with themes of violence and humiliation aimed against women sharply on the increase" (UNESCO, 1985, p. 38).

Studies of radio images in Hungary (Hanak, 1982) indicated that women tended to represent the "small world" of private life, and men the "large world" of public life.

In a study from Puerto Rico, women are shown as richer, and more often married than men. They are also less often involved with violence, more often with sexual innuendo, and less often portrayed as good characters (Canino, Bravo-Corrado, & Rubio-Stipec, 1985).

From whatever country, studies of sex roles in advertising show a particularly pernicious continuation of the portrayal of women as either household drudges or sex objects (e.g., Cuthbert, 1984—a study done in the Caribbean). In a recent British study, Manstead and McCulloch (1981) concluded the a recent British study, Manstead and McCulloch (1981) concluded that the portrayal of adults in British commercials is more sex role stereotyped than in American commercials. Compared to American ads, central female figures in U.K. ads much less often provided arguments in favor of the advertised products with which they were shown; they were less likely to be product users, and were more often depicted in home settings. In a Jamaican study (Royale, 1981), a direct comparison of men and women as sex objects showed that women exceeded men by a 5:1 ratio.

The situation in advertisements was summed up best by the Indian report: "Today our ads project the worst of Indian sexist attitudes. . . . On the one hand, the kitchen-confined housewife stereotype, and on the other the woman spread-eagled over a carpet in transparent underwear with the copy reading: Don't be a wallflower, use Peter Pan underwear" (Agarwal & Bhasin, 1984). This picture was echoed by Hoffman's (1984) study in Hungary, which found that the majority of advertisements were peopled by young women, whose sexual attractiveness was emphasized by portraying them prone on beds, floors, grass, and so on.

The above reports summarize the many states of women's media images elsewhere in the world, although primarily on television. It's a mixed bag; some situations are improving, some are getting worse, but most are about the same as they have been for decades, or at least as long as television has been available. These reports provide a useful alternative perspective to our typically parochial examination of U.S. media. Concerning the images of women in U.S. media, systematic content analyses show a great deal of stereotyping and inequality still persisting. And yet my casual sample of Monday night offerings gives much cause for optimism about the television portrayals of many types of women in highly varied sets of roles.

What We Don't See on TV

The elderly. It is surprising how seldom we think about the images we *don't* see on television. There is, for example, the paucity of old folks. Their presence on the screen is a small fraction of their rapidly increasing presence in the populations of many countries in the world.

Research in the U.S. finds that the old folks who appear on television are shown as quarrelsome, feisty, cranky, and not very physically active (Greenberg, Korzenny, & Atkin, 1980) or that they are typically foolish, eccentric, and held in low esteem (Gerbner, Gross, Signorielli, & Morgan, 1980). In both studies, old women were virtually absent, an empty cell—an especially strong contradiction of census figures.

What determines viewers' perceptions of old age has yet to be adequately examined. One U.S. study reported that heavy TV viewers put the onset of old age at a lower figure than lighter viewers, but both estimates were in the 50s (Gerbner et al., 1980). In a U.K. study, more survey respondents chose 70 as the first age at which they would describe a person as old, and there was no relationship between these estimates and amount of television viewing. More important, that study found that in the U.K. attitudes toward the elderly were not linked to amount of viewing, but rather to how old the viewer was (Wober, 1980). We do not know how these age estimates relate to perceptions of television characters. Specifically, do heavier viewers attribute the same or different characteristics to real-life "old" people as they do to "old" television characters, and how do those attributions compare with lighter TV viewers?

Another intriguing question is the perception of age by young viewers: What is old for a 6-, 10-, or 15-year-old? And does what is seen (or not seen) on television account for their attitudes (perhaps even behaviors) toward the elderly? In the absence of research evidence on this issue, it seems reasonable to anticipate that children may judge a 40- or 50-year-old television character as elderly and form their expectations of the aged accordingly. Consequently, there are two major reasons to favor having more elderly characters on television (arbitrarily stipulated as those in their 60s and 70s). One reason is to have models available for viewers of those actual ages. The other reason is to give a more realistic picture of old age to viewers who are younger. Since perception is subjective, viewers' perception of the traits of the elderly may not depend very much on their physical (or even their portrayed) reality. Consequently the few TV portrayals that do exist of the elderly may not be very contributory to public beliefs and feelings about the elderly.

Blacks on television. Systematic examination of blacks on television began in the late 1960s. One decade-long study used content samples from 1971, 1973, 1975, and 1980; during this period, black males increased from 6% to 9% of the male television character population, with no change found after 1975, and black females were 5-6% of the females in any given year (Seggar, Hafen, & Hannonen-Gladden, 1981). However, black appearances tend to be concentrated in a few shows; one study reported that 75% of the total time blacks were visible occurred in 18% of the shows (Weigel, Loomis, & Soja, 1980). However, in the daytime blacks have been consistently less visible; on soap operas, less than 3% of the speaking characters have been identified as nonwhite, and thus the black proportion would be even smaller.

The roles played by blacks have also been examined. In the multiple years examined by Seggar et al. (1981), major and supporting roles for black males *decreased* from more than 10% less than 5%, a decline verified by Gerbner and Signorielli (1979). Black females obtained 1-2% of such roles. Most typically, blacks were in situation comedies and largely cast in blue collar and service occupations. A final role attribute that persisted across studies was that younger blacks were more common. One-third of the whites and three-fifths of the nonwhites were under 35, and nonwhite teenagers were twice as frequent as white ones.

More interesting perhaps are the few studies in which cross-race portrayals have been examined, that is, blacks and whites on the same shows. First, cross-racial interactions were rare; only 2% of the human appearance time on a week's sample of prime-time shows involved such interactions, and they were almost exclusively in job-related contexts, compared with just half of the white-white interactions in that context (Weigel et al., 1980). In another study comparing 100 blacks with 100 whites on the same shows, half the blacks and none of the whites appeared on shows with 4 or more black characters (Baptista-Fernandez & Greenberg, 1980), again reflecting the ethnic segregation of programs.

Another content-analysis approach has been to characterize larger units of behavior, for example, families and work groups. For example, Greenberg and Neuendorf (1980) examined all TV representations of black and white families for 1 week. Black television families were more likely to be single-parent households; and black families seldom had kinfolk, whereas one-fifth of the white family members were cousins, uncles, and so on. But the major behavioral difference noted dealt with family conflict, which accounted for one-sixth of the interactions in black families and one-tenth in white ones.

Blacks have fared better in body counts of television advertising. By the mid-1970s, they typically constituted 12-15% of the characters in commercials, although there was a tendency for them to appear in crowd scenes with whites, rather than alone or with other blacks (Bush, Solomon, & Hair, 1977). Again applying their time-on-air measure, Weigel et al. (1980) found cross-racial appearances in commercials 5%

of the time and cross-racial interactions less than 2%. All-black commercials filled 2% of the time; all-animated commercials were twice that frequent.

On children's television, blacks have fared poorly; of 1,145 characters examined by Barcus (1983) in weekday and weekend programming directed at children, 3.6% were black. Again, they were distinctly more juvenile characters; 45% of the blacks compared to 24% of the whites were children or teenage characters. Weigel and Howes (1982) examined Saturday morning shows and found nearly half of the black appearances in a single program, and 85% concentrated in five shows.

Hispanic-Americans on television. Let us now consider the uncommon image of Hispanic-Americans. They remain a group seldom represented in television's regular or central characterizations. In the single published study of Hispanics on commercial television, they constituted less than 1.5% of the prime-time and Saturday morning fictional series characters, and none were identified in the Saturday morning shows. Further, these few Hispanics were clustered on just a few shows, a form of ghetto (or barrio) television described earlier regarding the black presence on television. There were five men to each women, exceeding the white gender imbalance, and most were cast as funny, crooked, or cops (Greenberg & Baptista-Fernandez, 1980).

Hispanics, who have not yet made strident calls for representation, remain marginally visible on U.S. TV. Whereas black Americans achieved a stable level of representation on television a decade ago (roughly 10% of the television character population) and then turned their attention to quality-of-portrayal issues, Hispanics have yet to progress through the several stages experienced by blacks and other demographic groups as they were introduced into regular television programming. The first stage of this image-analysis process is counting themselves to see if and where they can find themselves. Second comes concern about whether they are to be cast exclusively as clowns and buffoons in mid-size comic roles, or as children. It has been the pattern for minority characters to be introduced first in such roles, perhaps because programmers believe that such characterizations are less offensive and more palatable to majority-group viewers (but not, of course, to the real-life role holders being caricatured). It's hard to dislike a child, and it's easy to laugh at the pratfalls and woes of an unsympathetic comic character. Third, often concurrently more than sequentially, if the previous roles seem to have been accepted, minorities are likely to find new roles as cops and crooks in their next-to-last phase of television integration. Those are the first serious or semi-serious roles to be anticipated for adult actors of a minority group. Finally, at a stage still sought by those who find fault with the imagery of women and blacks on television, there is the hope to see more varied representations—sheer heterogeneity. At this stage, members of a group would not be typecast as anything in particular, but would enjoy a freedom of movement across roles, characterizations, story lines, and advertising spots.

Today Hispanics are the fastest-growing minority in the United States and predicted to be the largest minority before the end of this century, but they are still in the early stages of introduction into television programming. To date, we would still find perhaps only 2 Hispanic television characters out of 100, if it were a good week.

An Alternative to Head Counts

Having identified how "new groups" are introduced into the mainstream of television program content, let me propose that the next new group (or some not so new that are not yet satisfied with their imagery) consider an alternative route in its quest for equity or balanced representation. Let me also urge that researchers interested in the impressions formed from television images consider this route. I propose a diversion away from counting heads or bodies, and concentration on the question of whether there may be more impact from what can be termed "critical portrayals" than from the total number of portrayals.

If you were asked to close your eyes, to think about and visualize the TV portrayals of women you have greatly enjoyed or women you would want to be like—or old folks, or blacks—who would you think of? And what attributes or traits or behaviors are important in your judgment and recall? What characterizations have been most crucial in the vivid images you have developed? This group of portrayals significant to individual (and perhaps collective) memories should be examined more closely.

The drench hypothesis. The remainder of this chapter proposes that television may have more than a gradual, cumulative drip-drip-drip effect, although that is the prevailing assumption in the literature (aside from writers who posit no effect at all). On occasion, and perhaps more occasions than we acknowledge, certain role portrayals may generate a *drench effect.* Some characters in some series, or miniseries, or single programs may be so forceful as to account for a significant portion of the role images we maintain. It is those influential portrayals that should be pursued.

The primary hypothesis advanced thus far by others is that the incessant presentation of television characters in disagreeable roles or with unconscionable attributes—whether they be men or women, minorities or majority, gay or straight—develops in us a stereotype against which we assess real life as well as ideal images (Gerbner et al., 1980). That "cultivation hypothesis" has some limited research support. Yet it demeans the capacity of individual viewers to notice differences, in real-life or in the media, and it deprecates the television industry's ability to provide differing role portrayals.

My counterproposal is relatively simple. It asserts first that not all portrayals have the same impact. One woman is not every other woman on TV, one act of violence is not every other act, one minority character is not to be equated with every other minority character. Yet, typical content-analysis head counting assumes just that and specifically ignores individual differences in the power of performances. Counting presences serves principally to establish the overall level of visibility for some role or group, but arguing that equivalent group representation provides equity is a doubtful claim. That is why successive groups who have quested for more time and space in the media, whether in terms of fictional portrayals or news coverage, have become quickly disappointed with the additional faces presented and turned to quality-of-presentation issues. Innovative research approaches are needed to assess whether selected characters rather than the collected mass of role portrayals can have significant lasting impacts in their own right.

Take the current top-rated show on American television, "The Bill Cosby Show." A situation comedy about blacks? Yes. One featuring smart alecks or loudmouths, like "The Jeffersons" or "Sanford and Son"? No. Here the drench hypothesis would propose that, especially for young black and white viewers, the portrayals of blacks on the Cosby show may supersede or even overwhelm the black images derived from many other shows that have some blacks but in less distinguished, less interesting, and less positive characterizations. Do these other characterizations have less impact? The bulk of research has not focused on such possibilities, or only rarely, the miniseries "Roots" being an example (Poindexter & Stromen, 1981). To test these ideas, we could orient our research to focus on those role portrayals that stand out, are deviant, are intense, and thus are more important viewing experiences. Such research might begin with surveys of key viewing groups that attempt to determine key programs and characters with whom those viewers have especially chosen to identify, to favor (or to intensely dislike), rather than studying the mass of all programs available.

It seems likely that we viewers ignore most portrayals of most roles; they are minor parts of our total entertainment experiences, and we are resilient, perhaps resistant, to most of what we see. Probably we attend more closely to a limited set of portrayals, ones that become significant for us; but what is it that makes them significant—is it their intensity, their mood, the behavior they display? Are these significant elements common across viewers? These are important questions, for the significant portrayals are probably the ones we will carry with us in memory.

There are at least two practical dangers associated with this proposal. First, there could be an absolute reduction in female or black or other uncommon role presentations, which might be rationalized by the claim that "We're about to bring out a significant image." However, that loss could be countered by the kind of pressure already demonstrated by various activist groups monitoring television. Second, the proposal might lead to a surfeit of studies examining individual programs or characters or series, whereas a research strategy has yet to be identified that can explore potential *drench* candidates more inclusively. Such problems remain to be resolved.

Some Research Suggestions

Let us consider some initial thoughts about the kind of research efforts that might test these ideas. I would suggest commencing with open-ended interviewing, perhaps with young viewers who have a shorter history of television experiences. From these interviews we could extract the set of characters (or stories) identified as most important, most salient, most memorable. It might be prudent to start with a particular content area, such as women or blacks, although there is also merit in not delimiting the scope of inquiry too sharply at this stage. Respondents would be questioned as to why these particular characters have remained with them, and the character attributes they describe would be compared with those of other respondents, who may have chosen other characters.

Although this form of inquiry might generate a hodgepodge of characters more idiosyncratic than common across viewers, it is also likely to generate a relatively finite set of attributes used by a viewing group in making their assessments and discriminations. That key set of attributes would be an important discovery in its own right. An additional problem is that the viewers' responses may be overly based on current or recent television experiences. However, more intensive probing of recall could be used to offset that bias, using questions such as, "Of all the black people you have seen on television programs, who do you think is the most_____?"

Alternatively, one could begin this research with a more limited group of characterizations, utilizing more specific aided-recall strategies. For example, in the last decade or so, there have been a dozen medical shows in prime time to serve as a basis for assessing images of doctors, such as "M*A*S*H," "Ben Casey," "Trapper John," "St. Elsewhere," and several in the daytime as well, such as "General Hospital." One could compile a list of the doctors in these shows and then begin to determine which if any of these have had special impact, and why.

One also might approach the question more experimentally. For example, viewer ratings could be used to identify blockbuster attractions for a specific audience, such as children. Then selected episodes could be shown to a group of children in order to assess what it is that attracts them to the characters and/or situations. All the above suggestions could be formative stages in a programmatic research effort.

Returning to the question of Hispanics' presence on fictional television, the drench hypothesis would suggest working toward the development of a program or series that carefully crafts images of Hispanic characters for public consideration. It would suggest lessening the call for sheer numbers of Hispanics to be inserted into programming wherever it is convenient or where it makes no difference who plays the character—that is, let the call for large numbers follow rather than precede the attempt to establish initial, significant positive images. Finally, of course, the hypothesis requires conducting research to see whether the program or series makes a difference in either of two sets of critical perceptions: the self-perceptions of the Hispanic viewers.

The drench hypothesis, in its current, primitive form, asserts that critical images may contribute more to impression-formation and image-building than does the sheer frequency of television characters and behaviors that are viewed. The hypothesis provides an alternative to the no-effects hypothesis and to the view that the slow accretion of impressions cumulates across an indefinite time period. Finally, it also suggests that striking, new images can make a difference—that a single character or collection of characters may cause substantial changes in beliefs, perceptions, or expectations about a group or a role, particularly among young viewers. Whether those changes are lasting or temporary, or positive or negative, still remains to be demonstrated, as does the mechanism of the change process and the critical features of the characterizations.

REFERENCES

Agarwal, B., & Bhasin, K. (1984, August). Action for change. *Seminar,* pp. 38-42.

Anani, E. L. (1981). Sierra Leone. In *Women and the mass media in Africa: Case studies from Sierra Leone, the Niger and Egypt.* Addis Ababa: Africa Training and Research Centre for Women.

Baptista-Fernandez, P., & Greenberg, B. (1980). The context, characteristics and communication behavior of blacks on television. In *Life on television: Content analyses of the U.S. TV drama.* Norwood, NJ: Ablex.

Barcus, F. E. (1978). *Commercial children's television on weekend and weekday afternoons.* Newtonville, MA: Action for Children's Television.

Barcus, F. E. (1983). *Images of life on children's television: Sex roles, minorities and families.* New York: Praeger.

Bush, R. F., Solomon, P., & Hair, J., Jr. (1977). There are more blacks in TV commercials. *Journal of Advertising Research, 17,* 21-25.

Canino, G., Bravo-Corrado, M., & Rubio-Stipec, M. (1985). *The role of women in Puerto Rican television.* East Lansing, MI: Women in International Development.

Cuthbert, M. (1984). "Woman day a come": Mass media and development in the Caribbean. *Media Development, 31,* 18-21.

Downing, M. (1976). Heroine of the daytime serial. *Journal of Communication, 24,* 130-139.

Gerbner, G., Gross, L., Signorielli, N., & Morgan, M. (1980). Aging with television: Images on television drama and conceptions of social reality. *Journal of Communication, 30,* 34-47.

Gerbner, G., & Signorelli, N. (1979). *Women and minorities in television drama (1979-1978).* Philadelphia: Annenberg School of Communication, University of Pennsylvania.

Greenberg, B., & Baptista-Fernandez, P. (1980). Hispanic-Americans: The new minority on television. In *Life on television: Content analyses of U.S. TV drama.* Norwood, NJ: Ablex.

Greenberg, B., Korzenny, F., & Atkin, C. (1980). Trends in the portrayal of the elderly. In *Life on television: Content analyses of U.S. TV drama.* Norwood, NJ: Ablex.

Greenberg, B., & Neuendorf, K. (1980). Black family interactions on television. In *Life on television: Content analyses of U.S. TV drama.* Norwood, NJ: Ablex.

Greenberg, B., Richards, M., & Henderson, L. (1980). Trends in sex-role portrayals on television. In *Life on television: Content analyses of U.S. TV drama.* Norwood, NJ: Ablex.

Gunter, B. (1986). *Television and sex role stereotyping.* London: John Libbey.

Hammouche, A. (1984). Image of woman in the press and television. *Al-Raida, 1,* 27-28.

Hanak, K. (1982, August). The image of women in the radio. *Journal of the Hungarian Mass Communication Research Centre,* pp. 97-127.

Herouy, A. S. (1981). An overview of the mass media in Ethiopia and the role of women. In *Proceedings of the African women's features services workshop.* Nairobi: UNESCO Regional Population Communication Unit for Africa.

Hodges, K. K., Brandt, D. A., & Kline, J. (1981). Competence, guilt and victimization: Sex differences in attribution of causality in television dramas. *Sex Roles, 7,* 537-546.

Hoffman, M. (1984). *Gender advertisements in Hungary.* Paper presented at the 14th conference of the International Association for Mass Communication Research, Prague.

Hughes, M. (1986). *Lansing State Journal,* March 10.

Kalisch, P. A., Kalisch, B. J., & Scobey, M. (1983). *Images of nurses on television.* New York: Springer.

Keita, A. M. (1981). The Niger. In *Women and the mass media in Africa: Case studies from Sierra Leone, the Niger and Egypt.* Addis Ababa: Africa Training and Research Centre for Women.

Knill, B. J., Pesch, M., Parsey, G., Giltin, P., & Perloff, R. M., Still typecast after all these years: Sex role portrayals in television advertising. *International Journal of Women's Studies, 4,* 497-506.

Kundya, H. I. (1981). The state of mass media in Tanzania mainland. In *Proceedings of the African women's features services workshop.* Nairobi: UNESCO Regional Population Communication Unit for Africa.

Long, M., & Simon, R. (1974). The roles and statuses of women and children on family TV programs. *Journalism Quarterly, 51,* 107-110.

Manes, A. L., & Melnyk, P. (1974). Televised models of female achievement. *Journal of Applied Social Psychology, 4,* 365-374.

Manstead, A.S.R., & McCullough, C. (1981). Sex-role stereotyping in British television advertisements. *British Journal of Social Psychology, 20,* 171-180.

Maracek, J., Piliavin, J. A., Fitzsimmons, E., Krogh, E. C., Leader, E., & Trudell, B. (1976). Women as TV experts: The voice of authority? *Journal of Communication, 28,* 159-168.

McNeil, J. (1975). Feminism, femininity and the television shows: A content analysis. *Journal of Broadcasting, 19,* 259-269.

Miles, B. (1975). *Channeling children: Sex stereotyping on prime-time TV.* Princeton, NJ: Women on Words and Images.

Poindexter, P. M., & Stroman, C. (1981). Blacks and television: A review of the research literature. *Journal of Broadcasting, 25,* 103-122.

Rahman, A. A. (1981). Egypt. In *Women and the mass media in Africa: Case studies from Sierra Leone, the Niger and Egypt.* Addis Ababa: Africa Training and Research Centre for Women.

Royale, G. (1981). *Images of women in Caribbean TV ads: A case study.* Paper presented at the regional seminar on women and media decision-making, CARIMAC, Kingston, Jamaica.

Schechtman, S. A. (1978). Occupational portrayal of men and women on the most frequently mentioned television shows of pre-school children. *Resources in Education.* (ERIC Document Reproduction Service)

Seggar, J. F., Hafen, J., & Hannonen-Gladden, H. (1981). Television's portrayal of minorities and women in drama and comedy drama, 1971-80. *Journal of Broadcasting, 25,* 277-288.

Signorielli, N. (1984). The demography of the television world. In G. Melischeck, K. E. Rosengren, & J. Stappers (Eds.), *Cultural indicators: An international symposium.* Vienna: Austrian Academy of Sciences.

Siu, Y. (1981, Winter). TV images of Chinese women, *Asian Messenger,* pp. 39-42.

Turow, J. (1974). Advising and ordering: Daytime, prime time. *Journal of Communication, 24,* 135-141.

UNESCO. (1985). *Communication in the service of women: A report on action and research programmes.* Paris: Author.

Weigel, R., & Howes, P. (1982). Race relations on children's television. *Journal of Psychology, 111,* 109-112.

Weigel, R., Loomis, J., & Soja, M. (1980). Race relations on prime time television. *Journal of Personality and Social Psychology, 39,* 884-893.

Wober, M. (1980). *Television and old people: Viewing TV and perceptions of old people in real life and on television.* London: Independent Broadcasting Authority.

DIANA M. MEEHAN

9

THE STRONG-SOFT WOMAN:
Manifestations of the Androgyne
in Popular Media

One clue regarding what it means to be female in our society is provided by popular media. The behaviors, attitudes, and options permissible for women in our society are presented in the soaps and sitcoms, comic strips, and who-done-its of the popular media. Although the context is fanciful and exaggerated, these portrayals present the parameters of femaleness in our society, an index to acceptable womanhood.

Traditionally we've watered down the model passed to us from contributing cultures. In America, women characters have been weakened, the villains defanged, female heroes made to resemble damsels in distress. Cinderella in old-world versions of the tale is strong and cleaver; in America she has been translated as helpless and distraught (Yolen, 1983). Snow White is here represented as Disney's passive innocent; in European tales she represents "life-asserting qualities" (Kolbenschlag, 1979, p. 31). Moreover, Snow White has a sister in some versions, a foil, Rose Red, who is extroverted and active. She is missing in American stories.

Media analysts have noticed some change in female characters in the last decade. Daytime soap operas of the 1980s are less sex-typed than those of the previous decade (Cantor & Pingree, 1983). Radway (1984) found that recent romance novels represent female characters in male-dominated jobs, exhibiting behavior that is typically masculine, impelled by a desire for individuation and autonomy. These two genres are enormously popular and have been stereotypically "feminine" in appeal and approach. Their presentation of stronger, more autonomous females than in the past augurs well if it represents a trend in the media. I suggest that it does.

My analysis of various genres in several popular media has yielded a number of categories or types, one of which, the androgyne, is a strong, autonomous female image. It is a character who combines masculine-instrumental and feminine-expressive traits and behaviors, representing the full range of human potential (Bem, 1974; Heilbrun, 1973). Physically, she is frankly female—but is athletic, assertive, dominant, independent, and strong (masculine traits) and is also empathic, affectionate, gentle, nurturant, tender, and warm (feminine traits). This is a positive, balanced image of womanhood (Bem, 1975). Furthermore, it appears to be more popular than ever.[1]

Print Media

Print media offer some early examples of the type. In 1930 a pair of writers, Harriet S. Adams and Andrew Svenson, using the pseudonym Carolyn Keene, created a detective for the juvenile market, androgyne Nancy Drew. The female hero of this series of novels, still selling after more than 50 years, more than 50 volumes, and more than 50 million in sales, is a girl from River Heights in heartland America. Nancy is technically a teenager, 18 years old, but with abilities and circumstances a middle-aged hero could envy. Her lawyer, mentor, and male role model is her father; he treats her as an equal, inviting her advice on some of his law cases, providing emotional and financial support. Female support is provided by housekeeper Hannah Gruen, who worries about Nancy, cooks and cares for her "like a second mother," Nancy's biological mother being dead. Thus both male and female figures advise her and provide balance for Nancy.

A male-female balance is embodied in Nancy herself. Male character-istics include her work outside the home, where she has a reputation among professional criminologists as a good sleuth. Sleuthing itself would seem to be a masculine occupation the way she does it, since it is dominant (order-giving and judging) and rational rather than emotional. Another masculine attribute that Nancy possesses is independence; her financial status is moderate wealth, which provides her with clothes, car, free time, and a certain autonomy. She is also emotionally independent, linked to a boyfriend who is undemanding and occasion-ally helpful, an outside pillar to augment the support at home. Nancy is also athletic (without being obvious), able to swim, run, and mountain-climb; and she is active, dashing about in her own blue roadster, tracking clues, interviewing police.

Nancy's female characteristics are underscored by her physical form and hairstyle, which are feminine and conservative (and apparently timeless, as they've been serving her since 1930 without signs of age). She has shoulder-length, titian-colored hair and a large wardrobe including sports clothes and evening attire to cloak her trim figure. That she has a boyfriend reminds the reader she isn't gay, although her primary allegiance and time commitment is to her two female friends. She is loyal to her father, friends, and boyfriend, gentle with children and the elderly, and she does the dishes after dinner. She is also expressive, appreciating dainty cakes and tea, beautiful objects, comfort, and good manners. Manners are an important value in the novels, and their absence is a clue to criminal identity. Nancy asks politely, shows sympathy, avoids slang, uses titles, and displays the cues of feminine nonverbal behavior (Lakoff, 1975). By contrast, criminal suspects speak harshly and quickly, make noise, don't make eye contact. As a sleuth, her work may be as covert as theirs, but Nancy does it like a lady.

Whereas Nancy is a combination of masculine-feminine associations, her female friends are cousins who are polar opposites. One is fretful, decorative, comfort-loving; the other is impatient, impassive, forceful, and has a boy's name. Examples are evident in every novel:

> Bess and George were cousins but there any likeness ended. Bess, blond and pretty, had a penchant for second desserts and frilly dresses. She shared Nancy's adventure out of a deep loyalty to her but was constantly fearful of the dangers involved. George was as boyish as her name. Her hair was dark, her face handsomely pert. (Keene, 1967, p. 20)

> "I never turn down an invitation to anything exciting," George answered. (Keene, 1936, p. 81)

> "Here's his razor," said George, rushing in. Bess admitted that she was frightened. "The intruder certainly has a key to this house," she declared. (Keene, 1939, pp. 47-48)

> Suddenly one of Bess' turquoise earrings fell into her lap. "Oh this old earring makes me so mad. It's always falling off." "Why don't you tighten it?" George asked. She was apt to be impatient with her feminine cousin. (Keene, 1934, p. 5)

The cousins don't always get along with each other, but they both care very much for Nancy, endorsing her behavior with approval from both poles of masculinity and femininity. They provide a context within which to view the style and acts of the androgyne, a repeated motif in media representations of the androgyne. In the case of Nancy Drew, her positive traits are further emphasized by the support of the two adults, her father who praises and encourages her, and Hannah who nurtures her and serves her, making no demands (more in the manner of a godmother than a real mother). Thus Nancy has the blessings of both worlds.

Another androgyne was popular among readers of serial comic strips in the 1940s—the beautiful redhead, Brenda Starr. She is a newspaper reporter, flying to far lands to cover world events, ever stylishly coiffed and garbed. She has a beau, an elusive, romantic figure who is only occasionally met; but her primary supporters are two female friends—a mannish-looking colleague, Hank O'Hair, and her "pleasantly plump" cousin, Abretha Breeze, as round as Hank is angular.

As an androgyne, Brenda combines the ruthless pursuit of a rational order with a fabulous fashion sense. In comic strip simplicity, she has it all, the best of both dimensions. As with Nancy Drew and her cousins, Brenda Starr's appeal as a paragon is enhanced by the presence of her two friends, one somewhat masculine in dress and demeanor, the other overly feminine. Their portrayal of negative masculine and negative feminine features (O'Hair's aggressiveness and Breeze's weakness, for example) contrast with Brenda's positive portrayal.

Television

Television has had few androgyne characters in prime time until recently (Meehan, 1983). Then in 1970 the season opened with a series built around androgyne hero Mary Richards, named for its star "The Mary Tyler Moore Show." Mary Richards, in her early 30s, is older than Brenda Starr or Nancy Drew and more realistically and fully drawn as a character.

In many ways Mary is atypical of the television characterization of women. For example, Tedesco (1974) found that male TV characters generally surpass female characters in activity, independence, maturity, seriousness, power, and intelligence. Mary Richards, however, is more independent, emotionally and intellectually, than the male characters in her series. She possesses more power (by personality as well as position) than all but one of the male characters, and she is mature, serious, and intelligent. Her high activity level is evident in typical episodes of the 1974 season: Mary attends a broadcast convention (Lloyd, 1974a); Mary becomes the producer of the news (Lloyd, 1974b); Mary accepts a Teddy award for executive producer Lou Grant, who is too emotionally paralyzed to make the acceptance speech (Lloyd, 1974c). Except for male mentor Lou Grant (whom she calls "Mr. Grant"), Mary surpasses the men in positive male attributes.

Positive female attributes are also well represented, as Mary counsels, consoles, supports Lou in areas where he is weak, and encourages and cares for her coworkers, yet without acting the mother. She isn't one who pushes advice on friends, but one who expects friends to behave well:

> Murray: I thought I'd stop over at Judith's and look at that piano on the way home . . . So what do you think?
>
> Mary: Murray, don't do this to me . . . I think you want some sort of permission from me and you're not going to get it. (Silverman, 1974, p. 34)

With woman friends, Mary is affectionate and gentle; she is fond of Phyllis, her landlady, and warmly supportive of Rhoda, her closest friend. Without overmuch fanfare, Mary is supportive of women in general, sympathetic to the female condition.[2] In one episode she explains to Murray, "It's not fair to ask Marie [his wife] to have another child if she doesn't want one. Sometimes I think men have no idea of what's involved in caring for a baby, how much time it takes out of a woman's life" (Weinberger & Daniels, 1974, p. 24).

Mary's feminine attributes are shown physically by her slim woman's body, set off by stylish attire, earrings, shoulder-length hair. As with androgynes before her, all this is contrasted with the extreme attributes of her two female friends: Phyllis, the bony, angular apartment owner who is critical of others, argumentative, bold, and bossy; Rhoda, somewhat plump, artistic, insecure about men, whose work is nurturing plants. These two do not get along, but both admire Mary.

At work there are other female characters to contrast with Mary: Georgette, the news anchor's wife, a curly-haired waif with a little-girl voice; and Sue Ann, Mary's antagonist. Sue Ann is the reverse of the androgyne, a combination of the worst of masculine and feminine traits—overly sweet yet aggressive, dependent yet competitive. Sue Ann is a television chef, a job that combines domesticity and the spotlight in an ill-suited match, one that fosters a hearts-and-lace exterior and barely disguises the power-hungry businesswoman behind the scene. She sees Mary as competition for Lou and any available male in sight, but even with Sue Ann, Mary remains even-tempered, balanced, intrepid:

> Sue Ann: Competing with a man is both aggressive and unfeminine. I don't know what you hope to achieve, but your ambition is certainly obvious.
>
> Mary: Sue Ann, Mr. Grant has to stay here. (Lloyd, 1974a, p. 15)

When Mary went off the airwaves in 1977, the prime-time landscape emptied of strong adult women (with few exceptions). Mary was gone,

Maude was gone, bionic Jamie Sommers was gone. The most popular female-prominent shows were "Laverne and Shirley," "Charlie's Angels," "Alice," and "One Day at a Time," all of which showed female bondings, but none of which portrayed the strong-soft androgyne. Three of them were set in domestic or food environs, traditional female territory, while the characters on "Charlie's Angels" were sexual decoys or imp types whose forays into the violent world of men required constant rescues, if only by each other. The situation temporarily looked bleak.

Then in the early 1980s there came a corps of interesting television women who countered the drudges and decoys of the late 1970s. Many of the new characters were the creations of former or current writers from MTM, the production company that had invented Mary Richards: Elaine Nardo, the single, working mother of "Taxi"; Joyce Davenport, "Hill Street Blues" sassy, sexy lawyer; Dr. Annie Cavanero and female nurses, administrators, and resident physicians of "St. Elsewhere"; Laura Holt, detective-businesswoman of "Remington Steele"; and, finally, the androgyne Elyse Keaton of "Family Ties."

In the 1984 season chosen for review, Elyse Keaton is an architect (a field dominated by men), and Steven Keaton's wife, and the mother of their four children. The duality of her full existence is exemplified by this exchange:

Steven: So, how was your day?

Elyse: Well, let's see. First the Espositos decided that instead of a guest house they want a greenhouse. It seems they have more plants than friends. Then, when I got home Mallory and Alex were still arguing about the shirt and Jennifer was in the sixth straight hour of her phone-a-thon with Chrissy. I'd say the highlight of my day came when Andrew spit up his lunch.

Steven: I miss so much when I'm not here. (Reinhart, 1984, p. 21)

Elyse Keaton is a sexually mature, socially responsible adult woman whose life is characterized by a balance between masculine and feminine, between the outside world and the world of the family. She possesses all the androgyne attributes and, as two female foils, she has daughters Mallory and Jennifer.

Mallory is sensitive, socially active, obsessed with cashmere sweaters and clothing sales; her primary concern is matching her eyeliner with her outfit. Jennifer is the athlete, the good student, who punches the school bully for teasing her friend Adam. As their mother, Elyse participates in both worlds, advising Mallory on outfits and secretly enjoying Jennifer's victory over the bully. The ages of the other two females in the family serve to remind us that extremes in behavior are phases of growing up and that both dimensions are represented in the healthy adult. The aesthetic side of Elyse is expressed in her architecture career; the roles of tomboy and athlete have matured into a mate with a playful sense of fun:

> Steven: (throwing a football underhand lightly as Elyse enters)—Yo, Elyse, look alive!
>
> Elyse: (dropping a suit case and packages to make the catch)—Steven.
>
> Steven: And they say that pregnant women can't catch.
>
> Elyse: That's just an old wive's tale. (She throws the ball back to him.) (Weithorn & Bennett, 1984, pp. 1-2)

Androgyne Elyse Keaton appears on the second most popular television show in the country. The number one series, "The Bill Cosby Show," also has an androgyne lead in character Clair Huxtable, lawyer, doctor's wife, mother of five children. It is interesting to note that Clair Huxtable and Elyse Keaton between them mother nine children; it is as if their femininity is exaggerated to compensate for their success in masculine-identified professions.

By the mid-1980s, there are other androgynes, all in the most popular series on the airwaves: Maddie Hayes of "Moonlighting," a former fashion-model, owner of a detective agency, yet gentle, sensitive, and nonviolent; Jessica Fletcher, the post-prime-aged writer of murder mysteries, who is rational, independent, empathic, and nurturing in "Murder, She Wrote"; Amanda King, the housewife-spy whose mother and whose coworker Francine provide the polar opposites for her to play against in "Scarecrow and Mrs. King."

Films

Added to television's crop of androgyne heroines are those of the cinema. Joan Wilder is an adventurer and writer of romance novels in two recent releases, *Romancing the Stone* and *Jewel of the Nile;* she has a boyfriend who is a somewhat unreliable partner, a female literary agent who is brassy and supportive, and a sister who is more dependent than Joan and requires rescuing in the first film. In addition to having the positive attributes of the androgyne, she is occasionally defensive and demanding, indicating that she is still evolving.

Just Between Friends, a movie by writer-director Allan Burns (cocreator of "The Mary Tyler Moore Show" of the 1970s), has two female characters who are also evolving into androgyne women: Sandy Dunlap, assertive newscaster, and Holly Davis, an ex-dancer housewife. The film is about female bonding and becoming whole and balanced; each woman is incomplete as a solo operator but helps the other to fulfill her potential, even as they face the disturbing discovery that they've both loved the same man, Holly's husband. The two complement each other and contrast with other female types in the film: the sexpot at Sandy's station; the coach-owner of the exercise spa, who has little subtlety or sensitivity and the manner of a drill sergeant; and Holly's accommodating, dependent mother who discourages her daughter's attempts at autonomy. In spite of the obstacles, each principal finds strength to strive for autonomy, and the empathy and generosity to forgive the other.

Conclusion

At this stage we can only speculate as to what effects the androgynes have as role models on their audiences. On one hand, the positive images that androgynes portray may be largely offset by the crime-filled alleys and creaky elevators of the all-male spy-detective novels, the crime shows on television, and exploitative films in which women appear as cheerleaders or, worse, as victims.

Another drawback may be that the androgynes who do appear in popular media have always been of the fantasy variety: Clair Huxtable and Elyse Keaton with successful careers, happy husbands, and 4 or 5 children are clearly superwomen; Maddy Hayes is poor but fabulously chic; Jessica Fletcher has no dirty dishes, dust balls, or writer's deadlines to keep her from her avocation; and Amanda King has an obliging mother to do the chores. These are fantasy creatures removed from the struggles and difficulties of real life.

And yet their good points may still serve us well. They invite us to dream—which is at least 50% of role-playing. If they ignore the drudgery and the doubt of real women's lives, perhaps they may be forgiven in light of the aspirations, the desires, and dreams that they inspire. A plethora of strong-soft, assertive-affectionate women on small screen and large cannot be a bad thing. It may encourage real women and girls to be heroes in their own lives—heading families, heading corporations, conquering fears, and coping with change. Personally, I think we could not have had Geraldine Ferraro without Nancy Drew and Brenda Starr, and I expect Madame President of the future will be beholden to Mary Richards and Elyse Keaton.

NOTES

1. In a book entitled *Ladies of the Evening: Women Characters of Prime Time Television,* Meehan (1983) described and analyzed popular female characters who peopled evening episodic television from 1950 until 1983. She found 10 types: *Imp* (rebellious and rowdy), *Goodwife* (beneficent but banal), *Harpy* (aggressive single woman), *Bitch* (strong-willed, selfish, and destructive), *Victim* (one who suffered pain, disease, imprisonment, or death), *Decoy* (bait in chic clothing), *Siren* (insidiously sexy), *Courtesan* (an entrepreneur in painted face and peacock feathers), *Witch* (woman with special power), and *Matriarch* (prominent, competent, courageous older woman). The *Androgyne* appeared on television in the late 1960s in the short-lived "Ghost and Mrs. Muir" and then as the lead character in "The Mary Tyler Moore Show" discussed here. The type was relatively rare on popular prime-time programs until the 1980s, when such women appeared in major roles on "Taxi," "Hill Street Blues," "Cagney and Lacey," "Remington Steele," "St. Elsewhere," "Cheers," "Family Ties," "Kate and Allie," "The Bill Cosby Show," and "Golden Girls," among television's most popular, honored episodic programs.

2. "The Mary Tyler Moore Show" is pro-woman, but not necessarily pro-women's movement. Mary seldom endorses movement goals, other than equal employment, and the show steers a wide berth around issues such as abortion, lesbianism, and child care. The premise seems to be that women as individuals can fight for their rights and make great gains. The women's movement, however, specifically advocates group support for group gain. Mary may be liberated but she's no "women's libber."

REFERENCES

Bem, S. L. (1974). The measurement of psychological androgyny. *Journal of Consulting and Clinical Psychology, 42,* 155-162.

Bem, S. L. (1975). Sex role adaptability: One consequence of psychological androgyny. *Journal of Personality and Social Psychology, 31,* 634-643.

Cantor, M. G., & Pingree, S. (1983). *The soap opera.* Newbury Park, CA: Sage.

Heilbrun, L. G. (1973). *Toward a recognition of androgyny.* New York: W. W. Norton.

Keene, C. (1934). *The clue in the broken locket.* New York: Grosett & Dunlap.

Keene, C. (1936). *The mystery of the ivory charm.* New York: Grosett & Dunlap.

Keene, C. (1939). *The clue of the tapping heels.* New York: Grosett & Dunlap.

Keene, C. (1967). *Secret of the wooden lady.* New York: Grosett & Dunlap.

Kolbenschlag, M. (1979). Breaking the spell of feminine myths and models. In *Kiss Sleeping Beauty good-bye.* New York: Bantam.

Lakoff, R. (1975). *Language and woman's place.* New York: Harper & Row.

Lloyd, D. (1974a). Anybody who hates kids and dogs. *The Mary Tyler Moore show,* No. 7409.

Lloyd, D. (1974b). Mary the producer. *The Mary Tyler Moore show,* No. 7422.

Lloyd, D. (1974c). What are friends for? *The Mary Tyler Moore show,* No. 7425.

Meehan, D. (1983). *Ladies of the evening: Women characters of prime time television.* Metuchen, NJ: Scarecrow.

Radway, J. A. (1984). *Reading the romance: Women, patriarchy, and popular literature.* Chapel Hill: University of North Carolina Press.

Reinhart, R. (1984). Bringing up baby. *Family ties,* No. 60584-067.

Silverman, T. (1974). The affair. *The Mary Tyler Moore show,* No. 7401.

Tedesco, N. (1974). Patterns in prime time. *Journal of Communication, 24,* 119-124.

Weinberger, E., & Daniels, S. (1974). Baby, baby. *The Mary Tyler Moore show,* No. 7419.

Weithorn, M., & Bennett, R. (1984). Lost weekend. *Family ties,* No. 60584-049.

Yolen, J. (1983). America's Cinderella. In A. Dundes (Ed.), *Cinderella: A casebook.* New York: Wildman.

10

CHANGES IN WOMEN'S ROLES ON TELEVISION

In the postwar era of the '40s and '50s, the primary occupations for women were found in the service fields, particularly in service around the home. However, economics forced many middle-class married women into the work force. The evolutionary process began, and television as a newly acquired family member shared these changing times. May I introduce you to Alice and Ralph Kramden (Jackie Gleason and Audrey Meadows in "The Honeymooners"):

Alice: I'm the secretary. I'm the only girl in the office.

Ralph: You're the only girl in the *whole* office!

Alice: Yes.

Ralph: Boy! There must be a riot around that water cooler!

Alice: Listen, Ralph. I don't know what you're building in your mind but you're just being ridiculous. Millions of girls work in offices every day with men and nobody thinks a thing about it. First of all, those guys are all so busy they don't have time to give *me* a second thought. Though I couldn't very well tell them that I was married. They don't believe in hiring married women. That's an office rule.

Ralph: And so that Frank and Phil and Pete and George—they don't know you're married either?

Alice: Of course not. You see they think if they hired a married woman, you know, she might leave to raise a family, or her husband might just tell her to quit or something.

Ralph: Oh, they're *so* right! You are quittin'! You are quittin'! And this isn't your brother talking, this is your husband.

Gradually we saw more and more women's faces on the screen as we turned the dial, in leading roles in and around the home as well as in

AUTHOR'S NOTE: This script of a brief videotape produced by the CBS Television Network dramatically illustrates some of the points about women's changing roles on television made in the preceding chapters. Permission to print and © copyright by CBS Television Network.

supporting roles in all professions. But some things didn't change. Men continued calling the shots.

> Woman: Can I say something, if you will?
> Man: Only if it's what I want to hear.
> Woman: And if not?
> Man: Then let me hear silence.

Women in the news were rarely earth-shattering.

> Woman (talking to puppets): I'm Maria McLaughlin and I've come to talk to you about this time every day about the news.

By the late '60s, women's roles were changing. The focus remained on the home for many, but 41% of us moved into the work force and into positions previously reserved for men only. Economic recognition was another story.

> Mary Richards: I would like to know *why* the last associate producer before me made $50 a week more than I do.
> Lou Grant: Oh, because he was a man.
> Mary: Let me get this straight. The only reason he was paid more than I am is because he was a man?
> Lou: Well, sure, it has nothing to do with your *work*.
> Mary: Now wait a minute, wait a minute. You know, because I want to understand this—I'm doing as good a job as he did?
> Lou: Better.
> Mary: Better! And I'm being paid less than he was because . . .
> Lou: You're a woman.
> Mary: Well, Mr. Grant, there is no good reason why two people doing the same job at the same place shouldn't be making the same . . .
> Lou: He had a family to support, you don't. (Long pause.) Now why don't you come back when you have an answer to this? (Mary leaves and immediately returns.)
> Mary: Ah hah! Because financial need has nothing to do with it. Because in order to be consistent with what you're saying, you would have to pay the man with three children more than the man with two children, and the married man more than the bachelor, and Mr. Grant, hah!, you don't do that. So what possible reason can you give me for not paying me at least as much as the man who had this job before me?
> Ted Baxter (opening door): Say Lou.
> Lou: Yes, Ted.
> Ted: Oh, I'm sorry. I didn't know you were busy.
> Lou: Oh, we're not, we're not. Come on in, Ted. . . .

Lou: You know, Mary, I've been thinking. And there is no reason why you should be making $50 a week less than the person who had that job before. So, I'm raising you $25 a week.

Mary: Uh, well, Mr. Grant. I'm not sure you, you know, *fully* understand the principle involved here. I mean . . .

Lou: The whole $50, huh?

Mary: Right.

Lou: Okay, I'll try and get you $50 a week more.

Mary: Oh, thank you, Mr. Grant.

Ted: Why are you giving a $50 a week raise to someone who told me to shut up on the air?

Lou: It's all I can afford, Ted.

Even in the home, old rules were challenged.

Edith Bunker: Do you think that the work I do here in the house, the cookin' and the washin' and the cleanin' and the shoppin', is worth a dollar a week?

Archie: About.

Edith: Well I figured it all out, see. A dollar a week for 52 weeks, cause there's 52 weeks in a year, comes to $52 a year.

Archie: Well, that's close, yeah.

Edith: And we've been married 30 years, right? That's ten three's. And ten 52s is $520, and three $520s comes to $1,560, which *you* owe *me*.

Archie: Hold, hold, hold, hold it!

Edith: Let's make a deal. If you pay me right now $500, I'll let you keep the $1060 that's left.

Archie: What do you mean keep? When the hell did I ever have it?

Edith: When you didn't pay it to me.

Archie: But I don't see it nowheres. What did I do with it?

Edith: Well, how should I know? See? You don't have to tell *me* every time you spend your money. Why should I tell you?

Women are now moving into the forefront, exploring issues that cross gender lines.

Woman in group treatment: I got the sweetest husband in the whole wide world and you should see how I treat him. (Sigh.) I never was good for nothin' anyhow. My daddy always knew that. I don't mean to hurt anybody, you understand, but it just don't matter because I always seem to wind up doing it anyhow. (Sighs, whispers) And I lie. I lie something awful.

Therapist: Are you lying now?

Woman: Hell, no, I really am all those things (sobs).

Therapist: What would you like most in this world right now?

Group member: Other than a drink?

Woman: A bath. (Pause.) Well, me and some fellow members, I should say lady members, are going to start the first recovery house for women.

Programs began reflecting the changes in society.

Allie: When do you *really* feel divorced? I mean completely.

Kate: When your ex-husband is dead.

Allie: You know when Charles first told me that we were splitting up, I thought, oooh, this is how it feels to be divorced. And then when I got the final decree, I thought, hmmm, *this* is how it feels to be divorced. And then when he married Claire . . .

Kate: You thought oh, oh, *this* is how it feels to be divorced.

Allie: And now he's starting a family. You know at the rate I'm going, my divorce is going to last longer than my marriage.

To some the changes appear as a revolution. To others, more of a natural evolution.

Police lieutenant: You think a second whip can walk in and take over just like that? . . .

Cagney: I could learn to love this job. . . .

Lacey: You look right at home behind that desk. . . .

Police inspector: What was a woman that pregnant doing in the squad room? I want her out of here *today.*

Lacey: You know what's bugging Nelman? Pregnant is not a good image for one of his detectives. . . .

Cagney: Get your tail back here.

Cop: You know, you're real cute when you're angry, Cagney. . . .

Peetrie: You're on some sort of power trip.

Cagney: Okay, stop right there, Peetrie. . . .

Cop: Don't try muscling in to impress the department.

Cagney: I could bring you up for insubordination, detective.

Women are setting and achieving their own goals. Each step is expanding the options and presenting new challenges.

Man: It says, that the department is going to recommend that you be considered for tenure. Owing to the high caliber of your teaching and the exceptional quality of your poetry.

Woman: What? . . . And *without* a Ph.D. Hah, hah! That's what Marvin's so upset about. This is amazing.

Man: Well it would be except that there's this thing about the rumors. The one about the Longfellow award?

Woman: Awards make lazy artists.

Man: Well, you're already lazy so you'd make a perfect choice.

Woman: No, I don't believe in competition between artists. Besides who would say I was the best?

Man: Well . . . you, for example, have said so on many occasions. Barb, no woman has ever won this award in its *entire* history.

Woman: Now you're baiting me.

Man: No, I'm not. I'm only urging that because the Longfellow is so prestigious you ought to take it a little more seriously. Cause—the rumor is that you're one of the people they're thinking about giving it to.

On the newsfront we see women in positions only dreamed of 10 years ago.

Woman: I'm Diane Sawyer. Those stories, and Andy Rooney tonight on 60 Minutes.

Consistently women are not only reporting the news but making it. In the law courts, on the tennis courts. The victories keep on coming for women in every field of endeavor across this nation. After all, the sky's the limit.

11

MULTICULTURAL ROLE PORTRAYALS ON TELEVISION AS A SOCIAL PSYCHOLOGICAL ISSUE

Television as a Multicultural Door to the Universe

After 40 years of research and evaluation of television, most of us are aware that it is more than a medium that came to dinner one day, and that it will neither disappear nor be changed into the form that we individually might want it to have. Rather, we know that television is a permanent member of the family, and it actually is just the tip of the iceberg in relation to the other electronic media that are emerging or waiting in the wings.

After all these years, researchers, educators, parent groups, and professional communicators know a good deal about the findings regarding psychosocial effects of television on that very special audience, children. However, we must realize that television research challenges our statistical procedures and evaluation models because of the great variability in ways that children are socialized, and their selectivity in learning from television's cognitive and affective messages.

We know that, when well used, television can provide many benefits in entertainment, information, and education. Used carelessly or improperly, however, its power can confuse or mislead developing children through its special visual symbols, the level of its language usage, the power of its value-oriented messages, the behavior of its characters, the sophistication of its special effects, and the mixture of fantasy and reality sequences in its portrayals (Peel, Schauble, & Palmer, 1981; Rice, 1984; Stroman, 1984). In terms of both its positive and negative capabilities, television is not only a great "window to the world," but also a multicultural door to the universe.

The universe created by the portrayals of people, places, and events

AUTHOR'S NOTE: Special acknowledgment is made to Ann Benvenuti, Sally Cressani, and Kathy Silbert.

on television provides images and ideas that can have important meanings to all television viewers, and to the developing child in particular. With the turn of a knob or the push of a button, a child can learn day by day the number of new moons discovered around Uranus, the joy and eventual sorrow of Challenger, the courage of women such as Winnie Mandela and the late Marilyn Klinghoffer, the poverty and unemployment levels in our central cities, the despair in the farm country, the transfer of power in the Philippines, and information about people in far-off lands that would never have been known except through this door to the universe.

Purposes and Assumptions of This Chapter

The first purpose of this chapter is to point out the relationship between social attitudes acquired through the traditional agents of socialization and the multicultural attitudes that can be learned from a nontraditional socializing vehicle such as television. Second, I will offer a set of guidelines that suggest how various groups might be portrayed in order to transmit to young viewers a positive world view that shows the strengths of multicultural experiences. In considering these guidelines, it is important to note that they are not intended to restrict any First Amendment rights of broadcasters or to stifle any aspect of the creative process in writers or directors.

I make the basic assumption that, by its very nature, the content of commercial as well as public television is usually multicultural as well as cross-cultural. It is multicultural because television portrayals so frequently display similarities and differences among ethnic groups, religions, cultural and subcultural groups, genders, social classes, handicapped groups, sexual orientations, and generational groups. Moreover, it is cross-cultural because these portrayals are so often presented to audiences who have different demographic characteristics than the groups being portrayed.

Thus I am using the term *multicultural* to describe the diverse and sometimes special television portrayals of the following: (1) family roles, (2) general cultural and ethnic roles, (3) gender roles, (4) roles related to religions, (5) generational or age roles, and (6) roles of the disabled, mentally and physically challenged, or handicapped. Clearly, this view of multicultural portrayals is broader than the traditional inclusion of simply ethnocultural or racial groups. I emphasize this view of multiculturalism because of the very wide range of storytelling opportunities available to television programs, and the potential social learning along all these dimensions that television makes available to the developing child. Also, all of these types of roles have concerned researchers who have studied the effects of television portrayals on the attitudes of children (Berry & Mitchell-Kernan, 1982; Comstock, Chaffee, Katzman, McCombs, & Roberts, 1978; Murray, 1980).

Learning and Attitude Development in Children

Throughout history, children have learned about their own culture and themselves through the traditional agents of socialization: the family, school, religious institutions, and the peer group. It was through these institutions, especially the family, that children acquired many of their social attitudes and learned the values of their society. Research has shown that the medium of television, like traditional agents of socialization, can have a real impact on the views, values, attitudes, and behaviors of children (Comstock, 1978; Leifer, Gordon, & Graves, 1974; Liebert, Neale, & Davidson, 1973). Social attitudes, whether learned by traditional or nontraditional means, are important because they involve evaluative classifications and organized beliefs that are formed toward other people as role models (Bandura, 1977; Collins, 1983). Studies have shown that the more a child admires and believes in a role model whose behaviors are rewarded or recognized, the more he or she will imitate and identify with the model (Bandura, 1977; Berger, 1980; Miller & Dollard, 1941).

From many research studies we know that television programs offer intriguing value-oriented messages and attractive role models that are admired, believed, and potentially initiated by many children. According to Gerson (1966), television functions as a socializing force in at least two ways: by reinforcing existing values and attitudes, and by serving as a source of norms and values that offer solutions to personal problems. As Adler (1976) put it,

> Television is not a medium but a mediator between fact and fantasy; between our desires to escape and our need to deal with real problems; between our old values and new ideas; between our individual lives and the life of a nation and world. (p. 13)

However, Gross and Morgan (1980) have pointed out a limitation to television's potential impact:

In the matter of socialization, television has lot of competition. . . . In general television should be most influential when the viewer has either no contact (direct or mediated) with a given topic or when the television version is most congruent with the immediate environment. (p. 6)

Another limitation is present in the capability of our research instruments to detect subtle perceptions that may be absorbed by young viewers (Berry, 1982; Comstock, 1980). That is, the child may have his or her own unique frame of reference that affects what will be cognitively and affectively processed (Meringoff et al., 1983). Thus the way in which television's messages are learned and processed becomes complicated by being filtered through the young viewer's own "psychosocial attitudinal environment" (Dorr, 1983; Durkin, 1985; Salomon, 1983). As one example, some investigators have found that preschoolers process remarkably little of the complex information presented to them in certain programs (Collins, 1975; Singer & Singer, 1976).

Guidelines for Multicultural
Portrayals on Television

Whatever else commercial television is or does, one of its primary goals is to entertain. It is a tall order, therefore, to expect television scrupulously to offer the types of portrayals that capture the multifaceted aspects of human behavior and present desirable cultural depictions. Yet, because of television's power to define social reality about viewers' own groups, as well as about people and cultural groups that are different from viewers' own groups, it is important that its cultural lessons not be distortions of reality (Comstock et al., 1978; Greenfield, 1984; Wilson & Gutierrez, 1985). As Moody (1980) stated,

The child in the affluent suburb or the small midwestern town exists within his own limited reality. His experience with social problems or people of different races, religions, or nationalities is probably somewhat limited. It is precisely because he now relies so heavily on TV to define other realities for him that we must examine so carefully what those images are. If they are distorted, inaccurate, or unfair, then television's reality is potentially harmful. (p. 111)

There have been many studies that demonstrated television's power to foster both positive and negative multicultural attitudes in children (Allen & Chaffee, 1977; Berry, 1980; Comstock, 1975; Durkin, 1985;

TABLE 11.1
Guidelines for Family Portrayals

1. Program content portrays a variety of family constellations—such as nuclear, single parent, extended, and solely adult.
2. Program content avoids demeaning or patronizing portrayals of family constellations.
3. Program content shows families in a diversity of professional and vocational careers and roles.
4. Program content neither validates nor invalidates a particular family constellation.
5. Program content portrays families functioning throughout the range of socioeconomic conditions and life-style situations.
6. Program content does not define or limit role characterizations for family members in terms of their position in the family.
7. Program content portrays active, creative, and problem-solving roles for various family members.
8. Program content uses dialogue between various characters that is free of stereotypic language and demeaning labels/or retorts based on position within the family.
9. Program content focuses on the strengths of the depicted family constellation as well as their problems.
10. Program content does not stereotype personality traits based on a character's family position.

Gerbner & Gross, 1980; Greenberg & Atkin, 1982; Stroman, 1984). It is clear from the research that children can and do learn from both accurate and inaccurate cultural portrayals. Thus, as Graves (1980) has pointed out, programs that consciously include minorities in positive portrayals can change racial attitudes in a positive way.

Therefore this section of the chapter provides a set of guideline statements that can be used (1) by programmers as a reference point in analyzing the types of content portrayals they have included in a program, and (2) by researchers in devising cross-cultural content-analysis criteria for the evaluation of television programs.

The guidelines are divided into six major cultural and social areas that have provoked the most concern about television's multicultural portrayals:

(1) family portrayals that display the diverse patterns, situations, and behaviors that can make up a familly unit (presented in Table 11.1);
(2) portrayals of cultural and religious groups that reflect their diversity and

TABLE 11.2

Guidelines for Cultural and Religious Portrayals

1. Program content reflects religious and cultural diversity within historical and contemporary, international and American society.
2. Program content avoids demeaning or patronizing portrayals of customs, languages, and traditions of depicted religious, cultural, national, and international groups.
3. Program content shows members of various cultures and religions functioning in a diversity of professional and vocational careers and roles.
4. Program content neither encourages nor discourages the viewer's adoption of portrayed religious or cultural beliefs or practices.
5. Program content portrays members of various cultures and religions functioning throughout the range of socioeconomic conditions and life-style situations.
6. Program content does not define nor limit role characterizations for members of a particular culture or religion.
7. Program content portrays active, creative, and problem-solving roles for various members of the culture or religion.
8. Program content uses dialogue between various characters that is free of stereotypic language, demeaning labels, and/or retorts based on cultural or religious group membership.
9. Program content focuses on the strengths and contributions of various cultural and religious groups as well as the problems occurring in such groups.
10. Program content does not stereotype personality traits on the basis of membership in a cultural or religious group.

---

strengths, while avoiding stereotyped or demeaning depictions (Table 11.2);

(3) ethnic group portrayals that do not disparage persons because of their race, color, national origin, ancestry, or occupation (Table 11.3);

(4) female and male portrayals that show the contributions of both men and women in all types of roles (combined with ethnic group guidelines in Table 11.3);

(5) age or generational role portrayals that display diverse occupational, social, educational, and health-related behaviors within a framework of independence (Table 11.4);

(6) portrayals of handicapped and mentally and physically challenged individuals that reflect independence, intelligence, and the ability to function in society at many different levels (combined with age role guidelines in Table 11.4).

TABLE 11.3
Guidelines for Ethnic Group [Gender] Portrayals

1. Program content portrays various ethnic groups [both males and females] evenly in society, including depictions of historical, cultural, and current events.
2. Program content portrays various ethnic groups [both genders] evenly in their contributions to the arts and sciences.
3. Program content shows a diversity of professional and vocational roles and careers among various ethnic groups [each gender].
4. Program content does not define or limit occupational aspirations in terms of ethnicity [gender].
5. Program content portrays various ethnic groups [both genders] throughout the range of socioeconomic conditions and life-style situations.
6. Program content portrays both traditional and nontraditional activities performed by characters, regardless of ethnicity [gender].
7. Program content portrays active, creative, and problem-solving roles proportionally among various ethnic groups [males and females].
8. Program content uses dialogue between various characters that is free of stereotypic language, demeaning labels, and/or race-related [gender-related] retorts.
9. Program content portrays emotional reactions such as fear, anger, aggression, excitement, love, and concern regardless of ethnicity [gender].
10. Program content does not stereotype personality traits based on ethnicity [gender].

TABLE 11.4
Guidelines for Portrayals of Age Roles [Handicapped Persons]

1. Program content portrays elderly persons [handicapped persons] evenly in society, including depictions of historical, cultural, and current events.
2. Program content portrays evenly the contributions made by elderly persons [handicapped persons] in the arts and sciences.
3. Program content shows a diversity of professional and vocational roles and careers among elderly persons [handicapped persons].
4. Program content does not define or limit occupational aspirations in terms of age [handicapped conditions].
5. Program content portrays elderly persons [handicapped persons] throughout the range of socioeconomic conditions and life-style situations.
6. Program content does not define or limit role characterizations for elderly persons [handicapped persons] in terms of age [their handicapping conditions].
7. Program content portrays active, creative, and problem-solving roles proportionally for elderly persons [handicapped persons].
8. Program content uses dialogue between various characters that is free of stereotypic language, demeaning labels, and/or age-related [handicap-related] retorts.
9. Program content focuses on strengths and abilities as well as age-related [handicap-related] disabilities for elderly [handicapped] persons.
10. Program content does not stereotype personality traits based on age factors [handicapping conditions].

Concluding Thoughts

It is true that there is disagreement as to the amount of power and causal effectiveness of television in the development of social attitudes. However, there should be little controversy over the view that, whenever children are watching television, its explicit and implicit messages are always capable of teaching them something.

To the extent that television creates fair and accurate portrayals, it expands people's collective understanding and helps them to acquire a valid world view (Moody, 1980). The concern for assisting children to broaden their world view about people and cultures different from themselves is especially important because television can bring the universe into their living room. Proving positive multicultural and cross-cultural portrayals on television for children can guard against a "culturally encapsulated" view of people and cultures. Pedersen (1981) describes the encapsulated person as one who defines reality according to a noncultural set of assumptions and stereotypes, who is insensitive to cultural variations among individuals, and who becomes fearful or defensive when his or her assumptions are threatened by an alternative religion, political view, or cultural value. Some authorities fear that, if biased media portrayals are frequently presented with the social and psychological power of mass entertainment, they can threaten the strength and integrity of a society that is as culturally diverse as that of the United States (Wilson & Gutierrez, 1985).

Professional communicators who make the decisions about what is presented on television must always remember that they have a special responsibility to children, because these viewers are still in the process of forming their world view. However, television officials are not the primary people responsible for molding and shaping the multicultural attitudes of children toward themselves, other people, and the world; parents and other significant adults in the life of each child are the ones who must take the leadership in this area. Ideally, professional communicators, parents, researchers, and interested public groups should work together as mediators and "creative critics" to help television programming to live up to its quality potential, and to help children learn to be wise consumers of this potent medium.

REFERENCES

Adler, R. (1976). Introduction: A context for criticism. In D. Carter (Ed.), *Television as a cultural force* (pp. 1-16). New York: Praeger.

Allen, R. L., & Chaffee, S. (1977). Racial differences in family communication patterns. *Journalism Quarterly, 54,* 8-13.

Bandura, A. (1977). *Social learning theory.* Englewood Cliffs, NJ: Prentice-Hall.

Berger, S. (1980). *The developing person.* New York: Worth.

Berry, G. L. (1980). Children, television and social class roles: The medium as an unplanned curriculum. In E. L. Palmer & A. Door (Eds.), *Children and the faces of television* (pp. 71-81). New York: Academic Press.

Berry, G. L. (1982). Research perspectives on the portrayals of Afro-American families on television. In A. W. Jackson, *Black families and the medium of television* (pp. 47-59). Ann Arbor: Bush Program in Child Development and Social Policy, University of Michigan.

Berry, G. L., & Mitchell-Kernan, C. (1982). *Television and the socialization of the minority child.* New York: Academic Press.

Collins, A. (1975). The developing child as a viewer. *Journal of Communications, 25,* 35-44.

Collins, W. A. (1983). Interpretation and inference in children's television viewing. In J. Bryant & D. R. Anderson (Eds.), *Children's understanding of television: Research on attention and comprehension* (pp. 125-150). New York: Academic Press.

Comstock, G. (1975). *Television and human behavior: The key studies.* Santa Monica, CA: RAND Corporation.

Comstock, G. (1978, March). *Television and social values.* Paper presented at a meeting of the National Institute of Mental Health, Washington, DC.

Comstock, G. (1980). New emphases in research on the effects of television and film violence. In E. Palmer & A. Dorr (Eds.), *Children and the faces of television* (pp. 129-148). New York: Academic Press.

Comstock, G., Chaffee, S., Katzman, N., McCombs, M., & Roberts, D. (1978). *Television and human behavior.* New York: Columbia University Press.

Dorr, A. (1983). No shortcuts to judging reality. In J. Bryant & D. Anderson (Eds.), *Children's understanding of television: Research on attention and comprehension* (pp. 199-220). New York: Academic Press.

Durkin, K. (1985). *Television, sex roles and children.* Philadelphia: Open University Press.

Gerbner, G., & Gross, L. (1980). The violent face of television and its lessons. In E. Palmer & A. Dorr (Eds.), *Children and the faces of television: Teaching, violence, selling* (pp. 149-181). New York: Academic Press.

Gerson, W. M. (1966). Mass media socialization behavior: Negro-white differences. *Social Forces, 45,* 40-50.

Graves, S. B. (1980). Psychological effects of black portrayals on television. In S. Withey & R. Abeles (Eds.), *Television and social behavior: Beyond violence and children* (pp. 259-289). Hillsdale, NJ: Lawrence Erlbaum.

Greenberg, B. S., & Atkin, C. K. (1982). Learning about minorities from television: A research agenda. In G. Berry & C. Mitchell-Kernan (Eds.), *Television and the socialization of the minority child* (pp. 215-243). New York: Academic Press.

Greenfield, P. M. (1984). *Mind and media: The effects of television, videogames and computers.* Cambridge, MA: Harvard University Press.

Gross, L., & Morgan, M. (1980, March). *Television and enculturation.* Paper presented at the meeting of the National Workshop on Television and Youth, Washington, DC.

Leifer, A. D., Gordon, N. J., & Graves, S. B. (1974). Children's television: More than mere entertainment. *Harvard Educational Review, 44,* 213-245.

Liebert, R. M., Neale, J. M., & Davidson, E. S. (1973). *The early window: Effects of television on children and youth.* New York: Pergamon.

Meringoff, L. K., Vibbert, M. M., Char, C. A., Fernie, D. E., Banker, G. S., & Gardner, H. (1983). How is children's learning from television distinctive? Exploiting the medium methodologically. In J. Bryant & D. Anderson (Eds.), *Children's understanding of television: Research on attention and comprehension* (pp. 151-179). New York: Academic Press.

Miller, N. E., & Dollard, J. (1941). *Social learning and imitation.* New Haven, CT: Yale University Press.

Moody, K. (1980). *Growing up on television.* New York: Times Books.

Murray, J. P. (1980). *Television and youth: 25 years of research and controversy.* Boys Town, NE: Boys Town Center for the Study of Youth Development.

Pedersen, P. (1981). The field of intercultural counseling. In P. Pedersen, W. Lonner, & J. G. Draguns (Eds.), *Counseling across cultures.* Honolulu: University of Hawaii Press.

Peel, T., Schauble, L., & Palmer, E. (1981). A checklist of seven common production mistakes. *Television and Children, 4,* 33-37.

Rice, M. (1984). Television language and child language. In J. P. Murray & G. Salomon (Eds.), *The future of children's television* (pp. 53-58). Boys Town, NE: Boys Town Center for the Study of Youth Development.

Salomon, G. (1983). Television watching and mental effort: A social psychological view. In J. Bryant & D. Anderson (Eds.), *Children's understanding of television: Research on attention and comprehension* (pp. 181-198). New York: Academic Press.

Singer, D. G., & Singer, J. L. (1976). Family television viewing habits and the spontaneous play of preschool children. *American Journal of Orthopsychiatry, 46,* 496-502.

Stroman, C. (1984). The socialization influence of television and black children. *Journal of Black Studies, 15,* 79-100.

Wilson, C. C., & Gutierrez, F. (1985). *Minorities and media.* Newbury Park, CA: Sage.

QUESTIONS AND ANSWERS

Q: I've always found the area of television role portrayals to be quite short on effects research. Some speakers have said that these narrow and negative role portrayals can potentially affect people's multicultural world view. Others say that it remains to be seen what the effects are, but that more positive role portrayals couldn't hurt. But the whole area seems to be lacking in convincing studies of the effects of watching particular television content.

A related point is that television, by its very nature, seems to caricature people, and most of the research on role portrayals seems to examine only groups that have traditionally been the victims of social discrimination. However, if one examines, for example, the image of white males on television, you'll find that they are also caricatured— they tend to be inarticulate, terribly violent, and pretty helpless and infantile. A study in Canada of men's roles in television commercials found that, particularly in household-product commercials that were shown during the day, men were portrayed as helpless and bumbling. But then later in the evening, when more men were in the audience, men's roles in television commercials became much more competent, attractive, and powerful.

So what is the overall policy impact of research on role portrayals, in the absence of a strong body of effects studies, and in a media context where caricatures of certain groups are identified but not usually compared with caricatures of all the other groups portrayed on television?

Bradley Greenberg: On the issues of caricatures, an important question is how many caricatures there are—Is there a single caricature of a particular group as the word "caricature" suggests, or are there multiple portrayals? Within the United States at least, evidence shows increasingly varied role portrayals of women and of one minority group, black Americans.

For other groups, however, I think caricatures do still exist. For example, old people on television are still extremely rare, and they are portrayed as cranky, feisty, and quarrelsome, in England as well as in the U.S. Although "Golden Girls" may be the beginning of a breakthrough, for the most part, the portrayal of old people still is a caricature, a single distorted image, in several countries. Similarly, there is still a very limited number of role portrayals of Hispanic Americans on TV, and so we could call their image a stereotype or a caricature.

Gordon Berry: Research has shown that, when a particular cultural group is quite isolated from the rest of society, children's beliefs and feelings about these minority groups frequently are influenced by the way they are portrayed on television. So consequently, these groups should be portrayed on TV in a very meaningful way and very fairly.

Some cultural groups have had more media attention to the positive nature of their life-style and their culture than other groups. Thus, there are some groups that can stand more of the variety of portrayals that would include some negative ones, whereas other groups in our society by the current nature of things have to struggle to keep their life-style and the value of their culture evident to their young people. There's nothing wrong with showing the human foibles of minority groups as long as there is also a presentation such as "The Bill Cosby Show," for example, that displays their positive qualities as well.

Q: I'm concerned about the physical appearance of women portrayed on television. Though we now have a wider variety of role activities for women characters, still the appearance of women characters is by and large limited to our view of attractive women. One hypothesis is that that may mask some fears about homosexuality. In any case, I don't think children get realistic role models on television, either in appearance or in portrayals of role behavior.

Diana Meehan: That's also a concern of mine. One of the things that I noticed with the androgyne image is that we tend to equate grooming and beauty with femininity. So we have huge industries, the cosmetic industry and the fashion industry, which tell us that we're not all right the way we are, that we have to change ourselves. As a woman and a mother of two daughters, I'm unhappy that the media give this presen-

mother of two daughters, I'm unhappy that the media give this presentation of our society's values.

At this point in time, we find almost all of our heroes and heroines to be attractive. However, in "Cagney and Lacey" there is a character who is not as attractive as the traditional stereotype. When we start to see female heroes who look like Bella Abzug or Barbara Jordon or so on, then this greater range of portrayals will begin to show us that beauty isn't what counts. But at the moment we're still struggling.

Q: Several presentations have been about women's roles, but it seems to me that male roles on television are probably more of a social problem than female roles. This is true, for example, of violent roles where many males roles idealize violence, and also of the way that men treat women on TV. Furthermore, in completely focusing on women's roles, there's the implicit suggestion that women are somehow a problem and that men aren't.

I think we can't really solve women's problems, insofar as they have them, if we don't deal with the behavior of men. This is even true in the area of androgyny. I'm happy to see that there are more androgynous women on television, but what about androgynous men?—they are absolutely critical. Unfortunately, androgyny is often portrayed as going back to the superwomen role, which many women have worked long and hard to avoid—where the woman is taking two or three roles: career woman, housewife, and perhaps also mother, while the man still only has one role.

If women's roles are going to change, men's roles will have to change reciprocally. As long as television is only portraying changed female roles and not changed male roles, then we're missing half of the problem.

Diana Meehan: It's true that we have more research at the moment on women's roles, but I think men's roles in television have changed. For instance, the segment that I quoted from "Family Ties" is about the father trying to get home in time to spend some time with his wife. The father in "Family Ties" is an androgynous male. He is very much involved in his role as a father, as is the father on the Cosby show. I'd say that is one of the defining characteristics of those two prominent men on those two very popular shows. So I think the androgynous characteristics of some males in the media have shown noticeable positive changes over time.

ALICE M. HENDERSON
HELAINE DOKTORI

12

HOW THE NETWORKS MONITOR PROGRAM CONTENT

Program Practices is probably the least known department at each of the networks. We are responsible for determining the acceptability of all entertainment programs including sports, prime-time, daytime, and children's programming, as well as commercials. We work closely with those involved in the production of what is broadcast: writers, producers, and directors in program production; advertising agency executives as well as their clients, and production personnel for the clearance of commercials; and our own programming and sales executives.

We also meet with representatives of various recognized special interest groups who frequently offer insights to their specific areas of concern. Input from these organizations, our affiliated stations, and our viewing audience is given careful consideration in the formulation and application of CBS broadcast acceptance policy.

Organizationally, we are split into two primary sections: Commercial Clearance and Program Clearance. Program Clearance is further split between New York and Los Angeles to accommodate the production organization of different programs.

The department is composed of individuals with a wide range of experience in the broadcasting industry and others with specific training in such varied fields as pharmaceuticals, psychology, law, the performing arts, teaching, and communications.

We start with outlines and scripts, or storyboards for commercials, and suggest revisions where necessary in order to comply with our network guidelines. In the commercial clearance area, we review an average of 1,000 scripts, storyboards, roughcuts, or produced commercials each week. Each of the commercial clearance editors has developed expertise and is responsible for the clearance of commercials in specific product categories.

The categories include the following: corporate, institutional, political, carbonated beverages, publications, household appliances and furnishings, transportation, travel, hotels, public service announcements, statistics, schedules, insurance, medical products, vitamins, dental products, reducing aids and weight control, real estate, clothing, textiles, fabrics, toys, video games, computers, cereals, cameras, coffee and tea, personal products, automobiles and accessories, gasoline and petroleum products, room deodorizers, insecticides, tobacco products, luggage, shaving products, watches, clocks, jewelry, children's premiums, contests, banks and investments, credit cards, beer and wine, food products, baby food, telephone communication equipment, electronic entertainment, hardware/paint, mail order, office equipment, baby products, personal grooming, cleaning, pet food, household cleaning products, writing implements, sporting goods, billboards, motion pictures, records, restaurants, undergarments, hair products, cosmetics, paper products, candy and snacks.

Each submission from an agency is followed by a Commercial Clearance report, which indicates to the client agency whether approval has been given or withheld, details about the decision, or whether and what additional information/substantiation is requested. At this stage of the process prior to approval, we often work closely with our Research Department.

Program Clearance involves the review and approval for dramas based on fact, contest/award programs, theatrical films, children's programming, and new programs. Clearance includes script review, issuance of notes, research where appropriate, meetings, review of roughcuts/dailies, and attendance at shootings when necessary.

Many factors enter into the consideration of proposed programs. Some of these are set out in our *CBS Program Standards,* which are purposely broad to enable the exercise of subjective judgment in what is an extremely creative medium.

Generally speaking, our concerns in Program Clearance are that plots and characters be balanced in the presentation of ideas and issues and that sexual themes, violent action, and language be neither gratuitous nor exploitative. We also look at stereotyping and role portrayals, not only for women but of all people. Whether it is the elderly or women or an ethnic or religious group, Program Practices watches over their character development in each of the programs.

One of the most important factors used in our review is the audience's expectation. Not only does the viewing audience for individual programs vary—Saturday morning viewers are a different type and age from the viewers of prime-time programs—but every individual viewer brings a different attitude and background. Indeed, each of us brings different expectations to each of the programs we watch. The editors in Program Practices are trained to review program material with a view toward meeting this enormously complex set of audience expectations.

The detailed *Program Standards* that we follow are reprinted in Chapter 13.

13

PROGRAM STANDARDS FOR THE CBS TELEVISION NETWORK

The CBS Television Network has been dedicated since its inception to presenting the American television viewing public with entertainment and other programs of the highest caliber and standards. Over the years, this commitment has developed into an extensive case history of program-by-program judgments as to what constitutes material suitable for broadcast on CBS. Generations of Program Practices editors have conscientiously applied and refined them. Our broadcast standards tell an interesting and important story about the CBS sense of public and corporate responsibility toward its viewers. That story is reflected in this publication.

Introduction

In order to understand the CBS Program Standards and the process by which they are applied, it is necessary to understand certain characteristics of our medium, our industry, and CBS.

First, we exist for, and ultimately succeed or fail by, how well we serve the needs and interests of our viewing public. This public is vast, incredibly diverse, and, we believe, both knowledgeable and discriminating.

Second, we are built on human creativity—our business is not

EDITOR'S NOTE: These *Program Standards* are reprinted, with brief excerpts, by permission of and © copyright by the CBS/Broadcast Group.
The CBS TELEVISION NETWORK PROGRAM STANDARDS are subject to CBS's sole interpretation and may be subject to change from time to time. Thus the CBS TELEVISION NETWORK PROGRAM STANDARDS may not reflect current CBS practices, interpretation, or policy. The CBS TELEVISION NETWORK PROGRAM STANDARDS are reprinted with the permission of the CBS/Broadcast Group. All rights reserved. No portion may be reproduced without the prior written permission of the CBS/Broadcast Group.

derived from material resources but from people who strive to further human expression and development.

Third, we are a dynamic medium, never static but constantly evolving as the society we serve evolves around us.

Finally, we operate in an intensely competitive environment—the most advanced and prolific media marketplace in the world. To survive, we must search for new and rewarding ways to respond to our viewing public.

In this environment program standards must not only articulate important principles of responsibility to our audiences, they must do so in a manner that does not inhibit the responsiveness, dynamism, creativity, and innovation of the programs we are to present.

There is no way to feed a television program into a computer and determine whether it meets appropriate standards for the "typical television viewer." Indeed, there is no "typical viewer." Each year CBS broadcasts over 6,000 hours of programs to a vast audience of widely divergent backgrounds and interests. Every viewer brings a slightly different perspective to each program he or she watches. It would be impossible to anticipate and address in one set of standards each and every potential viewer reaction to that which we broadcast. Our standards address the "mass audience" that watches us, recognizing that, in the final analysis, it is the individual viewer that establishes his or her own standards, for it is in the viewer's power simply to change channels or turn us off.

The standards to which entertainment programs broadcast on the CBS Television Network are held are enunciated here. But it must be constantly appreciated that program review is ultimately a subjective and personal process of skilled and caring individuals—writers, producers, directors, actors, programming management, Program Practices editors, and viewers-interacting among themselves.

General Standards

A CBS television program is a guest in the home. It is expected to entertain and enlighten but not to offend or advocate. CBS entertainment programs are intended to conform to generally accepted boundaries of public taste and decorum, although as those boundaries change over time, programs will strive to be contemporary. In pursuing these goals, CBS takes into account the suitability of the time period in which a particular program is to be broadcast and the corresponding differences in audience composition and expectation.

Language. The language in a broadcast must be appropriate to a public medium and generally considered to be acceptable by a mass audience. Coarse or potentially offensive language is generally avoided and, if permitted for important dramatic reasons, cannot be employed flippantly or exploitatively. Blasphemy and obscenity are not acceptable for broadcast.

Nudity and sexuality. If consonant with prevailing societal standards, used for legitimate dramatic or historical purposes, and not perceived as exploiting the body for prurient interests, certain degrees of undress are acceptable.

The depiction of sexual intercourse is unacceptable for broadcast. Scenes or dialogue involving sexually oriented material necessary for reasons of plot or character development must be presented with good taste and sensitivity and cannot be gratuitous or exploitative.

Characterizations. Creative imperatives of the script will dictate the behavior and mannerisms of all characters. Character portrayals must be carefully crafted and sensitive to current ethnic, religious, sexual, and other prominent social concerns and unacceptable stereotypes. Care is also to be exercised when depicting characters subject to physical or mental disabilities to ensure that such persons are not demeaned.

Accuracy and misapprehension. A CBS television program must be what it purports to be.

Programs or scenes containing elements whose technical accuracy is important to maintaining public confidence in the integrity of a profession or institution must strive to be accurate in all material regards. Consultation with qualified advisors is encouraged.

Presentations that could convey the misapprehension that a dramatized of prerecorded event is occurring "live" or in the form of spontaneous news coverage of a contemporary event are not permitted. Use of words such as "bulletin" or devices such as "horizontal crawl" are unacceptable and reserved solely for the use of CBS News.

In any case where it may be unclear on its face what a broadcast purports to be, appropriate viewer advisories will be considered.

Violence. As a component of human experience, the dramatic depiction of violence is permitted. Here, violence is defined as "the use of physical force against persons, or the articulated, explicit threat of physical force to compel particular behavior on the part of a person." Accidents and incidents of comic violence are not included in this definition. Any depiction of violence must be relevant to plot and/or character development. It should not be gratuitous, excessive, or glamorized. Violence should not be used exploitatively to entice or shock an audience. The intensity and frequency of violent incidents should be consciously reviewed to ensure adherence to the foregoing standards. The use or portrayals of animals shall conform to accepted standards of humane treatment.

Substance abuse. Character portrayals and scenes depicting consumption of alcohol, drugs, cigarettes, and similar substances must be thoughtfully considered, essential to plot and role development, and not glamorized. When the line is crossed between normal, responsible consumption of a particular substance and abuse, the distinction must be clear and the adverse consequences of abuse specifically noted and explored.

Children and Television

Children watch television throughout the day, throughout the week. Parental supervision and interaction is the best means by which to ensure that children do not watch or are not confused or distressed by programs that are intended for an adult audience and that may contain mature themes and scenes. In certain cases CBS will broadcast and include in the promotional material for a particular program viewer advisories intended to alert parents to the need for special attention.

Programs intended for the child audience are reviewed with special care and, in some areas, according to different and perhaps more rigorous standards:

Role modeling. Protagonists, "heroes," should exemplify the most positive elements of social and personal codes of conduct such as honesty, fairness, compassion, and respect for authority. Attitudinally, such characters should show respect for important societal institutions, concern for distinguishing right from wrong, and commitments to such ideals as justice, ethics, and humanity. Characters that represent unacceptable social and personal conduct need not be avoided but must be clearly portrayed as undesirable.

Violence. Violence should not be portrayed as a socially acceptable means of conflict resolution. It should not be glorified, made to seem fascinating, amusing, or palatable. While villains may exhibit some violent behavior, this action should not be imitable, horrific, or extended in its presentation. Acts that carry the potential for violence should be clearly set in the realm of fantasy. Human beings should not be severely harmed or killed.

Jeopardy and peril. While a certain amount of jeopardy may be appropriate in a particular program, characters should not be placed in circumstances that provoke excessive or prolonged anxiety, or suggest gratuitous psychological pain. Characters should not be placed in hopeless situations, and those in peril should be presented with ways to overcome their predicaments.

Responsible social practices. Whenever appropriate, socially responsible attitudes and practices should be favorably portrayed and reinforced. When socially inappropriate or irresponsible behavior is portrayed, it should be disparaged and discouraged.

Commercialization. Program content and commercial messages must be clearly distinct. (See *CBS Television Network Advertising Guidelines.*)

Dramas Based on Fact

The artistic device of combining elements of fact with elements of fiction to produce a condensed dramatic whole is a longstanding and widely accepted one. It is found in literature, the theater, and cinema. It is equally appropriate to television.

There are many program forms that combine elements of fact and fiction. They can be placed along a continuum that begins with pure and unequivocal fact at one end and ends with pure fiction at the other. On this continuum are found programs based on legend, those adapted from specific autobiographies, those based on particular biographies or histories, and, finally, teleplays derived from original research.

A viewer who is aware of what kind of program is being presented is capable of evaluating the program in the light of his or her own knowledge and experience, taking into consideration the professed limitations and idiosyncrasies of that program form and the material on which it is based. Accordingly, the program and its promotional material should represent clearly to the viewer its genre and frame of reference. In some cases, viewer advisories that label or categorize the nature of the program or the material on which it is based, or present any other information that may be pertinent to a full viewer understanding of the program, may be helpful and will be used when appropriate.

Dramas based on fact adapted for television from another published source, and so denominated, must faithfully represent, in all material regards, the plot and characterizations of the original work. The nature of further review by Program Practices will depend on the type of literary work involved, its subject matter, and the background of the author. This review will seek to ensure proper viewer appreciation of the program according to the standards articulated above.

The original television drama based on fact, sometimes referred to as the "docudrama," is a particularly challenging program form. Its material factual components should be accurate and cannot be changed merely to enhance dramatic value. Fictionalized elements consistent with the events being presented may amplify or enhance the story, so long as they do not materially alter or distort history. Any presentation of a significant controversy should be done in a fair and balanced way. To ensure the achievement of these standards and thereby the integrity of this program form, the following guidelines are generally applicable.

- Unsubstantiated elements may be included only if they do not distort the material factual elements of the historical record.
- Omissions of historical information which materially distort the perception of historical events are not acceptable.
- Editing or condensation in the portrayal of historical events should maintain the accuracy or value of those events. Distortions of time, changes in the sequence of events or composite events which materially alter the historical record are to be avoided.
- All characters, including composite characters, based on real persons must accurately reflect those persons in reality and their actual roles and behavior in any significant events in which they are portrayed. Thus, in a composite character based on real persons, each of the characteristics and actions ascribed to the composite character(s) must be properly derived from the characteristics and actions of a real person or persons involved in those events. Composite or fictional characters used in roles essential to development of the main plot(s) must be carefully reviewed to ensure that their fictional or representative nature does not undermine in any material way the overall accuracy of the historical events portrayed.
- Care should be exercised in the employment of production techniques,

such as casting, character, and dialogue interpretation which have the potential to alter or distort the historical record.

These guidelines are applicable to all dramas based on fact. Any program project involving very sensitive themes, or events that occurred in or are presently surrounded by a highly charged atmosphere, or which is to be broadcast in close time proximity to the actual events on which it is based, is to be evaluated with great caution.

Theatrical Films

Standards for programs created for television are applicable to films originally created for theatrical release and subsequently broadcast on the CBS Television Network. Application of these standards to theatrical films will take into account the frequent inability to make changes for television in the film during its production and the limited ability to excise material after a film is complete without unacceptably altering its nature and creative integrity.

Game Shows

CBS has adopted and continuously refines rules and procedures to ensure that game shows are conducted honestly, fairly, and as they appear to the public. These procedures guard against contestant access to information that could jeopardize the fairness and integrity of the game. Steps are taken to ensure that no contestant is placed in advantageous or disadvantageous circumstances outside the game competition itself. Disruptions that necessitate editing of the broadcast must be disclosed. All programs must conform to Sections 317, 507, and 508 of the Communications Act of 1934.

Promotional Materials

All promotional material must accurately and tastefully reflect the content of the program to which it refers. Program material not cleared for broadcast cannot be included in the promotional material for that program. Certain elements, while acceptable in the context of the program, may not be suitable for inclusion in promotional materials. On-air promotion will be scheduled to ensure that it is appropriate to the program in which it is placed.

Procedures

Selection or creation of entertainment programs for broadcast on the CBS Television Network is the responsibility of the CBS Entertainment Division. Some programs are wholly produced by the division. Most programs are produced for the division by independent producers and production companies and licensed to CBS for telecast. The Program Practices Department reviews all of these programs for compliance with our *Program Standards*. Program Practices is not a part of the CBS Entertainment Division or the CBS Television Network but a completely separate and independent staff function of the CBS/Broadcast Group.

A television program begins with a spark of imagination in the mind of its creator. It takes form over a period of time through the collaboration of many people. Program Practices editors are involved in this process from the very outset and follow a program through all stages of its maturation to final approval of the completed project.

In many cases, the *CBS Program Standards* are clear and easily applied by the producers themselves with minimal guidance from our editors. In other cases—those involving novel themes or particularly sensitive subjects or program elements—more complex and sophisticated judgments must be made about the applicability of and compliance with the standards. Here, the involvement of Program Practices editors will be more extensive. Thus the timing and extent of program review is determined on a program-by-program basis.

Generally, an editor's observations on program compliance are offered at the concept, outline, script, rough-cut, and final cut stages. At the script stage, an editor will issue detailed, often page-by-page, scene-by-scene, or line-by-line, notes. Such notes might range from requested dialogue or scene staging changes to directional cautions on the execution of a particular scene. Often alternative approaches to problem areas are discussed with the creative team. This interaction between the Program Practices editor and the creative team continues through to the program's completion.

When advisable, qualified experts may be consulted to provide the information necessary to ensure accurate or appropriate portrayals. This is particularly true in the area of children's television where child psychologists are frequently consulted.

Original dramas based on fact are a unique and challenging program form and review procedures are structured accordingly. Most are produced by independent producers outside of CBS. The producer is expected to undertake extensive and reliable research into the factual elements of the drama and should have the ability and resources to do so. In applying the original drama based on fact standards, Program Practices will test the producer's research through an evaluation of that research and independent cross-checking, at times involving original research by Program Practices and, when appropriate, specifically including personal interviews of real persons portrayed in the program. The nature and magnitude of original CBS research and the process of factual verification will vary from project to project. Projects will also be reviewed by the CBS Law Department, and the nature and extent of that review will be tailored to the particular program.

Postscript

As noted at the outset, television is a dynamic medium. The *Program Standards* articulated here express the principles embodied in and the standards to which program broadcast on the CBS Television Network are held. But these standards cannot be immutable. For the ultimate principle to which we subscribe is that the viewer and society at large set the standards of acceptability. As cultural and social views change over time, we must be prepared to respond.

PART III

Television Violence

This part takes up the most thoroughly studied topic of television research: the amount of violence in television programming and its effects on viewers, particularly children. Despite all of the past research, this topic still remains one of the most controversial in the media field, as the following selections demonstrate.

All of the authors in Part III are researchers and authors who have written about television violence, but they have reached notably different conclusions about that topic. Several of them are academic researchers (Jonathan L. Freeman, Jerome L. Singer and Dorothy G. Singer, and Seymour Feshbach), while the others are employed by the NBC television network (J. Ronald Milavsky) and by the print media (Carol Tavris). However, their place of employment does not necessarily indicate their viewpoint concerning the effects of media violence. Several of the questions and comments at the end of this section, following Chapter 18, also come from researchers who have studied television violence.

Freedman and Milavsky are in close agreement that TV violence, though prevalent, has not been shown to have any causal effects on crime or aggression in our society. They emphasize that if it did have any effects, they would account for only a very small proportion of the variance; and moreover, they point to all of the other causes of social aggression, such as poverty or parental aggressive behavior, some of which have been well substantiated in research.

Singer and Singer agree that aggression has many other causes, but they see more strength in the evidence about television violence, particularly in the laboratory studies. In some instances they review the same studies as Freedman and Milavsky and reach different conclusions, but they also cite some additional and recent studies to bolster their views. Furthermore, they stress that the correlation findings are apt to be underestimates of the true effects, due to measurement difficulties. Singer and Singer express much concern about the whole television environment experienced by children, not just the violence, and they recommend that parents and educators join forces to monitor children's TV viewing and to train them to be more selective and critical viewers.

Despite these differences in conclusions, there are a number of points on which all of the following chapters agree. In terms of their personal values, they agree that there is too much violence and sex on TV, regardless of what their effects may be. They also emphasize that the "new media" (e.g., cable channels, and rented videotapes played on home VCRs) are much more extreme in their degree of violence and sadistic sexuality. Several authors also raise questions about the effects of U.S. television's format—for example, fast auditory and visual pacing, loud background noise, and quick shifts of subject—on children's attention span, cognitive style, and interest in other, slower-paced media.

Tavris expresses more concern about television's pacing and format than about the violence on network entertainment shows such as "Miami Vice," which she sees as more cartoonlike than realistic. She also stresses the impact of the actual, realistic violence seen in television coverage of sports such as professional football, which has been shown to encourage spectator violence—a point with which Feshbach agrees. Milavsky notes another possible danger of media public-service campaigns to publicize the problem of missing children, namely, that such reports may frighten children and help to convince them that the world is a dangerous place.

Feshbach's chapter raises a number of public policy issues regarding television violence. First he emphasizes that TV violence can either increase or decrease viewers' later aggression, depending on the environmental circumstances and the viewers' personalities. Research with other media such as newspaper front-page news stories has also shown effects of coverage of suicides and championship prizefights on the subsequent rate of suicides and homicides in the population at large. However, Feshbach stresses that public policy recommendations concerning regulation of media content must rest on public values and norms, not just on research findings, and he suggests that parents and educators should combine to advocate and encourage broadcasting and viewing of more desirable and educational programs. Policy issues concerning educational strategies for helping children to become active and critical media consumers are also discussed in the concluding questions and comments.

JONATHAN L. FREEDMAN

14

TELEVISION VIOLENCE AND AGGRESSION:
What the Evidence Shows

Television is a very prominent part of our world. With the possible exception of school, children spend more of their waking day engaged in television viewing than any other activity. Accordingly, it is hardly surprising that many people have speculated about what effect all of this is having on our children. It is perhaps less clear why so much of the speculation has centered on negative effects of television, but there is no doubt that it has. In particular, it has often been asserted that viewing television violence causes people, especially children, to become more aggressive. This chapter considers the evidence for that assertion.

Naturally, people are free to speculate all they want, but we must not confuse speculation with scientific facts. The only way we are going to find out whether television violence does cause an increase in aggression is to read the systematic research, do more research, and analyze what we have found. Also, because the issue is of such importance and because people care so much about it, it is especially important that we as scientists not make any pronouncements that are not solidly based on rigorous research. As private individuals we can speculate all we want; but when we speak as scientists, we must put aside our intuitions, political biases, personal hunches, and aesthetic preferences and talk only about the data. The only question for us is what the evidence shows—that is what we must present to the public and to each other, and only that.

Many psychologists, especially those who work in the area, are personally involved for one reason or another. They *care* about TV violence; they *dislike* TV violence. And who can blame them? Most responsible people dislike real violence and are offended that there is so much violence portrayed in the media. But of course, just because we dislike something, just because it strikes us as unpleasant or nasty, does not mean that it has any harmful effects. Virtually all North Americans are nauseated at the idea of eating ants, many feel the same way about raw oysters, but those who consume these items do not seem to suffer from them. The same may be true of violence in the media.

It is difficult to avoid sounding self-righteous about this, but let me ask readers to keep an open mind. Try to assess the literature as if it involved a topic that was entirely neutral, about which there were no personal concerns, no horrible crimes committed by 12-year-olds, no children growing up to be criminals. Expose yourself to the primary research and read it without preconceptions. In an earlier paper (Freedman, 1984) I tried to do this, helped by an outstanding group of fellow psychologists and graduate students, and I came to quite different conclusions from the common wisdom on this topic. Perhaps you will also.

The first discovery in a search of the literature is that almost every psychologist who writes about the issue takes the position that television violence causes aggression. Virtually every textbook that deals with the issue, including particularly books on introductory psychology (e.g., Atkinson, Atkinson, & Hilgard, 1983; Darley, Glucksberg, Kamin, & Kinchla, 1981; Smith, Sarason, & Sarason, 1982), developmental psychology (e.g., Elkind & Weiner, 1978; Kopp & Krakow, 1982; Leibert & Wicks-Nelson, 1979), and social psychology (e.g., Aronson, 1984; Baron & Byrne, 1984; Penrod, 1983), states with varying degrees of certainty that the evidence supports this causal relation. Some books hedge a little, saying that the evidence is not yet conclusive, while others say it is conclusive; but they almost all say that it is pretty strong.

This is hardly surprising because most of the primary sources, the research articles and books on the topic, take that position. The research articles begin with a brief literature review, which usually states in no uncertain terms that the evidence shows that television violence causes aggression. In these brief reviews, the few studies that obtained unmistakably negative findings are either criticized and dismissed or are not mentioned at all. There are some notable exceptions, such as one influential article (Leyens, Parke, Camino, & Berkowitz, 1975) that provides a very fair review of the literature, pointing out some of the difficulties and weaknesses in the previous research. Nevertheless, dozens of published articles and chapters begin with the more or less definitive statement that the research demonstrates the causal relation between TV violence and aggression. With this nearly unanimous position of the experts, it is natural for nonexperts to assume this is correct. In fact, quite recently the Council of Representatives of the American Psychological Association (1985) confirmed their belief in the overwhelming nature of the evidence.

Nevertheless, I shall argue here that the evidence provides little or no support for the notion that viewing television violence *causes* an increase in aggression, and that it might even be considered nonsupportive or contradictory to that idea. Even if one for some reason decided to give more weight to those studies that obtained supportive results than to those that did not, there is still no question that the research has produced inconsistent, weak results. At best, it offers some encouragement for the causal hypothesis; at worst, it refutes it.

A thorough review of this literature has already been published (Freedman, 1984), criticized (Friedrich-Cofer & Huston, 1986), and the criticism answered (Freedman, 1986). I will not repeat the review, the critique, or the rejoinder here. But perhaps a summary of the review, along with some of the discussion, will clarify the current state of the research. There are three sources of information about the effects of TV violence on aggression: experimental studies in the laboratory, field experiments, and correlational studies in the field. Each has something different to contribute to the argument.

LABORATORY EXPERIMENTS

The Findings

This is the most consistent set of studies. It indicates that showing children or adults violent programs in the laboratory can produce a momentary increase in scores on measures of aggression in the laboratory. On this we are all agreed. However, before discussing the significance of this research, we must put it into perspective.

To begin, it is important to realize that the findings are less consistent than they are usually thought to be. Many studies do find this effect; but quite a few do not. For example, Lovaas (1961), Hapkiewicz and Roden (1971), Hapkiewicz and Stone (1974), Collins (1973), Meyer (1972), Wotring and Greenberg, (1973) and Leifer and Roberts (1972) all obtain either no effect of television violence on aggression or get the effect in only some conditions or some studies. Given that the findings of the published studies are somewhat mixed, and that there is a strong tendency not to publish negative findings, it is not certain just how strong the results would be if all studies found the light of day in a journal. Thus I believe a fair summary of the findings is that a substantial majority of the published experiments do show the effect, but there are quite a few that do not.

Despite this somewhat mixed pattern, it seems reasonable to accept the effect. It is possible to increase responses to an aggression measure in the laboratory by first showing a violent film. The effect is less robust than one might expect, it seems to be susceptible to interference by various factors, known and unknown, but it is probably a replicable effect.

However, it is of considerable importance, and also of potential interest, that the conditions under which TV violence affects aggression vary from study to study. In the early years of this research, a popular theoretical analysis suggested that viewing violence should increase aggression only if the viewer were initially angry or upset. Sure enough, several studies found that pattern (Berkowitz & Geen, 1966; Berkowitz & Rawlings, 1963; Geen & O'Neal, 1969; Geen & Stonner, 1973; Hanratty, O'Neal, & Sulzer, 1972). On the other hand, there is a fairly large group of experiments (e.g., Hapkiewicz & Stone, 1974; Kniveton, 1973; Liebert & Baron, 1972; Savitsky, Rogers, Izard, & Liebert, 1971) in which anger was not deliberately aroused and yet TV violence was followed by an increase in aggression. Thus whether or not anger is a necessary precondition has not been decided.

There are several reasons why this lack of consistency about the necessity of prior anger is important. First, it is revealing that those studying the effect of TV violence on aggression do not seem concerned by these inconsistent results. They are rarely if ever mentioned in reviews of the literature, and they have not been followed up in detail. Second, the lack of consistency suggests that the effect is less clear or less robust than if the results had been consistent. One must ask why anger is apparently necessary in some studies and not in others. Failing to get an answer, it seems reasonable to ask whether we really understand the phenomenon being studied.

Third, and by far the most crucial, consideration is that the role of anger may be a key to the issue. If anger is necessary for the effect to occur, the most likely mechanisms are a release of impulses, or an arousal of drive that elicits a dominant response (which is aggression because the person is angry— or some combination of the two. In fact, a recent study (Mueller, Donnerstein, & Hallam, 1983) found that when a person was treated nicely and then shown violent TV, prosocial behavior increased (whereas aggressive behavior was unaffected). This result also suggests an arousal effect. What is more, it suggests that violent programs can increase any dominant response, not just aggression; and therefore, that there is no direct causal link, even in the laboratory, between TV violence and aggressive behavior.

From a more theoretical point of view, any evidence that suggests that the effect is due to *arousal* is inconsistent with the usual explanation of the effect of violent programs. The usual analysis is in terms of social learning (the person learns to be aggressive) or imitation (the person merely copies what is witnessed)—not in terms of an arousal or motivational process at all. This is vital, because if it is merely an arousal effect, any other exciting kind of program might have just as strong an effect. Since almost none of the experiments has equated programs perfectly on degree of arousal or excitement, it is possible that the effect of violent programs in the laboratory is due largely or entirely to the fact that they are more exciting or arousing than the control, nonviolent programs.

I am not claiming that this *is* true. Indeed, my own belief is that most of the effect in the laboratory is due to localized social learning: The subject in an experiment learns that it is all right, or perhaps even desirable, to be aggressive from the fact that the experimenter, a person in authority, has chosen to show a violent program. Thus some combination of arousal and social learning (also termed experimenter demand) may produce the increase in scores on the aggression measure. However, this is my own hunch, which has not been demonstrated. The fact remains that the role of prior anger is still uncertain, and if anger is necessary, the effects may be in doubt.

Generalizing from Laboratory Research

Let us pass quickly over the difficulties of generalizing from the laboratory to the outside world. Most psychologists know the problems of the short-term nature of the effects, the fact that aggression has been measured with all sorts of analogues of aggression but rarely with actual aggression (playfully punching a Bobo doll is not aggression in my book), and most of all, experimenter demand in laboratory settings. This last point is nicely illustrated by research (e.g., Borden, 1975) showing increased aggression in the laboratory in the presence of male observers (presumed to be more favorable to aggression) or observers who were explicitly described as pro-violence. When the observers left, aggression declined in both instances. Thus the assumed attitudes of observers can clearly affect the amount of aggression. It would be entirely reasonable for a subject to assume that an experimenter who showed a violent program was more in favor of violence than one who showed a nonviolent program, making this a troublesome alternative explanation of the result in the TV violence research. These are concerns that are present in varying degrees in almost all laboratory research. They explain why we have to be so cautious about generalizing from the laboratory to the real world.

In addition, there is one problem that is to some extent unique to this issue, namely, the possible difference between the effect of one violent program isolated in the laboratory and the effect of the mixture of programs people usually watch. The laboratory studies, taken as a whole and ignoring some of the inconsistencies, indicate that showing one violent program causes children to be more aggressive (ignoring the problems with the measures) than showing one nonviolent program. In the real world, however, children do not watch one program in isolation. They watch a mixture of violent and nonviolent, real and fantasy, exciting and boring, news and fiction programs. They watch programs that have messages and those that do not; violent programs in which the bad guys are punished and probably some in which they are not; violent programs with appealing characters and others with evil villains; news coverage of wars and beauty contests and earthquakes and manned space shuttles blowing up. The question is how this mixture of programs affects the children, or more specifically, how the effect of this mixture would differ from one in which the violent programs were omitted. The answer might be quite different from the answer as to how the effects of one violent program differ from those of one nonviolent program in the laboratory.

Although Friedrich-Cofer and Huston (1986) place considerable emphasis on the laboratory research, it would seem that, for the reasons stated above, this work has little relevance to the question before us. That question is how children are affected by the programs they really *do* see, under the conditions in which they really do see them. This is not a theoretical question; it is a practical one of great importance. But because it is not theoretical, the laboratory findings are of little help in answering it. Even if they were much more consistent and compelling than they are, they would tell us only that violent TV can increase aggression temporarily in the laboratory. This shows that violent TV has the potential to have this effect outside the laboratory— it does not show that it *does* have the effect. In order to show that, we must look at the real world and see what happens there.

FIELD EXPERIMENTS

The Findings

The best way to demonstrate a causal effect of television violence would be with experiments conducted in natural settings. The basic idea is to assign some people to a condition in which they see a lot of violent television and others to a condition in which they see less violent television, and then to measure their aggression at various times. The longer the assignment continues, the better. Unfortunately, as we all know, field experiments of this kind are extremely difficult. They require vast amounts of time, energy, and money, as well as a great deal of patience and persistence, and the kind of personality that can organize complex arrangements. Therefore, it is not surprising that there have been very few such experiments.

Despite the small number of field experiments, consistent, strong effects would certainly be helpful in resolving the issue. Unfortunately, the results are neither consistent nor strong. A few studies have found that subjects exposed to violent programs showed increased aggression compared to subjects who watched nonviolent programs (Leyens et al., 1975; Parke, Berkowitz, Leyens, West, & Sebastian, 1977). However, in these studies, the effect appeared on only some measures of aggression, occurred for some groups of subjects and not others, and was short-lived. Moreover, in all of these studies (there are three separate experiments in the two papers), only one or two cottages were in each experimental condition, and the authors treated the boys in each cottage as if they were independent of each other. It seems clear that when boys live together in a cottage and then engage in aggressive interactions with each other, the actions of one are to some extent dependent on and affect the actions of the others. For example, if Frank starts a fight with Bob and Bob fights back, Bob's aggressive behavior is dependent on Frank's. Thus one cannot consider their actions to be independent. As Friedrich-Cofer and Huston (1986) point out, to do so might greatly inflate the magnitude of an effect and distort the statistical significance of the analysis. Because of this, the statistical analyses presented in the papers are inappropriate, and the true reliability of the effects cannot be assessed. Therefore, these are in essence case studies rather than true experiments, and I believe that they should not be given much weight.

Yet, these are the only field experiments that produced even weak support for the causal hypothesis. The only other study in this set that is usually thought to support the idea of a causal effect of viewing television violence on aggression was conducted by Friedrich and Stein (1973). This was a very nicely designed study that involved quite a few subjects in a natural setting. Unfortunately, it obtained almost no significant effects on aggression. There were four measures and none of them showed anything. When a combined measure was used, there was still no significant effect. Finally, with the combined measure and an internal analysis into high and low aggressive children, there was a significant interaction that showed that high aggressive children *declined less* in aggressiveness after viewing a violent film than a neutral film; but that the low aggressive children *increased more* in aggressiveness after the violent film. It seems to be stretching the imagination to consider this pattern of results any support for an effect of television violence on aggression.

Other studies by Feshbach and Singer (1971) and Milgram and Shotland (1973) provide no support at all for the causal hypothesis. These studies have been criticized for various reasons (Comstock et al., 1978; Liebert, Sobol, & Davidson, 1972; Liebert, Sprafkin, & Davidson, 1982) and some of the criticisms are certainly sound. But these two studies are no less well designed than those by Leyens and Parke and their associates, and therefore must be considered in assessing the total picture. It is usually a mistake to place much weight on unpublished studies, but it is worth noting that in a replication of the Feshbach and Singer study, Wells (1973) also found no significant increase in aggression following violent television.

Thus this group of studies offers only the slightest support for the causal hypothesis. Moreover, it is important to note that not one of these studies obtained strong, consistent, lasting results. The strongest result consisted of a substantial increase in aggression in one of two cottages, with that increase lasting for a short while. I think it is fair to say that most psychologists would not consider this mixture of results convincing evidence of the existence of a phenomenon. Indeed, with most effects, if these were the results after this much research, most of us would give up the idea.

A Natural Experiment

I should add one study that might be called a natural experiment. During the years 1949 to 1952 there was a freeze on the introduction of television into American cities. By 1949 many cities already had television, but for those 3 years, no new cities got it. An ingenious study (Hennigan et al., 1982) capitalized on this by comparing the rates of crime in a large number of cities that had television with the rates in cities that did not have television. The authors looked at crime rates over a long period that included the crucial 3 years. They reasoned that if television affected crime, there should be an increase in crime in cities with television compared to those without it, and that this increase should then disappear after the freeze ended and television came to all of the cities. Although it was not a true experiment, in that the authors themselves had not randomly assigned cities to conditions, there was no reason to believe that the assignment has been affected by any systematic factors that would be involved in determining crime rates. Thus the study could assess the long-term effects of television on crime.

The results showed no effects on homicide or aggravated assault (violent crimes and crimes against persons) or on burglary or auto theft (serious instrumental crime). The only effect was some evidence that the amount of larceny (petty theft) increased after the introduction of television. Thus those crimes that are presumably related to aggression and to aggressive impulses were unaffected. The authors interpreted the effect on larceny as being due to relative deprivation, caused by viewers seeing the affluence on television.

The importance of this study is that it is the only serious attempt to assess the long-term effects of television as it is watched in the real world. It dealt not with one or five violent television shows watched in isolation, but with the full diet of television watched by a great many people. Although we do not know what shows people actually watched, we can surmise that most people watched a mixture of what was shown on television during that period. They presumably watched variety shows, news programs, wrestling and roller derby (both very popular then), westerns, cops and robbers, serious theater, and so on. And there was no evidence that that diet of television affected aggressive crimes. It could be argued that television then was less violent than it is now. Perhaps it was, but it did contain lots of violence, and there was no effect after years of exposure. No single study is definitive proof of the existence of an effect or the lack of an effect, but I find this study very impressive. For me, at least, it would take some pretty strong effects in short-term field experiments to balance the lack of effects in this natural experiment.

CORRELATION RESEARCH

The Basic Correlation

This brings us to the correlation research. Because there are so few field experiments, and because everyone agrees that they obtained mixed results, the burden of the causal case must fall largely on the correlational studies. Unfortunately, as we all know, it is the nature of correlational research that it is not designed to demonstrate causality, but only an association. Nevertheless, with sufficient ingenuity, it is sometimes possible to build quite a strong case for causality using correlational data, as long as they fall into the right pattern.

The procedure of most of the correlational studies is to obtain measures of TV viewing and aggression on the same people and them see if they are related. I will discuss some of the more complex studies later, but let us stop here for the moment. The basic fact that has emerged from this work is that watching violent television *is* positively related to aggression. That is, children who watch a lot of violent television also tend to be aggressive, while those who watch relatively little violent television tend to be less aggressive. The size of the relation tends to decrease when children are equated on total television watched, but the correlation still holds. Thus it is not just watching television that is related to aggressiveness, but watching violent television.

It is important to put this finding into perspective by noting that the magnitude of the correlation between TV violence and aggression is rather small. Different studies have obtained different results, but with a few exceptions the values have been between .10 and .20. In remarks reported in this part of this volume, Comstock suggests that these correlations may be underestimated do to the unreliability of the measures and other factors. It is difficult to assess this possibility. However, for the sake of argument, let us accept it and assume that the true correlations are 50% stronger than those reported. That would bring them to the range of 0.15 to 0.30. In terms of impact, the reported correlations would imply that between 1% and 4% of the variation in aggression may be accounted for by variation in viewing television violence, while the higher, assumed correlations would indicate that between 2.25% and 9% of the variance could be explained. In other words, by almost any standard, we are talking about a relatively weak relation. The highest figure, 9%, is by no means trivial, but is hardly overwhelming (and, of course, the research has not found correlations this high).

The magnitude of the correlation is not really important in terms of the scientific question of whether TV violence causes aggression, but it does have considerable practical and political significance. It means that, even if it could be demonstrated conclusively that there was a causal effect, viewing television violence is unlikely to be a very important factor in causing aggression. Compared with economic, ethnic, and cultural factors that have major effects on crime and aggression, viewing television violence would appear to be at most a relatively minor contributor. This does not mean that it should be ignored if the effect can be demonstrated, but it does mean that we should give it the amount of attention it deserves.

Nevertheless, the finding that the amount of television violence viewed is related to aggressiveness is extremely important. It shows that aggressive children prefer violent television, or at least are exposed to it more than nonaggressive children. This finding is absolutely essential for the causal hypothesis. If there were no such correlation between violent television and aggression, it would be almost impossible to demonstrate to anyone's satisfaction that violent television affects aggression. The existence of the correlation raises the possibility. It leads to the key question: Are children who watch a lot of violent television more aggressive *because* watching violent television causes them to be more aggressive?

That is, the existence of the correlation raises the possibility and allows us to ask the question. But of course it does not supply the answer, because the correlation by itself says nothing about causality. Television violence may cause aggression; aggressiveness may cause children to watch more violent television; or some third factor or group of factors may make children both watch a lot of violent television and be aggressive. Only additional research can resolve the issue.

Demonstrating Causality

Having said that, let us turn to the evidence from correlational research that relates to whether there is a causal link between viewing television violence and aggression. Making an argument for a causal effect from correlational data is naturally very complex. The basic strategy is to propose a pattern of relations that can be explained plausibly in terms of a causal effect and cannot be explained easily in any other way. To put it differently, the trick is to find effects that seem to indicate that A causes B and that would not occur if B caused A or if some third factor C caused both A and B. In terms of television violence and aggression, there have been several such proposals.

The Cumulative Effect of Television

The most convincing analysis, in my opinion, is based on a cumulative effect of viewing TV violence. The argument is that if watching violence on television causes aggression, the more violence that is watched (at least up to some point), the greater should be the increase in aggression. This kind of relation is almost always reasonable in cause-effect situations: If reinforcement leads to learning, more reinforcement should lead to more learning. If eating too much makes you gain weight, the more you eat, the more weight you should gain. There may be upper limits on all of these effects, but surely it makes sense that within some range they should increase with greater exposure to the causative agent.

This straightforward analysis leads to the simple expectation that the correlation between the amount of violent television that is watched and the level of aggressiveness should increase with age. If watching TV violence for a week or a month increases aggressiveness, watching it for a year should increase aggressiveness more; and watching it for years should have an even greater effect. There may be a ceiling to the strength of the effect, but it should increase from an early age to a later age. Since those who watch a lot of television violence should become more and more aggressive, while those who watch little should increase less (or not at all), the two groups should spread further and further apart in aggressiveness. This will produce stronger and stronger correlations between amount of television violence watched and aggressiveness. An opposing hypothesis is that television violence does not affect aggression and that their correlation is due merely to the fact that aggressive children prefer violent television more than do less aggressive children. Since there is no obvious reason why this preference should increase with age, this viewpoint suggests that the correlation between viewing television violence and aggressiveness should not increase over time.

Therefore, the causal hypothesis would receive considerable support if it were found that correlations between TV violence and aggression increased as children got older. As it happens, this does not occur. In one paper, Eron (1980) reported that the correlations did increase for boys from first to third grade, but for girls they decreased. However, later papers (Huesmann, 1982; Huesmann, Lagerspetz, & Eron, 1984) dealing with more complete data from the same study showed no pattern of increasing correlations. Similarly, studies by Singer and Singer (1980) and Milavsky, Stipp, Kessler, and Rubens (1982) indicate no hint of increasing correlations with age for either sex.

It might be argued that the lack of an increase is evidence against the causal effect of viewing TV violence. I would not go that far, because viewing television violence might have its maximum effect quite early in life or only during some critical period. Neither sounds very plausible and, if either were true, it would considerably weaken the case against television violence. Nevertheless, these are possible explanations for the lack of an increase in correlations over time. Therefore, although I consider the findings quite discouraging for the causal hypothesis, they are not strong evidence against it. In any case, it is clear that the evidence from this analysis does not provide any support for the causal effect.

Cross-Lagged Correlations

Another way of demonstrating causality depends on showing that the correlation between the amount of television viewed at one age and the amount of aggression some years later (one so-called cross-lagged correlation) is higher than the other cross-lagged correlation between early aggression and later TV viewing. Also, the first correlation must be higher than the correlation between TV viewing and aggression, both measured at the early age. This last result is necessary to suggest causality, because otherwise the cross-lagged correlation may simply reflect the fact that those who prefer television violence are also more aggressive (which we already know). To put this more concretely, the key pattern that would assist the causal hypothesis is for the amount of TV violence watched at, say, the age of 6 to be more closely related to the amount of aggression at, say, age 16 than to the amount of aggression at age 6. There are various difficulties with using these so-called cross-lagged correlations (Kenny, 1972, 1975), but a strong, consistent pattern of the kind just described would be evidence in favor of the causal hypothesis.

Once again the results have been disappointing. One study by Eron and his colleagues (Eron, Huesmann, Lefkowitz, & Walder, 1972) found the specified pattern for boys using one measure of aggression. But it did not find it for two other measures of aggression, nor for girls using any measure. Later studies by this group (Huesmann, 1982) failed to find this pattern for either sex, as did the study by Singer and Singer (1981). Thus this approach has not been successful in providing evidence for causation and, in fact, researchers in the area appear to have abandoned the use of cross-lagged correlations.

Other studies have examined the possibility of a causal relation based on the same logic but more sophisticated statistics. The basic idea is to show that, after controlling for the correlation between TV violence and aggression at age 6, the amount of TV violence watched at age 6 explains additional variance in the amount of aggression later. Huesmann et al. (1984) employed step-wise multiple regressions with data from boys and girls in the United States and Finland. They found positive effects for all four groups, but the amount of additional variance explained (i.e., over and above that explained by the stability in aggression) was significant only for girls in the United States (regression coefficient of .135). For boys in the United States, and for both sexes in Finland, the amounts of variance explained by early TV viewing were very small and not reliable.

The authors next attempted to show that aggression was caused by a multiplicative effect of TV viewing and identification with characters in TV programs. They performed a multiple regression analysis combining three factors: the linear effect of identification with characters on television, the linear effect of amount of television violence watched, and the interaction of the two. They found that this combination of factors made a significant contribution to aggression for boys in both the United States and Finland, but not for girls in either country. They argued that this indicated a multiplicative effect of identification and viewing, but it would seem that this particular analysis cannot show such an effect. Since neither the linear effect of TV violence nor the interaction was significant alone, all or much of the effect must have been due to the identification variable. But that may be largely a matter of the child's personality. Some identify more than others, and those who identify more are also more aggressive. Thus this cannot be used as evidence of a multiplicative effect involving TV violence. Moreover, none of the analyses controlled for total amount of television watched, so that the few effects the authors did obtain might have been due to television in general rather than to viewing violent television per se.

It should be recognized that this is an impressive study that provides an important set of data on the relation between television and aggression. It also does offer some results that might be interpreted as support for the causal hypothesis. However, it is weakened by the fact that the effects were significant for some groups with some analyses and for other groups with other analyses, that all of the effects were small, and that so many analyses (not described here) failed to produce any appreciable effect.

Another impressive study (Milavsky et al., 1982) also looked at the unique variance contributed by early TV viewing to later aggression using multiple regression and other statistical procedures. In this study, early TV viewing contributed little or nothing to the variance in aggression at a later date once the earlier relation between viewing and aggression was eliminated. The relations between early viewing and later aggression were mostly positive, but they were very small and the number of significant effects was at the chance level. Some authors (e.g., Cook, Kendziersky, & Thomas, 1983) have been impressed by this pattern, but given the unreliability of the measures and the increase in levels of aggression with age, it seems to me to indicate very little. Thus, in my opinion, this study offers no support for the causal hypothesis, and in fact should probably be considered evidence against it.

Overall, it seems clear that these attempts to use correlation data to demonstrate causality have been largely unsuccessful. There is one positive finding in the pattern of cross-lagged correlations in Eron et al. (1972), but it is inconsistent even in that study and does not replicate; there is some slight encouragement in Huesmann et al. (1984), but the effects are weak and inconsistent; and perhaps one could find solace in the number of positive effects in Milavsky et al. (1982). But, as with the field experiments, not one study produced strong consistent results, and most produced a substantial number of negative findings. Thus it seems clear that this approach to showing a causal relation between viewing television violence and aggression has provided at most weak and inconsistent support.

CONCLUSIONS

Once the studies are analyzed and the results presented, it is up to readers to draw their own conclusions. My own conclusion is that, considering all of the research—laboratory, field experiments, and correlational studies—the evidence does not support the idea that viewing television violence causes aggression. It seems to me that, giving the findings the most generous interpretation possible, there is at most some slight encouragement for the causal hypothesis. That is, there are some studies that seem to indicate that television violence may cause aggression, but there are also many studies that fail to find such a relation. And, of perhaps greater importance, no single study offers strong supporting evidence. The evidence seems to me to be so weak that, if this issue were of less importance, I might be tempted to conclude that the research findings constitute convincing evidence against a causal relation. However, because there have been relatively few really good studies, and because there have been some scattered positive results, my own mind is still open. For me, the causal hypothesis remains a possibility. It may be correct—but it certainly has not been demonstrated by the scientific evidence.

In his remarks in this section of this volume, Comstock argues that the different kinds of research on this issue involve such varied stimuli that, even when the results are not parallel, they are not in conflict. I agree entirely that media reports of suicides, for example, are conceptually different from violent scenes on weekly television programs or on the news, and that they may have quite different effects. However, it is not the conflicting results that are the problem, but rather the lack of substantial and consistent demonstrations that violence in any form on television affects aggressiveness.

Nevertheless, others may view the evidence somewhat differently. They may be more convinced by the positive findings, less bothered by the negative ones, and less worried about the possibility that unpublished studies tend to be negative rather than positive. Others may give more weight to the laboratory experiments and less to the field experiments. They may not mind that the positive effects have been inconsistent and have almost always appeared on only some of many measures and often for one sex and not the other. And they may not require one strong, consistent result in the literature. Certainly, what people need in order to be convinced about the existence of a phenomenon differs considerably. And so, some may decide on the basis of the available data that television violence probably does cause aggression.

However, I think even those who are most persuaded by the evidence must see that it is by no means overwhelming. We may be in a position where honest, objective scientists can disagree in their conclusions about what the evidence indicates, but it seems inconceivable that anyone reading all of the evidence would fail to recognize that it is not entirely consistent and that the effects are rather weak. Under the circumstances, I believe that the scientific community should make it clear to the public that the evidence is not terribly strong, that the results are not clear, and that those who believe in the causal hypothesis do so on the basis of relatively weak scientific evidence.

IMPLICATIONS

Having described the evidence and suggested conclusions about what it shows and does not show, where should we go from here? Some may feel that the possibility of a causal link between TV violence and aggression is sufficient to undertake some intervention, to put pressure on television stations to reduce the amount of violence in their programs, or even to pass legislation to require this. Those who favor such actions should understand that they would be acting on the basis of weak evidence that, at most, suggests a very small average effect. My own feeling is that, even if I believed that the causal relation had been demonstrated, which I obviously do not, I would be extremely hesitant to support any form of censorship. In the first place, we have no idea whether TV violence is related to any actual criminal activity or even to any really antisocial behavior. Virtually all of the research that has obtained positive findings has involved either the mildest forms of aggressive behavior, or in the case of the laboratory studies, only analogues of aggression.

Second, we have no idea whether other television programming has similar, better, or worse effects. If violence on television were reduced, what would replace it and still satisfy the audience? I personally believe that, even if violent programs on television have no harmful effect, it would be preferable to have them replaced with truly thoughtful and imaginative programs. However, it is more likely that reducing the number of violent shows would lead to an increase in soap operas, sitcoms, and quiz shows. Would that be an improvement? It may be that having children learn about life from these kinds of shows, and perhaps imitate the behaviors that occur in them, would be at least as harmful to our society as a slight increase in aggression due to violent programs, if such effects do occur.

The final argument against restricting violence on television, and I believe by far the most important, is that once we begin to tell the television stations to have less violence, it should be difficult to prevent the government from imposing still more restrictions on what can be shown. If violence on television is considered harmful because it encourages aggression, others will argue that programs dealing with divorce, family violence, sexuality, abortion, life in communist countries, or any other controversial issue are also harmful. It may also be true that children who regularly watch news reports on the major networks and on public broadcasting channels have more liberal political attitudes than those who do not watch the news, and they may be less automatically supportive of the federal government, whoever is in power. This too can be considered dangerous. Indeed, conservative governments typically complain that news coverage is biased against them. If we allow restrictions on violent programs, perhaps the next restriction would involve the news. Once censorship starts, who is to say where it will stop?

Therefore, given the minimal evidence indicating any harmful effects of watching television violence, given the lack of knowledge of the effects of alternative programming, and given the grave consequences of beginning censorship in any form, I believe there should be no attempt to legislate a reduction in violence on television. Naturally, people can express their aesthetic preferences both by their viewing habits and by social pressure, but it should be clearly understood that they are doing so on the basis of personal preference and belief rather than scientific proof.

REFERENCES

American Psychological Association. (1985, February 22). News release.

Aronson, E. (1984). *The social animal* (4th ed.). San Francisco: Freeman.

Atkinson, R. L., Atkinson, R. C., & Hilgard, E. R. (1983). *Introduction to psychology* (8th ed.) New York: Harcourt Brace Jovanovich.

Baron, R. A., & Byrne, D. (1984) *Social psychology: Understanding human interaction* (4th ed.). Boston: Allyn & Bacon.

Berkowitz, L., & Green, R. G. (1966). Film violence and the cue properties of available targets. *Journal of Personality and Social Psychology, 3,* 525-530.

Berkowitz, L., & Rawlings, E. (1963). Effects of film violence on inhibitions against subsequent aggression. *Journal of Abnormal and Social Psychology, 66,* 405-412.

Borden, R. J. (1975). Witnesses aggression: Influence of an observer's sex and values on aggressive responding. *Journal of Personality and Social Psychology, 31,* 567-573.

Collins, W. A. (1973). Effect of temporal separation between motivation, aggression, and consequences: A developmental study. *Developmental Psychology, 8,* 215-221.

Comstock, G., Chaffee, S., Katzman, N., McCombs, M., & Roberts, D. (1974). *Television and human behavior.* New York: Columbia University Press.

Cook, T. D., Kendziersky, D. A., & Thomas, S. V. (1983). The implicit assumptions of television: An analysis of the 1982 NIMH Report on Television and Behavior. *Public Opinion Quarterly, 47,* 161-201.

Darley, J. M., Glucksberg, S., Kamin, L. J., & Kinchla, R. A. (1981). *Psychology.* Englewood Cliffs, NJ: Prentice-Hall.

Elkind, D., & Weiner, I. B. (1978). *Development of the child.* New York: John Wiley.

Eron, L. D. (1980). Prescription for reduction of aggression. *American Psychologist, 35,* 244-252.

Eron, L. D., Huesmann, L. R., Lefkowitz, M. M., & Walder, L. O. (1972). Does television violence cause aggression? *American Psychologist, 27,* 253-263.

Feshbach, S., & Singer, R. (1971). *Television and aggression.* San Francisco: Jossey-Bass.

Freedman, J. L. (1984). Effect of television violence on aggressiveness. *Psychological Bulletin, 96,* 227-246.

Freedman, J. L. (1986). Television violence and aggression: A rejoinder. *Psychological Bulletin, 100,* 372-378.

Friedrich, L. K., & Stein, A. H. (1973). Aggressive and prosocial television programs an the natural behavior of preschool children. *Monographs of the Society for Research in Child Development, 38,* (no. 4, Serial No. 151).

Friedrich-Cofer, L., & Huston, A. C. (1986). Television violence and aggression: The debate continues. *Psychological Bulletin, 100,* 364-371.

Geen, R. G., & O'Neal, E. C. (1969). Activation of cue-elicited aggression by general arousal. *Journal of Personality and Social Psychology, 11,* 289-292.

Geen, R. G., & Stonner, D. (1973). Context effects in observed violence. *Journal of Personality and Social Psychology, 25,* 145-150.

Hanratty, M. A., O'Neal, E., & Sulzer, J. L. (1972). Effect of frustration upon imitation of aggression. *Journal of Personality and Social Psychology, 21,* 30-34.

Hapkiewicz, W. G., & Roden, A. H. (1971). The effect of aggressive cartoons on children's interpersonal play. *Child Development, 42,* 1583-1585.

Hapkiewicz, W. G., & Stone, R. D. (1974). The effect of realistic versus imaginary aggressive models on children's interpersonal play. *Child Study Journal, 4,* 47-58.

Hennigan, K. M., Del Rosario, M. L., Heath, L. , Cook, T. D., Wharton, J. D., & Calder, B. J. (1982). Impact of the introduction of television on crime in the United States: Empirical findings and theoretical implications. *Journal of Personality and Social Psychology, 42,* 461-477.

Huesmann, L. R. (1982). Television violence and aggressive behavior. In D. Pearl, L. Bouthilet, & J. Lazar (Eds.), *Television and behavior: Ten years of scientific progress and implications for the eighties: Vol. 2. Technical reviews* (pp. 220-256). Washington, DC: National Institute of Mental Health.

Huesmann, L. R., Kagerspetz, K., & Eron, L. D. (1984). Intervening variables in the TV violence-aggression relation: Evidence from two countries. *Developmental Psychology, 20,* 746-775.

Kenny, D. A. (1972). Threats to the internal validity of cross-lagged panel inference, as related to "Television violence and child aggression: A follow-up study." In G. A. Comstock & E. A. Rubinstein (Eds.), *Television and social behavior* (Vol. 3, pp. 136-140). Washington, DC: Government Printing Office.

Kenny, D. A. (1975). Cross-lagged panel correlation: A test for spuriousness. *Psychological Bulletin, 82,* 887-903.

Kniveton, B. H. (1973). The effect of rehearsal delay on long-term imitation of filmed aggression. *British Journal of Psychology, 64,* 259-265.

Kopp, C. B., & Krakow, J. B. (1982). *The child: Development in a social context.* Reading, MA: Addison-Wesley.

Leifer, A. D., & Roberts, D. F. (1972). Children's responses to television violence. In G. A. Comstock & E. A. Rubinstein (Eds.), *Television and social behavior.* (Vol. 3, pp. 43-180). Washington, DC: Government Printing Office.

Leyens, J. P., Parke, R. D., Camino, L., & Berkowitz, L. (1975). Effects of movie violence on aggression in a field setting as a function of group dominance and cohesion. *Journal of Personality and Social Psychology, 32,* 346-360.

Liebert, R. M. & Baron, R. A. (1972). Some immediate effects of televised violence on children's behavior. *Developmental Psychology, 6,* 469-475.

Liebert, R. M., Sobol, M. P., & Davidson, E. S. (1972). Catharsis of aggression among institutionalized boys: Fact or artifact? In G. A. Comstock, E. A. Rubinstein, & J. P. Murray (Eds)., *Television and social behavior. Vol. 5. Television's effects: Further explorations* (pp. 351-358). Washington, DC: Government Printing Office.

Liebert, R. M., Sprafkin, J. N., & Davidson, E. S. (1982). *The early window.* New York: Pergamon.

Liebert, R. M., & Wicks-Nelson, R. (1979). *Developmental psychology.* New York: McGraw-Hill.

Lovaas, O. I. (1961). Effect of exposure to symbolic aggression on aggressive behavior. *Child Development, 32,* 37-44.

Meyer, T. P. (1972). Effects of viewing justified and unjustified real film violence on aggressive behavior. *Journal of Personality and Social Psychology, 23,* 21-29.

Milavsky, J. R., Stipp, H. H., Kessler, R. C., & Rubens, W. S. (1982). *Television and aggression: A panel study.* New York: Academic Press.

Milgram, S., & Shotland, R. L. (1973).*Television and antisocial behavior: Field experiments* New York: Academic Press.

Mueller, C. W., Donnerstein, E., & Hallam, J. (1983). Violent films and prosocial behavior. *Journal of Personality and Social Psychology, 9,* 84-89.

Parke, R. D., Berkowitz, L., Leyens, J. P., West, S. G., & Sebastian, R. J. (1977). Some effects of violent and nonviolent movies on the behavior of juvenile delinquents. In L. Berkowitz (Ed.), *Advances in experimental social psychology* (Vol. 10, pp. 135-172). New York: Academic Press.

Penrod, S. (1983). *Social psychology.* Englewood Cliffs, NJ: Prentice-Hall.

Savitsky, J. C., Rogers, R. W., Izard, C. E., & Leibert, R. M. (1971). Role of frustration and anger in the imitation of film aggression against a human victim. *Psychological Reports, 29,* 807-810.

Singer, J. L., & Singer, D. G. (1981). *Television, imagination and aggression: A study of preschoolers.* Hillsdale, NJ: Lawrence Earlbaum.

Smith, E. R., Sarason, I. G., & Sarason, B. R. (1982). *Psychology: The frontiers of behavior* (2nd ed.). New York: Harper & Row.

Wells, W. D. (1973). *Television and aggression: Replication of an experimental field study.* Unpublished manuscript, University of Chicago Graduate School of Business.

Wotring, C. E., & Greenberg, B. S. (1973). Experiments in televised violence and verbal aggression: Two exploratory studies. *Journal of Communication, 23,* 446-460.

J. RONALD MILAVSKY

15

TELEVISION AND AGGRESSION
ONCE AGAIN

There are many psychological researchers who believe that television violence is a cause of real violence. Generally, sociological researchers tend to be more skeptical of this link. Sociologists began the study of mass media effects a bit earlier than psychologists did, searching for political effects. The early studies did not find clear ones and, as a result, sociologists largely have abandoned mass communication studies. In contrast, the laboratory experiments of Bandura and Berkowitz in the early 1960s kindled psychologists' interests, and the flame they lit has burned brightly ever since.

Nevertheless, I remain unconvinced that television has anything to do with real-world violence. One can interpret this declaration on an *ad hominem* basis and point to the facts that I am employed by a television network and that I am a sociologist. But there is a substantive argument to be made based on the existing research literature on the subject.

This research literature is far less extensive than is generally believed. The publicity generated by NIMH after their 1982 review of the research literature mentioned a figure of 2,500 studies (NIMH, 1982, p. iii). However, this 2,500 figure is hyperbole because it includes virtually anything that deal with television or violence, empirically, theoretically, or journalistically.[1] The relevant literature, which attempts to deal with a possible causal link between exposure to television violence and aggression empirically, is closer to 100 studies (Freedman, 1984). And most of this empirical literature consists of laboratory experiments in the tradition of Bandura and Berkowitz. Psychologists disagree about the generalizability of results of such experimental studies to real-world behavior.

A Major Panel Study

One of the 100 or so empirical studies is a longitudinal panel study of TV's effects on children and teens in the real world that took more than 10 years to complete (Milavsky, Stipp, Kessler, & Rubens, 1982). It is worth examining the data of this study very carefully because they are of the same order of magnitude that can be found in other studies of similar design.

Some 3,200 young people—a sample of elementary school children and a sample of teenage boys—were surveyed over a 3-year period, from May 1970 through December 1973. Data were obtained at six different points in time from about 2,400 boys and girls in the elementary school sample through questionnaires administered to the children in their classrooms. Their parents and teachers also were interviewed so that the possible effects of television could be analyzed in the context of the children's home and school environments. The other sample consisted of about 800 teenage boys in grades 7 through 12, with data being obtained in five waves, as well as from their parents and their peers.

All of these children lived in two midwestern cities. The intent of this selection procedure was to maximize opportunities for the occurrence and detection of television effects on aggression at that point in history. Thus cities were chosen, with their higher crime rates, rather than rural areas; two cities rather than one; and cities in the Central Time Zone because the more "adult" programs are shown an hour earlier there than in the East or West, creating more opportunity for children to view them. Both cities had independent TV stations in addition to the three networks affiliates, thus making available a full array of network and independent programming. Finally, within those cities, schools were chosen that would draw into the study children with diverse socio-economic and ethnic backgrounds. Thus it is difficult to argue that the impact of television violence would have been less for this sample than elsewhere.

One of the reasons that the study took so long to complete was that the results were weak and inconsistent and therefore difficult to interpret. Relationships in the data between prior exposure to violent television programming and later aggressive behavior were examined in many different ways to see whether some substantial evidence of a true relationship could be uncovered. For example, measures of violence exposure were conceptualized in eight different ways, the data were corrected for random and correlated measurement error, and effects were sought among every theoretically plausible subset of the sample, such as children who had a history of prior aggressive behavior, children without fathers, poor children, children who lived in families and cultural groups where aggressive behavior was normative, and children whose parents disciplined them with physical punishment.

No matter what was examined, the data for elementary school

children, and also those for teens, showed tiny effect-size numbers. However, in the elementary school sample, the numbers, though tiny, at least showed a positive sign pattern. That was the strongest result found. Although the sign pattern could not be conclusively tested to see whether it was genuine or spurious, when a few outside variables were controlled, the numbers always got smaller, and in the case of one of the control variables, the positive sign pattern disappeared.

Based on this result, our conclusion was that any effect of watching television violence on children's aggression either did not really exist or was very small. The data did not permit a firm choice between these two interpretations, but based on what happened when controls were introduced, our judgment was that it was somewhat more likely that the effect was zero than that it was small. Other researchers may or may not agree with this interpretation. Both positions were taken by those who reviewed the book in the academic journals (Cook, Kendzierski, & Thomas, 1983; Felson & Morgan, 1984; Kenny, 1984; Rossi & Wright, 1983). Readers are invited to make up their own minds; the data are all there. An objective observer will reach the conclusion that they are not clear enough to compel any judgment with great certainty.

Other Research

Studies similar in design with similar empirical results exist in the literature. There are differences in interpretation even among these, however. Leonard Eron and Rowell Huesmann have played a coordinating role in studies in the United States, Finland, Israel, Poland, Australia, and the Netherlands that used identical or nearly identical methodology (Huesmann & Eron, 1986). They interpret results in all countries as supporting the television effect hypothesis. However, a recently published book on the Netherlands data clearly indicates that there is disagreement between the American and the Netherlands researchers about the interpretation of those data. The Netherlands group's interpretation of their data is virtually identical to the interpretation we have made of our data. They write,

> Milavsky conducted a longitudinal survey to investigate the influence of aggressive television models on the aggressive behavior of children and came to the conclusion, as we did, that there was hardly any empirical support for a causal relationship between viewing aggressive television models and a lasting increase in aggressive behavior. The interesting question is, who is in fact correct? In reading the conclusion of Huesmann and Eron very carefully, one discovers that they too were unable to find

the effect they sought originally. (Wiegman, Kuttschreuter, & Baarda, 1986, p. 153)

Indeed, they go on to disagree with Huesmann and Eron's interpretation of the results in the other countries participating in the cross-national study.

People will continue probing data like these, and it is inevitable that some investigators will think that there is evidence for television effects in them. However, it is well to keep in mind the sage observation attributed to Peter Rossi: "If you torture data long enough, sooner or later they confess."

In sum, the assertion that television violence has little or nothing to do with violence in the world is based in part on looking at data like those just described. But the assertion is also based on seeing what has happened recently in the real world.

Greater Violence in the New Media

When our study was done, virtually all television available to viewers had been produced with the involvement of the networks, which means that all the programs had gone through an intensive review and censorship process performed by the networks' standards departments. This process starts in the concept stage, when editors in these departments point out possible problems, and continues through drafts of scripts to the final production. Nothing gets on network air until the standards department approves. You may or may not agree with their claim that they make conservative judgments and, for example, try to eliminate any violent acts that might possibly be imitated, insofar as this can be judged. However, their censorship is a highly documented fact.

Today, there is a great deal of programming available to television viewers that can be seen in pure "uncensored" form. Pay cable services show uncut movies, and about 25% of all TV households subscribe to such services.[2]. In the month of March 1986 alone, you could have seen the highly acclaimed but nevertheless extremely violent film *The Killing Fields* six times just on HBO. And *Missing in Action* was so successful that each pay service also brought you Part II five or six times. Altogether, my program guides show that you could have watched 64 violent movies 208 times on Long Island's Cablevision in that month. If you only subscribed to HBO and selected their most violent category, "graphic violence," you would still have had 10 movies with 39 showings.

The households that subscribe to such cable services tend to have proportionally more children than those who do not. In fact, over 30% of all children have such services available in their homes.[3]

Videocassette recorders, also in homes with proportionally more children, are now in at least 30% of all homes, and penetration is growing rapidly. Today, 40% of children have VCRs in their homes.[4] In the United States, there are now over 20,000 video stores that rent cassettes, and most urban and suburban residents live no more than a 20-minute walk from one of these.[5] Most of those stores feature a prominent display of horror/slasher movies of the type studied by Malamuth and Donnerstein (1982). In most cases, this is the largest display. Why? Obviously it is because teenagers are very attracted to them. Buy why are they? One researcher thinks it is because such material provides teenage boys the opportunity to "show off" their ability to tolerate horror and thereby impress girls.[6] Or are they closet sadists? We don't know, but we do know that young Ned and Jane now get a great deal of graphic gore with their violence, more than they ever got before. For example, the Family Video Center in New York City has a choice of 274 titles in their "horror" collection. (If you want your violence in a different form, you can also rent film on "martial arts," "war," and "mystery and suspense." Most stores classify their movies in this way and carry similar titles.) The horror section includes the classic *Texas Chainsaw Massacre,* all parts of *Friday the 13th*, other movies used in research by Malamuth and Donnerstein such as *I Spit on Your Grave* and *Maniac*, as well as titles geared toward the interests of young customers such as *Sleepaway Camp and Christmas Evil.* Some stores also stock the notorious *Faces of Death*, which claims to portray real killings, not just make believe. This kind of stuff makes "The A-Team" look like a fairy tale.

Thus there is a real-world experiment already underway—a period of very rapid increase in availability of and exposure to forms and genres of vicarious violence that have never been experienced before by mass audiences. We have to wonder why, if such fare does affect people, we don't have "Apocalypse Now" or at least some real-world signs. If not now, the results should be seen soon, because we can expect availability of these things to keep on increasing rapidly in the future. So far, I do not see any such effects in violent crime rates for the United States, which have been dropping during this period of rapid change in the media. Crime rates are still high, but they are lower than in 1980, when the new media were not a factor. For example, homicide rates have dropped from 10.2 (per 100,000 persons 12 years and older) in 1980 to 7.9 in 1985. Aggravated assault rates dropped from 25.8 (per 1,000 persons 12 and older) to 24.2 during the same period. Rates for rape have fluctuated over this period, but the trend is unmistakably down. Data for juveniles are less reliable, but here, too, there is no sign of an increase (U.S. Department of Justice, 1985a, 1985b).

There are undoubtedly many reasons for the observed declines in violent crime rates, such as the shrinking proportion of people in the young age groups most prone to commit crime. However, whatever the causes, it is clear that recent trends in the kinds of antisocial behavior measured by these statistics run counter to the changes in availability of violent films that have come about by the advent of the new media. In other words, whatever the power of the media to influence crimes such as assault and rape, the effect is not strong enough to show up in these social statistics.

Some may argue that the increasing availability of new kinds of violence brought about by changes in the media should affect attitudes before they affect behavior. Trend data in sources such as Roper, Gallup, and surveys of high school students have not shown any such trend yet (e.g., Johnston, Bachman, & O'Malley, 1984). However, these data were collected for other purposes, and it is possible that a panel tracking study designed to focus on this issue might detect some signs of change.

Needed Research—A Question of Priorities

The U.S. media mix has changed enough since the time when the major studies of TV violence were conducted that it may perhaps warrant another attempt to see whether more robust data would emerge. This suggestion should not be interpreted as pointing the finger away from the networks to the other competitive media. That is not the intention. In fact, based on the trends we see occurring in real-world violence, the probability still is that new research on these other media would also show no effects. No one can be sure until a real-life study is done like the one described above, but taking account of the new media viewing availabilities.

There are other studies regarding television that are worth doing, however. And since everything uses resources, choices have to be made among all the worthwhile studies. Perhaps it is time to devote more research resources to other issues.

For example, there is another trend we have experienced that is till continuing. All the media—television, radio, newspapers, milk cartons, bumper stickers—have been trying to do what many critics of television have said television ought to do: use their power to solve a social problem. The problem that they took on was finding all those millions of missing children. There was even a syndicated TV news program service offered to stations around the country, called the Missing Children Network. Now it seems that all that power really may not have been needed because we have learned that in all probability there are not millions, but perhaps only some thousands of missing children, with many of these held by one parent without knowledge of the other parent ("Experts Question Data," 1985; "How Many Missing Kids," 1985).

Few people have stopped to ask what the effect of this media blitz about missing children has been on the children who are not missing. It is possible that they now have an abiding worry that at any moment they may be snatched away from their loved ones by some stranger. If so, there are probably few fears worse than this for young children to have. Do we know whether the degree of risk of children being abducted is commensurate with the media coverage, and the fear it might have produced? Such effects should have been studied, but to the best of my knowledge, they have not been.

We can expect that the demand to use television as well as other media to solve social problems will continue and may increase. The list of current problems the media are called on to address includes drug and alcohol abuse and teenage pregnancy. It is quite possible that some of the efforts to address such problems with mass media messages may actually backfire and increase rather than decrease the problems because of the lack of research in this area.

In short, there are other important issues besides violence regarding television's impact, and we may well ask whether scarce research funds might be better used to address them.

NOTES

1. Reports citing this erroneous figure include the following: "An Overwhelming 'Violence-TV Tie,'" *New York Times*, May 6, 1982; "A New Indictment of TV Violence," *Newsweek*, May 17, 1982; Eugene H. Methrin, "TV Violence: The Shocking New Evidence," *Reader's Digest*, January 1983.

2. NBC Research estimate for March 1986 based on data by the A. C. Nielsen Co. and an NBC-sponsored study by Statistical Research, Inc. (both unpublished).

3. NBC Research, as cited in Note 2.

4. NBC Research, as cited in Note 2.

5. In March, 1986, *Video Business* magazine estimated 22,000 "video specialty stores." In the November 17, 1986, issue, *Time* magazine estimated the number of outlets to be 35,000.

6. The *New York Times* reported (September 16, 1986) that researcher Dolf Zillman,

at the Institute for Communication Research at Indiana University, found that to be one reason for watching such movies, especially among the less appealing young men.

REFERENCES

Cook, T. D., Kendzierski, D. A., & Thomas, S. U. (1983). The implicit assumptions of television research: An analysis of the 1982 NIMH report on television and behavior. *Public Opinion Quarterly, 47,* 161-201.

Experts question data on missing children. (1985, August 18). *New York Times.*

Felson, R. B., & Morgan, M. (1984, March). Book review, *Television and aggression: A panel study. Contemporary Sociology, 13* (2).

Freedman, J. L. (1984). Effect of television violence on aggressiveness. *Psychological Bulletin, 96,* 227-246.

How many missing kids. (1985, October 7). *Newsweek.*

Huesmann, L. R., & Eron, L. D. (Eds.). (1986). *Television and the aggressive child: A cross national comparison.* Hillsdale, NJ: Lawrence Erlbaum.

Johnston, L. D., Bachman, J. G., & O'Malley, P. M. (1984). *Monitoring the future: Questionnaire responses from the nation's high school seniors.* Ann Arbor: Survey Research Center, University of Michigan.

Kenny, D. A. (1984). The NBC study and television violence. *Journal of Communication, 34,* 177-188.

Malamuth, N. M., & Donnerstein, E. (1982). The effects of aggressive-pornographic mass media stimuli. *Advances in Experimental Social Psychology, 15,* 103-135.

Milavsky, J. R., Stipp, H. H., Kessler, R. C., & Rubens, W. S. (1982). *Television and aggression: A panel study.* New York: Academic Press.

National Institute of Mental Health. (1982). *Television and behavior: Ten years of scientific progress and implications for the eighties: Vol. 1. Summary report, Vol. 2: Technical appendix.* Washington, DC: Government Printing Office.

Rossi, P. H., & Wright, J. D. (1983). Review and comment, *Television and aggression: A panel study. Television Quarterly.*

U.S. Department of Justice. (1985a). *Sourcebook of criminal justice statistics 1984.* Washington DC: Author.

U.S. Department of Justice. (1985b) *Uniform crime reports for the United States.* Washington, DC: Author.

Wiegman, O., Kuttschreuter, M., & Baarda, B. (1986). *Television viewing related to aggressive and prosocial behavior.* The Hague: Stitchig voor Onderzoek van het Onderwijs.

JEROME L. SINGER
DOROTHY G. SINGER

16

SOME HAZARDS OF GROWING UP IN A TELEVISION ENVIRONMENT:
Children's Aggression and Restlessness

Should Television Viewing by Children Be a Matter of Indifference to Parents and Society?

Children in the United States and increasingly throughout the world are growing up in a new kind of environment. In addition to their exposure to the behavior of parents, siblings, and extended family members, young children now are confronted from their earliest years by a new source of stimulation. The television set in every home is tuned in for an average of about 6 hours a day, and is watched as much as 4 hours a day through the week by children aged 3 or 4 (Pearl, Bouthilet, & Lazar, 1982; Singer & Singer, 1981). In addition to learning their national language, gesture behavior, and social attitudes from the family group (and somewhat later from peers and teachers), children can now observe models of child and adult behavior and attitudes in the figures that appear on the television screen.

Yet parents and authorities in our society on the whole have taken a curiously ambivalent stand toward the regular viewing of television by young children. On the one hand, there are occasional outbursts from groups of parents stimulated by organizations such as Action for Children's Television or the National Council on Television Violence as well as by congressional committees such as that headed by Senator Pastore in the late 1960s. These critics decry the heavy exposure of child viewers to an excessive demonstration of violent behavior as the regular fare of television. On the other hand, we have indications that parents prefer not to look closely at what their children are watching or to consider television as a potential influence or hazard because of its

AUTHORS' NOTE: Some of the authors' research reported in this chapter was supported by grants from the National Science Foundation, the Spencer Foundation, and the John D. and Catherine T. MacArthur Foundation.

highly effective "baby sitting" properties. The appropriate committees of the federal government that began in the late 1970s to show some concern about these issues have moved, under the Republican administration of the 1980s, to almost total deregulation of any phase of advertising or of requirements for public service and programs for children by the private businesses that are licensed to control the television airwaves. It remains to be seen whether the Wirth-Lautenberg Bill, which mandates local stations to produce an hour of children's programming daily in order to maintain a license, can make any progress through Congress.

The same parents, who would probably be furious if they learned that teachers were using books such as *Fanny Hill* or *Lady Chatterley's Lover* as texts in the elementary schools, seem relatively uninterested when their children watch heavy doses of evening television where themes of sexuality, flirtation, and seduction are commonplace. Would such parents tolerate teachers who spent a good deal of time demonstrating to children how to race automobiles and use them as lethal weapons, or how to punch, stab, or shoot others who might be viewed as hostile? If, as common sense as well as considerable research in cognitive psychology suggests, a picture is worth a thousand words, why are parents more likely to march on school boards to ban books such as *Catcher in the Rye* or *Down These Mean Streets*, but to respond with relative indifference to the excessively violent content that characterizes daily television programming?

The television industry, confronted with concerns by psychologists and other behavioral scientists, as well as by some religious leaders and consumer advocates, about the quality of programming available generally, and specifically programming for children, calls for clear social science evidence that viewing of such materials produces any effect at all on children. Thus we have the intriguing paradox of a tremendously successful industry that earns its income through the sale of advertising time, using claims that a company's influence, brand recognition, and sale of products are enhanced through regular viewing of these commercials—yet at the same time, industry representatives assert that heavy viewing by children of a variety of frightening or antisocial behaviors on the same medium will not influence their behavior! Each new study by social scientists that suggests that viewing aggressive materials may indeed have some influence on the overt behavior of children or on their attitudes is greeted by an extremely critical analysis, and by arguments that such effects cannot be demonstrated in the laboratory and that field studies show only extremely modest results. We have personally observed an instance in which a senior executive of one of the networks, testifying before some members of the Federal Communications Commission, argued that television can have important positive effects on children by giving an example of a child who, having recently seen only one demonstration on TV of the Heimlich maneuver (a method for dislodging bones or other objects in the throat that threaten suffocation), was able to use it shortly afterward to save the life of another child. Clearly he was arguing that just one demonstration on television could produce a valuable social learning experience. At the same time, he went on to deny that the aggressive content on television had any influence on teaching children aggressive responses. Thus the industry argues that advertising information and "prosocial" behaviors can be learned from television, while denying that the heavy doses of aggressive materials that characterize daily programming have any impact on the aggressive responses of young viewers.

The television industry has cleverly put the pressure on its critics to demonstrate any learning effect from the medium, but it avoids systematic efforts to demonstrate whether advertising on television actually produces increases in viewer recognition and sales (McGuire, 1985). Social scientists have sprung to the bait and have attempted in a whole series of studies to determine whether television viewing by children is correlated with or predictive of either prosocial or aggressive behavior. Extensive reviews of the literature such as those by Comstock, Chaffee, Katzman, McCombs, and Roberts (1978), Comstock (1982), Huesmann (1982), and Murray and Kippax (1979) conclude that heavy television viewing, especially of more violent content, can be influential on children's overt behavior. This conclusion was also reached by the authors and advisory panel for the recent update of the Surgeon General's Report on Television and Behavior (Pearl et al., 1982). A critical analysis by Cook, Kendzierski, and Thomas (1983) of this last report, while noting the relatively small size of effects, nevertheless agreed that despite an occasional apparently negative finding (e.g., Milavsky, Stipp, Kessler, & Rubens, 1982), the bulk of the evidence leads to the belief that there may indeed be a causal relationship between heavy viewing and overt aggressive behavior in children and adolescents. Another recent review by Freedman (1984) seems to lead to a negative conclusions. However, careful examination of Freedman's review shows his neglect of the implications of the extensive experimental literature in this field, his omission of some significant recent studies (which are described below), and his failure to examine in greater detail the efforts by persons carrying out field studies to account for alternative explanatory variables (Friedrich-Cofer & Huston, 1986).

An extensive recent review by McGuire (1985) of a vast amount of literature on attitude change comes to the conclusion that the data do support consistent but low-level relationships between television viewing and overt aggressive behavior. McGuire is concerned that these correlations from field studies may be too modest, due to inherent difficulties in field research. He provides 14 arguments to demonstrate why field studies in general show only weak effects of television on a variety of attitudes and behaviors, including aggression. In view of the extensive documentation of a consistently high level of violent content in television programming, and of indications that heavy viewers are particularly susceptible to excessive fear of victimization (Gerbner, Morgan, & Signorielli, 1982; Morgan, 1983), McGuire points out the difficulties confronting researchers in the social sciences who must attempt to demonstrate effects in the natural environment. It seems to us that the television industry representatives, by putting such a heavy burden of proof onto social science researchers in the area of television viewing and violence, and by taking little responsibility for reexamining programming or developing regular age-specific shows for children, are able to "laugh all the way to the bank."

Some Theoretical Issues:
Sources of Influence on the Developing Child

Let us first consider some theoretical issues. What particular set of influences may play a role in the emergent attitudes, beliefs, cognitive structures, and overt behaviors of a growing child? In his remarkable analysis, McGuire (1985) has identified 16 theories of how attitudes are changed and organized them into a 4×4 matrix, which includes active and reactive stability models, active and reactive growth models, cognitive models that are internal and external in their state, and affective models that are internal and external in their state. These models are not mutually contradictory except with respect to a few specific hypotheses that might be generated by each. Rather they encompass, as McGuire suggests, the range of possible ways in which the complex nature of human thought and action can be modified or can develop, as a function of interaction with others or as a function of the inherent way that we organize our cognitive and affective experiences.

The position we are taking reflects a combination of these theoretical approaches, which may be best summarized in terms of the cognitive developmental theory proposed by Zigler and Child (1969). In this position it is assumed that social experience within the family or in school settings, overlaid on the specific cognitive stage of the child's development, influences the patterns of personality organization in the child. Of course, one must also consider inherent temperamental variations that are constitutionally determined or genetic (Scarr, 1981). In the research on television that we and others have done, there has been no opportunity to estimate such genetic factors, and obviously these must necessarily reduce at least some of the possible influence of television on variables such as restlessness and aggression. We have elsewhere outlined a series of family variables as well as characteristics of the child's "television environment" that might be assumed to interact or to function independently in predicting later attitudes, cognitive capabilities, or motor behaviors of the child (Desmond, Singer, Singer, Calam, & Colimore, 1985; Singer & Singer, 1983b). Among such family variables we have included measures of parental values and personal styles such as emphasis on resourcefulness and imagination, stability and conventionality, as well as sociability and relationships. We have also included estimates of parents' views of child discipline, including especially the emphasis on power-assertive child rearing methods and the use of physical punishment. We have also considered parents' use of what we have called "mediation," an approach emphasizing discussion and explanation, in contrast to one that primarily involves moral injunctions and prescription or commands. Other family variables considered include the organization of the home, regularity of mealtimes and other family routines, availability of a variety of cultural resources, sleep patterns of the child, and so on.

One might argue that other influences on children, in past history or in other countries, would be the extended family members such as grandparents, uncles and aunts, and cousins. For an increasing number of children in our society, the television set has in effect replaced the extended family. The television environment is one in which children are exposed from the earliest ages to a dazzling potpourri of miniaturized adults, children, and animated figures who laugh, shout, jump around, and belabor each other, with a background of loud music. What can children make of all of this? We can estimate the role of the television environment by taking into account the amount of viewing by the child, the kinds of programming viewed regularly, the relative availability of television, availability of cable and VCRs, the extent to which parents themselves watch regularly (thus setting an example for children), the extent to which there are or are not rules about television viewing imposed on the child, and finally the extent to which parents discuss material from television with children (Singer, Singer, & Rapaczynski, 1984b).

Possible influences of television. Television might have several kinds of influence on the child. For example, a more passive form of learning may occur simply by exposure, involving the inherent human tendency to categorize even fleeting or incidental experience. A more active form of learning may also involve the child's attempting to form schemas or categories and to organize ultimate action scripts based on the kinds of experiences encountered with the television medium. Quite apart form the content of what is presented, one might also argue that the rapidity, quick-cutting, and loud music of television may foster children's beliefs and expectancies that other social situations will have some of these same properties. Teachers complain increasingly that children are impatient with any extended lectures or discussions and seem to be oriented in their manner to the short-sequence approach that characterizes American television. With respect to content, heavy exposure to the medium also means heavy exposure to an inordinate amount of aggressive behavior carried out by both "good guys" and "bad guys." As children actively seek to organize scripts about human actions, either through direct imitation or through the formation of ongoing cognitive structures, they must inevitably—if they are heavy TV viewers—begin to see violence as the major form of problem solution. It might be argued that television viewing simply fosters the children's natural tendency for imaginative play and provides a vicarious substitute for overt action. However, available research (Singer, 1982; Singer, Singer, & Rapaczynski, 1984b) suggests that TV viewing, because of its relatively easy availability to the child, preempts other forms of self-entertainment and precludes the child's development of play skills as an alternative to overt aggressive actions.

Why Should We Be Concerned About Children's Aggression?

Some people have questioned whether we ought to be disturbed even if television does increase children's aggression. They propose that aggression is basic for children in self-protection and in dealing effectively with a competitive world. One must, however, make a distinction between assertive or self-defensive behavior and aggression as it is defined by researchers in the television field. Most studies either directly observe overt aggressive behavior by children that is essentially unwarranted or obtain reports from peers or parents about such aggressive behavior. A distinction is also made in these studies between verbal aggression and physical actions such as punching, pushing, breaking up others' materials—generally a delivery of "noxious stimuli" to others without adequate cause. Only the most extreme "Rambo" mentality would argue that boys and girls in the preschool or early elementary school ages benefit from being encouraged to engage in such overt aggression. Available research literature suggests that such aggression persists over time, as the work of Olweus (1979), Parke and Slaby (1983), Huesmann, Eron, Lefkowitz, and Walder (1984), and Farrington (1979) have shown. Indeed, one might argue that early disruptive behavior in the form of aggression or extreme restlessness by a child puts the child at risk when it must inevitably confront the restraints of the early elementary school situation. Teachers begin to label such aggressive youngsters as "troublemakers"; the children themselves become increasing unpopular with peers, and their restless and abrupt behaviors often make it more difficult for them to engage in the concentrated attention necessary to master simple reading skills.

No serious and responsible social scientists would argue that viewing of television is a major cause of violence in children, youth, or adults in the world or in our society generally. Research evidence is clear in indicating that parental aggressive behavior is the best predictor of later aggressive behavior by children (Patterson, 1982; Singer, 1984). Instead, the question is whether heavy viewing of television contributes *further* to the prediction of later aggressive behavior of our children over and above the influence of parental power-assertive child rearing methods or parental modeling of aggression. Despite Freedman's (1984) proposal that some as yet undefined "other" variable may be accounting for the correlation between heavy television viewing and aggression in children, social scientists have been at pains in each study to examine such factors as parental influences before drawing conclusions about the possible role of the television medium. As a matter of fact, one of our own studies investigated the variable *hours of sleep* of the child. One might argue that 7- or 8-year-old children watching the most violent action-adventure programming, shown usually at 9:00 or 10:00 p.m., are not getting as much sleep as other children. Therefore their aggressive or restless behavior may be accounted for primarily by insufficient sleep (Singer et al., 1984a). As it turned out, hours of sleep *was* a relevant predictor, but viewing of action television proved to be linked to subsequent aggressive behavior even when the sleep factor was taken into account statistically.

In summary, even with relatively modest correlations or predictive equations, the link between heavy television viewing and children's aggression must be taken seriously when we consider the millions of children who watch regularly. The aggression in the nursery school or schoolyard may not in itself put society at risk, but ample data suggest that children who show such behaviors are soon in difficulties and alienated from teachers and peers. The longitudinal studies make it clear that childhood fighting and bullying is correlated with adult violence and antisocial and self-destructive behavior (Friedrich-Cofer & Huston, 1986; Huesmann, Eron, et al., 1984).

A CLOSER LOOK AT SOME
OF THE RESEARCH

Investigators in the television field have generally agreed that four types of research evidence are relevant to the issue of television viewing and aggression. These include (1) laboratory experiments, (2) experimental studies in field settings, (3) field research involving correlations and predictions across time, and (4) surveys of "contagion effects," that is, increases in the incidence of suicides, acts of violence, or dangerous driving by adults following extensive media coverage of such events (Comstock, 1982; Friedrich-Cofer & Huston, 1986; Huesmann, 1982; Huesmann, Eron, Berkowitz, & Chaffee, in press). Since the contagion-effects research, such as that of Phillips (1974, 1979, 1982, 1983), is largely focused on adult violence, we will not address it further in this chapter. As Comstock (1982) has noted, however, studies of this phenomenon provide some of the clearest cases that television-viewing can be associated with subsequent serious violence in daily life.

Laboratory Experiments

More clearly than other types of research, laboratory experiments, in which children exposed to violent programs (in contrast to those seeing "control" shows) increase their aggressive behavior, permit more definitive causal statements. There are now well over 50 reasonably well-controlled laboratory studies that indicate that children, adolescents, or young adults will imitate or increase aggressive behavior following exposure to violent programming (Andison, 1977; Bandura, 1973; Hearold, 1979). Work such as that of Parke, Berkowitz, Leyens, West, and Sebastian (1977), Ellis and Sekyra (1972), and Steuer, Applefield, and Smith (1971) suggests that laboratory measures of aggression have "field validity." Johnston, Deluca, Murtaugh, and Diener (1977) showed that results of analogue studies using "shock" machines with children (as in studies on delivery of "hurtful" effects to others after frustration or aggressive films) correlated with the actual aggressive behavior shown by the children in other settings.

The experimental studies have considerable theoretical importance for understanding how aggressive behavior is stimulated. They cannot of course demonstrate that children who are heavy viewers at home will be more prone to aggression in daily social interaction. But they make a crucial theoretical point: Aggression, which was once viewed in Freudian terms as a cyclical, appetitive drive, is better understood as a socially stimulated behavioral response. The experiments make it undeniable that imitation of aggression, arousal, or reduced inhibition of aggression are all *possible* outcomes of natural television viewing, especially when the programs are full of violent acts in fiction, cartoons, and the news (Bandura, 1973; Friedrich-Cofer & Huston, 1986; Huesmann, 1982; Singer, 1984).

Experimental Studies in Field Settings

This group of studies involves some form of experimental intervention with controls, carried out in settings such as schools or residential treatment settings. The experimental features allow for causal assertions, but the difficulty of instituting all of the desirable control conditions often weakens the clarity of outcomes. Thus an experiment by Feshbach and Singer (1971) offered evidence that boys in residential treatment centers exposed to a nonviolent diet of programming actually showed more aggression afterward, compared with boys who saw a normal (relatively violent) diet of programs for 2 weeks. Since the boys seemed in general to prefer violent shows, the change in their diet might in itself have accounted for the greater aggression of boys "deprived" of their preferred programming. An attempted replication of this study by Wells (1973), including base-line data, showed an *opposite* result from the previous study. Boys who were initially more aggressive demonstrated significantly more aggressive behavior after the violent TV diet, and those boys who liked the aggressive programs more were more aggressive afterward, while those who liked the nonviolent shows showed lower aggression after viewing such programs. Two studies, one in Belgium and one in the United States, also found evidence of increased aggressive behavior after about 5 days of violent TV viewing (Leyens, Parke, Camino, & Berkowitz, 1975; Parke et al., 1977).

Field experimental studies carried out with preschoolers and early elementary school-agers have shown that television viewing can have both prosocial and aggressive effects. Friedrich and Stein (1973) demonstrated that exposure of preschoolers to 2 weeks of nonviolent programming ("Mister Rogers' Neighborhood"), compared to controlled alternative viewing, moderated aggressive responses in the children subsequently. Initially aggressive children who saw more aggressive programming failed to show the decline in subsequent aggression that characterized children watching neutral programming. Two comparable field experiments that we carried out demonstrated the prosocial effects possible after viewing the "Mister Rogers' Neighborhood" shows, and also indicated reduced disruptive or negative affective responses by the children who saw this show as compared with "neutral" control programming (Singer & Singer, 1976; Tower, Singer, Singer, & Biggs, 1979). The demonstration of such prosocial effects in field settings is important because it points out the influence of *particular* program content on later behavior. Ethical considerations necessarily prevent exposure of young children in field experimental settings to really heavy diets of violent programming of the type they actually *do* watch at home.

Two larger-scale field experiments may be mentioned because they sought to moderate aggressive behavior of TV-viewing children or to increase prosocial responses by special training procedures for parents or children. Singer and Singer (1981), in a year-long study, used parent-training groups and controls to see if children's heavy viewing could be reduced, and imagination and cognitive skills improved, by having parents use the television viewing patterns of children in more constructive ways. Their results indicated some effects, including less aggression when parents encouraged more imaginative or cognitive play in children, as well as a number of increased prosocial behaviors a year later for the appropriate experimental groups.

Even stronger results emerged from a study with early elementary schoolers by Huesmann, Eron, Klein, Brice, and Fischer (1983). They used an imaginative play format to provide experimental-group children (part of a field study group) with fresh ways of looking at the aggressive behavior shown on TV and with opportunities to explore alternatives to such violent solutions. Various control and placebo conditions with other children were also included in the design. By the end of the second year, children in the experimental training conditions were rated by their peers as significantly less aggressive, and the correlation between viewing violent TV and overt aggressive behavior was significantly decreased for this group.

In summary, while experiments in the field present enormous logistical and control problems, the bulk of data from such studies again points to the potential influence of television on aggressive behavior, while also indicating that viewing of prosocial programs may increase positive affect, sharing, imagination, and cooperation. Major reviews of studies in these areas by Hearold (1979) and Rushton (1982) indicate that children can and do learn social behaviors from television. The problem we confront in the United States is that consistent, carefully designed, age-specific, prosocial programming is almost unavailable through most networks or local stations. Instead, children are exposed to violent cartoons on Saturday morning and generally watch adult-oriented programming including action-adventure shows during the week. Thus the *learning potential* demonstrated by both laboratory and experimental field studies is mainly channeled toward violent behavior examples, which characterize so much of regular commercial television programming.

Naturalistic Field Studies

Most investigators in the television field concur in the necessity for supplementing the laboratory and field experiments with correlational studies examining the link between children's natural home viewing patterns and evidence, either from direct observation or peer ratings, of children's behavior at school or home. The problems of such field studies are considerable. One must (1) find ways of staying in contact with a large enough sample; (2) establish dependable methods, through parent logs or other procedures, for estimating children's viewing over a reasonable time period; and (3) have raters make direct observations of children's behavior without knowledge of their TV viewing; or (4) use peer ratings by other children, a method that has been shown to have considerable validity (Huesmann, Eron, et al., 1984). Field studies must rely on statistical methods such as partial correlation, multiple regression, or causal modeling to estimate the relative contributions to the child's aggression of other variables such as social class, parental child rearing methods, and other potential "third variables" that might explain away any correlations between TV viewing and aggression.

Every field study so far carried out has indicated that heavy television viewing, especially viewing of more violent programming, is positively correlated with concurrent and subsequent aggressive behavior. Even a study sponsored by the National Broadcasting Company, which involved follow-up of boys over several years, showed 12 of 15 correlations as positive (Milavsky et al., 1982). Although the authors of that study drew a negative conclusion, a review of available field studies including theirs by Cook et al. (1983) reached the conclusion that a positive though modest link between television viewing and overt aggressive behavior, probably of a causal nature, is supported by the array of field studies. The reviews by Cook et al. (1983) and by Huesmann (1982) did not include additional studies by Granzberg and Steinbring (1980), Hennigan et al. (1982), Huesmann, Eron, et al. (1984), Singer and Singer (1980), Singer et al. (1984a), and Williams (1986). The data range from studies of preschoolers (Singer & Singer, 1980; Singer & Singer, 1981) through elementary school ages (Huesmann, Eron, et al., 1984; Huesmann, Lagerspetz, & Eron, 1984; Singer et al., 1984a), and adolescents (Belson 1978).

The most extended study over time has been one under the continuing direction of Leonard Eron (Huesmann, Eron, et al., 1984, Huesmann & Eron, 1984). Data from this study involved a 20-year follow-up of boys in an upstate New York county, with indications that heavy TV viewing at ages 9 or 10 continues to predict aggressive behavior, including grossly antisocial acts of child abuse, at age 30. A subsequent study with a Chicago-area sample and with a sample of Finnish elementary school students also provided further evidence of the television viewing and aggression association over several years' time, based on rather sophisticated statistical analyses (Huesmann, Lagerspetz, et al., 1984).

Our own research has involved two separate year-long studies of preschoolers, one representing a somewhat more middle-class sample (Singer & Singer, 1981), one with a more blue-collar group (Singer, & Singer, 1980). In both studies we were at great pains to obtain repeated samplings of television viewing, through logs kept daily by mothers for 2-week periods several times through the year, and also to have the children observed and rated for aggression and other behavioral and affective variables by trained teams of observers who were blind to the children's TV viewing patterns and to the hypotheses of the study. For both boys and girls, early heavier TV viewing was correlated significantly with later aggressive behavior, even with a number of other variables partialed out. Indeed, in the 1980 study (actually carried out after the one published in 1981), we looked at specific programming viewed by the children and found that watching violent cartoons was a strong predictor of later aggressive behavior by these preschoolers.

In these studies we also carried out more intensive interviews and observations with subsamples of the children ($N = 40$). We selected those children who could be classified over the years as *High Aggressive-High TV Viewing, High Aggressive-Low TV Viewing, Low Aggressive-High TV Viewing,* and *Low Aggressive-Low TV Viewing.* Interviewers visited the homes of these children and reported in detail on daily routines, life-styles, and parent discipline. What stood out as a highly discriminating feature of the families of High Aggressive-High TV Viewing children was the report by parents that television or movies were the major source of recreation, that there was more parent-child co-viewing, but that the *children* controlled the TV viewing. The type of programming viewed was again relevant: The High Aggression children, *including* those who were Low TV Viewers, averaged four times as much time watching adult-oriented action-adventure programming (the more violent shows) as did Low Aggressive children. By contrast, the Low Aggressive children watched the peaceful "Mister Rogers' Neighborhood" show significantly more often than did High Aggressives.

Can we find any clear indications that there are modeling influences in the home that might play as much of a role in the child's subsequent aggressive behavior at school as do the very striking differences in the television viewing patterns? It is certainly true that children in both of the High Aggressive groups are more likely to be punished by spanking than are children in the Low Aggressive groups, and they are also less likely, according to mothers' reports, to be rewarded by praise. Beyond these differences, there were few indications of differences between the families and no indications that the High Aggressive children in our samples came from disrupted, stressed, or violent families. These home interviews further supported the indications that television viewing was implicated in the later aggressive reactions of the children (Singer & Singer, 1981).

In a third study we followed a group of 63 children from preschool to early elementary school, a period of up to 6 years. In this study we examined parental values, disciplinary practices, social class, and control of television, as well as a number of "television-environment" factors including parents' viewing, number of TV sets, and purchase of cable (then more rare). Our criteria were separate scores of children's aggression (based on mother's reports of their day-to-day behavior), school behavior adjustment, and restlessness, which was observed directly in our laboratory. We found that that, even though factors such as children's sleep patterns or parental use of physical force were predictors over the years of children's aggression, school disruptive behavior, or observed restlessness, our data indicated that heavy viewing (especially of the more violent programming) strongly predicted these variables. Indeed, even controlling for earlier levels of aggression shown by the child did not change the predictive role of TV viewing (Singer et al., 1984a).

In a more recent study with 5- to 7-year-olds, we looked more intensively at parental attitudes and communication patterns with children. A canonical analysis was carried out, with family patterns, TV viewing, and demographic variables (IQ, SES, gender, etc.) as one cluster of variables, and the child's cognitive and behavioral performances as the other cluster. A highly significant bipolar canonical variate emerged. Parents who established rules about TV, who showed more positive (supportive or pleasant) responses to the child, who engaged in more discussion and explanation rather than abrupt prescriptions with the child, and who also used less physical punishment and watched TV less themselves, were grouped together with children who watched less television. Such a cluster was significantly linked to lower aggression and less observed restlessness in the child's behavior (Desmond et al., 1985).

A Naturalistic Experiment

A final field study of great significance has just been published (Williams, 1986). This work has some of the characteristics of a natural experiment, for it involves a study of three neighboring Canadian towns, quite comparable in almost all characteristics, but which differed in the availability of television to each. One community (labeled Multitel) had access to United States commercial stations as well as to the single Canadian network, the second (Unitel) had access only to Canadian programming, and the third town (Notel) had no television until late 1973. Williams and her group were in a position to obtain measures of child and adult behavior, children's cognitive performance, and children's aggression in Notel as well as the other towns both before and after the regular availability of television in Notel. Direct observations of the aggressive behavior of the children made it clear that such reactions increased after the introduction of television, and this effect was still observable 2 years later. Effects were found for both boys and girls and across age levels, and for verbal as well as physical aggression. Results could not be attributed to IQ differences or to social class factors. Considerable care was taken in this study to examine alternative hypotheses, but the researchers were led to a firm conclusion that it is exposure to television that influences aggressive behavior, and that their findings cannot be explained away by stating that aggressive children simply prefer to watch more television or more violent programming. General television viewing rather than specific violent programs seemed critical, but content analyses showed a sizable level of aggression in the newly introduced television content, even in government-sponsored documentaries.

Some Conclusions and Implications

In summary, the field studies are generally consistent in supporting the experimental research, although field data almost certainly underestimate effects because of their greater logistic difficulty and control limitations. Except for the 20-year follow-ups of Huesmann and Eron (1984), we only have data over short periods—3 to 4 years at most. Thus we can only guess at the *cumulative impact* of a lifetime of viewing. For the shorter run, we must conclude that heavy television viewing puts children at risk of increased aggression and restlessness, with all of the negative cognitive and social consequences of such a behavior pattern (Friedrich-Cofer & Huston, 1986; Huesmann & Eron, 1984; Singer, 1984). Those of us who have been active over more than 15 years in studying a variety of aspects of the television medium in a reasonably scientific fashion cannot fail to be impressed with the significance of this medium for the emerging consciousness of the developing child. In its present form, both from the standpoint of content and of its fast-paced, fragmented format (Singer, 1980), we can only conclude that the frequent unmonitored television viewing by young children puts them at risk. Groups such as the National Council on Television Violence may be criticized for *appearing* to place the blame on television for many forms of social violence, but we would emphasize that their position is more responsible than that of industry representatives (or parents) who are quick to minimize any potential negative effects of viewing.

We have elsewhere reviewed many of the constructive possibilities of the medium and have prepared parent manuals and school curricula to encourage adults to take television seriously and to train children in a more critical approach to what they watch (Singer & Singer, 1983a). With the competition of a television set in the home attracting their growing children, parents are going to have to decide early on whose values they want their children to develop, the parents' or the television's world of violence.

REFERENCES

Andison, F. S. (1977). TV violence and viewer aggression: A cumulation of study results 1956-1976. *Public Opinion Quarterly, 41,* 314-331.

Bandura, A. (1973). *Aggression: A social learning analysis.* Englewood Cliffs, NJ: Prentice-Hall.

Belson, W. (1978). *Television violence and the adolescent boy.* Hampshire, England: Saxon House.

Comstock, G. (1982). Violence in television content: An overview. In D. Pearl, L. Bouthilet, & J. Lazar (Eds.), *Television and behavior: Ten years of scientific progress and implications for the eighties* (pp. 108-125). Washington, DC: Government Printing Office.

Comstock, G., Chaffee, S., Katzman, N., McCombs, M., & Roberts, D. (1978) *Television and human behavior.* New York: Columbia University Press.

Cook, T. D., Kendzierski, D. A., & Thomas, S. V. (1983). The implicit assumptions of television research: An analysis of the NIMH report on television and behavior. *Public Opinion Quarterly, 47,* 161-201.

Desmond, R. D., Singer, J. L., Singer, D. G., Calam, R., & Colimore, K. (1985). Family mediation patterns and television viewing: Young children's use and grasp of the medium. *Human Communication Research, 11,* 461-480.

Ellis, G. T., & Skeyra, F. (1972). The effect of aggressive cartoons on the behavior of first grade children. *Journal of Psychology, 81,* 37-43.

Farrington, D. P. (1979). Longitudinal research on crime and delinquency. In N. Morris & M. Tondry (Eds.), *Crime and justice: An annual review of research* (Vol. 1, pp. 289-348). Chicago: University of Chicago Press.

Feshbach, S., & Singer, R. D. (1971). *Television and aggression.* San Francisco: Jossey-Bass.

Freedman, J. L. (1984). Effect of television violence on aggressiveness. *Psychological Bulletin, 96,* 227-246.

Friedrich, L. K., & Stein, A. H. (1973). Aggression and prosocial television programs and the natural behavior of preschool children. *Monographs of the Society for Research in Child Development, 38* (4, Serial No. 151).

Friedrich-Cofer, L., & Huston, A. C. (1986). Television violence and aggression: The debate continues. *Psychological Bulletin, 100,* 364-371.

Gerbner, G., Morgan, M., & Signorielli, N. (1982). Programming health portrayals: What viewers see, say, and do. In D. Pearl, L. Bouthilet, & J. Lazar (Eds.), *Television and behavior: Ten years of scientific progress and implications for the eighties* (pp. 291-307). Washington, DC: Government Printing Office.

Granzberg, G., & Steinbring, J. (1980). *Television and the Canadian Indian: Impact and meaning among Algonkians of Central Canada.* Unpublished manuscript, University of Winnipeg.

Hearold, S. L. (1979). *Meta-analyses of the effects of television on social behavior.* Unpublished doctoral dissertation, University of Colorado.

Hennigan, K. M., Del Rosario, M. L., Heath, L., Cook, T. D., Wharton, J. D., & Calder, B. J. (1982). The impact of the introduction of television on crime in the United States. *Journal of Personality and Social Psychology, 42,* 461-477.

Huesmann, L. R. (1982). Television violence and aggressive behavior. In D. Pearl, L. Bouthilet, & J. Lazar (Eds.), *Television and behavior: Ten years of scientific progress and implications for the eighties* (pp. 126-137). Washington, DC: Government Printing Office.

Huesmann, L. R., & Eron, L. D. (1984). Cognitive processes and the persistence of aggressive behavior. *Journal of Aggressive Behavior, 10,* 243-251.

Huesmann, L. R., Eron, L. D., Berkowitz, L., & Chaffee, S. (in press). Effects of television violence on aggression: A reply to Freedman. *Psychological Bulletin.*

Huesmann, L. R., Eron, L. D., Klein, R., Brice, P., & Fischer, P. (1983). Mitigating the imitation of aggressive behaviors by changing children's attitudes about media violence. *Journal of Personality and Social Psychology, 44,* 899-910.

Huesmann, L. R., Eron, L. D., Lefkowitz, M. M., & Walder, L. O. (1984). Stability of aggression overtime and generations. *Developmental Psychology, 20,* 1120-1134.

Huesmann, L. R., Lagerspetz, K., & Eron, L. D. (1984). Intervening variables in the TV violence-aggression relation: Evidence from two countries. *Developmental Psychology, 20,* 746-775.

Johnston, A., Deluca, D., Murtaugh, K., & Diener, E. (1977). Validation of a laboratory play measure of child aggression. *Child Development, 48,* 324-327.

Leyens, J. P., Parke, R. D., Camino, L., & Berkowitz, L. (1975). Effects of movie violence on aggression in a field setting as a function of group dominance and cohesion). *Journal of Personality and Social Psychology, 32,* 346-360.

McGuire, W. J. (1985). Attitudes and attitude change. In G. Lindzey & E. Aronson (Eds.), *Handbook of social psychology* (3rd ed., Vol. 2, pp. 233-346). New York: Random House.

Milavsky, J. R., Stipp, H. H., Kessler, R. C., & Rubens, W. S. (1982). *Television and aggression: A panel study.* New York: Academic Press.

Morgan, M. (1983). Symbolic victimization and real-world fear. *Human Communication Research, 9,* 146-157.

Murray, J. P., & Kippax, S. (1979). From the early window to the late night show: International travels in the study of television's impact on children and adults. In L. Berkowtiz (Ed.), *Advances in experimental social psychology* (Vol. 12, pp. 253-320). New York: Academic Press.

Olweus, D. (1979). The stability of aggressive reaction patterns in human males: A review. *Psychological Bulletin, 85,* 852-875.

Parke, R. D., Berkowitz, L., Leyens, J. P., West, S., & Sebastian, R. J. (1977). Some effects of violent and nonviolent movies on the behavior of juvenile delinquents. In L. Berkowitz (Ed.), *Advances in experimental social psychology* (Vol. 10). New York: Academic Press.

Parke, R. D, & Slaby, R. G. (1983). The development of aggression. In P. H. Mussen & E. M. Hetherington (Eds.), *Handbook of child psychology. Vol. 4: Socialization, personality, and social development* (4th ed., pp. 547-641). New York: John Wiley.

Patterson, G. R. (1982). *A social learning approach. Vol. 3: Coercive family process.* Eugene, OR: Casstalia.

Pearl, D., Bouthilet, L., & Lazar, J. (Eds.). (1982). *Television and behavior: Ten years of scientific progress and implications for the eighties.* (Vols. 1-2). Washington, DC: Government Printing Office.

Phillips, D. (1974). The influence of suggestion on suicide: Substantive and theoretical implications of the Werther effect. *American Sociological Review, 39,* 340-354.

Phillips, D. (1979). Suicide, motor vehicle fatalities, and the mass media: Evidence toward a theory of suggestion. *American Journal of Sociology, 84,* 1150-1174.

Phillips, D. (1982). The impact of fictional television stories on U.S. adult fatalities: New evidence on the effect of mass media on violence. *American Journal of Sociology, 87,* 1340-1359.

Phillips, D. (1983). The impact of mass media violence on U.S. homicides. *American Sociological Review, 48,* 560-568.

Rushton, J. P. (1982). Television and prosocial behavior. In D. Pearl, L. Bouthilet, & J. Lazar (Eds.), *Television and behavior: Ten years of scientific progress and implications for the eighties* (Vol. 2, pp. 248-257). Washington, DC: Government Printing Office.

Scarr, S. (1981). *Race, social class and individual differences in IQ.* Hillsdale, NJ: Lawrence Erlbaum.

Singer, D. G. (1982). Television and the developing imagination of the child. In D. Pearl, L. Bouthilet, & J. Lazar (Eds.), *Television and behavior: Ten years of scientific progress and implications for the eighties* (Vol. 2, pp. 39-52). Washington, DC: Government Printing Office.

Singer, D. G., & Singer, J. L. (1980). Television viewing and aggressive behavior in preschool children: A field study. *Annals of the New York Academy of Science, 347,* 289-303.

Singer, J. L. (1980). The powers and limitations of television: A cognitive-affective analysis. In P. Tannenbaum (Ed.), *The entertainment function of television.* Hillsdale, NJ: Lawrence Erlbaum.

Singer, J. L. (1984). *The human personality.* San Diego, CA: Harcourt Brace Jovanovich.

Singer, J. L., & Singer, D. G. (1976). Fostering creativity in children: Can TV stimulate imaginative play? *Journal of Communication, 26,* 74-80.

Singer, J. L., & Singer, D. G. (1981). *Television, imagination and aggression: A study of preschoolers.* Hillsdale, NJ: Lawrence Erlbaum.

Singer, J. L. & Singer, D. G. (1983a). Implications of childhood television viewing for cognition, imagination and emotion. In J. Bryant & D. R. Anderson (Eds.), *Children's understanding of television: Research on attention and and comprehension.* New York: Academic Press.

Singer, J. L., & Singer, D. G. (1983b). Psychologists look at television: Cognitive, developmental, personality, and social policy implications. *American Psychologist, 38,* 826-834.

Singer, J. L., Singer, D. G., & Rapaczynski, W. (1984a). Family patterns and television viewing as predictors of children's beliefs and aggression. *Journal of Communication, 34,* (2), 73-89.

Singer, J. L., Singer, D. G., & Rapacznyski, W. (1984b). Children's imagination as predicted by family patterns and television-viewing: A longitudinal study. *Genetic Psychology Monographs, 110,* 43-69.

Steuer, F. B., Applefield, J. M., & Smith, R. (1971). Televised aggression and the interpersonal aggression of preschool children. *Journal of Experimental Child Psychology, 11,* 442-447.

Tower, R. B., Singer, D. G., Singer, J. L., & Biggs, A. (1979). Differential effects of television programming on preschoolers' cognition, imagination, and social play. *American Journal of Orthopsychiatry, 49,* 265-281.

Wells, W. D. (1973). *Television and aggression: Replication of an experimental field study.* Unpublished manuscript, Graduate School of Business, University of Chicago.

Williams, T. M. (Ed.). (1986). *The impact of television. A natural experiment in three communities.* Orlando, FL: Academic Press.

Zigler, E., & Child, I. (1969). Socialization. In G. Lindzer & E. Aronson (Eds.), *The handbook of social psychology* (2nd ed., Vol. 2). Reading, MA: Addison-Wesley.

17

BEYOND CARTOON KILLINGS:
Comments on Two Overlooked Effects of Television

I begin this commentary with excerpts from a letter by a network official in charge of program practices to the producer of a typical shoot-'em-up TV entertainment. This document, given to me by someone connected with the show, reveals a great deal about the negotiation of violent images on television. (I have deleted the specific scene and page numbers that follow each point of the letter.)

1. There is an overabundant use of "hell" and "damn" which must be appreciably reduced. Additionally, please delete "Chrissakes" [11 citations in script follow], "goddamn" [two citations], "numbnuts," "Christ," "friggin," "ass," "scumbag," "bastard," "son of a bitch," and "cabrones." . . .

2. It is important for all action scenes to be brief, with impact occurring off camera (page 32, impact to stomach, not crotch). Please avoid the morbid or grotesque when showing victims of shootings and temper the use of "blood" make-up and sound effects . . . It is [network's] policy not to have guns or other lethal weapons held to the head or neck as indicated on [five citations follow] . . . Action must also be considerably modified in scene which calls for [hero] to begin "banging him viciously against the driver's window, utterly out of control" [two scenes]. . . .

3. *Action* [each statement refers to specific scene in script]:

- Eliminate shot of two men as they are hit by bullets.
- Eliminate one of the two gunshots to Second Bodyguard.
- Eliminate shot of men's bodies during explosion.
- Eliminate second gunshot.
- Eliminate shotgun blasts and delete shot of man as he receives gunshot in stomach.
- Eliminate this second shot of barrel of gun aiming directly into camera.

4. Finally, all animal action must be staged in accordance with the American Humane Association standards . . . [the association] has been notified of the presence of an animal actor (alligator).

I often think that if alligators and other animals were treated on television the way people are, the uproar would be so great that violence would be completely eliminated.

What are we to make of this effort to censor and control the violence on a show that is, nevertheless, one of the most "violent" there is? I do not doubt the network's good intentions, but I think what we have here is an elaborate game, rather like counting how many damns and deaths can dance on the head of a pin. The scriptwriters double the scenes of violence and throw in lots of cuss words; the network cuts the numbers in half; and everyone goes away happy.

And yet . . . the violence of this show is cartoon violence, the modern equivalent to all those "whoops" and "bangs" that used to appear in "violent" funnies like "Terry and the Pirates" or "Dick Tracy." In contrast, think of the public outpouring of anger and sadness that emerged when "M*A*S*H" killed off Col. Henry Blake, the character played by MacLean Stevenson, who was leaving the series. According to Larry Gelbart, the show's creator and one of its greatest writers, people can tolerate 5,000 killings on TV shows, but not one *meaningful* death of a character they love.

The cartoon-reality difference, I think, accounts for one of the major problems in trying to pinpoint the effects of TV violence. Is violence on television harmful? I am persuaded that it does affect the attitudes and negative world view of some adults; heavy viewers of TV violence, for example, exaggerate the frequency of violence in the world around them (Gerbner, Gross, Signorielli, Morgan, and Jackson-Beeck, 1979). And I am persuaded that it does increase the aggressiveness of some children (Huesmann & Eron, in press; Huesmann, Eron, Berkowitz, & Chaffee in press). But does violence on television have a harmful effect on *most people?* I am equally persuaded that it does not. Even the researchers who believe strongly in the harmful effects of TV violence acknowledge that they are talking about a small percentage of the variance, which ranges, in different studies, from 3% to 10% or 15%. Most people aren't affected one way or the other; they watch television, as Ellen Langer would say, mindlessly. Some are actively repelled by scenes of violence. If I were to be taken to *Rambo,* the only kicking and screaming I would do would occur as a result of being forcibly dragged there, not as an aftereffect of having seen it.

In this discussion, I want to raise two ideas regarding possible consequences of American television that I believe are more serious and influential than the cartoon violence of TV "sitkills." (We speak of sitcoms; why not a term for the formula of situation killings?) In doing so, I will draw comparisons with English television, the other system with which I am most familiar. I think such cross-cultural comparisons are necessary, because we all too often speak of the influence of "television" as if the medium were the same in the United States as in England, France, Norway, or China.

THE PACE RACE: FORM OVER CONTENT

The first point concerns the effects of commercials and pace: The way people watch a television story may be more damaging than what they see. Years ago I interviewed Stanley Milgram, who had just finished a massive, complicated, and inconclusive study on the effects of a TV show on its audience (Milgram & Shotland, 1973). (The audience watched an antisocial act—a character stealing money from a charity box—that had been included in a real program, "Medical Center," and were later given an opportunity to imitate what they saw. They didn't do so.) Milgram said, "Actually, it occurs to me that perhaps it is not the content of TV but its form that constitutes the real affront to human sensibilities: I mean the constant interruption of cognitive processes every 12 minutes by irrelevant material—commercials. I wonder what decrement in appreciation and understanding comes about when children watch a show with such interruptions" (Tavris, 1974, p. 74).

If you watch the news, you don't even get 12 continuous minutes. I recently timed a half-hour program on my local CBS station. It consisted of 7 minutes of news, 2 minutes of ads; 4.5 of news, 2 of ads; 7 of news, 2 of ads; 2.5 news, 3 of ads. Even those minutes of commercials are broken into 15- and 30-second segments advertising several different products.

Over the years, as networks competed more fiercely for viewers and as viewers switched channels with remote-control abandon, there has been a rapid escalation of quick-and-shiny gimmicks. Shows now "must" begin with grabbers, must give the entire store away, must move at a rapid-fire pace with no time to develop characters. The "news" must be entertaining, complete with the intrusive beat of music (sometimes over the announcer's voice, as in sports reporting). There is no room, no *time*, for subtlety or complication. It is axiomatic among television programmers that audiences no longer have the patience to watch and see for themselves. They have to be led by the hand (Postman, 1985).

I realize that some researchers have tried to measure the effects of commercial interruptions and pace, with unsuccessful results. But this is like trying to measure the effects of air; it is very difficult, because no one doesn't breathe. American television is our visual air. The greatest confirmation of the hypothesis that pacing affects thinking comes from the fact that slower-paced shows do not survive. Even PBS now feels obliged to "give away" what's to come by showing glimpses of forthcoming scenes. There is no time now for documentaries, in-depth reports, or experimental dramas. The occasional English import—a show, such as "Tinker, Tailor, Soldier, Spy" or "Edge of Darkness," that is murky, mysterious, slow, and provocative—is inevitably accompanied by advice from critics to "have patience" and "stay with it." How insulting! How condescending! How . . . necessary?

It is only by getting out of the air—say, by watching television in other countries—that one is shocked out of one's complacency about the incessant intrusion of commercials and the rapid-fire pace of our shows . . . and the resulting effects on our attention span. Lest we assume that the rating system or commercial interruptions are inevitable, I think television reformers would do well to consider alternatives from other nations. In France, commercials are bunched together between shows, and people watch them anyway. In England, television owners pay a yearly fee that helps subsidize the BBC, which is required to include public service shows along with the usual sitcoms. The result is a mix of programs instead of the relentless uniformity that tends to mark American television.

Why do social policy activists think only of tinkering with the content of television and never with changing its form or economy? Why add one drop to a leaky bucket, instead of repairing the bucket? I am all in favor of getting more good shows on the air, with more good messages and more parts for minorities, but a greater contribution to art and public welfare would be the abolition of the Nielsen ratings. (You couldn't abolish critics; shows would still be reviewed!) No one need fear that advertisers would stop advertising their wares entirely, simply because they couldn't target their products quite as specifically as they used to. Advertisers and television need each other in our system, and that would continue even without ratings.

Abolition of ratings might accomplish another revolution and permit real writers to write for television. As a writer, I am sensitive to the fact that the English do not despise their writers, but acknowledge and celebrate them. In contrast, can you name one eminent, accomplished American novelist or playwright who has written for television since the old days of "Playhouse 90"? Good American writers must choose between affluence from schlock writing for TV, and penury from good writing for books and plays. Good English writers do not have to make such a devil's choice. The likes of John Mortimer and Jack Rosenthal can write classic television stories that don't have a *single car chase* in them.

I offer a story that contrasts the American and English systems perfectly. Jack Rosenthal (a family friend of mine) is known in Hollywood for having written *Yentl* with Barbra Streisand, but in England he is considered the Chekhov of English television. Jack wrote "Bar Mitzvah Boy," "The Evacuees" (a story of the children who were evacuated from London to the countryside during the blitz), and "The Knowledge" (a story of ten Londoners studying to earn licenses to drive a cab; this is a year's course in England). After *Yentl* Jack was prevailed upon by this agent to come to Hollywood and consider film offers. Reluctantly, he went.

"Look, this is what we want for our movie of the week," a television producer explained to Jack. "*Heart*—romance and passion. *Stomach*—nerves, excitement, thrills. *Groin*—lots of sex and desire. That's what you have to give us: heart, stomach, and groin." "I'm afraid I'm not the person for you," said Jack. "You see, I do elbows."

American television has no room for elbows: for subtlety and nuance. But the reason is not that we lack writers or ideas or alternatives to violence. The reason is that our shows depend on ratings. Any art form that depends only on ratings will suffer a lack of imagination and variety, and will end up pandering to that infamous lowest common denominator.

SPORTS ON TELEVISION: THE UNSPOKEN MESSAGES

The second influence on television I wish to discuss is its coverage of sports—real-world, noncartoon activities that increasingly glorify violence and conflict. Television has promoted the McEnroe model of competition, because temper tantrums, rudeness, and racket-hurling are more photogenic and lively than self-control and playing by the rules. (They make a better story.) Temper tantrums also give those ubiquitous commentators something to talk about, and of course American commentators feel it necessary to comment *all the time*. Compare the difference between American and English coverage of Wimbledon tennis, figure skating, or any other sport, and you will see my point. On English television you actually get to watch the sport yourself, with only the thock-thock of the tennis ball and an occasional (informative) remark from the announcer. On American television you are assaulted with relentless chitchat. Geoff Mason, an NBC producer, called the British telecasts of Wimbledon "a little bit sterile" for

Americans. "We have to focus on emotion, be superaggressive and get closer to the action," he said. "Reserve and respect are not our way of doing it" (Tavris, 1982, p. 177). Golf remains one of the few American sports in which commentators have to shut up—or at least whisper— and in which players can't afford to have temper tantrums because self-control is essential to good play.

Although some researchers doubt that television's *entertainment* violence has a significant or long-lasting effect on the overwhelming majority of its viewers (Freedman, 1984, and this volume; Milavsky, this volume), there is extensive and convincing evidence that *sports* violence does (Goldstein, 1983). The usual effect is increased anger, but some studies also find greater violence, destructiveness, and even national tendency toward war.

In recent years U.S. sports commentators have increased their attention to and praise of "playing dirty," inflicting pain, rules violations, and "winning at any cost." Studies of sports coverage find that commentary stressing conflict among players has increased significantly in recent years, and praise about exceptionally rough plays in football exceeds negative comments by 5 to 1 (Bryant & Zillmann, 1983). A feedback loop is created: Male viewers' enjoyment of televised football increases as a function of the degree of roughness and violence involved (Bryant, Comisky, & Zillmann, 1981).

The Question of Catharsis

It is time to put a bullet, once and for all, through the heart of the catharsis hypothesis. The belief that observing violence (or "ventilating it") gets rid of hostilities has virtually never been supported by research (Averill, 1982; Goldstein, 1983; Russell, 1983). Fans may want to see angry displays, emotional ventilation, and violence, but they can't call on science to justify the catharsis hypothesis of viewing.

For example, violence on the playing field doesn't reduce an "aggressive drive," it begets further aggression. Richard Sipes (1973) selected 20 societies around the world and rated them for the frequency of their wars and the presence or absence of combative sports (sports that involve body contact, the real or symbolic gaining of territory, and any "warlike" action). In contradiction to the catharsis hypothesis, Sipes found that the societies that had the most violent games had the *most* wars. In the United States itself between 1920 and 1970, Sipes showed, interest in football and hunting rose during World War II and the Korean War; affection for baseball drops during war years and rises afterward (as it did after Vietnam). Even war doesn't "get rid of" aggressive "impulses": a nation's murder rate tends to *rise* after a war, not decrease (Archer & Gartner, 1976).

Similarly, a recent study investigated the relationship between a nation's participation in the Olympic Games of this century and the number of wars in which it was involved (Keefer, Goldstein, & Kasiarz, 1983). The greater the participation (in number of athletes and events entered), the more frequent the wars. This finding is not confounded with the nation's standing as a world power; many small nations are frequently at war with neighbors too.

None of this, of course, is to suggest that combative sports cause wars. But this work does show that aggressive sports do not "drain off" any warlike motives. Rather, they are simply a microcosm of society—if a society rewards violence or is involved in combat, its sports are violent too.

What about spectators of aggressive sports? Psychologists have measured the effects of sports on the players' and spectators' hostility and aggressiveness. Male spectators at an Army-Navy football game and an Army-Temple gymnastics meet were interviewed before and after the games (Goldstein & Arms, 1971). The football fans were more hostile after the game than they had been going in, regardless of which team they supported (even fans of the winning team). The men who watched the gymnastics meet did not feel angrier afterward.

In a replication of this study that controlled for degree of competitiveness of the sport, possible personality differences among fans, and the effects of a "stylized" form of aggression (wrestling), young men and women were randomly assigned to watch a hockey game, a wrestling match, or a competitive but nonaggressive swimming meet. The findings support the conclusion that spectator hostility increases as a result of the aggression observed on the playing field, and not from other extraneous factors. The spectators' hostility levels rose after the hockey and wrestling, but not after the swim meet (Arms, Russell, & Sandilands, 1979; Russell, 1983). It seems that violence and displays of temper do not "displace" such tendencies among fans; they teach fans how to behave. A large proportion of incidents of fan violence are preceded by aggression by players.

Of course, some games require combativeness and competition, and no one would say that watching a terrific football game is enough to make everyone want to kick the cat or wreck the TV. Spectator hostility does depend on the perception of the beholder, and on whether the beholder enjoys violence or abhors it. For instance, hockey fans who agree that "fighting should be allowed to go unpenalized because it is an important part of the game" become more hostile and angry after watching a game than fans who dislike hockey violence (Harrell, 1981). Fans who believe that boxers are *unfairly* trying to injure one another become more belligerent after watching a bout than spectators who think the boxers are just behaving professionally in order to win. In a contrasting vein, students of karate—who acquire a passive and peaceful philosophy along with their lethal skills—become less aggressive with increased training (Nosanchuk, 1979).

The prevailing belief in America—that it is bad to suppress anger and instinctive and healthy to ventilate it—confuses two things: the physical state of high energy and excitement generated by many games, and what players do with that energy (Mandler, 1984). But intensity can be controlled and directed in many ways. No instinct links energy with violence, and players have plenty of "outlets" that do not require taking swings at each other. They can, for example, use the energy of arousal to play the game better. (This is one of the enjoyable uses of anger in sports, as when Reggie Jackson, furious at a pitcher who strikes him out, and Pete Rose, provoked by opposition fans waving signs saying "this Rose is a weed," hit the ball out of the park.) In 1984 the New York Rangers made a concerted effort to play nonviolent hockey, even against the fierce Philadelphia Flyers, and they beat them twice. "We knew they would come out in the first period and play the way they did," said Barry Beck in an interview in the *New York Times*, "trying to intimidate us, trying to get us to fight, but we're just not going to play that way. We're smart, we're intelligent, and that's why we beat them."

I believe that the lessons portrayed by television sports—which can glamorize violence and aggressive players, or glamorize the games and players that are "good sports"—influence children and adults far more than all the sitkills do. We are a nation that celebrates the individual over the team, the emotion over its control, rule-breaking over the rule, competition over cooperation; and these values are apparent in the sports we most enjoy and the players we pay most highly. I do not object to competition that is part of the game, or to the enjoyment of caring who wins or loses. But I do object to the win-at-all-costs model of sports that is currently enjoying such popularity, and to the pacing and structure of television that tends to foster mindless viewing (see Langer & Piper, this volume).

Television cartoons such as "Miami Vice" are not, I think, the problem. More serious problems are the violence that television does to thinking, and our thinking that violence is a desirable way to win.

REFERENCES

Archer, D., & Gartner, R. (1976). Violent acts and violent times: A comparative approach to postwar homicide rates. *American Sociological Review, 41,* 937-963.

Arms, R. L., Russell, G. W., & Sandilands, M. L. (1979). Effects of viewing aggressive sports on the hostility of spectators. *Social Psychology Quarterly, 42,* 275-279.

Averill, J. R. (1982). *Anger and aggression.* New York: Springer-Verlag.

Bryant, J., Comisky, P., & Zillmann, D. (1981). The appeal of rough-and-tumble play in televised professional football. *Communication Quarterly, 29,* 256-262.

Bryant, J., & Zillmann, D. (1983). Sports violence and the media. In J. H. Goldstein (Ed.), *Sports violence.* New York: Springer-Verlag.

Freedman, J. (1984). Effect of television violence on aggressiveness. *Psychological Bulletin, 96,* 227-246.

Gerbner, G., Gross, L., Signorielli, N., Morgan, M., & Jackson-Beeck, M. (1979). The demonstration of power: Violence profile No. 10. *Journal of Communication, 29* 177-196.

Goldstein, J. H. (Ed.). (1983). *Sports violence.* New York: Springer-Verlag.

Goldstein, J. H., & Arms, R. L. (1971). Effects of observing athletic contests on hostility. *Sociometry, 34,* 83-90.

Harrell, W. A. (1981). Verbal aggressiveness in spectators at professional hockey games: The effects of tolerance of violence and amount of exposure to hockey. *Human Relations, 34,* 643-655.

Huesmann, L. R., & Eron, L. (in press). *Television and the aggressive child: A cross-national comparison.* Hillsdale, NJ: Lawrence Erlbaum.

Huesmann, L. R., Eron, L., Berkowitz, L. & Chaffee, S. (in press). Effects of television violence on aggression: A reply to Freedman. *Psychological Bulletin.*

Keefer, R., Goldstein, J. H., & Kasiarz, D. (1983). Olympic games participation and warfare. In J. H. Goldstein (Ed.), *Sports violence.* New York: Springer-Verlag.

Mandler, G. (1984). *Mind and body: Psychology of emotion and stress.* New York: W. W. Norton.

Milgram, S., & Shotland, R. L. (1973). *Television and antisocial behavior.* New York: Academic Press.

Nosanchuk, T. A. (1979). *The ways of the warrior: The effects of traditional martial arts training on aggressiveness.* Working paper, Department of Sociology and Anthropology, Carleton University, Ottawa.

Postman, N. (1985). *Amusing ourselves to death.* New York: Viking.

Russell, G. W. (1983). Psychological issues in sports aggression. In J. H. Goldstein (Ed.), *Sports violence.* New York: Springer-Verlag.

Sipes, R. (1973). War, sports and aggression: An empirical test of two rival theories. *American Anthropologist, 75,* 64-86.

Tavris, C. (1974, June). The frozen world of the familiar stranger: "We are all fragile creatures entwined in a cobweb of social constraints." (Interview with Stanley Milgram). *Psychology Today,* p. 70-80.

Tavris, C. (1982). *Anger: The misunderstood emotion.* New York: Simon & Schuster.

SEYMOUR FESHBACH **18**

TELEVISION RESEARCH AND SOCIAL POLICY:
Some Perspectives

There are many groups of individuals, with rather different roles—researchers, child clinicians, educators, members of the television industry, policymakers, social activists, parents—who are concerned with the interaction between the child and television. Although these groups may have different perspectives, it can be assumed they all have a common interest in the welfare of children. They also share a similar consciousness of the change that has occurred in the past several decades in the role of the mass media, especially television, in the lives of our children. But their views may differ as to the significance and implications of that change.

We know that television has become an integral part of our cultural experience, that almost every child (and adult), rich and poor, urban and rural, has access to a television set. We also know that television is not only a pervasive experience for the future but often a pervasive experience for the individual. Whereas cinema viewing, even before the advent of television, was typically limited to a few hours once or twice a week, television viewing encompasses much more of the average child's life experience. Estimates of children's TV viewing indicate that children spend about as much time interacting with the television set as they do with the classroom teacher (Comstock, Chaffee, Katzman, McCombs, & Roberts, 1978), and it is a commonplace observation that most children have more than an idle involvement in the transaction with television. They like to watch it and do not like to be deprived of television, especially the viewing of their favorite program (see reactions to TV schedule excluding "Batman" in Feshbach & Singer, 1971). Parents, educators, and legislators want to know what to do about this new object in the lives of children and await the verdict of research to provide the basis for social policy regarding the child's transaction with television.

I am reminded of an incident that occurred in one of our studies of television and the young child. We had just completed a project at a preschool and, in the process of loading equipment into our station wagon, had left a television set in the schoolyard. When we returned to the yard, a group of about 12 preschoolers were gathered around the TV set, staring at the blank screen. When asked why they were sitting there, the children indicated that they were thinking about the program being shown on the television set, even if they could not see it. We then carried the set to the car and, as we drove off, several children came up to the wire fence that bounded the schoolyard, waving their hands, saying "Goodbye, TV set."

That incident conveys something about the meaningfulness and import of television for these children. But is this impact something positive or negative? Should the children's interest in and attachment to television be the occasion for parental concern? Should the concern be limited to particular kind of programming content? We look to research for the answer to these and myriad other questions regarding the influence of television on children's emotional, social, and intellectual development. We would like research to tell us whether television is causing a decline in children's reading skills and school performance or, conversely, whether it stimulates children's curiosity and increases the range and scope of their knowledge. We are concerned that exposure to violence on television may contribute to delinquency and aggressive behavior in youth. We worry whether television is fostering social isolation and passivity among our children, and whether the advertisements they watch encourage materialism and poor consumer habits. We wonder whether their conception of the world is misshapen by television's images, whether theirs is a world fraught with danger and magical solutions, with distorted notions of sex roles, of blacks and other minorities, and of the way in which people relate to each other and resolve their conflicts. We may also wonder about television's image of the child, whether television promotes in adults attitudes and conceptions regarding children that are conducive to children's growth and development. And we look to research to help us resolve these questions and concerns.

These are important questions that have significant implications for entertainment practices, regulatory policy, and child rearing. However, it is my contention that we expect too much from research: that we cannot expect research to resolve the social policy issues with which the omnipresence of television confronts us. An unrealistic need for more definitive research may be used as a mechanism for delaying polity change, much as administrators often turn over troublesome issues to committees as a method for delaying action. Second, unrealistic expectations may result in minimizing people's attention to research when the findings are complex or qualified. Third, researchers themselves, in an effort to be heard, may become overzealous in their interpretations and fail to distinguish between inappropriate scientific inferences and legitimate policy recommendations drawn from the same set of data. Policy recommendations cannot await the verdict of definitive research findings. Science is always incomplete; policy is in the here and now. Those involved in policy formulation and change—legislators, broadcasters, parents, advocates—must make decisions on the basis of the information that is currently available to them. They use that information in conjunction with economic values, social values, political considerations, and personal constraints either to maintain or to modify some extant policy or behavior with regard to television programming and the exposure of children to that programming.

The Television Violence Debate

It can be argued that the concern with definitive research findings has served to obfuscate and impede the implementation of meaningful social policy in the child-television arena. The controversy over the effects on children of television's depiction of violence is a case in point. The amount of research that has been addressed to this issue is enormous. No other area of television effects has received as much attention. Yet, despite the conclusion of national commissions and probably most behavioral scientists that frequent exposure to television violence is a significant cause of aggressive behavior in children (Pearl, Bouthilet, & Lazar, 1982), the question is far from resolved. Several distinguished social psychologists have recently taken strong issue with the assertion that a causal relationship between violence on television and aggressive behavior has been demonstrated (Freedman, 1984; McGuire, cited in Coughlin, 1985). Perhaps my presumption of the prevailing view of most behavioral scientists that "TV violence stimulates aggression" is incorrect. On this point, let me quote from a letter of rejection by an editor of one of our more prestigious academic journals concerning an article that reported a form of aggression-inhibiting effect of violent TV. I had served as one of the reviewers of this article and, incidentally, had recommended that it be published. The editor wrote, "This study presents one more field experiment that contradicts laboratory findings—it adds to the debate, but does not resolve it." The editor referred here to the discrepancy between laboratory findings, which generally reflect an aggression-stimulating effect of TV violence, and field studies, which usually indicate no effect or an opposite effect (Kaplan & Singer, 1976), as did the study in question.

And so the debate goes on, to the dismay of parents and professionals concerned about children, while network executives and advertisers remain content with the status quo. The situation is additionally complicated by the likelihood that the cartoons and television dramas that have been the primary object of study constitute only one category of potential aggression-stimulating fare that can be observed on television, and perhaps not even the most potent of such stimuli. For example, I would hazard a guess that observation of "Monday Night Football" would elicit significantly more aggression than any of the programs presented on Saturday morning.

The intriguing and provocative series of studies carried out by Phillips is relevant here (Phillips, 1977, 1979, 1982, 1983). His initial research addressed the effects of publicity given to incidents of suicide. He first identified the suicides given front-page accounts by newspapers throughout the United States for the period 1946-1968. He then determined the number of suicides that were recorded in the United States during the month of a publicized suicide and, as a control, the number of suicides in the corresponding month the previous year and the following year. He found an increase in suicides after 26 front-page suicide stories in contrast to a decrease after 7 such stories. Moreover, he repeated the study with television news stories and obtained similar findings. In subsequent research, using data from the State of California, he found an increase in motor vehicle fatalities following news reports of suicides. In these studies he used as controls the number of fatalities recorded the week before and the week after the critical week in which the suicide occurred.

Phillips then turned to a very different kinds of news event, heavyweight championship prize fights, and determined the dates on which all such prizefights took place between the years 1973 and 1978. He assumed that a great deal of media attention is given to these sporting events, and that communities throughout the nation would be exposed through television, radio, and newspapers to descriptions of the fights. He employed standard time-series regression analyses to determine whether there was any systematic relationship between the occurrence of a heavyweight championship bout and frequency of homicides during the period following the bout. After controlling for variables known to be correlated with homicide incidence, such as day of the week, month, year, and holidays, he found a significant increase in number of homicides following heavyweight championship prizefights (Phillips, 1983). The largest peak in homicides occurred on the third day following the event. While the explanation for this lag in effect is not evident, a similar phenomenon was observed in the previously cited studies of the effects of published suicide stories. Further analyses of the data revealed rather remarkable relationships between the race of the prizefight combatants and the race of the homicide victims. "White loser" fighters were followed by significant increases in young, white male homicide deaths, but not in black male homicides. In contrast, "black loser" prize fights were followed by significant increases in young, black male homicides, but not white male homicides. Whether or not the provocative results of this series of studies by Phillips are substantiated by research employing other kinds of methodologies, these data point to the possible aggression-instigating role of non-dramatic or nonfictional forms of TV violence.

Interestingly, Phillips found no effects for reports of murders, indicating that one cannot automatically assume that media descriptions of all kinds of violence will stimulate violence in viewers and readers.

Policy Implications of Television Violence Research

What are the policy implications of these findings concerning the potential aggression stimulating properties of certain news and sporting events, and of my prior suggestion that effects of the depiction of violence in television cartoons and dramas are varied and still not well understood? Censorship of the news is objectionable to most of us and would raise even more thorny constitutional issues than do attempts to influence the degree of aggressive program content depicted on television. However, this does not mean that we should desist from efforts to modify the kind of television programming to which children in the United States are currently exposed. Nor do we have to await the verdict of research before attempting to bring about changes in children's television environment. The data required for social policy recommendations and social action are less demanding that those required for scientific conclusions.

This assertion that the database for social policy advocacy need not be as strong as that required for scientific validity may seem to run contrary to a prevalent view among scientists that only strongly supported scientific conclusions should be used as a basis for advocating policy decisions. The conflict is more apparent than real. Scientists do object to the misuse of their findings, to exaggerated assertions regarding the strength of relationships, and to failures to acknowledge conflicting data when advocates cite the results of "scientific" studies to support some policy option. However, social policy is always under consideration in the present, and social policy advocates are obligated to utilize whatever information is presently available, including tentative empirical generalizations. Decisions not to "act," or to delay some action, or to plan a future change represent present choices on the part of decision makers. These decision options are usually somewhat linked to extent to which scientific data are compelling, but the introduction of change usually requires a stronger scientific base than the maintenance of the status quo. For example, a great deal of scientific evidence was required before policymakers were willing to control smoking in public places and to limit tobacco advertisements. However, if the elders of a society were confronted with a decision regarding the introduction of tobacco to their society, then they would need less strong scientific evidence of negative effects to prohibit the importation of tobacco. There are obviously other factors also that enter into the determination of the costs and benefits of policy options. Nevertheless, the point remains that social policy decisions cannot await scientific certainty, and that scientific propositions of varying certainty can enter into rational policy decision making, providing that the scientific probabilities are appropriately represented.

It is proper that behavioral scientists should be debating the issue of the effects of violence in the media on the behavior of the viewer. As scientists, we need to be able to reconcile the conflicting findings that have been reported in the literature and to understand better the conditions under which television and other media violence stimulates, has no effect on, or decreases aggressive behavior. While we can expect our research findings to have policy implications, nevertheless we have a basis for advocacy of changes in television programming without having to become immersed in the intricacies of research design and conflicting research findings.

Social advocacy and social policy in the television arena should emerge from and be rooted in the basic datum that underlies all of the issues and concerns regarding television's influence on children—namely, the enormous amount of time that children, particularly children in the United States, spend watching television—more than 25 hours a week for the average preschool and elementary school child (Comstock et al., 1978; Price & Feshbach, 1983). This concrete reality poses a responsibility for all of us—parents, those involved in the media, and professionals concerned with children's development and welfare. How we address this responsibility in part depends on the perspective we take in viewing the issue.

An Alternative Policy Perspective

In considering policy changes in the television arena, we have typically focused on the question of the harmfulness of extant programming practices, assuming that the justification for advocating programming changes rests on the demonstration of negative effects. An analogue is cigarette smoking: Cigarette production is profitable; cigarette smoking is pleasurable; people choose to smoke. Therefore, before attempting to modify smoking behaviors and advertising practices, we have to demonstrate that smoking is harmful. Similar considerations might appear to hold for television programming.

However, the cigarette smoking analogue may be the wrong one. I think education is a better one. This does not mean that television should be educational in the "three Rs" sense of schooling; but like education, it has a significant socializing function and takes up a major part of the child's daily life. Those in the television industry see television as primarily an entertainment medium, but the social reality is otherwise. Children's involvement in television compels us to view television, not merely as an entertainment medium, but as a major medium of socialization. Our legislators need to assume this perspective in considering the kinds of policies that are appropriate to a free society, and appropriate to the development of our children, just as much when they examine television practices as when they address formal schooling. They do not need research to tell them that most of what children are exposed to in their many hours of television viewing, especially on Saturday morning, is banal and aesthetically impoverished. Nor do I think that broadcasters or advertisers would disagree with the appraisal that most of what children see is hackneyed and cheaply produced. Those involved in the media industry perceive their options as limited by the constraints of a market economy, and while they are as desirous as parents and educators to improve the quality of children's television, they must deal with the harsh reality that the programs that attract the widest audience and cost the least to produce are the most economically advantageous.

How can the community most effectively respond to this economic issue? One approach, which might entail some legal difficulties, is implementing regulations that limit profits on programs broadcast on Saturday mornings and perhaps some weekday afternoon hours. A second and perhaps more acceptable approach is community support, in which parent-teacher associations and the various professional groups and organizations that have been concerned with the role of television in children's lives would endorse those programs that are judged as fostering the child's development. They need not be educational in the narrow sense. But they should stimulate the child's imagination, or enlarge his or her horizons, or promote active rather than passive skills. And, if they also happen to elicit prosocial responses, enhance cognitive skills, or foster better consumer and self-care behaviors, so much the better.

Thus teachers, school administrators, and parent groups could well assume a broader role in this area. They might recommend particular programs, in addition to the manifestly educational ones that are shown after school and during prime time. Teachers could use homework assignments as a means for stimulating in children a less passive and more perceptive attitude in their television viewing behavior. The selection of television programs for recommended viewing would be on the basis of criteria similar to those used in recommending supplementary reading material to children. The quality, style, and interest value of a program would enter into recommendation decision, along with age appropriateness, moral and character implications, and related developmental considerations. One consequence of the schools adopting an active role in bringing particular television programs to the attention of children would be the recognition that television is a significant facet of the child's culture and, along with written materials, ought to be integrated into the educational curriculum.

If schools, parents, and professionals joined together in formulating television policies that would influence children's program viewing behavior, we might be able to attract large audiences to more positive, productive kinds of program content. And, in so doing, we would provide a spur to the entertainment industry to produce more programming compatible with its socialization function. Similarly, advertisers would be motivated to pay for quality programs in order to earn the support of the community. This positive approach of endorsement seems to me preferable to and, in the long run, more effective than the negative one of developing a list of taboo programs or boycotting the advertisers. Positive economic support could bring about substantial changes in what children see on television. As scientists, of course, we would want to evaluate the effects of these changes in programming and viewer exposure. But we need not await the outcome of research to begin the implementation of these changes.

REFERENCES

Comstock, G., Chaffee, S., Katzman, N., McCombs, M., & Roberts, D. (1978). *Television and human behavior.* New York: Columbia University Press.

Coughlin, E. K. (1985, March). Is violence on TV harmful to our health? Some scholars, a vocal minority, say no. *Chronicle of Higher Education.*

Feshbach, S., & Singer, R. D. (1971). *Television and aggression.* San Francisco: Jossey-Bass.

Kaplan, R. M., & Singer, R. D. (1976). Television violence and viewer aggression: A reexamination of the evidence. *Journal of Social Issues, 32,*(4), 35-70.

Freedman, J. L. (1984). Effect of television violence on aggressiveness. *Psychological Bulletin, 96,* 227-246.

Pearl, D., Bouthilet, L., & Lazar, J. (1982). *Television and behavior: Ten years of scientific progress and implications for the eighties* (Vols. 1-2). Washington, DC: Government Printing Office.

Phillips, D. P. (1977). Motor vehicle fatalities increase just after publicized suicide stories. *Science, 196,* 1464-1465.

Phillips, D. P. (1979). Suicide, motor vehicle fatalities, and the mass media: Evidence toward a theory of suggestion. *American Journal of Sociology, 84,* 1150-1174.

Phillips, D. P. (1982). The impact of fictional television stories on U.S. adult fatalities: New evidence on the effect of the mass media on violence. *American Journal of Sociology, 87,* 1340-1359.

Phillips, D. P. (1983). The impact of mass media violence on U.S. homicides. *American Sociological Review, 48,* 560-568.

Price, J., & Feshbach, S. (1983, April). *Demographic characteristics related to children's television viewing frequency: Theoretical and practical implication.* Paper presented at the meeting of the Eastern Psychological Association, Philadelphia.

QUESTIONS AND ANSWERS

Guy Lometti, Director of ABC Social Research: I'd like to make a point about television violence and the public's perception of television violence. After the NBC study, we at ABC conducted our own study, slightly different in intent and content. We found that when we asked people about the amount of violence on television, a large number of them—in this national sample somewhere in the neighborhood of 50%—indicated there was too much violence on television. However, we went further and asked people about their perceptions of the amount of violence on particular programs and whether they thought that violence was acceptable. When we did that, we found "The A-Team" was perceived to be the most violent television program, but on an absolute scale of violence it was given a relatively low number. And the level of acceptability of that violence was very high—85% of the people in the sample told us that the violence in that program was acceptable. Asking further about other television programs, and then about movies that were available on cable services, we found that a great deal of violence was perceived in those pay movies—twice as much or more than was perceived on broadcast television. And also, the level of acceptability was reduced greatly—to less than half of the level of acceptability for violence that was portrayed on the networks.

So it's important to realize that when we ask a very general question, especially about television and violence, we find (1) that there's social desirability in answering that question, and (2) that the perception of television now is very different than it was just a few years ago, given the advent of the larger number of independent television stations as well as the large numbers of motion pictures that are broadcast or provided on pay services.

Q: In an attempt to test out the special, more complicated factors that might in fact make television sometimes dangerous to some people, I've done a field study recently with 400 8-year-old boys engaged in a violent sport, a floor-hockey game. I found, across the board, no effects of violent television; but when the circumstances were just right, there was an increase in aggression. First, there had to be frustration before the television. Second, there had to be a cue associated with the violence that was clearly apparent when the floor hockey game began. In a four-way interaction, the group that accounted for virtually all the aggression were the kids who had seen the violent television, had been exposed to the cue, had been frustrated, *and*, probably most important of all, had been identified (independently, by their teachers) as the most highly aggressive kids in the class. This was about 15% of the kids.

At first I thought that that was a small effect and not very important, but then I realized that most of the aggression in that school is probably going to be accounted for by those few kids, that 15%. If you frustrate them, they are more likely to be aggressive, and especially so if they've just seen violent television. That is going to affect the life of my child and all of the other children in the school. It will make their world more aggressive, more violent.

Jonathan Freedman: It is difficult to comment on a study unless you've read it carefully. Let me just mention two things. First, I think the notion about teasing the data long enough might apply here. If you look hard enough, and examine many interactions, you usually can find some effect. Second, I would be loathe to generalize from that study to conclude that even the findings for the special conditions you described would hold up in other studies.

There have now been a number of studies comparing high and low aggressive children, and overall there is no evidence that television violence increases aggression more among kids who are highly aggressive to begin with. Sometimes the opposite is found, so I wouldn't put too much weight on a single study.

Carol Tavris: I'd like to comment about the end of that possible causal chain, which is the effects of playing hockey on aggressive children. I would say that the boys who are disposed to aggression would do well to go out for track and swimming, rather than bashing each other with hockey sticks. I'm persuaded that the effects of playing a very aggressive, very energizing, very competitive sport are absolutely clear—such sports increase the aggressiveness and hostility of children, and of adults.

Seymour Feshbach: From a scientific point of view, the important question is not whether violence on television stimulates aggressive behavior, but rather *under what conditions* that effect or other differing effects will occur. There are studies in the literature that are oriented toward those more complex questions. But there results are less dramatic and appear less germane to social policy issues than more simplistic statements such as "It produces violence" or "It doesn't produce violence."

Q: For the most part, you've discussed the effects of violence on aggression, or at least on behavioral outcome measures. What are the research findings about the effects of seeing so much violence on beliefs and attitudes about violence being good or bad?

Jonathan Freedman: In reading the evidence I focused on the effects on actual aggression, but there is a substantial amount of evidence on attitudes. It is difficult to sort out the effects. The typical findings are that there are some small effects, which often interact with the family environment in which the television is used—for instance whether or not the parents criticize what they see on television. My own feeling about that evidence is that the research is not substantial enough, and has not been done carefully enough, to reach any firm conclusions.

However, I would add that there is no question that television is a very powerful medium. Anyone who thought that television did not affect the attitudes and values of children in our society would be making a claim that is almost impossible to imagine. Certainly television must play a role in shaping us, so it's very unlikely that what we see on television doesn't to some extent affect our attitudes and values. But then the question is, what is it on television that has an effect? If you think it's violence, you might be right. But of course there are news programs, there's a spacecraft blowing up right in front of you, and a million other things. We live in a society that has a great deal of violence, a great deal of crime, and great many terrible things happening. It's hard to imagine (and this is purely intuitive, not based on evidence) that watching violent shows is a terribly important aspect of that. My guess is that it is the exposure of children and adults to what's going on in our world, rather than specifically watching "The A-Team" or something like that, that has an effect.

Seymour Feshbach: I can think of one body of literature that shows such effects, and that's the literature on sexual violence and its effects. There is a fair amount of data indicating that it does modify attitudes toward women, decrease negative attitudes toward rape, and the like (e.g., Donnerstein, E. [1984]. Pornography: Its effect on violence against women. In N. Malamuth & E. Donnerstein [Eds.], *Pornography and sexual aggression*. New York: Academic Press).

Q (to Alice Henderson): I'd like to know whether your Program Practices department has considered the issue of the way violence is portrayed on TV. Violence frequently is shown, or sudden death, or somebody being beaten up, and then it stops. That is, we do not see the funeral, the bereaved children, or the widow or widower. If somebody is beaten up, we rarely see them spending months in a hospital, or permanently injured and having to alter their life-style. Do you see that as an issue?

Alice Henderson: Yes, I do see it as an issue, more of an issue now than 10 or 15 years ago. We in the television industry get accused of two things in the area of violence: One group says that we don't show enough of the impact, the blood and pain and agony of it; but another faction says that we're already showing too much. Our general positions is this: We try to show that knives and guns do hurt, that people do end up in the hospital, or that they may die. But we try not to linger on it. Perhaps we have not struck the best balance yet; it's very difficult to find the right balance. But we don't like to have someone die in a car crash, or be shot, and never show what has happened to the family. If it's at all possible, we try to show the result of the actions as well as the action.

Q: In response to Professor Freedman's comment, I think it would be sad if we couldn't think of any programming to replace the violent programs that are on television, and I would like to make a suggestion. I'm from Madison, Wisconsin, and I represent the National Telemedia Council, which is involved in teaching critical viewing skills and developing media-literate young viewers. We have done an experiment, which is now an ongoing movement. We feel education *is* the answer, as Professor Feshbach mentioned, and we are educating by involving children in active participation in television. We have developed a children's channel on cable, where children are actually doing everything from conceptualizing the ideas, to going out and producing the programs, to being the camera operators, and acting in front of the camera. They run the channel, they manage it. These children are becoming media-literate, and I would be very happy to see psychologists begin to investigate that area as a prosocial, positive approach to children and television.

Jonathan Freedman: I agree with you that we're all looking for something better, but it's hard to know what we could suggest to the television networks that would be better because it reduced violence and would still attract the audience that they are looking for. Educational programs are terrific, but most of them are notoriously unpopular. If you put a lecture on the air, very few people would watch it. It's very hard to make shows that the public will like and that are of high quality.

Carol Tavris: I strongly disagree that it's hard to specify alternatives to violent TV other than a dull lecture. Have we really become so inured to violence that we can't imaging anything else the public will like? It is *not* very hard to make shows the public will like. It *is* hard to make shows that the *entire* public will like. There are many publics, each with different tastes. It is *not* hard to specify what "something better" would be; just look at the stories on English television. The problem is that if "only" 15 million people like a thoughtful show, that's not enough to keep it on the air in the U.S. That's what guarantees mediocrity and kills the chances for genius.

Q: I want to question the evidence about the effects of aggression. This pattern of inconsistent research findings is very typical of a lot of areas; for instance, it's true of sex and gender effects. But the technique of meta-analysis can test a large body of studies statistically to see if there is in fact a consistent effect across studies. I would like to know if this has been done for TV violence. When it has been done for sex and gender effects, we find effects about the size Dr. Freedman mentioned, 1% to 5% of the variance. But we also find that there are certain circumstances that evoke the effect.

So, I would suggest that there may be certain circumstances that have not yet been teased out, possibly because we're looking for the wrong variables. Two variables that I think might be very important are the issue of showing domestic violence as opposed to public crimes, and the issue of tolerance of aggression. I've seen several studies that indicate that kids watching violent TV don't necessarily become more aggressive themselves, but they become more accepting of higher and higher levels of aggression. As an illustration, they now go into video stores and rent these absolutely ghastly movies and don't bat an eye.

Seymour Feshbach: The fact that adolescents will go into a video store and select *Chainsaw Massacre* or some horror films doesn't prove that it was exposure to television that caused them to become inured to violence. They might have selected movies like that 30 or 40 years ago if they had been available. However, I agree that contemporary television violence and movie violence can have a negative effect. In my view, one of the great dangers about contemporary media presentations is that they have become so realistic and so gory and clear and explicit. There are good theoretical reasons, I think, that those kinds of programs can have deleterious effects. But I think that, as psychologists, we should also be asking such questions as, Who is it that watches these films? Why do they watch them? What functional value do they have in their lives? Those are quite different questions than the question of effects, but they are psychologically interesting ones and important to understanding the role of the media in our daily lives.

Jonathan Freedman: There has been at least one meta-analysis of the laboratory studies, and these laboratory studies do hold up, although not terribly well. No one would bother with a meta-analysis of studies outside the laboratory because there aren't enough of them, and you have to have at least some findings in the right direction to justify doing a meta-analysis. One thing I did not say in my review is that there is *not one* study that produced a clear, consistent effect, and we require that at the very least.

[Editor's Note: As the author of a meta-analysis on TV violence and behavior, George Comstock was asked to comment on that subject.]

George Comstock: On the basis of my own personal experience, I'm a counterexample to Dr. Freedman. Before I worked for the Surgeon General's Committee, I was (and I still am) a lover of media violence. I think it includes some of the greatest fiction and the greatest literature. I am a connoisseur of violence, and I came to that committee strongly believing that there would be no evidence to suggest that violence—in films, television, or literature—had any bad effects. I've had a lot of years of work in this area, and I became convinced that the evidence did point in that direction.

On the topic of meta-analyses, there are two of them, one published in *Public Opinion Quarterly* (though not technically following the Glass tradition), and there is one by Susan Hearold that's been in the literature for a long time. There's another by her in the first volume of *Public Communication and Behavior,* which I'm editing, which compares 1,043 effect sizes. The data show that the effect size for the laboratory experimental literature is about one-third of a standard deviation, which in meta-analytic circles is considered pretty large. The effect size of the survey literature is identical. When these studies are evaluated objectively in terms of study quality and external validity, the effect sizes decline, but they do not drop to nonsignificance. The field experimental literature, as Dr. Freedman suggested, has a zero effect size.

I differ with Dr. Freedman's paper in this area, because he treats all external tests—field experiments, surveys, and time series—as conceptually very similar. I feel that each of these has particular methodological strengths and problems, and so basically there are four great strains of research in this area: laboratory experiments, field experiments, time-series analyses, and surveys. Clearly, time-series analyses that investigate different kinds of media stimuli like publications about suicides, or violent prizefights, are not conceptually in conflict when the results are not parallel, because the stimuli are different.

Dr. Freedman's paper does not deal with any of the reasons why these various strains of literature are strong or weak. He concludes in his paper that the literature suggests a small, positive correlation between viewing TV violence and aggression. Another important point is that, because of unreliability or measurement, there is an excellent possibility that small correlations are underestimates. He also doesn't discuss the fact that it's impossible in this society to compare people who are zero or really low in exposure to violent stimuli, so we are always dealing with people who have substantial exposure versus people who have very high exposure. Thus from simple measurement issues, there are problems that suggest that obtained correlations would be underestimates.

Q: I think the reason that we're not getting any clear research results is that we're taking the violent acts out of context, and that is bound to distort their meaning. Our television and our films support the most conservative kinds of ideology; they support society. People learn that crime doesn't pay. The violence is shown as being perpetrated by bad people, and it's punished. As Dr. Greenberg said, if we count up all these actions, we're doing the drip, drip, drip studies, but not the drench studies—ones that show the essential nature of stories in the media and how these are affecting people.

In our fictionalized versions of things, whether it's "Masters of the Universe" or Don Johnson on "Miami Vice," crime doesn't pay. But things like missing children, or TV sports, or the shuttle explosion, those are stories that don't have a pat answer, and those stories are going to affect the children much more vividly. For instance, stories about missing children tell kids, "There are bad people out there that can grab me. And Don Johnson isn't going to be there to rescue me." I think that we have to take a look at how real life is portrayed in media, not just at fictionalized life that always ends up on the side of right and order.

Q: My background is public health, and so I'm surprised that no one has been looking at the effects of television violence in the way that a social epidemiologist might look at this problem. I'm wondering what kind of an attack rate you require in order to be convinced. You see, we spend enormous amounts of money and energy on combatting physical illnesses that have an incidence in the area of 20 to 50 per 100 thousand. To take the example that Dr. Milavsky used, for instance, the actual number of stranger-child abductions in the United States is not in the thousands, it's only 67 per year. But when you bring in the family, the child's schoolmates, the principal and teachers, and the police officers who work on the case, the repercussions of one stranger-child abduction are staggering because they ripple out into the community a long way for a long period. So I think the people who are considering the violence that results from television need to decide what is an acceptable incidence rate as opposed to one that they will worry about and try to combat.

PART IV

Prosocial Values and Television

Part IV presents the "flip side" of the preceding debate about the antisocial effects of television violence. Here we ask, can television present and inculcate prosocial values? As a starting point, what does "prosocial" mean, and what prosocial values are we most concerned about? If television can affect them, which ones can it influence most successfully, and how can this be accomplished? What changes in television programming and procedures are needed if television is to fulfill these objectives? Or must the necessary changes occur in viewers' uses of and reactions to television? Also, how fully is television already transmitting prosocial themes and models?

In contrast to the area of television violence, this is an area that has had very little research, but the authors in this part present original research findings as well as creative suggestions and speculative ideas concerning television's potential prosocial role in society. These authors are all researchers who have studied various aspects of television and child development and personality. In addition, several of them have served as consultants to the television industry, and one (Barbara Lee) is the director of social research for the CBS Network. Other issues about prosocial uses of television are raised by the questions and comments at the end of the section.

In the first chapter, Charles Winick points out that television is the most mass medium, since almost everyone in the United States has access to it in their homes without charge, and many people use it several hours a day. Television serves many different and important functions, and his research shows that, when television is suddenly removed from people's lives, they realize that several of these functions are relevant for them.

Barbara Lee reports the results of an original study of prosocial actions, themes, and values in network prime-time programming. Defining prosocial behavior to include altruistic actions, display of affection (including empathy), and control over negative predispositions, she found from three to five prosocial actions per hour of programming. She also found that about one-quarter of the programs studies had an overall prosocial theme or moral. These findings do not answer the question of whether this a good or a bad record. Some basis for comparison is needed in order to interpret the desirability of this level of prosocial programming, and commentators may differ in their answers.

Ellen J. Langer and Alison Piper stress that television, like any stimulus situation, can be responded to mindfully or mindlessly. They start from the research findings that show the importance that a feeling of choice and control makes in people's health and longevity; and they point out that television can be used as a stimulus that contributes to one's sense of control. However, many people view television mindlessly and thereby lower their own feelings of competence and self-esteem. The authors report the result of original research showing how mindful television viewing can lead to more flexible thinking and awareness of complexity in the world, and also how mindless acceptance of information can be prevented.

Norma Deitch Feshbach focuses on a prosocial characteristic little studied by communication researchers—empathy—and stresses television's potential for developing it in children. She emphasizes the typically low level of empathy portrayed in television programming, a conclusion that seems somewhat at odds with Lee's content analysis findings. Feshbach goes further by suggesting innovative ways that various aspects of empathy can be portrayed on television, and she speculates that both adult and child viewers would find such portrayals satisfying and be attracted by them. Certainly this is an area that merits more research and programming attention.

In the final chapter of this section Halford H. Fairchild gives a fascinating behind-the-scenes account of his actual experience over several years in creating, producing, and evaluating a prosocial pilot television program. The objectives of this program included reversal of gender and ethnic stereotypes, and portrayal of multiracial, equal-status cooperation in common efforts to solve important problems. The results of the pilot program are assessed, and practical suggestions are offered about how this approach to prosocial programming could be improved and extended in ways that would be acceptable to network television.

CHARLES WINICK

19

THE FUNCTIONS OF TELEVISION:
Life Without the Big Box

During the January 1986 television presentation of the football Super Bowl, the most widely watched regular single program, there was one minute of silence. This was so very unusual that the effects on viewers of having even one minute with nothing to watch became a subject for considerable speculation and concern on the part of commentators ("Talk of the Town," 1985).

What are the effects on television viewers of having nothing to watch for an extended period of time? Some answers to this question have been sought by an investigation of how people deal with the loss of television, resulting from theft or breakdown of the set.

In a number of other social research areas, it has proven productive to study the attractions and functions served by an activity through examining reactions to its absence. Thus the study of divorced persons has contributed to knowledge about marriage (Hayes, Stinnett, & DeFrain, 1980), work gratifications have been clarified by investigating the unemployed and retired (Komarovsky, 1940; Winick, 1964), sexuality has been explored by studying incarcerated men deprived of traditional sexual outlets (Kinsey, Pomeroy, & Martin, 1948), alcohol's gratifications have been examined by interviewing former drinkers (Fox, 1958), and opiate addiction's satisfactions have been explored by withdrawal of the drug from addicts (Wikler, 1952).

RESEARCH ON THE ABSENCE
OF A MASS MEDIUM

A number of previous investigations, usually with small samples, have explored users' responses to loss of a mass medium that had become temporarily unavailable to the community. In Berelson's (1949)

AUTHOR'S NOTE: I want to acknowledge support from the Social Science Faculty Research Fund of the City College of the City University of New York and the Research Award Program of the National Association of Broadcasters. Students in my courses in

217

well-known study, 60 New York city residents were interviewed 2 weeks into a newspaper strike about how they were coping. Berelson identified six noninformational functions of the medium: relaxation, prestige, social contact, reading for its own sake, protection against anomie, and satisfaction of a compulsive reading habit. In another New York newspaper strike study (Kimball, 1959), two additional gratifications were cited: stimulation of the reader's interest in violence, and simply passing the time. A later newspaper strike investigation concluded that the availability of alternate media cushioned readers' reactions, and that newspapers provided tools for daily living as well as entertainment and news (Newspaper Advertising Bureau, 1979). A Swedish study explored how viewers reacted to a television strike (Windahl & Hedinsson, 1982).

There have been several investigations in Europe and the United States in which people were paid not to view television. In Munich in 1973, under the auspices of the Institute for Rational Psychology, five families were paid $150 a month for an open-ended period of time not to watch television. In England in 1974, a BBC program paid five families $200 a month, for an indefinite period, not to watch television. Both studies were terminated within 2 months because the subjects' need for television was so great that no family was able to continue the period of nonviewing, in spite of the payment.

Subjects were paid a small amount not to watch television in two U.S. university towns, for relatively short periods of time. In Madison,, Wisconsin, Walters and Stone (1971) conducted a study of 76 households, half of which had sets under repair. The results were ambiguous because of the disproportionately high number of college-educated and upper-income persons, and of homes with two sets that still had one set working while the other set was under repair. Tan (1977) paid 51 households in Lubbock, Texas, $4 a day not to watch television for a week. During the week of deprivation, most respondents used newspapers for news analysis and consumer purchase information; radio became their leading medium for entertainment and current events news; and there were increases in visiting and socializing with others and in family social activities.

A Detroit newspaper paid $500 to each of five families not to view television for a month (Trost & Grzech, 1979). The same amount was also paid, by a public television program, to five Minneapolis families

mass communications and popular culture at City College contributed to data collection. An earlier version of this article was presented at the annual meeting of the American Association for Public Opinion Research at Buck Hill Falls, Pennsylvania, in May 1983.

that made a similar commitment (Moyers, 1979). Neither of these situations was a systematic study because each involved a small and unrepresentative sample of paid participants, who knew that their purpose was exploitation by media competing with commercial television. They also know that the nonviewing period was finite and they would subsequently be interviewed by reporters and become media personalities themselves.

In possibly the first American communitywide effort to turn off television, families in Farmington, Connecticut, pledged to eliminate or reduce viewing time for the month of January 1984. One-fourth of the families reported having done no viewing, 50% to 60% reduced their viewing, and 15% continued to watch more than 30 hours a week (Moritz, 1984). The program's sponsor explained that "Our goal was . . . to make people aware of all the other terrific things they could do with their time" (Markey, 1986). The Farmington program has sold over 600 kits on "How to Organize a TV Turn-Off" to other interested communities.

In addition to the general social science and media-deprivation literature, there is a substantial body of knowledge on people's uses of and gratifications from the mass media (e.g., Blumler & Katz, 1975; Galloway & Meek, 1981; Rosengren, Wenner, & Palmgreen, 1985). This research approach deals with audience needs and expectations that lead to self-selection of media, and the resultant need gratifications.

STUDY DESIGN

How viewers adapt to and deal with the absence of television for varying periods of time has been the focus of an ongoing program of research (Winick, 1985). This program has included interviews with the following groups: persons in situations where television has been unexpectedly unavailable for whole populations, as in the case of a strike by station personnel; persons living in areas where a hurricane eliminated television reception; residents of countries where there has been no television for specific days of the week (e.g., Austria), or months of the year (e.g., Iceland); and Orthodox Jews in the United States who voluntarily do not watch television for one day a week.

The present report concerns a group of persons living in the metropolitan New York area who owned a television set but became deprived of its use through its breaking down or being stolen. During the period of unavailability of television to these persons, they were interviewed in their homes concerning their general social and personal functioning and use of various media at that time. They were also asked about their use of media and patterns of behavior during the previous period in which their television sets had been available. On the basis of these interviews, it was possible to develop a picture of how these persons had used television, and of the values represented by television viewing experience itself.

This chapter deals with the prosocial dimensions of viewing television. The study is built on the various earlier social science investigations of the impact of different kinds of media deprivation, by collecting data on the uses made of television. The interviews with persons whose televisions had become unavailable took advantage of the natural experiment provided by loss of the set, which created relative deprivation combined with substantial awareness of personal reactions (Stouffer et al., 1949).

The names of persons who had a set break down (81%) were obtained from informal sources, repair services, and stores. The names of persons who had experienced theft of a set (19%) were obtained from individuals, community groups, and law enforcement agencies.

Over a period of 6 years (1976-1982), interviews were conducted in 680 metropolitan New York area homes with 1,614 persons whose television sets had become unavailable. In each such home, there had only been one set available at the time of its loss. At the time of the interviews, the respondents had been living without television for from 1 to 21 weeks, with an average of 6 weeks. All the homes had had their sets for at least 3 years.

There is a reason to believe that the respondents represented a reasonable cross-section of the population of the area, since the distribution of sets breaking down or being stolen appeared to be random. The demographic characteristics of the sample interviewed closely approximated those of the general population, as shown in census data. In terms of socioeconomic status, 17% were classified as lower class, 30% as lower middle class, 41% as middle class, 9% as upper middle class, and 3% could not be classified. As to ethnicity, 22% were black, 6% were Asian, 16% were Hispanic, and 56% were other/white. Of the adults, 13% had completed college, 10% had finished up to three years of college, 34% had graduated from high school, and 43% had less than 4 years of high school.

There was probably an undersampling of households with television "superfans," who either had several sets or, if they had one set, presumably would have rented or otherwise obtained a set during the period of waiting for repairs, or arranged to get another set when theirs was stolen. During the years of this study, the average American home still had only one set. The proportion of homes with more than one set has increased relatively slowly, from 42% in 1975 to 51% in 1981, according to A. C. Nielsen Company surveys.

A pilot investigation developed an interview guide that covered pre- and post-television-loss behavior. After it was established through telephone contact that the household had previously had a single television set, that it was no longer available and had not been replaced, arrangements were made to conduct an interview in the home. All available persons in the household were interviewed during the home visit or visits. The interviews ranged form 1 to 3 hours each, with an average of 1½ hours for each person.

During the interviews, information was obtained on pre-loss uses of other media and television viewing behavior, based on the respondents' recollections. Aided recall, using television program listings, was utilized if necessary. Questions on procedures for choosing programs, favorite programs, how respondents felt about television, and specific programs that were regularly viewed, were asked of all interviewees, including children. Respondents described their pre- and post-loss use of all media and the larger patterns of social behavior in the home.

HOW PEOPLE RESPONDED TO LOSS OF TELEVISION

Most respondents were easily able to verbalize the details, nature, and intensity of their responses to loss of their television sets. For those who did not do so, direct questioning was employed. In general, how people dealt with and responded to the loss of their television sets was a function of a variety of factors, including socioeconomic status, other work and leisure activities of the viewer, the age and number of persons in the home, the kinds of programs that had been viewed, established patterns of media activity, other ways in which the respondents had been spending their time, and the functions of television viewing for members of the household.

The sequence of respondents' reactions to the loss of television was, to some extent, similar for many households. The first 3 or 4 days for most persons were the worst, even in many homes where viewing was minimal and where there were many other ongoing activities. In over half of all the households, during these first few days of loss, the regular routines were disrupted, family members had difficulties in dealing with the newly available time, anxiety and aggressions were expressed, and established expectations for the behavior of other household members were not met. People living alone tended to suffer greatly and to be bored and irritated. Over four-fifths of the respondents reported moderate to severe dislocations during this period.

The 5th to the 8th day represented, in many cases, some form of readjustment to the new situation. By the 2nd week, a move toward adaptation to the situation was common.

In general, those persons who were home the most, such as unemployed and retired persons, young children and their mothers, nonworking spouses, and senior citizens, were the most discomfited by the deprivation experience. Respondents who had social, work, and other activities outside the home were able to cushion the shock to some extent. Of the ethnic groups, blacks experienced the loss most intensely and Hispanics next most urgently. Households where the set was on for the longest number of hours tended to miss it the most.

Households with a relatively high level of education were more likely than those with lower levels of education to handle the loss of the set with relative equanimity. Persons who belonged to a number of voluntary organizations and participated in activities outside the home were better able to adapt to the loss than others not so involved in the community. The degree of participation in religious activity was not related to how people coped with the loss of television.

The theory of crisis developed by Caplan (1964) and his associates seems relevant to our data. In a normal situation, a person is likely to operate in a consistent pattern with minimal self-awareness and strain. When his or her equilibrium is upset, there is the possibility of crisis, which is characterized by inner tension, unpleasant affect, and disorganization of behavior. Over half the households interviewed reported reactions consistent with Caplan's definition of a crisis.

A four-way classification of the households' overall reactions to loss of their sets was established. About one-fourth (24%) experienced extreme disruption and discomfiture, akin to the reaction of mourning after the death of a beloved person (Freud, 1925) or to *atonie*, an apathy and lack of responsiveness to stimuli and to the environment, which often characterizes people who have become unemployed (Winick, 1964). A third of these, or approximately 8%, reported an extreme level of depression or melancholia, a withdrawal of interest in others combined with a sense of internal loss. The second group experienced substantial disruption (39%), involving explicit symptoms of anxiety and unhappiness. Moderate disruption occurred in the third group (29%), and little disruption was reported in 8% of the households. In almost three-fifths (58%) of the households, all of the members had the same level of reaction.

SOME FUNCTIONS OF TELEVISION

On the basis of the respondents' discussion of television in general, their comments on specific programs, their description of the pre-television-loss behavior in the household, and their reports on post-loss behavior, six basic functions served by television were identified. The six categories, and the proportion of respondents to whom they applied, are the following:

(1) Surveillance and information—83%
(2) Relaxation and entertainment—82%
(3) Conversation—72%
(4) Social cement—71%
(5) Punctuating the day and week—63%
(6) Companionship—60%

Surveillance and Information

Although over four-fifths of the respondents reported that they regularly read newspapers and over two-thirds had listened to radio news when their TV sets were functioning, 83% of the households had also watched local and/or network news programs and indicated that they learned information from television. Many of the respondents spoke feelingly of their favorite news personalities and reporters.

Viewers tended to regard news on television as not competitive with the other media. Five aspects of news programs were mentioned by the respondents; the average respondent talked about three of these. In descending order of importance, these were the dimensions:

(1) The on-camera reporters, anchorpersons, and other presenters who humanize the news, and with whom viewers often develop a trusting emotional relationship.
(2) The tone and style, the flow and pace of the material presented on the programs.
(3) The visual aspect of the news—what is shown on the screen.
(4) The people and situations presented on the programs.
(5) The wide range of many different kinds of subject matter presented with immediacy: "You can see it happening and it is closer to you than in any other way." The regularity of news programs contributed to the viewers' feelings of confidence in their utility.

Almost half (46%) of the persons interviewed indicated that they regularly derived information on various dimensions of social behavior from programs other than news and public affairs. It is possible that this unplanned or casual learning accounts for the discrepancy between the 34% of a national sample (Bower, 1973) who said that they usually watched television "because I think I can learn something" and the 83% of the respondents in the current study for whom this function was relevant. Our respondents may have become aware of obtaining information from television even if they had not planned on doing so.

Over one-third of the respondents were able to describe the special characteristics of individual stations, in terms of news and other programs. A station cited for interesting news programs was not necessarily mentioned for its attractions in other program or viewer-use areas.

About 21% of the persons interviewed had significant ties to another culture. Over half of these persons used television either to obtain information about and maintain ties with their minority culture, and/or to obtain information about the language and ways of life of the American majority culture.

Persons interviewed around election times tended to mention the information function of television with greater frequency than at other times of the year. A number of people suggested the importance of being able to see and hear candidates on television before voting: "When I saw Carter debate Reagan, I could see how they really handled themselves, and it was important in helping me make up my mind."

This surveillance function was particularly important for two different groups: those who spent most of their time at home, and those whose occupation brought them into contact with others. It was also especially important for parents, students, and persons with less than a college education.

There was a clear tendency, in the absence of television, to spend somewhat more time with other information services that had previously been used when television was available. Typically, more time was devoted to radio news and newspapers. Very few people, however, began giving time to news media that had not previously been utilized. Many respondents noted that none of the other media provided information in a manner that could compete with television.

Relaxation and Entertainment

One of the most potent attractions of television derived from its provision of many forms of relaxation and entertainment. Of the eight different dimensions of this function mentioned, the average respondent talked about four. In descending order of frequency of mention, the main features of television entertainment were the following:

(1) Release from tension into a different and gratifying kind of experience; "After the stresses of the day, I need it."

(2) Antidote to boredom, fatigue, and inadequate satisfaction in other aspects of social life; "It takes me out of a rut, especially when I feel blah."

(3) Escape, expressed both as getting away and as an active choice of a socially sanctioned kind of enjoyment; "I can be in totally different settings by turning the dial."

(4) Raising spirits, generating arousal, excitement, and stimulation; "Watching a football game revs me up and turns me on."

(5) Mood modification by program choices; the availability of a wide range of moods from different kinds of program content; "Whatever I feel like feeling like, I can get."

(6) Connoisseur gratifications derived from knowledge of the range of performer portrayals within each program, and curiosity about how each appearance will represent a variation within the range experienced in the past; reexperiencing the past; "I know Archie Bunker real well, but every week you see a different side of him."

(7) Enjoying different kinds of relationships with the characters in serial programs such as situation comedies and dramas as the series moved through their life cycles. In the newer programs there was interest in the unfolding of the characters. Older series provided the gratification of anticipating and recognizing the familiar and dealing with changes. "In 'All My Children,' Liza Colby was rich and beautiful and everybody admired her. When she found out her mother was sleeping with her boyfriend, she became like the town drunk and an alcoholic."

(8) Television viewing is the only activity that provides free entertainment where the consumer continually can make choices. "With TV, you have a choice, and you don't have to ask what it will cost."

Over a third (37%) of the respondents mentioned the entertainment values of news and news-related programs: "The news programs are so interesting that I enjoy them even more than comedies or dramatic shows."

Approximately 12% of the respondents, mostly under 20 years of age, indicated that they increased their attendance at movies during the absence of television. During the period of television unavailability there was no significant increase in reading for pleasure or in any other media activity designed for the purpose of relaxation and entertainment.

Conversation

Talking during and about television programs emerged as a significant use of the medium in 72% of the homes. Programs provided a continuously available subject for conversation, especially where the same program was seen by several members of the family.

The conversations were conducted during programs as well as during commercial breaks. They ranged from casual chitchat, to serious matters involving family members, and local and other problems.

Conversations while watching television, when visitors were in the home, were reported by 41% of the respondents. In the presence of visitors, the set might be left on as a general background to which persons paid slight heed. In the case of some programs like sports events, the visitors might give close attention. Many respondents reported on conversations in which visitors were involved, that were mediated and/or inspired by the program that was being watched at the time.

About two-thirds (68%) of the respondents reported discussing some aspect of viewing with associates, friends, or others in a work, school, or other social situation. "People are always talking about different shows at the office, " said a 22-year-old clerk. Conversation about television is a social facilitator by which many viewers are assisted in relating to others, and it provides a widely accepted currently of discourse. Conversation about television provides a continuing vehicle for connecting oneself to and affiliating with others. Households tended to use television as a contributor to the desired level of conversational interaction—to facilitate, blunt, enhance, or otherwise influence levels of conversation.

A number of parents with children of elementary school age or younger noted that their children spoke less in the absence of television. The very young children might have been used to speaking to the people on the screen, and school-age children sometimes integrated material from programs into peer conversational activities. Television provided content that could be shared by parents and children, or even grandparents and children.

About one-tenth of the males recalled their conversational interaction with the set during the presentation of sports events, during which they would urge specific athletes on, respond emotionally to what was happening during the event, and offer other verbal comments about the sports activity.

A number of teenagers enjoyed watching soap operas because their content provided daily opportunities for conversation. "They're so current, they have stuff about cocaine users and dykes. Everybody calls up everybody else to talk about what's happening. It's not too heavy and you get the latest." Such teenagers achieved status enhancement by being able to discuss current social issues presented in soap operas. In addition to teenagers, persons over 55, office workers, and blacks and Hispanics were especially likely to mention conversation as a significant aspect of their television viewing.

During the period of television deprivation, no other mass medium or institution or form of social interaction was cited by the respondents as providing a substitute subject for conversation, or acting as a facilitator or background for conversation.

Social Comment

In over two-thirds (71%) of the households, television served a centripetal function of social cohesion, which might be termed social cement: "social" because it involved relationships and interactions and participation in a larger group, and "cement" because it provided a binding foundation on which other activities rested and depended. The set offered a reassuring and predictable framework for the routines and interactions and role behavior of the home.

In terms of systems theory, in these homes television can be said to perform a significant role in the maintenance of the family system (Moos & Moos, 1976). Television use can be an important theme in family relationships and a central concern of shared family interaction as defined by the persons in the household (Hess & Handel, 1959). Similarly, when they revisited Middletown, Caplow et al. (1982) reported that the phenomenon of a husband and wife watching television together is now found throughout the community—a significant development in family life—in contrast to the pervasive class differences in marital behavior reported there earlier in the century.

This social cohesion function was found not only in all socioeconomic status groups but in households of all sizes. For the person living alone, television often represented a major way of dealing with reality, as important as the spine of a book in holding its pages. In homes with more people, the TV set served to absorb impulses that were otherwise difficult to express, provided a satisfying shared activity, facilitated interaction, and presented a previously tested range of experiences. Television often offered a model for successful resolution of disputes, since many households had coped with conflicts over the choice of programs, and it provided programs in relation to which other activities were scheduled. Television not only contributed substantially to the construction of many families' social reality, but it frequently represented a considerable component of that reality.

In describing what happened to these functions when the television set became unavailable, respondents used phrases such as "the whole house fell apart," "we didn't know what to do," "every evening was hell." In such homes, the loss of television typically led to increases in free-floating anxiety and hostility, acerbity among family members, decreases in sexual activity, difficulties in falling asleep and sleeping, and similar manifestations of disharmony and discomfort.

In general, relationships between husbands and wives that had been relatively positive when television was available tended to remain positive or even to improve somewhat in the absence of the set. However, couples who had been experiencing difficulties tended to deepen their problems and disagreements. A pattern found in a number of homes was a temporary increase in sexual activity, followed by its total disappearance. "The first week or so that we didn't have the set, every night, you could say, was X-rated; but after that we just lost interest and were depressed." In these homes, the television set provided a social equilibrium. When the set ceased to be available, the balance of forces was disrupted and socioemotional problems developed.

The decline in family cohesiveness and communication that occurred without the set did not lead to any systematic use of other approaches to coping with the situation. Only a handful of the households attempted any systematic program that would provide substitute activities for the members of the household in the absence of television. Hardly any parents developed alternate activities either for their children or for other members of the family during the period of deprivation.

This lack of alternate activities is not surprising, considering the relatively small proportion of the day that most U.S. parents devote to "quality time"; interactions, such as reading to children, or playing or conversing with them. In the most careful national study of its kind, University of Michigan researchers found that the average working mother spends an average of 11 minutes each weekday and 30 minutes on weekend days in such activities. Homemaker mothers gave 30 minutes on weekdays and 36 minutes on weekend days, and fathers typically spent 8 minutes on weekdays and 14 minutes on weekend days, in interactions primarily directed to children (Juster & Stafford, 1985). In view of the surprisingly small amount of time devoted to nontelevision relationships between parents and children, it would clearly be difficult for parents to draw on any reservoir of previously fulfilling nontelevision activities with their children to help in coping with the loss of the television set.

Punctuating the Day and Week

Punctuating the day and week was important as a function of television for nearly two-thirds (63%) of the households interviewed. The set helped to establish the rhythm of the day and week, contributed to the mental set for different parts of the day and evening, served to distinguish one day from another, and provided a predictable ritual.

"First thing I do when I come home from work is turn the set on when I come in the door," said a 35-year-old office worker. "I would know that I'm going to feel good every Tuesday evening because I looked forward to 'Happy Days' and 'Laverne and Shirley,'" said one 31-year-old woman. "Monday night was football night and it kicked off the week for me and helped to carry me into the regular week," said a 40-year-old man. "The day began for us with 'Captain Kangaroo' every morning," said a 33-year-old mother of two toddlers. For a 47-year-old woman, "Saturday night was movie night—I looked forward to seeing a movie every Saturday, after a day of shopping and errands." A 53-year-old man stressed that "Sunday night was '60 Minutes'—I always had dinner just before the program so I could enjoy it more. It was a good beginning for the week and a nice ending for the weekend."

At least one end of the day was demarcated by television in one-sixth of the homes. A typical comment was "I woke up to the 'CBS Morning News,' and it helped me to get ready in the morning, before I went out." Or, "I always watch the 'Tonight Show,' and it relaxed me so that I could fall asleep."

For some people, television literally bracketed the day. One 25-year-old actor said, "I sleep in a loft bed with a TV set at the foot. I turned the set on for a while, not too loud, before going to sleep at night. If I went to sleep early, I watched the late news. If I was tuning in later, I watched Johnny Carson. In either case, after watching for a while, just as I felt that I was going to fall asleep, I hit the button with my foot to turn the set off. When I woke up in the morning, the first thing I did was to turn on the morning news. It helped to get me going in the morning in the same way that it helped me to nod out at night."

Once particular television viewing patterns of marking the ebb and flow of a day or week developed, they gained additional strength by virtue of repetition and habit. Punctuating the day was particularly important for housewives, students, middle-class homes, and larger families. No other medium or other activity was able to replace television in performing this function.

In terms of discomfort resulting from television deprivation at different times of the year, the winter was clearly the most difficult season, with spring next most trying, fall in third place, and summer least difficult. Winter made outdoor activities less possible, and by then viewers had generally settled down into a predictable pattern of watching a mix of new and older programs.

Companionship

Television's companionship, relevant in 60% of the homes, included the provision of company or an association or relationship for family activities. The associated activity might include the performance of household chores, or children doing their homework, or adults or the whole family having dinner. The set could be turned on when guests came, to provide an additional kind of companionship, as when male visitors watched a football game, or it could be relatively unobtrusive in providing a kind of pleasant background to accompany something else.

The television set was a source of companionship that was often important for both mother and child. "The only way I could do house cleaning in peace was if my 3-year-old could watch 'Sesame Street.'" At the other age extreme, older persons found television to be a pleasant companion for the day. "Without my set, I feel the house is empty, and I am so lonely and alone," said a 62-year-old widow. Over half the respondents engaged in parasocial interaction with specific personalities, especially talk show hosts, local newscasters, and game show hosts.

For over two-fifths of the respondents, television provided an opportunity to pass time and have companionship during time that would otherwise have been flat or empty. Said a 34-year-old homemaker, "Now that I don't have a set, the whole day is dead time; I don't know how I am managing to get through the days and nights. When the set was here, I felt alive and like I was involved with others."

One woman noted, "The set kept me company for everything I did during the day. I'd watch the morning news show while getting my children ready for school and have my morning coffee with a 9 o'clock talk show. I would dust while watching talk show and do the floors with another program. I did exercise to another program and cooked while the soap operas were on, and we'd have dinner while the evening news was on."

A 14-year-old girl said that "TV always kept my company while I did my reading, because it helped me to concentrate better. Because it was on, I could pay closer attention to what I was studying. When a friend came over, we would always have the set on when we hung out in the living room."

A 68-year-old woman observed, "With television, even though I live by myself, I felt that I was not really alone. The TV set always kept me company." Another woman who lived alone said, "I turned on the set as soon as I got up. I had the set on all the time that I was home." For senior citizens and homes without children, the companionship provided by television was especially significant. For them, as for the other respondents, this function was not fulfilled by other media or activities during the unavailability of television.

A special form of companionship as a function of television was mentioned by approximately one-tenth of the respondents, who cited the set's use as a way of getting away from other members of the family. "Sometimes I just didn't want to have to deal with my family, and I turned on a show that I liked but that had no special interest for them," said a 21-year-old college student.

Even with such viewers, who turned on their sets to tune out other things or other people, there was a strong overall tendency to watch specific programs, in contrast to watching television in general. Very few people turned on the set just to "watch television." The viewer usually either knew what was available on a particular day and time, checked the listings, or turned the dial in order to make a choice. Hardly any instances of people choosing to watch television but not finding a suitable program were mentioned.

SOME COMPLEXITIES
OF TELEVISION FUNCTIONS

Perhaps the most noteworthy feature of the six functions summarized is that each one characterized most households. Although a very broad range of relationships to television was represented in the sample and many different kinds of people were interviewed, no simple typology of discreet and nonoverlapping types of viewers emerged in terms of basic functions provided by television. Most people used television for different purposes in different circumstances, depending on the time and day, the interpersonal situation, their mood, and other factors. The typical respondent mentioned four of the functions summarized above as germane to his or her viewing.

Generalizing about the functions served by television is difficult because each member of a household may be deriving something different from the very same program as each watches it. A woman might watch the 7 o'clock network news to keep abreast of current happenings, her husband could be partially attending to the program while reading a newspaper, and their 10-year-old child's imagination might be stimulated by the same newscast. Or, a family group might watch a situation comedy, with a 5-year-old regarding it as a fantasy, a parent relaxing with it, and a teenager talking to a friend in the same room.

In over half (53%) of the homes in which two or more persons indicated that they had watched the same program, the program's functions differed for different viewers. Since residents of a household share the same socioeconomic status, such differences in program perception and cognition are noteworthy. The same program is perceived differently by, and has different meanings for, adults and children at each developmental epoch (Winick & Winick, 1979).

There was no consistent correlation between any program type and any single function. Earlier researchers have pointed out that practically any kind of content can serve any function (Rosengren & Windahl, 1972).

Another problem in generalizing about function is that the same person might primarily derive information from one program, entertainment from a second program, parasocial interaction and companionship from a third program, and a subject for conversation from a fourth in the course of one evening. It was not difficult for viewers to adapt their expectations to different programs. Most programs represent known quantities so that viewers usually have a sense of what is coming, and they shift their mental sets accordingly. Another consideration is that the very same program could fulfill several functions simultaneously. Thus a 14-year-old girl who watched a situation comedy while studying was accompanying another activity, being entertained, and engaging in an established after-dinner ritual that contributed to the household's homeostasis.

There were relatively few cases—less than 10%—in which only one or two functions primarily characterized a person's overall viewing. However, these persons, for whom television performed a limited number of functions, did not spend less time with television. Indeed, there was a tendency for them to devote more time than the average to their sets. There was also a tendency for them to be more uncomfortable because of the set's loss, perhaps because the one or two functions involved had been so salient.

Generalizability

The functions identified in the present study were found in the social system existing in the metropolitan New York area. The culture of this area shares many characteristics with urban communities elsewhere in the United States, but it also differs in various ways from the culture of other communities. Although generalizations about the functions of television and other media can be made with reasonable confidence about a small homogeneous country, such generalizations should be made with more diffidence about the range of viewer types, regions, climates, subcultures, and communities in the United States.

It is possible, however, that the four decades of television availability have helped to obliterate traditional regional and socioeconomic differences. In the current study, there was no single background variable that was significantly related to viewers' responses to television deprivation. For instance, degree of viewing, socioeconomic status, and even education did not significantly influence responses to deprivation. Nationwide, television is overwhelmingly the preferred leisure activity for practically all groups, and the only recreational activity shared by all members of the family, especially by parents and children. Viewing television represents approximately one-fourth of all the time that parents and children spent together in the present study, and also in a national survey conducted in 1975 and 1981 (Juster & Stafford, 1985). Thus to an extent that is not true of any other medium, television is clearly a vehicle of *mass* communication, and this fact may allow more generalizability than is possible for other media of communication.

METHODOLOGICAL ISSUES

A number of recent uses-and-gratifications studies have employed sophisticated statistical techniques to analyze various dimensions of media use, by presenting viewers with lists of gratifications and then cross-tabulating or factor-analyzing the gratifications reported. Such studies help to achieve quantification and to identify interrelationships in media functions. In contrast, the approach in the current study has been to determine the relative importance of some dimensions of use that are probably more easily identified by an indirect method.

Both the direct and indirect approaches have their special capabilities, and their findings should be complementary. Rubin (1983), on the basis of an interview study of midwesterners' television-viewing behavior and attitudes, identified two viewer types: (1) those who use television out of habit and to pass time, for amusement and enjoyment, and (2) those who use television for information and to learn. In the present study, however, viewing choices had multiple determinants and did not identify discrete types of viewers.

Most studies of uses and gratifications provided by media, in whatever sections of the United States and other countries, assume that subjects can identify and verbalize their specific needs. In the current study, subjects typically were able to talk clearly about three of the functions: surveillance, entertainment, and companionship. Most interviewees for whom it was pertinent gave the details of the punctuation function, although none used that term. The conversation function was also described by the respondents for whom it was important, though it was not necessarily conceptualized by them as a function. The social cement function, however, was largely latent and emerged on the basis of the households' reporting of the pre- and post-loss behavior.

Direct questions on reasons for watching television may yield different results from those reported in an indirect approach. For example, this study found the companionship function to apply to 60% of the homes and the conversation function to be relevant to 72% of the homes. Yet, in response to a direct question in one of the few relevant national studies (Bower, 1973), these functions were selected from a list of 15 "reasons for watching television" by only 34% (combining "keep me company when I'm alone" and "background while I'm doing something else") and 9% ("I want to be able to talk about it afterwards"), respectively. The element of social desirability may make such "less acceptable" reasons unpopular with the respondents in a situation involving choosing from a list, or such reasons may be less accessible to consciousness, or they may not emerge clearly via a list. Another possibility is that interviewing persons who have been deprived of television may make it easier for them to recall positive functions rather than dysfunctions, although every opportunity for voicing the latter was provided in the current study.

SOME IMPLICATIONS

For each typical television viewer, there existed a cluster of functions that the medium performed. This cluster might vary from day to day, or in different parts of the same day, or at different times of the year, or in terms of particular social and other contexts. The viewer would, at any particular time, (1) decide to view television and then (2) decide which program/channel to view. The decision process, which was the focus of specific questioning, was as active as the decision to spend time with any other medium. Viewers were questioned about their response for choosing the programs on their television "diet" rather than about the possible entries on the "menu." There appeared to be hardly any viewing by default, in terms of selecting a program because it was the least objectionable of those available. By choosing a program or channel, a viewer was choosing not to expose himself or herself to other programs or channels. There was no interviewee who simply turned on one channel and kept it on.

A number of the functions served by television were probably performed by radio in the past. Mendelsohn (1964) reported on interviews with a sample of radio listeners in the metropolitan New York area, and concluded that radio provided an important and versatile presence that fulfilled three psychological needs (mood accompaniment, psychological release, and friendly companionship) as well as its utilitarian information role. It is possible that some of the functions of television were taken over from analogous functions formerly fulfilled by radio.

More than 98% of the households in this study expected either to recover their repaired television sets, buy a new set, or replace their stolen sets. The gratifications available through living without television, for these persons, were not attractive or compelling enough for them to decide to continue without the medium. Television was like a public utility that fulfilled a range of needed social, psychological, and information functions. Public utilities perform necessary functions that are generally taken for granted until some disaster temporarily removes access to them, at which time their importance emerges; and the same is true of television.

However, some critics have raised questions about the implications of Americans' considerable dependence on television and have suggested that television may help to neutralize society's stresses by draining off emotional and intellectual energy that might otherwise be directed toward social amelioration (Gurevitch, 1983). Ball-Rokeach and DeFleur (1976) argue that media dependency increases at times of social change and conflict.

Television has become so salient to most people that it is taken for granted and its functions become less and less accessible to conscious awareness. The kind of natural experiment provided by a period of temporary deprivation offers a unique look at the needs that are met by television, and at the factors that motivate viewers to watch it on a regular basis. Taking advantage of the research opportunities provided by a situation of television deprivation can open up access to data that are not available in any other way.

The approach taken in this study could be applied to any community, although the proportion of single-set households is declining slowly. A logical extension of the present study would be to explore the incidence of these six functions of television in other populations in the United States. Another approach would be to replicate it in the New York area later in this decade, because the period studied may represent the end of one era and be accompanied by a peak or plateau in the functions provided by television. The increasing availability of cable services and the surge in use of videocassette recorders (VCRs) in recent years may be modifying how people use television.

Employing some version of the deprivation approach in future studies could be of special interest because of the inconsistency between what different groups of viewers say about television programs and what they actually watch (Bower, 1973). Attitudes toward the medium and toward specific programs, which are expressed in answers to direct questions, may not be significantly correlated with people's viewing behavior. Obtaining data on how viewers cope with the absence of the medium permits access to dimensions of gratification that are not otherwise available, about which it may otherwise be difficult to verbalize, and in which the element of social desirability is less likely to be important.

REFERENCES

Ball-Rokeach, S. J., & DeFleur, M. L. (1976). A dependency model of mass effects. *Communication Research, 3,* 3-21.

Berelson, B. What missing the newspaper means. (1949). In P. F. Lazarsfeld & F. Stanton (Eds.), *Communication research 1948-49* (pp. 111-129). New York: Harper.

Blumler, J., & Katz, E. (Eds.). (1975). *The uses of mass communications.* Newbury Park, CA: Sage.

Bower, R. T. (1973). *Television and the public* New York: Holt, Rinehart & Winston.

Caplan, G. (1964). *Principles of preventive psychiatry.* New York: Basic Books.

Caplow, T., et al. (1982). *Middletown families: Fifty years of change and continuity.* Minneapolis: University of Minnesota Press,

Fox, R. (1958). Treatment of chronic alcoholism. *Medical Clinics of North America, 42,* 804-814.

Freud, S. (1925). *Mourning and melancholia.* London: Hogarth.

Galloway, J. J., & Meek, F. L. (1981). Audience uses and gratifications: An expectancy model. *Communications Research, 8,* 435-449.

Gurevitch, M. (1983, May). *Television research.* Discussion presented at meeting of American Association for Public Opinion Research, Buck Hill Falls, PA.

Hayes, M. P., Stinnett, N., & DeFrain, J. (1980). Learning about marriage from the divorced. *Journal of Divorce, 4,* 23-29.

Hess, R. D., & Handel, G. (1959).*Family worlds: A psychosocial approach to family life.* Chicago:

University of Chicago Press.

Juster, T. F., & Stafford, F. P. (1985). *Time goods, and well-being.* Ann Arbor, MI: Institute for Social Research.

Kimball, P. (1959). New York readers in a newspaper shutdown. *Columbia Journalism Review, 2,* 47-58.

Kinsey, A. C., Pomeroy, W. B., & Martin, C. E. (1948). *Sexual behavior in the human male.* Philadelphia: W. B. Sanders.

Komarovsky, M. (1940). *The unemployed man and his family.* New York: Dryden.

Markey, J. (1986, February 27). TV withdrawal's a cinch, just give it a few years to work. *New York Post,* pp. 19-20.

Mendelsohn, H. (1964). Listening to radio. In L. S. Dexter & D. M. White (Eds.), *People, society, and mass communications* (pp. 239-260). New York: Free Press.

Moos, R. H., & Moos, B. S. (1976). A typology of family social environments. *Family Process, 15,* 357-371.

Moritz, O. (1984, February 5). Turning the TV off and turning life back on. *New York Daily News,* p. 41.

Moyers, B. (1979, April 23). *Bill Moyers' journal.* New York: Public Broadcasting System, Channel 13.

Newspaper Advertising Bureau. (1979). *One of our media is missing.* New York: Author.

Rosengren, K. E., Wenner, L. A., & Palmgreen, P. (Eds.). (1985). *Media gratifications research: Current perspectives.* Newbury Park, CA: Sage.

Rosengren, K. E., & Windahl, S. (1972). Mass media consumption as a functional alternative. In D. McQuail (Ed.), *Sociology of mass communications* (pp. 166-194). Middlesex, England: Penguin.

Rubin, A. M. (1983). Television uses and gratifications: The interactions of viewing patterns and motivations. *Journal of Broadcasting 27,* 37-51.

Stouffer, S. A., et al. (1949). *The American soldier: Adjustment during army life.* Princeton, NJ: Princeton University Press.

"Talk of the Town" (1985, December 30). *The New Yorker,* pp. 15-16.

Tan, A. S. (1977). Why TV is missed: A functional analysis. *Journal of Broadcasting, 21,* 371-380.

Trost, C., & Grzech, E. (1979, August). What happened when 5 families stopped watching TV? *Good Housekeeping,* pp. 94-99.

Walters, J. K., & Stone, V. A. (1971). Television and family communication. *Journal of Communication, 15,* 409-414.

Wikler, A. (1952). A psychodynamic study of a patient during self-regulated readdiction to morphine. *Psychiatric Quarterly, 26,* 270-293.

Windahl, S., & Hedinsson, E. (1982). *Perceived deprivation and alternate activities during a television strike.* Paper presented at a media panel, Lund, Sweden.

Winick, C. (1964). Atonie: The psychology of the unemployed and the marginal worker. In G. Fisk (Ed.), *The frontiers of management psychology* (pp. 269-386). New York: Harper & Row.

Winick, C. (1985). *Living with television, living without television.* New York: Television Information Office.

Winick, M. P., & Winick, C. (1979). *The television experience: What children see.* Newbury Park, CA: Sage.

20

PROSOCIAL CONTENT
ON PRIME-TIME TELEVISION

"Prosocial" has now become the accepted shorthand for designating television programming that is seen as having positive social content. The term "prosocial" has been used to encompass a multitude of virtues—ranging from cooperation, to good health habits, to equality of the sexes. The complexity of the question of what behavior, content, and values should be deemed prosocial has been little explored. However, the first use of the term occurred in a context quite different from the current one.

Originally, "prosocial" came into use as a qualifier of the term "aggression." More than 20 years ago, psychologists in the field of child development employed the phrase "prosocial aggression" to distinguish aggressions "for the purposes that the culture defines as desirable" from the clearly antisocial kind (Wispe, 1972). This differentiation was intended to take into account the circumstances and consequences of aggression—for instance, to separate the spanking administered by a well-intentioned parent from brutal actions designed to harm.

Thus while we usually think of prosocial behavior as antithetical to aggression, the original use of the term provides a useful reminder that there are times and occasions when aggressive action is necessary or desirable. We honor the valor of police officers, soldiers, and biblical heroes, and social psychologists have studied how people vary in their definitions of acceptable violence (Blumenthal, Kahn, Andrews, & Head, 1972). Yet, for the world of television, commentators frequently make a simplistic contrast between violent and prosocial programming. The word "violent," attached to a program, has the automatic connotation of something bad to be eliminated, and contradictory to desirable prosocial programming—an unrealistic distinction that ignores the complexity of television drama.

This approach has been fostered by an emphasis on inventorying violent actions through content analyses of television (e.g., Pearl, Bouthilet, & Lazar, 1982, pp. 108-125). Relatively few attempts have been made to analyze prosocial content in a systematic way. Probably the first foray into this area was the work of Liebert and his colleagues in the mid-1970s (Poulos, Harvey, & Liebert, 1976), followed by Greenberg et al.'s (1980) analysis of 3 years of television content for both prosocial and antisocial behaviors. The categories of prosocial behavior (e.g., cooperation, friendliness, sharing, etc.) used in these studies were mainly derived from earlier experimental investigations designed to induce such behaviors in children (Wispe, 1972).

The analysis of prosocial content of television that we are now conducting in the CBS Office of Social and Policy Research parallels these earlier studies, expanding on them by incorporating more global measures of thematic content and overall values. Following the approach suggested by Bradley Greenberg in his illuminating chapter in this volume, we hoped to capture not only the "drip, drip, drip" of individual incidents but also the possible "drench" impact of a story that builds to a specific moral. We also wanted to go beyond the past emphasis on modeling of good behavior, designed with children in mind, to the larger issue of what are the *implicit values* in television content. Though this attempt has only been partially successful, it has provided some insights into the problems of dealing with the multiplicity of meanings inherent in television programs.

Coding System for Prosocial Content

In the schema that my colleague, Luis Torres-Bohl, and I have developed, prosocial behavior is broadly defined as models of positive social relations. Operationally, coders were instructed to scan each individual scene for specific prosocial behaviors. (A scene was defined as a sustained dramatically continuous event, with essentially the same group of participants and with no major interruptions in continuity.) On a more global level, coders also evaluated whether the program, as a whole, had an overall prosocial theme, and if so, what message or moral was presented. The types of behavior that we defined as prosocial were grouped into three categories:[1]

(l) Altruistic actions, such as sharing, cooperating with, or helping others. Here the commonality is that the activity is directed toward the well-being of the other person at some cost to oneself, either in material resources, effort, time, or even personal risk.

At the extreme in this category would be *heroic altruistic acts,* in which one places the good of others above one's own self-interest, as, for example, a passerby jumping into a freezing lake to save a drowning child. *Sharing* encompasses all acts of generosity or charity that were performed with no quid-pro-quo motive. *Cooperation* was defined as people working together for mutual benefit or to resolve a common problem, as, for example, townspeople getting together to build a new school. *Helping* was defined as voluntarily providing assistance to others in attaining their goals.

Excluded from the category of altruism were those actions that are obligatory or routine (e.g., firemen habitually cooperate and rescue people) or directed to antisocial or illegal ends. We also arbitrarily exclude all acts of physical aggression, even those initiated for prosocial purposes, as, for example, a rescue effected by violent means.

(2) Socially approved affective behavior, where expressions of feeling and emotion are paramount—such as showing affection, empathy, and sympathy.

Showing affection consisted of both physical and verbal expressions of love and caring, as, for example, the affection shown by a parent for a child. In some instances, such gestures between adults might lead to sexual behavior, but only those acts in which this was not the primary intent were scored in this category. *Sympathy/empathy* was defined as positive acts of reassurance and understanding directed toward others. Examples would include a friend consoling another for his father's death, or a woman sharing the joy of her coworker's promotion. Also included in this overall category were expression of *remorse* in which a person showed contrition for wrong or mistakes. However, perfunctory or conventional behavior with little emotional content (such as an incidental apology or casual goodbye kiss) was not scored in this category.

(3) Control over negative predispositions, of oneself or others. This includes such actions as resisting temptation or using reasoning as a way of resolving conflict or problems.

Use of reasoning was defined as providing rational explanations or objective reasons directed toward the positive solution of problems, as, for example, a father persuading his son to live up to his responsibilities. *Resisting temptation* involved acting oneself (or advising others) to control impulses toward harmful, amoral, or unlawful acts (e.g., an official refusing to accept a bribe). *Controlling aggression* referred specifically to the restraint of one's self or others from physical or verbal coercion.

Though several types of prosocial behavior could occur within a single scene—as, for example, a benefactor who was both sympathetic and generous—only one incident of prosocial behavior was coded for each scene. Coders were instructed to select whichever type of behavior had the most impact on the recipient. Also coded for each incident of prosocial behavior were the reaction of the person who benefited from these actions, the relationship between the benefactor and recipient, and how effective the behavior was in resolving the problem (if there was one.)

Procedure

In this study, 4 weeks of network prime-time television entertainment programming in the 1985-1986 season were analyzed. The weeks selected were scattered across the season to better capture the diversity of programming, since program series are dropped and added throughout the year. In total, 235 entertainment programs were analyzed. Sports, documentary, and news programs were not included.

Initially, the project directors reviewed the coding instructions in detail and analyzed sample programs with the two coders. The results of the first week's analysis were also reviewed by one of the project directors to provide any further clarification needed. Each coder viewed and analyzed each program independently. Overall, there was perfect agreement on 81% of the judgments on the occurrence of a prosocial incident, and 80% agreement on the presence of a prosocial theme. All instances in which there was disagreement between coders were discarded from the analysis. For each program judged to have a prosocial theme, the coders provided a detailed description of the theme and identified the crucial incident that embodied it.

RESULTS

Prosocial Incidents

Almost all (97%) of the programs analyzed included at least one prosocial incident. As shown in Table 20.1, of the total of 1,035 prosocial incidents, more than half (57%) fell into the affective category. Within this category, incidents involving the expression of sympathy or empathy predominated—over one-third of all prosocial incidents were of this nature. The showing of affection was less frequent, while expressions of remorse rarely occurred.

One-fifth (21%) of the prosocial behaviors recorded were of an altruistic nature, predominantly heroic altruistic acts and helping others. The third category, control, which included 22% of all prosocial incidents, mainly comprised the use of reasoning. Rather than showing internal control, such as resisting temptation, television is more likely to focus on interactive discourse—dialogues rather than monologues.

It is not surprising that the affective category dominates, given the nature of prime-time television. As in any dramatic form, television devotes considerable attention to feelings and emotions: People are shown trying to reach mutual understanding, expressing their affection for one another verbally and physically, sympathizing and consoling. The heroes and heroines on television—as friends, lovers, coworkers, parents, or even just regulars at a bar—are often shown as people who, beneath their disagreements or banter, are concerned about the feelings of their companions. Perhaps one of the appeals of television is that it portrays the kind of understanding behavior that we would like more of in real life.

Prosocial behaviors were usually depicted as successful in working out whatever conflicts existed and easing people's problems. In over half (56%) of the incidents, the prosocial behavior was intended to resolve an immediate problem or conflict. In eight out of ten of these cases, the prosocial behavior was rated as completely or partially successful in problem resolution.

Most prosocial behavior on television occurs among those who are relatives or friends—three out of four incidents involved these groupings. Situations between coworkers, teachers and students, and other types of relationships accounted for the remainder. Incidents of prosocial behavior occurred in all program types, but were more frequent in situation comedies and dramas (five incidents per hour) than in action-adventure programs (three incidents per hour).

Overall Prosocial Themes

Going beyond individual scenes, each program as a whole was evaluated for the presence of an overall prosocial theme or moral. One-quarter of the programs (60 of the 235 analyzed) were judged to have such prosocial themes. These themes most commonly appeared in situation comedies, but also occurred in dramas, movies, and detective programs.

Four themes predominated, accounting for almost half of the prosocial themes. One frequent message was the importance of overcoming one's fears. For example, a child's anxieties about a school

TABLE 20.1
Types of Prosocial Behavior in Prime-Time Television Entertainment
(Base: 1,035 prosocial incidents in 235 programs)

Content Category	Percentage
Affective behavior	
Sympathy, empathy	37
Showing affection	15
Showing remorse	5
Altruistic actions	
Heroic altruism	8
Helping	8
Sharing	3
Cooperation	2
Control over negative predispositions	
Use of reasoning	15
Resisting temptation	5
Controlling aggression	2

project and an adolescent's concerns about the demands of college were the central themes in two of the programs. In other instances, adult anxieties were the focus: an elderly woman who had become abnormally apprehensive as the result of a mugging, or a stroke victim who had lost hope of recovery.

A second frequent theme was the priority of people over material gain. In one movie, a doctor decided to give up his well-to-do practice to help poor people; in two separate situation comedies, the protagonists' relationships with people overrode their desire for a better job. The decision of townspeople to oppose a place that created toxic wastes, even at the risk of their jobs, was the subject of another dramatic program.

Other themes that appeared in several different programs were the destructive effects of deceit and lying, and the lesson of tolerance or the acceptance of differences. For example, the plot of one detective program concerned the distrust of the local people for an inner-city camp in their area and their mistaken assumption that the campers were responsible for a wave of thefts.

In many of the programs with prosocial themes, the moral of the story was drawn explicitly—a character would explain why he or she must do the "right" thing or tell someone else the lesson he or she had learned. In some cases, the message was more implicit, as in a cautionary tale, with the moral embodied in the responses of others or the outcomes for the actor. However, in order to be coded, the intended meaning had to be manifest in the sense that an intelligent viewer, asked to summarize the plot, would probably include such themes. This method of analyzing prosocial themes did not deal with the latent content in television programs (e.g., the values the programs contain). Thus, for example, several episodes of "The Cosby Show," even though they generally promoted positive family relations, did not qualify as having a specific prosocial theme.

Implicit Values on Television

Beyond prosocial content, there is the larger issue of the values presented by television—a topic that is frequently discussed, but usually on the basis of subjective impressions rather than empirical analysis.[2] For our analysis, we searched for an overall scheme that was broad enough to encompass the whole range of values that occur on television, without any prior categorization as "good" or "bad."

The system that seemed most appropriate and nonjudgmental was one developed by Milton Rokeach (1975). His lists of values, defined as guiding principles or enduring beliefs about what is important in life, have been used in several studies to compare different groups of people. Two types of values are specified: *instrumental*, referring to modes of conduct, such as independent, honest, or helpful; and *terminal*, referring to desirable end-states of existence, such as freedom, self-respect, or an exciting life.

In the work Rokeach has done, respondents are asked to rank order the values on these lists, indicating their relative importance. We adapted the method to our purposes by instructing the coders to select the three instrumental and terminal values that guided the major characters and were most favored or prevalent in the program. However, unlike the other categories in our analysis, this effort failed since there was very little agreement on what values were central. Despite intensive discussions of the reasons for these differences in judgments, we were unable to reach acceptable levels of reliability.

What made it difficult to identify the values inherent in the programs? One problem is that these implicit values are more intangible than specific behaviors or overall themes. But another source of the difficulty in objectively defining the values that television presents may be the multi-valued nature of television itself. For instance, Newcomb and Hirsch (1984) have described television as a "cultural forum." Arguing against those who see a monolithic, dominant point of view in television content, they describe the television text as "dense, rich and complex," full of opposing meanings. They emphasize that "conflicting viewpoints of social issues are, in fact, the elements that structure most television programs."

Thus, for example, if the theme of a program is the conflict between the urge for freedom and responsibility to one's family, one or the other may prevail, but both sets of values will be aired and given support—the conflict of values itself become the focus. On television, as Newcomb and Hirsch (1984) noted, "the raising of questions is as important as the answering of them." Television's portrayal of a diversity of life paths, each with its own appeal, hinders generalizations about the values that television fosters, even for a single program, and certainly for the broad range of possibilities that television presents.

To take a familiar example, "The Odd Couple" was a long-running program that featured two main characters, with quite opposite personalities and values. Oscar was a careless, easy-going person whose major goal in life was enjoyment; Felix was a model of self-control, concerned with propriety and security. In any single episode, one or the other might be shown to be foolish, but neither was labeled totally wrong. Thus what a viewer might take from this program would depend on his or her own experience and outlook. Even for programs such as "All in the Family," where there was a clear intent on the part of the producers to convey certain messages, the audience members may supply their own, radically different interpretations (Vidmar & Rokeach, 1974).

To investigate the complexity of television values further, we intend to take a different approach. Using ordinary viewers, we plan to explore how much, if any, commonality exists in the values attributed to specific television programs, and the relationship of such perceptions to the viewer's own beliefs.

The diversity of television content presents a challenge to the researcher. Utilizing strictly defined categories, limited to those aspects of behavior that are considered desirable (or undesirable), provides one way of looking at television. But we should not confuse an examination of its parts with a comprehension of the whole. Nor should we make an even greater leap of faith by assuming that our categories define and contain all that viewers take away from the programs they see.

NOTES

1. A fourth category (civility), initially included in the analytical scheme, proved to be rarely the focal point in a scene, and the category was dropped from the analysis. It

involved showing respect for authority or courteous consideration for others.

    2. For example, an article on "The State of American Values" in *U.S. News & World Report* (December 9, 1985) quotes a Clark University philosophy professor on the role of TV: "Teaching values has always been a cooperative effort by the family and the social institution. Parents could count on honesty being taught in the church or synagogue, or in the Boy Scouts. Now, you have TV instead, but it is hard to see what moral values, if any, are taught by TV." (p. 57)

REFERENCES

Blumenthal, M. D., Kahn, R. L., Andrews, F. M., & Head, K. B. (1972). *Justifying violence: Attitudes of American men.* Ann Arbor, MI: Institute for Social Research.

Greenberg, B., et al. (1980). Antisocial and prosocial behaviors on television. In *Life on television: Content analyses of U.S. TV drama* (pp. 99-128). Norwood, NJ: Ablex.

Newccomb, H., & Hirsch, P. (1984). Television as a cultural forum. In W. Rowland & B. Watkins (Eds.), *Interpreting television: Current research perspectives* (pp. 58-73). Newbury Park, CA: Sage.

Pearl, D., Bouthilet, L., & Lazar, J. (Eds.). (1982). *Television and behavior: Ten years of scientific progress and implications for the eighties, Volume 2: Technical reviews.* Washington, DC: Government Printing Office.

Poulos, R., Harvey, S., & Liebert, R. (1976). Saturday morning television: A profile of the 1974-75 children's season. *Psychological Reports, 39,* 1047-1057.

Rokeach, M. (1975). *The nature of human values.* New York: Free Press.

Vidmar, N., & Rokeach, M. (1974). Archie Bunker's bigotry: A study in selective perception and exposure. *Journal of Communication, 24,* 35-47.

Wispe, L. G. (1972). Positive forms of social behavior: An overview. *Journal of Social Issues, 28,* (3), 1-19.

ELLEN J. LANGER
ALISON PIPER

21

TELEVISION FROM A
MINDFUL/MINDLESS PERSPECTIVE

Television held great promise when it first entered people's lives. It was considered *the* medium that now controlled the message. However, despite its unquestionable popularity among the public at large, television has been repeatedly criticized for the dulling effects it purportedly has had on people's minds. It is alleged to limit imagination and creativity (Harrison & Williams, 1977), lead to unrealistic understanding of the world (Gerbner & Gross, 1976; Gerbner et al., 1977), teach one to be aggressive (Bandura, Ross, & Ross, 1963; Eron, 1982; Singer & Singer, 1983), lead to an incorrect belief in the discontinuity of life (Postman, 1986), perpetuate negative stereotypes (Hartmann & Husband, 1974), and contribute to more limited intellectual growth because it spoon feeds and therefore provides little to think carefully about (Morgan & Gross, 1982).

In this chapter we will argue instead that there may be good reason for television's popularity with the public. We base this argument on research from the literature on perceived control, and on a reconsideration of the negative intellectual consequences of television based on research on mindlessness/mindfulness. We suggest that television may enable control and that it may be watched mindfully. Research specifically addressing the impact of mindful television viewing, or televiewing, suggests unusual positive consequences of watching TV. This work leads us to conclude that *how* one watches TV may matter more than *what* one watches.

The Importance of Choice and Control

In work assessing the effects of choice (e.g., Glass & Singer, 1972; Langer, 1983; Langer & Rodin, 1976; Sherrod, Hage, Halpern, & Moore, 1977; Seligman, 1975; Wortman & Brehm, 1975), it has become clear that this variable plays an extremely important role in one's well-being, both psychologically and physiologically speaking. For example, research suggests that choice plays a part in stress reduction, in improving task performance, and in health and longevity.

In work on the illusion of control (Langer, 1975; Langer & Roth, 1975) it was found that the chance to manipulate the object in question, be it a coin in a coin-flipping task or a stylus in a random-path-following game, had the effect of increasing people's feelings of confidence. Not only active involvement increased confidence, but so did the more passive involvement inherent in just thinking about an event. The positive consequences of control became even more apparent when participants were given control over the decisions they made, even though these decisions would not, to an observer, seem substantive (see Langer, 1983).

The importance of control in these ways becomes most clear in research with populations such as elderly adults, who are characteristically denied a good deal of control. In order to experience feelings of mastery, one simply has to be consciously mastering something. Yet elderly adults are too often asked to live in environments that have already been mastered. Thus they are robbed of the opportunity to experience control. All obstacles are removed to make life easier, decisions are made by others to save them from stress and the possibility of deciding poorly, and work becomes a thing of the past to make life struggle-free. With nothing to master, it is difficult to feel masterful (Langer & Avorn, 1981; Piper & Langer, 1986).

In research conducted in a nursing home environment, we found that encouraging participants to make even seemingly unimportant choices and providing these sorts of choices for them to make (e.g., which night to see a movie, which room to use for visiting with friends) resulted in important improvement in intellectual and physical functioning (Langer & Rodin, 1976). People randomly assigned to this group became more active, more alert, and in general experienced an increase in well-being.

In a follow-up to that experimental investigation, we found that those participants who were given this control-enhancing treatment actually lived longer. Only half as many of them had died as those in the comparison group (Rodin & Langer, 1977). Similarly, in another experiment, we increased control for nursing home residents by making their responses matter; rewards were made contingent on remembering and reporting self-chosen items of information (Langer, Rodin, Beck, Weinman, & Spitzer, 1979). As a result memory and well-being improved. In the follow-up to that study, we again found an increase in longevity as a result of the experimental treatment (Langer, Beck, Janoff-Bulman, & Timko, 1984).

Schulz (1976) also found just how important choice is. In his study with elderly adults, participants either chose when they wanted to be visited, or were able to predict when the visitor would come, or had neither of these options. Both predictability and control improved the well-being of these elderly participants. Thus exercising even seemingly trivial sorts of control appears to have important consequences.

If one considers television in this light, a different picture emerges. It is not hard to see how television may provide the opportunity actually to exercise control. At the least, it provides for the opportunity to engage in conscious instrumental responding. One turns the TV on and a picture appears; one can change the channel and remove an unwanted stimulus or attain a desired outcome; one can change one's mind and make a person reappear; one can make people speak louder or softer, or even change the color of their faces and clothes. If simply being free to choose among random events results in an increase in self-confidence, then it is not hard to imagine how deciding carefully which of various television programs to watch may lead to all of the benefits mentioned above.

The control that television may enable surely does not end there. Watching game shows may lead to feelings of efficacy in the same way any learning does. Commercials keep one informed of current styles, choices, and societal expectations. And such information, whether tacitly or overtly learned, can be used in social exchanges, thereby directly and indirectly increasing feelings of control and self-efficacy. Watching serials may lead to feelings of predictability and safety. Viewers often feel that people on these shows become their friends, which may be especially important to those for whom mobility is restricted. Predictability has been taken by many to be an essential ingredient of control (e.g., Pervin, 1963; Staub, Tversky, & Schwartz, 1971). Indeed, psychological and physiological measures (e.g., self-reports of improvement, and galvanic skin response) show that the effects of providing predictability are virtually equivalent to those of directly enhancing perceived control. Thus as long as these television shows are not totally predictable (see Piper & Langer, 1986), they should provide some positive benefits for the individual viewer.

As with most things, in order to assess whether television is good or bad, one must ask "with respect to what?" It is unlikely that television is popular with the public because of the potential harm it might do or the ways it can teach them to be aggressive or prejudiced. Television is popular, not because the average viewer has the mind of a 12-year-old, but rather because it may increase viewers' perceptions of control in a world in which many people frequently feel helpless. It is condescending to overlook consequences like these when trying to understand the appeal of TV.

Mindfulness and Control

Recent research has suggested that in order to understand when and how control will be effective, and to encourage more of it, one should examine control from the perspective of mindlessness/mindfulness theory (Chanowitz & Langer, 1980; Piper & Langer, 1986). As mentioned above, predictability will result in positive consequences as long as the event is not completely predictable (in which case it is psychologically equivalent to a nonevent).

Consider turning on a light switch. Once the behavior was meaningful to each of us, but now, for most adults, it may be enacted without any thought. For an event to yield meaningful feelings of mastery, the individual must be in the process of mastering. Events that have already been mastered do not result in these feelings. To master is to go from not knowing to knowing, from the unpredictable to the predictable. Herein lies the essence of control.

The work on mindlessness/mindfulness has led us to new views of televiewing. However, to clarify these ideas, a brief overview of this work is needed. When we speak of *mindfulness*, we are referring to the process of drawing distinctions, creating categories, making the unknown known, or making the novel familiar. When people are *mindless*, on the other hand, they are relying on rigid distinctions or on familiarity without an awareness of other ways the object (person, event, idea) might exist. When one first learns how to turn on the light, one notices many new things about the light switch and many aspects of one's response to it. Once one makes it familiar and knows just how to turn on the light reliably, one no longer pays any attention to it. One does not notice new ways of viewing the switch or the ways one light switch may be different from another, and one does not consider new ways to flip the switch. One now just responds to it mindlessly. When responding mindlessly one is treating the stimulus as having only one meaning, which is completely known. In contrast, when one is mindful, the stimulus is not rigid and fixed, and one is sensitive to contexts.

Effects of Mindlessness

Work conducted to assess negative consequences of the mindlessness that occurs with repeated exposure illustrates the rigidities of mindlessness. Langer and Imber (1979) studied how responses to events become rigid over time and the effects this may have on self-esteem. When one is first exposed to a task (situation), one attends to many of its different aspects. Upon repetition, these individual aspects coalesce into larger and larger units until the task is overlearned (or the situation is "completely" known). The individual aspects no longer exist for someone acting mindlessly. Now the person no longer thinks about how the task is performed; it is just performed. If anything in the environment leads her or him to question her or his competence at the task and the person tries to recall the individual steps of the task as evidence, she or he may not immediately find them. If the person doesn't find them, she or he is likely to conclude erroneously that she or he is incompetent. When the task is so well learned that it can be performed mindlessly, the individual steps, no longer exist in awareness. They have been subsumed into larger, more global steps and are not available for conscious consideration any longer.

In the Langer and Imber (1979) study, people performed a task so that it was either overlearned, moderately learned, or novel. They were then led to question their competence. This group who had not yet learned the task was appropriately lacking in confidence, and they displayed poor performance. The group who had overlearned the task was inappropriately nonconfident, and this similarly resulted in poor performance. In contrast, the moderately practiced group, for whom individual parts of the task were still available and fluid, the mindful group, performed well.

A good deal of research now suggests that mindlessness may lead not only to heightened vulnerability to competence-questioning aspects of the environment, but also to poor speech, and to not seeing nor hearing what is present in a situation to be seen or heard (see Langer, in press; Langer, Bashner, & Chanowitz, 1985; Langer & Imber, 1979; Langer & Newman, 1979; Langer & Weinman, 1981). Once one has an overlearned script or a rigid structure to respond to, one need not pay attention to the ongoing situation. However, this reliance on the past is costly. And there are most costs than the ones just mentioned.

Other studies have found that excessive mindlessness is bad for one's health. In fact, we reinterpreted the studies dealing with elderly adults mentioned earlier, emphasizing the principle that only mindful control is likely to be effective. We also assessed the effects of mindfulness on health in a prospective experimental study, in which participants practiced the mindfulness treatment they were taught for 20 minutes twice a day for 12 weeks. Essentially this entailed creating novel thoughts. The result was an increase in health, longevity, and perceived control (Alexander, Langer, Newman, Chandler, & Davies, in press).

To be mindful is to form discontinuous categories from continua. However, a corollary to this view is that, although we conceptualize most things as discrete, there may be some advantage to recognizing them as continuous. All of our experience may be continuous until we act on it, to make it discontinuous. Making it discontinuous is mindful; but overly relying on the discrete categories created is mindless. For example, consider the variable of age. There are many sensible ways people could be divided into age groups. In fact, if people were mindfully evaluated on each attribute indicating age, they would probably line up very differently on different attributes. In contrast, consider how we act toward a continuum of people, and break them down into smaller groups by age, for employment purposes. By deciding in the past according to some criteria that 65 was a sensible retirement age, we created the category "old" as anyone 65 and older. In our present society, we know that 65 is not old. However mindful that initial decision may have been, it has contributed to feelings of loss of control and to premature death for many people who incorporated it into their self-images (see Seligman, 1975). After using the age of 65 mindlessly as the reason to retire people, policymakers began to notice that people may be effective after age 65, and the mandatory retirement age was raised to 70. Now people are often mindlessly misjudged once they turn 70.

A *mindless* response is one that is made without any choice or any awareness that the situation could be understood differently. The point here is that the world that we experience in some singular, absolute way may be experienced in many alternative ways, once one pays attention to it. For example, imagine that you are walking along and you spot a lion before you. If you are like most people, fear would quickly overtake you and would seem quite absolute and uncontrollable. Now assume, instead, that you are on that same walk, and you see that same lion, but now you look up and see a sign that says "Safari Park." Now you probably would not be afraid. In one context the stimulus of the lion single-mindedly leads to fear, in another it does not. But who controls the context? Perception is an active constructive process, but one that we take for granted. Each situation we are in may be seen in many different ways, some that are similar to the way the situation is typically viewed, some that are different, and some that account for all the same data but are completely opposite to the familiar view. A rancher may look at a piece of steak as a product of good work; a nutritionist may see it as a cancer-causing killer; a starving child may see it as a life-giving godsend; and one can only guess how a cow might see it. It is clear that each of these perceptions can be simultaneously true (Langer, in press).

The individuals above are all likely to view the stimulus from their own vantage point in a singular way, often oblivious to alternative views. No doubt they would agree that each of these perspectives is viable if they stopped to consider alternative perspectives. The problem is that, when dealing with the world mindlessly, alternative conceptions do not spontaneously occur. It does not occur to people that each stimulus is simultaneously many stimuli, depending on the perspective one takes.

The Many Faces of Television

Television, like all stimuli, is not simply smart or stupid. In saying that, we do not mean merely that it has aspects that are smart and others that are stupid. Rather, we mean that each aspect of each show may be simultaneously smart or stupid, or anything in between that the mindful viewer makes it. Television is good or bad, enlightening or dulling, scintillating or boring, depending on how we view it. Television can be a mindful, creative process that provides food for thought, or it can be a substitute for thought.

Csikszentmihalyi and Kubey (1981) compared reading and watching television and concluded that a person expends greater cognitive effort when reading. They maintain that reading involves concentration, more challenges, more skills, more alertness, and less passivity than televiewing. If TV is preconceived to be less demanding than print, it is likely that people will expend less effort processing the material they view on television than they do when reading. Morgan (1980) has shown that heavy televiewing results in preferences for material that is like common television fare. Similarly, Watkins, Cojuc, Mills, Kaitek, and Tan (1981) have found that writing styles are also influenced by television. The narratives written by heavy televiewers are less fluid, contain fewer words per sentence, and describe more external, superficial elements than those written by light televiewers.

All of this work makes the assumption that people have no control over the way they watch television. However, we would maintain that television may be watched mindfully or mindlessly. Indeed, Salomon (1984) has repeatedly found that Israeli children watch television very differently than do American children, investing more effort and retaining more of the material. With this issue in mind, we ran the following study.

A Study on Mindful Televiewing

Essentially we tested the hypothesis that television could be viewed in many different ways, with discernible consequences of a mindful versus a mindless mode of viewing (Piper & Langer, 1986). We asked adults between the ages of 20 and 60 to commit themselves to watch 1 hour of television a day for 1 week at a time they chose in advance. Two groups of participants were treated in the same manner except for the instructions they were given regarding the manner in which they should watch the television. One group was told we were interested in relaxation and that we felt television was often relaxing. They were told that television is familiar, that familiarity and predictability often make people feel more secure, and that feeling secure enables one to relax. Therefore, we told them, we wanted them to watch television in a familiar way. In contrast, the mindful group was told that we were interested in perspective-taking, so we wanted them to watch television from a different perspective each night, their own and then one we would suggest. As perspectives for each respective viewing occasion, we asked them to watch television as though they were a lawyer, a child, a physician, an athlete, a psychologist, an actor, and a politician. In each case they were to try to think and feel just like the role they were playing and to contrast that with the way they would have watched had we not intervened.

At the end of the viewing period several measures were taken. To assess creativity in a comparable way, all participants were asked to watch the next episode of the television program "Dynasty." We did not provide any particular perspective from which to watch this show for either group. We wanted to see whether the mindful group's televiewing would have enabled them to see more possibilities and to break away from what the writer of the program might have prepared to seem inevitable. Participants were told we were interested in their ideas and not their writing styles or ability, so they could just outline their answer for us. They were also given a list of 300 adjectives on which their task was to check off each word that was related to themselves. This was taken as a test of flexible thinking: the more words checked off, the more flexibility in one's self-image. The mindful group significantly outperformed the comparison group on this task.

A detailed television questionnaire followed. Among the questions included, we asked how much they enjoyed the target program, and we found the mindful group enjoyed the program more than the comparison group. We asked a number of questions about their view of the complexity of the characters in the target program, hypothesizing that the more mindful the viewer, the more complex the characters would seem, since complexity is in the mind of the perceiver. The mindful group saw the characters as significantly more complex—not simply as good or evil—whereas the comparison group saw the characters in a more stereotypical way.

The mindful group also described the episode significantly differently. They saw more action and more subplots than the comparison group and their memory for details of the program was also better. We asked several multiple-choice questions and presented alternative answers that included "it depends"—an answer that we took to indicate awareness that circumstances are complex. Consistent with our hypothesis, the mindful group circled significantly more of these answer than the comparison group.

Finally, participants were given a mindfulness/mindlessness questionnaire to complete, the MMQ. This scale asked a number of general questions, the alternative answers to which included "it depends." Again, the more times "it depends" was circled, the more mindful participants were taken to be. Consistent with the previous measure, the mindful group was significantly more aware of complexity than was the comparison group.

In summary several converging measures in this study suggest that watching television in a mindful way apparently results in greater flexibility in one's thinking. Thus it seems that mindful televiewing may indeed be beneficial. However, the question remains: Who is going to supply the varied perspectives to be used in viewing mindfully? Surely, if one repeatedly looks at something the same way day in and day out, even if initially the perspective is novel, eventually mindlessness will result. One possibility would be for parents or teachers to provide a novel perspective each week. A better strategy, however, would be to prevent mindlessness in the first place.

How Mindlessness Comes About

To see how to prevent mindlessness, one might first consider the ways in which it comes about. Our research suggests that mindlessness not only occurs through rigid structures that emerge over time and are relied on mindlessly, but it may also arise on first exposure to information *if* that information is given in particular ways (Chanowitz & Langer, 1981; Langer & Piper, in press). Again, in this situation, when a structure is accepted, it is relied on without awareness of alternative ways that the information could be understood. As an example, when information is presented with no apparent reason to consider it carefully, it may be accepted as unconditionally true. If so, and if later conditions arise under which the information may be false, it is relatively unlikely for the person not to question it. Some of the contexts that encourage this rigid acceptance of information are when the information is apparently irrelevant, when it is presented by an expert, and when it is presented in a linguistic form that suggests that it "is" unconditionally true.

We have called this acceptance of structured information on initial exposure to it a *premature cognitive commitment*. Our research has shown that premature cognitive commitments encourage mindlessness. In the first of these studies (Chanowitz & Langer, 1981), participants were told about the symptoms of a fictitious disorder that they were led to believe was either relevant or irrelevant to them. We assumed that if people were given information that was perceived to be irrelevant, they would not take the time to think about it actively. Instead, they were expected to accept the information unquestioningly and form a premature cognitive commitment to it.

The problem with unconditionally accepting information that is irrelevant today is that it may turn out to be relevant tomorrow. If so, and if it has become mindlessly relied on, we hypothesized that it wouldn't occur to participants to reconsider it, even if it was to their advantage to do so. In this study, everyone took tests and thereby discovered that they had the disorder they had read about. They then took other tests that required an ability that people with this disorder purportedly lacked. Those participants who made premature cognitive commitments about the symptoms of the disorder displayed those symptoms and performed poorly. In contrast, participants who initially had reason to think about the information because it was relevant to them did not show this debilitation. Thus mindlessness may come about on a single exposure to information.

One cannot mindfully consider everything at one time. However, dealing with something mindlessly so that one can mindfully deal with something else apparently sets the stage for trouble. At the least, this is problematic when the information that was set aside mindlessly comes to need mindful attention. As examples related to television, researchers who study the deleterious effects of television, people who fear that television is a substitute for reading (which, by the way, is also an activity that can be enacted either mindlessly or mindfully; see Radlick, 1980; LaBerge & Samuels, 1974) and those who have lost significant others to the company of the television set all may have made a premature cognitive commitment about the nature of television. In so doing, they may have given up a useful source of stimulation, if they had only learned to see it that way.

Research we have done with children (Langer, Bashner, & Chanowitz, 1985) suggests that mindlessness may be reversed by teaching multiple views of events. In that study we asked children to make finer and finer distinctions among people and events. Doing so resulted in less stereotypic discrimination against people. That is, mindfulness training decreased prejudice. This study demonstrates essentially the same point as our television study. Both taught multiple views and both reduced mindlessness. But what about prevention?

Preventing Mindlessness

The way most of us are probably taught about most things takes the linguistic form of an unconditional truth: "This *is* an X." However, if there is actually a continuum of experience we abstract from to create categories, then objects may be simultaneously many things. If so, then this unconditional form of teaching may belie the truth or, at the least, obscure a more useful world view (Langer, in press). If we consider that scientific facts are probability statements, that there are multiple perspectives to virtually everything depending on the context in which we embed it, and that all we know about anything may be turned inside out by something new yet to be discovered, then it makes sense to teach a view of the world that is more conditional, more probabilistic, and less absolute.

We have conducted research to assess the effects of teaching more conditionally (Langer & Piper, in press). These studies were very straightforward. Participants were introduced to novel or familiar objects either unconditionally ("This is an X") or conditionally "This could be an X"). Later an unexpected need arose, for which the target object was suited but not traditionally used. Only those people who were introduced to a novel object in a conditional way later thought to use it creatively. For example, in one study the conditional group was told, "This could be a dog's chew toy." Of this group 40% later thought to use it as an eraser, whereas one in the absolute group thought to do so. When a second different need arose, many participants in the conditional group used the object in yet another novel way. This work suggests that people are able to learn conditionally, and that to learn in this way encourages mindfulness.

People may be taught to view television programs more mindfully, and television itself may be programmed to be more conditional, in order to encourage even more mindfulness. This greater mindfulness should have all the positive consequences found in our previous work.

To show the link most dramatically, however, we are conducting our most recent investigation on the topic of mindfulness and health. Here again, people are being asked to view television very mindfully or, as people typically do, somewhat mindlessly. However, here our research participants are hospital patients, and the question is whether even this brief mindful televiewing will result in health benefits. Participants are being given essentially the same instructions as in our previous television study, with the added exception that mindfulness or relaxation, depending on the condition, may be good for one's health. Whatever the results of this brief mindful exposure to television turn out to be, there is good reason to believe that mindful televiewing over an extended period should be good for one's health.

In light of all the above research findings, let's reconsider one of the more important issues regarding television: television and aggression. It may be true that whether television leads to aggression or not may depend on whether a viewer formed a premature cognitive commitment or not. That is, mindful televiewing may prevent what otherwise might be a powerful link between what viewers see and what they believe or do.

In any event, television need not be the medium that controls the message, and this conclusion is especially important for those who disagree with the current message. While waiting for television fare to represent one's own values better, one can still enjoy watching and learn *how* to watch television. Watching television mindfully returns control to the individual viewer. This mindful control may result in important psychological and physical benefits—perhaps even important enough to be reported on TV!

REFERENCES

Alexander, C., Langer, E., Newman, R., Chandler, H., & Davies, J. (in press). Aging, mindfulness, and Transcendental Meditation. *Journal of Personality and Social Psychology.*

Bandura, A., Ross, D., & Ross, S. (1963). Imitation of film-mediated aggressive models. *Journal of Abnormal and Social Psychology, 66,* 3-11.

Chanowitz, B., & Langer, E. (1980). Knowing more (or less) that you can show: Understanding control through the mindlessness/mindfulness distinction. In M.E.P. Seligman & J. Garber (Eds.), *Human helplessness.* New York: Academic Press.

Chanowitz, B., & Langer, E. (1981). Premature cognitive commitment. *Journal of Personality and Social Psychology, 41,* 1051-1063.

Csikszentmihalyi, M., & Kubey, R. (1981). Television and the rest of life: A systematic comparison of subjective experience. *Public Opinion Quarterlyl, 45,* 317-328.

Eron, L. D. (1982). Parent-child interaction, television violence and aggression of children. *American Psychologist, 37,* 197-211.

Gerbner, G., & Gross, L. (1976). Living with television: The violence profile. *Journal of Communication, 26,* 173-199.

Gerbner, G., Gross, L., Eleey, M., Jackson-Beeck, M., Jeffries-Fox, S., & Signorielli, N. (1977). TV violence profile No. 8. *Journal of Communication, 27,* 171-180.

Glass, D., & Singer, J. (1972). *Urban stress.* New York: Academic Press.

Harrison, L. F., & Williams, T. M. (1977, June). Television and cognitive development. In J. M. Williams (Chair), *The impact of television: A natural experiment involving three communities.* Symposium presented at the meeting of the Canadian Psychological Association, Vancouver.

Hartmann, P., & Husband, C. (1974). Racism and the mass media. In D. Pearl, L. Bouthilet, & J. Lazar (Eds.), *Television and behavior: Ten years of scientific progress and implications for the eighties.* Washington, DC: Government Printing Office.

Laberge, D., & Samuels, J. (1974). Automatic processes in reading. *Cognitive Psychology, 6,* 293-323.

Langer, E. (1975). The illusion of control. *Journal of Personality and Social Psychology, 32,* 311-328.

Langer, E. (1983). *The psychology of control.* Newbury Park, CA: Sage

Langer, E. (in press). Minding matters: The consequences of mindfulness/mindlessness. In L. Berkowitz (Ed.), *Advances in experimental social psychology.* New York: Academic Press.

Langer, E. (in press). *Mindfulness/mindlessness.* Reading, MA: Addison-Wesley.

Langer, E., & Avorn, J. (1981). The psychosocial environment of the elderly: Some behavioral and health implications. In J. Seagle & R. Chellis (Eds.), *Congregate housing for older people.* Lexington, MA: Lexington.

Langer, E., Bashner, R., & Chanowitz, B. (1985). Decreasing prejudice by increasing discrimination. *Journal of Personality and Social Psychology, 49,* 113-120.

Langer, E., Beck, P., Janoff-Bulman, R., & Timko, C. (1984). The relationship between cognitive deprivation and longevity in senile and nonsenile elderly populations. *Academic Psychology Bulletin,* 211-226.

Langer, E., & Imber, L. (1979). When practice makes imperfect: The debilitating effects of overlearning. *Journal of Personality and Social Psychology, 37,* 2014-2025.

Langer, E., & Newman, H. (1979). The role of mindlessness in the typical social psychological experiment. *Personality and Social Psychology Bulletin, 37,* 2003-2013.

Langer, E., & Piper, A. (in press). The prevention of mindlessness. *Journal of Personality and Social Psychology.*

Langer, E., & Rodin, J. (1976). The effects of enhanced personal responsibility for the aged: A field experiment in an institutional setting. *Journal of Personality and Social Psychology, 34,* 191-198.

Langer, E., Rodin, J., Beck, P., Weinman, C., & Spitzer, L. (1979). Environmental determinants of memory improvement in late adulthood. *Journal of Personality and Social Psychology, 37,* 2003-2013.

Langer, E., & Roth, J. (1975). Heads I win, tails it's chance: The illusion of control as a function of the sequence of outcomes in a purely chance task. *Journal of Personality and Social Psychology, 32,* 951-955.

Langer, E., & Weinman, C. (1981). When thinking disrupts intellectual performance: Mindlessness on an overlearned task. *Personality and Social Psychology Bulletin, 7,* 240-243.

Morgan, M., & Gross, L. (1982). Television and educational achievement and aspirations. In D. Pearl, L. Bouthilet, & J. Lazar (Eds.), *Television and behavior: Ten years of scientific progress and implications for the eighties.* Washington, DC: Government Printing Office.

Pervin, L. A. (1963). The need to predict and control under conditions of threat. *Journal of Personality and Social Psychology, 31,* 570-587.

Piper, A., & Langer, E. (1985). Aging and mindful control. In M. Baltes & P. Baltes (Eds.), *Aging and control.* Hillsdale, NJ: Lawrence Erlbaum.

Piper, A., & Langer, E. (1986). *Mindful televiewing.* Unpublished manuscript, Harvard University.

Postman, N. (1986). *Public discourse in the age of show business.* New York: Viking.

Rodin, J., & Langer, E. (1977). Long-term effects of a control-relevant intervention among the institutionalized aged. *Journal of Personality and Social Psychology, 35,* 897-902.

Salomon, G. (1984). *The processing roles of coding properties and learners' perceptions: A matter of divided labor.* Unpublished manuscript, Tel Aviv University.

Schulz, R. (1976). Effects of control and predictability on the psychological well-being of the institutionalized aged. *Journal of Personality and Social Psychology, 33,* 563-573.

Seligman, M. (1975). *Helplessness.* San Francisco: Freeman.

Sherrod, D., Hage, J., Halpern, P., & Moore, B. (1977). Effects of personal causation and perceived control on responses to an aversive stimulus: The more control, the better. *Journal of Experimental Social Psychology, 13,* 14-27.

Singer, J. L., & Singer, D. G. (1983). Implications of childhood television viewing for cognition, imagination and emotion. In J. Bryant & D. R. Anderson (Eds.), *Children's understanding of television.* New York: Academic Press.

Staub, E., Tversky, B., & Schwartz, G. (1971). Self control and predictability. *Journal of Personality and Social Psychology, 18,* 157-162.

Watkins, B., Cojuc, J. R., Mills, S., Kaitek, K., & Tan, Z. (1981). *Children's use of TV and real life story structure and content as a function of age, and prime-time television viewing* (First Annual Report to the Spencer Foundation). Ann Arbor: Children's Media Project, University of Michigan.

Wortman, C., & Brehm, J. (1975). Responses to uncontrollable outcomes. In L. Berkowitz (Ed.), *Advances in experimental social psychology* (Vol. 8, pp. 278-332). New York: Academic Press.

Zuckerman, D. M., Singer, D. G., & Singer, J. L. (1980). Television viewing and children's reading and related classroom behavior. *Journal of Communication, 30,* 166-174.

NORMA DEITCH FESHBACH **22**

TELEVISION AND THE
DEVELOPMENT OF EMPATHY

Inquiries regarding the possible influence of television viewing on children's development have usually been framed unfavorably: Does television viewing make children more aggressive, less social, more hyperactive, or less achieving? Other complaints voiced by teachers and parents include mental health concerns and the erosion of good taste. While there is considerable literature on some of these debatable topics, only rarely have questions been raised regarding possible positive outcomes derived from watching television (Comstock, Chaffee, Katzman, McCombs, & Roberts, 1978; Dorr, 1986; Greenfield, 1984).

Does the medium of television have the potential for fostering positive characteristics? Specifically, can television viewing enhance empathic development in a young audience? Superficially, it would appear that television is a particularly compatible medium for the teaching and learning of empathy. Empathy is an important dimension that should be fostered in the developing person, especially because of its relationship to the child's prosocial and emotional development. The portrayal of empathy on television should be intrinsically engaging to children because of the affective quality of much of television content (Feshback & Feshbach, 1984, 1986).

The basic issue addressed in this chapter is whether exposure to television influences the development of empathy in children. Studies directly investigating this relationship are almost nonexistent. However, there has been a considerable amount of theorizing and research on the effects of television viewing on processes and behavior that are postulated as components of empathy or are related to empathy.

The Construct of Empathy

First, let us consider what empathy is and why it is important. Empathy has become a popular concept in today's vernacular. A good teacher is referred to as an "empathic" teacher. A responsive person is an "empathic" listener. Is empathy the antonym of narcissism, hedonism, and selfishness? Is empathy an all-embracing trait that includes nurturance, caring, altruism, and love? The answer is both yes and no.

Empathy is a shared emotional response between the viewer and the viewed—between the subject and the object in an interaction. For example, I perceive a person in my environment as unhappy, and I feel unhappy. I observe a happy individual, and I respond by feeling happy—perhaps not with the same intensity of emotion that is being observed, but with the same general feeling.

Empathy is a basic ingredient of social understanding and social harmony. Although the empathic response is affective, it is contingent upon cognitive factors. It entails the ability to make important discriminations regarding other people's affect (how they look, the behavioral cues they display) and the capacity to take the role of another person, to appreciate their point of view, to share their feelings, whether those feelings are of happiness, pride, fear, sadness, or anger (Feshbach, 1975, 1978). Because of our capacity to empathize with people in distress, empathy is closely linked to sympathy and compassion. The empathic process helps us to appreciate the pain of individuals whom we punch or hurt, and empathy functions to restrain and modulate aggressive behavior (Feshbach, 1978; Feshbach & Feshbach, 1987).

Empathy has still another remarkable quality. The display of empathy by one person in a social relationship tends to evoke positive feelings in the other member. When someone has responded empathically to us, we feel that we have been understood; we feel validated (Kohut, 1971). This feeling of being validated by another's empathic response is an important tenet in a number of psychotherapeutic approaches (Rogers & Truax, 1967). Moreover, empathy can disrupt a cycle of conflict and discord and initiate a cycle of positive social interaction.

Empathy sometimes is seen as the opposite of egocentrism. Being egocentric is perceiving a situation one-sidedly or having a viewpoint that is narrowly restricted. Being able to take the role of another, a prerequisite for empathy, allows a person to hold multiple perspectives of the same situation.

Relevant Research

According to the model of empathy that has guided this analysis, two of the three major components of empathy involve critical aspects of the child's emotional experience—the ability to discriminate and identify different emotions, and the capacity to experience and feel different emotions.

Drama elicits emotional responses in the audience. Its emotional properties are an essential feature of the dramatic experience (and of other forms of entertainment as well). Television is no exception to this rule. The emotional impact of television has been extensively reviewed by Dorr in a series of publications (Dorr, 1981, 1982, 1983; Door, Doubleday, & Kovaric, 1983). As these comprehensive reviews make evident, television elicits a range of affects, including negative emotions such as fear, sadness, and disgust, and positive reactions of pleasure and mirth. Children, like adults, appear to enjoy the process of arousal and resolution of these feelings. They enjoy and value programmatic content that elicits affective reactions of excitement, mirth, and social warmth (Zillman, 1982).

Children attend to cues that convey the emotions being experienced by television characters. There are important age differences in the subtlety and range of cues to which children are sensitive. Preschoolers and young children are especially guided by the facial expression of the characters. Older children are more responsible to situational cues and are more able to understand the emotional implications that particular symbols and metaphors are intended to convey (Harris, Olthof, & Terwogt, 1981).

Because television evokes a kaleidoscope of emotions, and because children can discriminate among varying affects portrayed on the television screen, does it therefore follow that children become more emotionally sensitive and responsive as a consequence of television viewing? Not necessarily. It can also be argued that children's affect may become blunted and desensitized by repeated exposure to the emotion-eliciting stimuli of movies or television (Dysinger & Ruckmick, 1933). After extensive television viewing children can become even less emotionally sensitive.

There is some evidence that these divergent consequences may be dependent on the types of program content viewed (Thomas, Horton, Lippincott, & Drabman, 1977). One of the explicit goals of a program such as "Mister Rogers' Neighborhood" or "Sesame Street" is to teach children to recognize and label their own and others' emotions. Research has shown that heavy viewers of "Sesame Street" are better able to associate particular emotions to relevant affective situations than are light viewers, though the effect is rather weak (Bogatz & Ball, 1971).

Although the evidence concerning the impact of television on affective components of empathy is ambiguous, there is little doubt that exposure to visual-media stimuli can significantly modify affective responses. In clinical laboratory studies, procedures have been developed that employ visual stimuli to foster desensitization to a fear-arousing situation. More directly germane to the question of television influence, a decrement in fear of large dogs has been observed in some children following repeated viewing of "Lassie" (Bandura, Grusec, & Menlove, 1967). Other data bearing on desensitization to aggression provide further evidence of the potential influence of television in the conditioning and deconditioning of emotions (Cline, Croft, & Courrier, 1973; Drabman & Thomas, 1974).

Empathy entails the capacity to assume another's perspective, a skill that involves an act of imagination. Therefore, the impact of television programming has implications for children's empathy. If a television program is effective in stimulating children's imagination, it might also enhance their empathy. In a well-designed study, Singer and Singer (1976) experimentally varied exposure of preschool children to "Mister Rogers' Neighborhood." They found enhancement of imaginative play skills in one of their experimental groups; however, the effect was contingent on the presence of a "mediator" who interpreted events in the program and directed children's attention to relevant program cues. No significant effects were found for the children who watched "Mister Rogers' Neighborhood" without a mediator present. Friedrich and Stein (1975) have also reported increases in 3- to 5-year-old children's imagination following exposure to "Mister Rogers' Neighborhood" programs. Again, other elements in the experimental treatment such as teacher training and relevant play materials may have been primarily responsible for the experimental effects.

Prosocial behaviors are believed to be mediated by or closely related to empathy. Helping individuals who are economically less fortunate is an example of a behavior that is related to empathy and that has been shown to be enhanced by exposure to experimentally prepared videotapes depicting a model engaging in acts of generosity (Bryan, 1975). A similar kind of effect has been demonstrated for an actual television program. A group of 5-year-old children, randomly assigned to viewing a "Lassie" program in which Lassie's master risked his life to save Lassie's pup, displayed a greater willingness than comparison groups to help puppies in distress when it involved some cost to the children (Sprafkin, Liebert, & Poulos, 1975).

Generalized prosocial effects of television were also found in an impressive experiment by Moriarty and McCabe (1977), in which children participating in various team sports were assigned to prosocial, antisocial, or control video presentations of the relevant team sport in which they were engaged. Although exposure to the antisocial, aggressive content did not change player behavior, significant increases in prosocial behavior were observed in children who had been exposed to television content portraying cooperative and sympathetic behaviors, affection, reparation for wrong-doing, and concern for others.

A variety of studies have indicated that exposure to prosocial program content can enhance socially desirable behaviors, as summarized in Rushton's (1982) review of the literature. However, the stability and generality of these effects are less well established. It is possible that, after prolonged exposure, prosocial stimuli may lose their potency, and viewers may become indifferent to or bored with the content. This may also be true for the direct and indirect learning of empathy. The studies by Singer and Singer (1976) and Friedrich and Stein (1975) suggest that television content may have to be reinforced by other socializing influences to sustain its impact.

In summary, although there have been almost no studies directly bearing on television's influence on the development of empathy, there are a number of studies that reflect the impact of television viewing on the individual facets involved in empathy. A variety of children's emotions are evoked by watching television. Children learn to label and discriminate different affects, and they can also acquire imaginative skills. These effects are enhanced if learning these behaviors is an explicit program goal and/or if there are adjunct mediators such as teachers who help implement the behaviors. An unresolved question is whether extensive television viewing can make children less rather than more empathic. Another is whether prosocial behaviors related to empathy, acquired by viewing television, generalize beyond the specific learning context. It seems possible that additional use of role-playing strategies can facilitate the learning of empathy and prosocial behaviors.

Television and Empathy:
Research and Programming Directions

The study of media influences on children's empathy poses an interesting set of issues and challenges. Longitudinal data would provide insights into these influences by showing the effects of repeated and prolonged exposure to particular kinds of television content. It would be of interest to compare the relative influence of interpersonal, social programming content, as depicted in family situations and even soap operas, with that of strongly action-oriented content, or predominantly cognitive and educational programs. Longitudinal studies would also allow the application of causal models to these data in order to determine the likely causal direction of relationships between empathy and particular kinds of television exposures. Findings regarding the kinds of television content that appear causally linked to the development of empathy in children would, then, provide a basis for introducing changes in television programming that would foster empathy.

In terms of the theoretical model of empathy that has been described, it would be especially important for significant television figures to engage in role-playing and perspective-taking, and to manifest empathy in their social interactions. These figures would not simply function as models for imitation, although this in itself would be quite desirable. More important, through their empathic reactions to the feelings of others, these dramatic characters could provide an opportunity for viewers to experience vicariously the processes that contribute to empathy—to be cognizant of another person's emotions, to see situations from another person's perspective, and to experience the feeling that the other person is experiencing. Also, depiction of contrasts between the interactions of an empathic television character and those of a nonempathic character could be a dramatic device that illuminates for viewers the role of empathy in facilitating communication and resolving misunderstandings. This might enable viewers to see the possibility of alternative interpretations of the same situation and alternative ways of coping.

Contemporary television, especially television that is intended for children, offers very few opportunities for this kind of vicarious experience. And yet portrayal of empathy processes could be readily incorporated into current programming without requiring major content changes. For example, television programs directed toward children are typically characterized by a high degree of action: Heroes and other characters fly robot ships, attack adversaries, perform physical feats, play games, commit pranks. Meanwhile, the feelings, ideas, motives, and perspectives of either the main or supporting players are usually given little, if any, attention. For example, take a scene in which a child is fearful because a parent—or friend, or pet, or some other love object—is in danger, and the television hero or heroine is called on to rescue the love object. Sometimes the distress of the frightened child is conveyed through facial expressions and demeanor, but the feelings of the characters are almost never verbally articulated. There are usually no statements about the attachments of the child to the endangered love object, nor the feelings of loss or helplessness.

It would not be necessary to reduce or eliminate the exciting action, but action could be punctuated or accompanied with scenes in which the inner world of the protagonists is given attention—the feelings with which they are struggling and the attributions they are making about themselves and others. Action depicted on television does not inevitably require a psychological analysis of the emotional state of the individual engaged in the action. However, much more could and should be done to depict the feelings and perspectives of television characters in children's programming.

I am proposing that sensitivity to other people's feelings and viewpoints, and the understanding and sharing of emotional experiences, be integrated into standard television fare. Obviously, incorporating empathic material will create some changes in content. For example, when a television figure is sensitive to the feelings and viewpoints of another character, it is more difficult for the figure to aggress against that other character. The depiction of empathy in conflictual contexts may lead to responses and resolutions such as compassion, mercy, and compromise. Thus the integration of empathy into traditional television programming might also lead to an increase in prosocial content and in prosocial behavior of viewers.

Although aspects of empathy can be evoked and learned through television viewing, "true" empathy may result only rarely and be very difficult to monitor. Nevertheless, it should be possible to evaluate the influence of television on the development of empathy by assessing viewers' responses to secondary as well as main characters, by measuring the responses of children varying in their degree of empathy, and through longitudinal studies that reflect the long-term influence of exposure to particular kinds of program content.

An important question should be raised at this point. Will the portrayal of these themes on television attract a large audience? I believe that it will. Children, as well as adults, are intrigued by and attracted to the world of feelings and desires, though not to the same degree. The question of the ideal mix of action and emotion will have to remain unresolved until empathy themes are more systematically introduced into television programming and then evaluated. As yet, studies bearing directly on the relationship between empathy and television are almost nonexistent, but the study of this relationship can be approached reciprocally: by evaluating the effect of the media on the development of children's empathy, and by evaluating the role of empathy in determining children's affective and cognitive responses to the media. Until relevant research findings are available, it seems reasonable to predict that programs focusing on relationships or misunderstandings, on conflicts and their resolution, on empathy, caring, and compassion, will have wide appeal. All of us have to cope with conflicts in relationships that are important to us—with family members, colleagues, and friends—and the experience of empathy and caring, even if only vicariously through television, is positive and reinforcing.

By confronting this challenge of making television a more meaningful medium for children, we will begin to explore and expand the richness and range of experiences that television can provide its audience. It seems likely that, once we broaden the nature of our attitudes and expectations, television programming can simultaneously serve the industry and also the best interests of children.

REFERENCES

Bandura, A., Grusecc, J. E., & Menlove, F. L. (1967). Vicarious extinction of avoidance behavior. *Journal of Personality and Social Psychology, 5*, 16-23.

Bogatz, G. A., & Ball, S. (1971). *The second year of Sesame Street: A continuing evaluation.* Princeton, NJ: Educational Testing Service.

Bryan, J. H. (1975). Children's cooperation and helping behavior. In E. M. Hetherington (Ed.), *Reviewing of child development research* (Vol. 5). Chicago: University of Chicago Press.

Cline, V. B., Croft, R. G., & Courrier, S. (1973). Desensitization of children to television violence. *Journal of Personality and Social Psychology, 27*, 360-365.

Comstock, G., Chaffee, S., Katzman, N., McCombs, M., & Roberts, D. (1978). *Television and human behavior.* New York: Columbia University Press.

Dorr, A. (1981). Television and affective development and functioning: Maybe this decade. *Journal of Broadcasting, 25*, 335-346.

Dorr, A. (1982). Television and affective development and functioning. In D. Pearl, L. Bouthilet, & J. Lazar (Eds.), *Television and behavior: Ten years of scientific progress and implications for the eighties* Washington, DC: Government Printing Office.

Dorr, A. (1983). No shortcuts to judging reality. In J. Bryant & D. R. Anderson (Eds.), *Children's understanding of television: Research on attention and comprehension.* New York: Academic Press.

Dorr, A. (1986). *Television and children.* Newbury Park, CA: Sage.

Dorr, A., Doubleday, C., & Kovaric, P. (1983). Emotions depicted on and stimulated by television programs. In M. Meyer (Ed.), *Children and the formal features of television: Approaches and findings of experimental and formative research.* Munich: K.G. Saur.

Drabman, R. S., & Thomas, M. H. (1974). Does media violence increase children's toleration of real-life aggression? *Developmental Psychology, 10*, 418-421.

Dysinger, W. S., & Ruckmick, C. A.(1933). *The emotional responses of children to the motion picture situation.* New York: Macmillan.

Feshbach, N. D. (1975). Empathy in children: Some theoretical and empirical considerations. *Counseling Psychologist, 4*(2).

Feshbach, N. D. (1978). Studies of empathic behavior in children. In B. A. Maher (Ed.), *Progress in experimental personality research* (Vol. 8). New York: Academic Press.

Feshbach, N. D., & Feshbach, S. (1984). *The humanistic potential of television: A mechanism for stimulating and developing empathy.* Paper presented at the NIMH workshop on the Role of Media in the Prevention of Violence, Los Angeles.

Feshbach, N. D., & Feshbach, S. (1987). Television and empathy in children. In A. Dorr (Ed.), *Emotions and television.* Unpublished manuscript.

Feshbach, S., & Feshbach, N. D. (1986). Aggression and altruism: A personality perspective. In C.

Zahn-Waxler, M. Chapman, & M. Radke-Yarrow (Eds.), *Aggression and altruism: Biological and social origins* New York: Cambridge University Press.

Friedrich, L. K., & Stein, A. H. (1975). Prosocial television and young children: The effects of verbal labeling and role playing on learning and behavior. *Child Development, 46,* 27-38.

Greenfield, P. M. (1984). *Mind and media: The effects of television, video games and computers.* Cambridge, MA: Harvard University Press.

Harris, P. L., Olthof, T., & Terwogt, M. M. (1981). Children's knowledge of emotion. *Journal of Child Psychology and Psychiatry, 22,* 247-261.

Kohut, H. (1971). *The analysis of the self* (Psychoanalysis of the child, Monograph No. 4). New York: International Universities Press.

Moriarty, D., & McCabe, A. E. (1977). Studies of television and youth sport. In *Report of Ontario Royal Commission on Violence in the Communications Industry* (Vol. 5). Toronto: Queen's Printer for Ontario.

Rogers, C. R., & Truax, C. B. (1967). The therapeutic conditions antecedent to change: A theoretical view. In C. R. Rogers (Ed.), *The therapeutic relationship and its impact: A study of psychotherapy with schizophrenics.* Madison: University of Wisconsin Press.

Rushton, J. P. (1982). Television and prosocial behavior. In D. Pearl, L. Bouthilet, & J. Lazar (Eds.), *Television and behavior: Ten years of scientific progress and implications for the eighties* (Vol. 2). Washington, DC: Government Printing Office.

Singer, J. L., & Singer, D. G. (1976). Fostering creativity in children: Can TV stimulate imaginative play? *Journal of Communication, 26,* 74-80.

Singer, J. L., & Singer, D. G. (1983). Psychologists look at television: Cognitive, developmental, personality, and social policy implications. *American Psychologist, 38,* 826-834.

Sprafkin, J. M., Liebert, R. M., & Poulos, R. W. (1975). Effects of a pro-social example on children's helping. *Journal of Experimental Child Psychology, 20,* 119-126.

Thomas, M. H., Horton, R. W., Lippincott, E. C., & Drabman, R. S. (1977). Desensitization to portrayals of real-life aggression as a function of exposure to television violence. *Journal of Personality and Social Psychology, 35,* 450-458.

Zillman, D. (1980). Anatomy of suspense. In P. H. Tannenbaum (Ed.), *The entertainment functions of television.* Hillsdale, NJ: Lawrence Erlbaum.

Zillman, D. (1982). Television viewing and arousal. In D. Pearl, L. Bouthilet, & J. Lazar (Eds.), *Television and behavior: Ten years of scientific progress and implications for the eighties* (Vol. 2). Washington, DC: Government Printing Office.

23

CREATING POSITIVE
TELEVISION IMAGES

This project was motivated by the convergence of three related bodies of literature: research on the effects of media violence, the portrayal of minorities and women in the media, and the prosocial potential of television.

By far, the bulk of scholarly attention to television has been devoted to the effects of violence on the viewing audience. The results of several decades of research in this arena clearly reveal that violence in the media can affect the violent attitudes and/or behaviors of at least a portion of the viewers (Roberts & Bachen, 1981; Withey, 1980).

A related concern has been the effects of stereotypic portrayals of American ethnic minority groups and nonminority women. Indeed, the mass media have presented stereotypic portrayals of black and other minority Americans throughout their entire history (see Bayles, 1985; Berry, 1980; Graves, 1980; Poindexter & Stroman, 1980; Staples & Jones, 1985). Equally problematic has been the lack of television programming depicting cross-race interaction. Weigel and Howes (1982), for example, reported that cross-racial associations constituted only 1% of children's network programming.

Images of women have been constrained in their adherence to traditional sex-role stereotypes (e.g., Morgan, 1982; Weigel & Loomis, 1981; Zuckerman, Singer, & Singer, 1980). Women characters are typically portrayed as passive, domestic, or in traditional "women's roles" (e.g., teacher, nurse, secretary).

Thus despite television's admitted socialization potential (e.g., Abeles, 1980; Berry, 1980; Rushton, 1979), its use to date has been dominated by violence and by negative images of minorities and nonminority women. In addition to being incomplete and stereotypical, these images can negatively affect the self-esteem of members of the stigmatized groups (Abeles, 1980).

This use of the medium is even more frustrating because of television's prosocial potential. A substantial body of research on the effects of prosocial television has now demonstrated the medium's ability to enhance interpersonal empathy, cooperation, nonviolent problem resolution, and reversal of racial or gender prejudices and stereotypes (see Rushton, 1979, for a review). The general conclusion that emerges is that television, whatever its content, can have a demonstrable impact on its viewers. A major problem, however, has been the lack of adequate programming of a prosocial nature (Houser, 1978; Rushton, 1979).

CREATING "STAR CRUSADERS"

In order to help in redressing this problem, I gave some time to "creative writing" and developed the concept for an educational television program that would address each of the concerns outlines in the preceding pages. In beginning this creative endeavor, I saw a number of needs: The program would have to be attractive and appealing to its target audience, it should promote interracial harmony and positive multicultural exchanges, it must reverse the stereotypical images of minorities and nonminority women, it should provide positive role models and vicarious cross-ethnic experiences, and it should develop an appropriate prosocial value base.

The creation of the original "Star Crusaders" concept has been detailed elsewhere (Fairchild, 1984). In summary, the pilot television program involved an interracial and cross-gender team of skilled young adults, cast in counter-stereotypical roles, who traveled to other planets to solve problems of intergroup conflict. The program incorporated the conditions for reducing prejudice specified in the "contact hypothesis," developed in race relations research (Allport, 1954): The team of protagonists shared equal status and common goals, they cooperated in a fairly intimate context, and they enjoyed successful outcomes.

This formula for "Star Crusaders" was then articulated in a treatment and a shooting script, and was later produced by a public broadcasting station in Los Angeles (KCET-TV, Channel 28) with funding from the U.S. Department of Education (see Fairchild, 1984). "Star Crusaders" aired in Los Angeles in the summer of 1981.

The program introduced five Star Crusaders: Logan (adult black male), Jim (young adult black male, and the leading protagonist), Susan (young adult Asian female), Tom (young adult white male), and Miguel (young adult Mexican-American male). Each of the Star Crusaders possessed a unique and useful skill or ability (e.g., telepathy, history, computer sciences, acrobatics).

The pilot program pitted the Star Crusaders against a Hitlerian demogogue who was preaching racial, ethnic, and age separation. In a dramatic debate, Jim defeated the demagogue and his separatist ideology.

EVALUATING "STAR CRUSADERS"

In order to evaluate the effects of the program on viewers, a three-phase method was developed to assess (1) program content, (2) viewer perceptions of that content, and (3) the effects of the content on interpersonal attitudes and behaviors.

The first study, a detailed and objective content analysis, calculated the proportion of "total human appearance time" that various ethnic and gender groups were portrayed. Results indicated that whites were involved in scenes 64% of the time, blacks 59%, Asians 25%, Hispanics 25%, males 87% and females 46%. Interracial interaction accounted for 40% of the total human appearance time.

The second study, an audience perception analysis, involved 104 university undergraduates who judged the themes and impact of the program. These students viewed the program in small group settings, and then evaluated the program on an open- and closed-ended questionnaire. In reporting up to four themes, the students accurately perceived the prosocial themes in the program with peaceful living mentioned by 62%. Other themes reported to have high salience in the program were interpersonal cooperation (32%) and racial harmony (35%). Although nearly half (43%) of the students said that the program had little or no impact on them, some students said that the program reinforced their existing attitudes (15%), increased their sensitivity to racial discrimination (24%), or increased their concern for problems on earth (14%).

The third study was a larger field experiment involving 948 students in the public schools. Of these students, 494 were in the 5th and 6th grades (about 10-11 years of age), and 454 were in the 7th and 8th grades (about 12-13 years of age). The schools were predominantly black and Hispanic. Students in intact classrooms were exposed to one of three conditions: "Star Crusaders" without a discussion, "Star Crusaders" with a discussion, or a control film about animals ("Wild Kingdom"). The use of a discussion condition was motivated by the research literature, which has demonstrated the positive benefits of media-related discussions and activities (e.g., Wade & Poole, 1983).

Students were given a closed-ended questionnaire that assessed appeal, agreement with themes in the program (10 Likert-type items), character evaluation and identification (students were shown pictures of the seven key characters and asked, "How good do you think this person is as an actor or actress?" and "How much would you like to be like this person?"), and a "feeling thermometer" for four ethnic/racial groups (Asians, blacks, Mexican-Americans, and whites). Questions were worded so as to be suitable for both treatment and control conditions.

Results indicated that students found "Star Crusaders" more appealing than "Wild Kingdom" (the discussion condition was most liked by elementary school students, and the no-discussion condition was most liked by the junior high school students). Exposed students typically endorsed the themes in the program (e.g., "It is best to solve problems by working together," and "Some leaders can turn people against each other"). Students also more favorably evaluated and identified with the "Star Crusaders" characters if they had seen the videotape. This latter finding was particularly true for the lead character, Jim (the young adult black male). As expected, gender was related to character identification, with female students more likely to identify with female characters, and male students more likely to identify with male characters. Students' feelings toward their own and others' ethnic groups were not related to exposure to "Star Crusaders" (See Fairchild, 1984, for details).

These studies provided evidence of the potential of the "Star Crusaders" concept to capture and hold the attention of a youthful audience, and to form a basis for the adoption of positive values concerning racial and gender groups.

In many respects, however, research on "Star Crusaders" was limited in nature because the videotape was a *constant*. Although containing a variety of content, the tape as a whole presented a constant stimulus to viewers. As a result, some of the more interesting research questions could not be addressed—for example: What features of the program are related to which results?

RE-CREATING "STAR CRUSADERS"

After 7 years of creative and research work, I had produced a 30-minute pilot tape and data from a series of investigations demonstrating the tape's efficacy in schools. I could continue research with that tape, but I felt enough research had already been devoted to an admittedly modest pilot television program. What I now needed was a new direction—an effort to improve on the original concept and develop a television series that would be suitable for either broadcast or classroom use. This, certainly, is not the typical work of a social psychologist!

In reconceptualizing "Star Crusaders," I was concerned with four issues: (1) maintaining the appeal of the program, (2) maintaining prosocial themes in the program, (3) creating sets and plots that could be feasibly produced, and (4) developing a research agenda to be incorporated into program production.

I was also concerned about the quality of the pilot program itself. Although it had been positively received by viewing audiences, I was dissatisfied with several aspects of the program. First, the program was not entirely consistent with respect to its "counter-stereotypical" images. In certain scenes, conflict on the alien planet was depicted using some minority actors in stereotyped activities. Second, the pilot was too "preachy" in presenting its prosocial themes. The debate between the demagogue and Jim was too didactic, and too non-action-oriented.

Third, the casting of the "Star Crusaders" did not allow for the portrayal of certain groups. Black and Hispanic women, and Asian men, were all but nonexistent. Moreover, the content analysis demonstrated a lack of equal time (and therefore probably also of equal status) in the presentation of various group members.

These issues were difficult to overcome, and "Star Crusaders" sat on a back burner for several years, until I returned again to "creative writing." The result of this creative work is "Star Crusaders: An Animated Space Adventure." The title of the series tells a lot about the proposed program: A group of youthful protagonists are the nexus for the series. These youth, born in space as part of a moving colony, conduct space exploration in the course of their training and engage in conflict resolution as their raison d'être. The program will utilize state-of-the-art animation techniques, thus avoiding many of the prohibitive costs associated with live-action and science-fiction production.

The program is to have a triple purpose: to entertain, to present prosocial themes, and to inform. Concerning the latter, "Star Crusaders: An Animated Space Adventure" will feature "real science" in the context of space exploration. Information in the program will be correct in terms of current knowledge about astronomical processes and other scientific areas. The more subtle, prosocial messages of the program will be embodied in the modeling of cross-ethnic, and cross-gender egalitarianism.

Although the series is targeted to a youthful audience (early childhood through adolescence), it will use "adult" dialogue and situations, and will therefore attract older audiences as well. Other successful programs have this same cross-age appeal (e.g., *E.T., the Extraterrestrial*; "Star Trek").

The Concept

Time. Approximately 200 years in the future.

Setting. On board "The Ariel," a space vehicle for exploring the far reaches of space. Because of the distances (and therefore travel time) involved, space travel is multigenerational. The Ariel is huge (built in space, it is more than a cubic kilometer), and rotates in order to simulate gravity. Population: 1,553.

Protagonists. The first children born in space, the Star Crusaders have been specially trained for space exploration. The first cohort is composed of 16 crusaders. They are divided equally in gender, and the major racial groups are represented. In addition, they are multinational and multilingual.

One emphasis will be the development of harmonious Soviet/American relationships. Key characters will be of Soviet and American origin, and will work harmoniously together. Other key characters will represent the people of the world. In a sense, the Ariel is to be a traveling United Nations.

The Star Crusaders will be specialists with respect to their vocational training (e.g., astro-navigator, gravitational physicist, electrical and mechanical engineers, biologists, botanist, etc.).

Activities. The Star Crusaders are explorers of space. Part of their training includes knowledge about the solar system, and animated holograms provide them, and the viewing audience, with an education about the planets. After the development of a Star Drive (allowing for space/time transformations exceeding the speed of light), the crusaders explore the far reaches of space: black holes, X-ray stars, binary star systems, other galaxies, pulsars, neutron stars, and other worlds. Material will be presented as entertaining lessons in astronomy, and will adhere to current scientific theory and facts. Fictional material will include contacts with other life forms and civilizations (an emphasis on scientific plausibility will be maintained). The Star Crusaders will encounter disasters and perils that require intelligence and cooperation to solve.

Considerable attention will be given to "life in space." New forms of recreation, physical exercise, and communal living will be explored.

Prosocial themes. The series is intended to provide positive models for interpersonal relations, especially cross-gender and cross-ethnic relationships. Characters will be cast in "equal status" roles, and will demonstrate cooperative efforts in achieving common goals. Some programs will explicitly deal with the peaceful resolution of conflict between life forms encountered in space. For example, in one treatment, the Star Crusaders bridge the gap between two warring factions and bring peace to a world at war.

Appeal

"Star Crusaders: An Animated Space Adventure" capitalizes on the immense popularity of science fiction with young and old audiences alike. The use of computer-assisted animation heightens appeal, especially for young viewers. As an action adventure, the program will capture the attention, and the imagination, of children and adolescents. By presenting veridical science (true explanations and theorems concerning the structure of the universe), the program will appeal to adults as well. A dynamic music score will heighten appeal.

DISCUSSION

The foregoing program proposal provides a glimpse of the potential of the "Star Crusaders" concept. Of course, a number of challenges remain: obtaining funding, determining a production house, writing scripts, and so on. These are not small items, and I recognize the great improbability of the series' eventual production. Nevertheless, the first step is the articulation of the proposal, and this chapter has accomplished that.

What is a social psychologist doing creating television programming? Should this not be left to the appropriate industry experts? My answer is that television, as one of the most pervasive socialization influences in our society, must be part of the social scientist's work and concern. Experts in human behavior should become directly involved in creation of the material being offered to audiences. Social psychologists (and social scientists more generally) should apply knowledge in real-world contexts and toward the resolution of real-world problems.

And what of research? My background as a social psychologist demands a comprehensive research program despite the methodological and conceptual complexities involved. As Gans (1980) noted, the media researcher has the "insuperable task of isolating the impact of the mass media from the impact of other institutions, and obviously, methodological problems abound" (p. 57).

But it is precisely the potential of "Star Crusaders: An Animated Space Adventure" that excites me as a researcher. With a continuing series of programs, it becomes possible to study the myriad influences on children's social behavior in longitudinal and/or experimental designs. Such studies, at a minimum, must include the following classes of variables: characteristics of the viewer, including personality, cognitive development, group membership(s), and television viewing habits; content analyses of the programming itself; characteristics of the viewing situation (time, day, location, and social influences); the processes involved during or after exposure (e.g., attention, information processing, follow-up activities); and the complex cognitive, affective, attitudinal, and behavioral outcomes that may result.

Summative research, as described above, must distinguish between direct and indirect effects, short-term and long-term effects, and the effects of cumulative exposure to the prosocial television programming. Formative research would seek feedback and input from students, teachers, and others during the production of the programs. Here, comparatively less sophisticated research designs would be geared toward providing rapid responses to questions that pertain to the quality and messages of the programs as they are being developed.

Also, the researcher must control for "selective exposure" and "selective avoidance" problems in media effects research. A substantial number of studies have demonstrated that efforts to change attitudes and behaviors of viewers are thwarted by the tendency for viewers to attend media selectively in a way that fortifies their existing attitudes, beliefs, and/or behaviors (Wallack, 1981).

CONCLUDING COMMENTS

My creative engagement in children's television programming has not been without professional costs. Time devoted to creative writing subtracts from time available for pure research, and research is the currency of evaluation for most social psychologists. My work on "Star Crusaders" has been devalued by some because it demonstrated my "lack of commitment to research" or my "failure to obtain robust results."

Social scientists committed to social change and social improvement must be aware of the inherent difficulties and impediments to success. Social problems are difficult to study, and certainly difficult to change.

Indeed, the fact that we may *want* to create social change is cause for alarm to many. Traditional biases within science for "objectivity," and "detachment" from the object of inquiry lead to a depreciation of the applied social scientist's work. Commitment to the resolution of continuing social problems may require a deviation from the traditional paths to academic rewards. The risks are great, but the potential rewards, it seems to me, are greater. Television can be a pathway to peace by creating a sense of world community, promoting intercultural understanding, and impeding the formation of the enemy image.

If "Star Crusaders: An Animated Space Adventure" has any potential for changing the normative climate of American/Soviet relations, or intercultural relations, or gender relations, then it deserves the effort required to bring it to fruition.

REFERENCES

Abeles, R. P. (1980). Beyond violence and children. In S. B. Whithey & R. P. Abeles (Eds.), *Television and social behavior: Beyond violence and children.* Hillsdale, NJ: Lawrence Erlbaum.

Allport, G. W. (1954). *The nature of prejudice.* Cambridge, MA: Addison-Wesley.

Bayles, M. (1985). Blacks on TV: Adjusting the image. *New Perspectives, 17,* (3), 2-6.

Berry, G. L. (1980). Television and Afro-Americans: Past legacy and present portrayals. In S. B. Withey & R. P. Abeles (Eds.), *Television and social behavior: Beyond violence and children.* Hillsdale, NJ: Lawrence Erlbaum.

Fairchild, H. H. (1984). Creating, producing and evaluating prosocial TV. *Journal of Educational Television, 10,* 161-183.

Gans, H. J. (1980). The audience for television—and in television research. In S. B. Withey & R. P. Abeles (Eds.), *Television and social behavior: Beyond violence and children.* Hillsdale, NJ: Lawrence Erlbaum.

Graves, S. B. (1980). Psychological effects of black portrayals on television. In S. B. Withey & R. P. Abeles (Eds.), *Television and social behavior: Beyond violence and children.* Hillsdale, NJ: Lawrence Erlbaum.

Houser, B. B. (1978). Use of audiovisual media in reducing prejudice. *Psychology in the Schools, 15,* 116-121.

Morgan, M. (1982). Television and adolescents' sex role stereotypes: A longitudinal study. *Journal of Personality and Social Psychology, 43,* 947-955.

Poindexter, P. M., & Stroman, C. A. (1980). Blacks and television: A review of the research literature. *Journal of Broadcasting, 25,* 103-122.

Roberts, D. F., & Bachen, C. M. (1981). Mass communication effects. *Annual Review of Psychology, 32,* 307-356.

Rushton, J. P. (1979). Effects of prosocial television and film material on the behavior of viewers. In L. Berkowitz (Ed.), *Advances in experimental social psychology* (Vol. 12). New York: Academic Press.

Staples, R., & Jones, T. (1985, May/June). Culture, ideology and black television images. *Black Scholar,* pp. 10-20.

Wade, B., & Poole, R. A. (1983). Responses to educational television: A case study. *Journal of Educational Television, 9,* 21-32.

Wallack, L. M. (1981). Mass media campaigns: The odds against finding behavior change. *Health Education Quarterly, 8,* 209-260.

Weigel, R. H., & Howes, P. W. (1982). Race relations on children's television. _Journal of Psychology,_ _111,_ 109-112.

Weigel, R. H., & Loomis, J. W. (1981). Televised models of female achievement revisited: Some progress. _Journal of Applied Social Psychology, 11,_ 58-63.

Withey, S. B. (1980). An ecological, cultural, and scripting view of television and social behavior. In S. B. Withey & R. P. Abeles (Eds.), _Television and social behavior: Beyond violence and children._ Hillsdale, NJ: Lawrence Erlbaum.

Zuckerman, D. M., Singer, D. G., & Singer, J. L. (1980). Children's television viewing, racial and sex-role attitudes. _Journal of Applied Social Psychology, 10,_ 281-294.

QUESTIONS AND ANSWERS

Q: In terms of its formal features, television seems to be very well suited to portray action and not well suited to portray inner reflections and thoughts of characters, because it's a visual medium and can't show things going on inside very well. It seems to me that other media are better suited to that, especially print, because there the inner reflections can be transformed into words on a page in a way that is much more difficult to do with television.

Norma Feshbach: I think your point is well taken and presents a challenge. However, we really haven't compared yet whether television or radio or magazines or books are optimal ways of stimulating internal feelings and thoughts.

Q: You [the questioner] have been seeing too much American television. You should observe Readers' Theater, Chamber Theater, or Story Theater, where they're doing creative things in staging prose and narrative literature. That can be done on television as well. That is some of the best theater that's current because it opens up a whole new realm of literature to performance, and it could be done on television.

Q: Dr. Winick, in your study did you look at the possibility of teaching families coping skills, things they could do together that would increase family cohesiveness and communication more than television does? As a teacher in a liberal arts college, I have a concern about how many books our students read. Recently I asked a freshman how many books he'd read last year, and he said he hadn't read any.

Charles Winick: There was a small amount of interaction of the sort you've described, but on their own very few people did those things. That kind of approach, however, is exactly what the Farmington, Connecticut, type of programs seek to achieve: that is, to present organized substitute activities that can be engaged in by the whole family. By and large these programs have not been very successful. I think the first one in the country was at the Horace Mann School in New York, a very prestigious school and difficult to get into. There the parents were told that, if their preschoolers watched more than 5 hours of television a week, the children would be dropped from the school. Even that had no effect! In other words, even with the parents doing everything possible to encourage the child to engage in desirable activities other than television, the children simply did not do so.

Q: Would you comment on the issue of whether television is destructive or supportive of American family life? You have some interesting findings on that issue.

Charles Winick: The social cohesion factor was shown in Caplow and his associates' follow-up of the Middletown studies. There you will find practically nothing on the effect of television in spite of the fact that it's the greatest single change in Middletown since the two previous studies. But they briefly describe one significant change: Just about the only thing that couples and members of families do together that cuts across all class and caste lines is watching television together. That is the unique development since the 1920s and 1930s, and that seems to be the major effect of television, namely holding the family together. In my study, I found this to be a very central function and one that was cited in over three-fifths of the homes.

PART
V

Social Science Research
and Future Visions
of Television

This part discusses several themes. They include how social science research on television is typically done, how it should be done, what some of its substantive findings are, and what its findings suggest about the future of television and the visual media in general. Also discussed are issues of how research can feed into media policy decisions, how television program "quality" can be assessed and improved, and how technological advances are likely to affect television programming, viewer behavior, and public policy controversies.

The authors in this section represent a rich range of backgrounds. Several of them are professors who are widely known for their media research (Aimee Dorr, Elihu Katz, George Comstock, and W. Russell Neuman). Several have been network or broadcasting industry officials as well as media researchers (Philip A. Harding, Elihu Katz, and John Abel), while John P. Blessington was a longtime educator before becoming a network official. In addition, the commentary section includes contributions from Guy Lometti and Horst Stipp, who are the directors of social research for ABC and NBC, as well as ideas from other well-known media researchers.

The first chapter in the section, by Aimee Dorr, includes a brief but thorough overview of the many classes of broadcasting employees who have some say in the process of producing a program, and the limited impact that any of them can have. This underlines the complexity of the broadcasting system and the reasons that it may seem like a foreign culture to academic researchers. The chapter also points out the discouraging limits of social science knowledge that can be clearly applied to programming questions and indicates why the activities of academic researchers may not be welcomed by broadcasters. For those who are eager to work with broadcasters, however, it outlines ways to be professionally useful while avoiding complete cooptation by the system.

The next chapter, by Philip A. Harding, describes the little-known research efforts of the television networks as important mechanisms of social responsibility. Similarly, the commentary later in this section by other television network researchers points out the variety of questions they try to answer and how programmers may use their findings. Harding also responds to the attacks of critics who condemn the low "quality" of network programs that are enjoyed by millions of viewers, and thus he raises the issued of how program quality can be appropriately judged and whose standards should be used in the judging. Regarding the role of research on media policy issues, the chapter emphasizes the key importance of the "fit" between the policy questions and the research design and data that attempt to answer those questions. Harding offers several examples of research and interpretations that he considers too simplistic, and he particularly emphasizes the viewer's active role in perceptually shaping and modifying the incoming TV stimulus material. Finally, he makes some stringent recommendations concerning the desirable scope of any research that attempts to measure the social effects of media content.

Elihu Katz's chapter bears on the above points in its declaration that the "fit" of research findings should not be judged solely against the questions that broadcasters want to have answered. Drawing on his personal experiences as a broadcasting official as well as a researcher, Katz points out instances where the goals of the two groups may diverge, and other examples of situations where the input of researchers is particularly welcome. He particularly stresses the important role of critical research, which may ask questions uncomfortable to broadcasters about the basic structure and functions of the media—but questions that are very important to the society in which the media operate.

The chapter by John Abel points out a different dichotomy, that between media researchers and public policy officials who make decisions about media legislative and/or regulatory policies. He stresses the importance of marketplace theory in these policy decisions under the current administration, and he recommends that researchers should base their research questions on its principles. However, the following commentary raises contrasting assumptions about what is desirable programming and how the media preferences and needs of various societal groups should be met—particularly, how can children's programs be improved in both "quality" and prosocial content? This leads to important questions about whether research should have to prove harmful effects of media in order to bring about programming changes, or on the other hand, whether broadcasters' interest in serving the public should extend beyond the financial bottom line and the ratings.

George Comstock's chapter reviews the results of much research on the media and organizes them under 10 major propositions. Some of the key conclusions he reaches are that public opinion regarding the media is often inconsistent with viewer behavior, that people's liking or disliking for television is little related to their use of the medium, but that available time and prevailing social norms influence media use significantly. Though people's concern about the media as a political issue is generally low, audiences are likely to perceive television news reports as biased against their own viewpoints; and furthermore, most citizens have a poor understanding of the First Amendment right of free speech, which is so crucial to mass media policy in the United States. From archival and survey research findings such as these, Comstock makes predictions about future media trends and related policy implications.

W. Russell Neuman extends Comstock's analysis in the area of video technology, comparing the abundant promise of new technologies with contrasting trends in television programming and viewer media use. His prediction of an "empty cornucopia" is based on past observations that increased availability of video programming has led, surprisingly, to less diversity in typical citizens' viewing. He points out how these findings stem from the economics of the industry and the psychology of viewer behavior. He also warns of the resulting risk that the media's sense of public trusteeship may be lost or dimmed, and he concludes that new public policies and private initiatives may be needed to avoid these dangers.

Finally, John P. Blessington suggests that the future of television will be much like its past and present, with continuing debates and arguments about its desirable or undesirable effects. Based on his experience as an educator, he advances the sanguine view that television has very little of the harmful effects that its critics perceive, particularly because viewers' moral values stem from their upbringing and cannot be distorted by television or other media. Consistent with this view, he is also skeptical of the often-claimed great potential of TV for education and child development. Following in the media-uses-and-gratifications tradition, he considers television as a tool that viewers actively use in many different ways, some of them beneficial and some detrimental. Children who have grown up with television, he suggests, will use it more wisely and be less fearful of it than the current older generation.

AIMÉE DORR

24

WHEN SOCIAL SCIENTISTS COOPERATE WITH BROADCASTING

The relationships of social scientists with the broadcasting community are many and varied. Few are easy. Some are rewarding. All are intriguing. Here, I will explore only a few such relationships—those of independent social scientists who work cooperatively with the television industry as consultants or applied researchers focusing on television content and/or broadcast schedules.

The terms "social science" and "social scientist" in this chapter are a shorthand way of referring to those with formal training in social science who are concerned with television content and broadcast schedules. They do not refer to social scientists concerned with organizational structure, employee relations, stress, or any of the myriad other social science areas that are also relevant to the television industry. Some of the points to be made here no doubt apply to these social scientists as well as to those concerned with content and scheduling, but my comments are limited to the areas in which I have personal expertise and experience.

In my experience, social scientists are often frustrated that television creators and broadcasters do not want them and their knowledge. Therefore, I begin the chapter with a short analysis of the circumstances under which some cooperative relationship is likely between social scientists and the television community. I then briefly describe the complexity of the broadcasting system and illustrate the challenges social scientists experience when they enter this new and different culture. After emphasizing the very real limits of social science knowledge as a source of advice for broadcasters, I discuss the social scientist's dual, equally important goals of being useful and of escaping cooptation. It will be apparent that many essentially unresolvable difficulties attend cooperative relationships between social scientists and broadcasters, and some social scientists will surely choose to avoid such relationships. However, this chapter summarizes what can be done to foster a cooperative relationship.

NEEDING AND GETTING
AN INVITATION

In the United States, the television industry is not in any way required to work with social scientists. It can operate alone and usually does. It has its own culture, life-style, and products, and it is rich in resources. It succeeds in several important ways: Its members make lots of money; its products are very popular; and virtually everyone feels they are better off with television than without it. Those who create and broadcast television programming feel a commitment to and membership in the industry, and they find much of which to be proud.

Social scientists very often feel that those who create and broadcast television are impoverished in many of the areas in which social scientists are rich. We openly proclaim that they need our knowledge and research techniques, and privately we may believe they need our values as well. With our knowledge, we feel, they could create programs that convey valuable information, promote desirable social attitudes and behaviors, combat negative stereotypes, and generally contribute to personal and societal well-being. There is a clear and immediate need, we think, for us to play a role in broadcasting.

With such a common presumption of moral and intellectual superiority, social scientists are not very attractive to members of the television community. They do not believe their social values are any less meritorious than ours. They do not take kindly to social scientists' frequent attitudes of superiority, and they are loath to enter a relationship in which they might be treated as inferior. They take advantage of only a small portion of what we so willingly offer, limiting our input, and limiting even more the extent to which they take our input seriously.

If U.S. broadcasters are going to make use of the riches we social scientists have to offer, this must occur at their invitation so long as the current broadcasting structure and regulatory system remain in place. Right now we can point out broadcasting's needs, offer our assistance, make our resources known, and advertise our wares. But we would do well to assume a cooperative, respectful posture, for we cannot make them accept us and our goods. Those who create and broadcast television content will decide what their needs are, who they want to meet them, when they will be met, and how this will be done. If they believe we can help them to achieve *their* goals, they will invite us in. The invitation will almost certainly be for more limited action and influence than we would like, and final authority will rest with broadcasters, not us. If we accept the invitation, we will finally have our opportunity to assist broadcasters—at least in some ways. And we will encounter the following new problems.

CULTURAL COMPLEXITY

The social scientist who enters the television industry to serve as a consultant or researcher encounters a complex system. There are many participants in many different roles, interacting in a wide variety of ways. Each has a specialized jargon and a well-understood but not easily articulated knowledge of the processes and principles by which television content is created and broadcast. I will not provide a primer here on the production and scheduling process. In recent years there have been several excellent analyses and case studies published (e.g., Barnouw, 1977, 1978; Brown, 1971; Cantor, 1971, 1974, 1980; Elliott, 1972; Gitlin, 1983; Johnston & Ettema, 1982; Lesser, 1974; Turow, 1984). However, a brief outline of industry organization and operation will illustrate the complexity of the environment in which the social scientist must strive to make an impact.

Models of the industry vary, but most consider broadcasting to consist, at a minimum, of program creators, advertisers and advertising agencies, stations, networks, regulators, and audiences. The number and variety of roles, functions, and interactions within each of these types of organization are large, and the linkages between organizations are complex.

For social scientists concerned with television content and scheduling, the most important parts of the industry are program creators, advertisers and advertising agencies, networks, and stations. Program creators develop ideas for all kinds of content except advertising, obtain financial support for their proposals, secure broadcasting outlets, create the content, and deliver it to the broadcaster. Advertisers and advertising agencies develop products and advertising campaigns, create commercial advertisements, purchase advertising time on commercial television stations, and provide support to public stations in return for acknowledgment. In the early days of television, advertisers actually supported the production of particular programs or series (e.g., Campbell Soup supported "Lassie"). Today, some help support public Broadcasting System (PBS) programming and some support animated series for children (e.g., "He-Man" and "Masters of the Universe").

The three major commercial networks and a few other smaller commercial systems perform several different functions. They produce some programs themselves (e.g., news, morning news and talk shows, specials, sports) and involve themselves intimately with most of what is produced by others to be broadcast over network stations. They suggest ideas to creators, alter creators' ideas, work with creators to shape a program or series, censor language, action, and images, and concern themselves with accuracy and impact. In short, they have a hand in program production from beginning to end, even though the production company is an independent organization. Networks also conduct research to assist in developing or improving programming and to aid in marketing. They create the schedule for most of each broadcast day and for all of prime time, when most Americans watch television. The networks promote themselves, their stations, and their programs; and they sell time for commercials that meet their standards for fairness, accuracy, and presentation techniques.

Television stations broadcast program content (most of which they buy), advertising (for which they sell time), and other nonprogram content (which they produce or receive from other providers), and usually produce some content of their own (e.g., local news, a Sunday talk show, an afternoon children's show). Most stations are affiliated with one of the three major networks, the Public Broadcasting System, or a "minor" network. In larger cities, there are independent stations as well, commercial stations supported by the sale of advertising time in the local market. The most-watched television content is broadcast on a station owned and operated by or affiliated with a major network, and the great majority of programs broadcast on independent stations were first created for and broadcast on network stations.

In the past few years broadcasting has become further complicated by a proliferation of broadcasting outlets, diversification of program producers, and intermingling of participants and processes once quite separate. Today, cable, direct broadcast satellite, pay over-the-air and cable television systems, and video recorders supplement the traditional outlets of local over-the-air commercial and public stations. The total amount of programming needed for these many outlets is truly phenomenal. Many cable systems and pay channels are involved in the production of new programming for their own use, as a means of both increasing their supply of good material and differentiating themselves from competitors. While some are doing for themselves what used to be done for them by others, others are finding new ways to intermingle. Movie companies produce for theaters, television, and home video; television companies produce movies; toy companies support the production of cartoon series featuring their products; and networks buy into a product line based on a television series.

The major regulator of television is the Federal Communications Commission (FCC), created by Congress in 1933. The FCC is responsible for ensuring that television stations, which the FCC licenses, operate in the public interest, convenience, and necessity. It may not directly regulate content, but it may stipulate what patterns of performance constitute fulfillment of a broadcaster's obligations. The FCC has typically been concerned that community interests and issues be represented in local programming, that the programming needs of various groups (e.g., children, cultural or linguistic minorities) be met, that informational functions be fulfilled, that overcommercialization be avoided, and that opposing viewpoints (and politicians) be given fair and equitable representation. The Federal Trade Commission is responsible for truth and fairness in the commercial advertising that is broadcast on television. Other federal agencies oversee the business function of the participants in broadcasting, making sure, for example, that the networks do not create a monopoly or cooperate in their scheduling.

The audience comes last, even though it is probably first in the hearts of social scientists. Audiences are what networks and commercial stations are selling to advertisers. Station and network income depends on having a very large number of people, with expendable incomes, tuned in to their programs. In this way, audiences also influence what is produced, when it is broadcast, and how long it survives. Programs that will be watched by the largest possible number of consumers are what will be produced and broadcast on commercial stations. Even PBS stations need many viewers and subscribers if they are to survive, and their most popular programs are again the most likely to be supported for more production.

This is indeed a complex, interacting environment in which many, many people directly shape content, and they do not all have the same set of priorities, perspectives, and abilities. It is hard to put one's finger on any individual who is the person in charge, the power behind the throne, the party responsible for program content, the villain, the culprit, or the meritorious one. In the heyday of concern about televised violence, most social scientists knew little about broadcasting. They were baffled—even outraged—when virtually every participant in broadcasting claimed to be interested in "doing good television" and avoiding violence, and pointed the finger at other participants as being responsible either for thwarting efforts to do good television or for contributing to violence in television (see, for example, Baldwin & Lewis, 1972).

OPERATING IN A COMPLEX SYSTEM

Today, there is much more formal knowledge about the broadcasting industry and about the processes and players involved in creating and scheduling television content. We understand the dynamics and complexities better. Few would now be shocked to learn that each participant felt that others in the system directly and indirectly constrained his or her choices, options, and opportunities. Few individuals are fully prepared for the challenges involved in serving effectively as a consultant or applied researcher in such an environment, particularly when their ideas run counter to conventional broadcasting wisdom or practice.

Suppose that a social scientist is hired to give advice or to conduct applied research that should affect the development of a television series. Many people will definitely have a direct, identifiable role in determining whether the social scientist's input is used or used well. Among the program creators, the writers, story editor, director, producer, camera people, tape-film editor, animators and actors for animation, and actors for live action will make contributions to the realization of a series to which the social scientist is providing input. At the network, the program department staff member in charge of this series, several levels of programming executives, the broadcast standards staff member in charge of this series, and one or more levels of broadcast standards executives will also make a difference. At a bare minimum, this amounts to at least 16 people who will directly affect the way in which a social scientist's input will be handled.

In reality, many more people are likely to have a hand in determining the fate of the social scientist's contribution. Usually more than 16 program creators and network staff will be directly involved. It is also quite likely that findings from network program research with representative audiences will make a difference, and fairly likely that input from the social research, community relations, marketing, and sales divisions of the network will matter. Whether advertisers and advertising agencies will have any direct impact depends on the particular arrangements under which the series is being produced. Ordinarily, advertisers' impact comes indirectly through subtle shaping of content by production companies and networks to conform to their images of programs that advertisers will find attractive when buying commercial time. Similarly, the impact of stations, regulators, and audiences on program development is ordinarily mostly indirect, in that program creators and the networks are aware of their interests and attempt to take them into account.

Given the large number of people from different units and organizations and the multiplicity of perspectives and interests directly affecting program production, the social scientist finds it hard to function in such a way that the finished program is different from what would otherwise have been created. A consultant's suggestion accepted by network programming staff may be consciously rejected or altered by broadcast standards or by any number of program creators. Suggestions may be imperfectly or even inaccurately realized by well-meaning program creators, who did not fully understand the point or did not have the artistic skill to realize it in the program. Scheduling suggestions that are liked by programming may be rejected by sales or public relations people or by station managers, with whom the social scientist has no interaction. Such experiences are commonplace for the social scientist who serves as a consultant or applied researcher for broadcasting, especially because he or she often suggests something different from the norm for those who make their living in broadcasting.

A further complication in affecting programming or scheduling is that it takes many months, sometimes even years, to develop a program idea, get it produced, and have it aired on television. Each step in the process is another chance for a "misfire," and—whatever the choice—each step tends to narrow options and restrict flexibility for revision and repair. The social scientist, then, cannot just step in once for a short time and be certain that whatever has been agreed on will actually be implemented down the road. Nor can he or she just step in anywhere in the process and expect that any suggestion could be implemented. There are windows within the production and scheduling processes where people are ready to make choices or changes of a particular type and where such choices and changes can be made without undue costs. Outside these windows, the same input is likely to get little serious attention.

CULTURAL DIFFERENCES

As if the complexity of the broadcasting system were not enough, the social scientist who attempts to work cooperatively with it soon recognizes some essential differences in the operative goals, values, knowledge, and skills of most social scientists and most broadcasters. No matter what material is being produced for whom, social scientists are likely to give less weight to entertainment, creativity, artistry, production quality, budget, deadlines, marketing, and distribution, and more weight to enlightenment, education, and communicative clarity than are those in broadcasting. Particularly in commercial broadcasting, the need to attract very large audiences is one that social scientists ignore much more easily than do broadcasters. Of course, their jobs, not ours, depend on achieving this goal.

Those who create programs—especially entertainment programs— often complain that social scientists want to take the heart out of television. They see us as ignoring feelings in favor of logic and dry facts and as eschewing pleasure in favor of boring didacticism. They also see us, as have some of our own (Gans, 1974), as insufferable elitists who fail to appreciate the positive features of popular culture and perhaps even disdain any cultural product that succeeds in appealing to the masses, simply because it does appeal to them. And they know we are not artists or members of a creative community and thus cannot possibly place proper value on artistic expression and creativity. They also realize that their reference group is other members of the television industry, while ours is other social scientists.

There are very substantial differences in the knowledge and skills of most social scientists and broadcasters. We notice that they have little formal knowledge of perception, attention, linguistics, cognition, learning, instruction, persuasion, social influence, socialization, child development, social roles, or any other area of social science. Knowledge in any one of these areas could legitimately inform program development and make content more accurate, useful, understandable, and impactful.

Some have argued explicitly or implicitly (e.g., Cantor, 1972; Noble, 1975; Siegel, 1980) that those who produce children's television would do a far better job if they at some time had some formal training in child development. Others (e.g., Ettema, 1980; Lesser, 1974) have sought means of bringing the disparate knowledge and skills of program creators and social scientists together into a functional system in which the final product profits from the specialized contributions of each. So far, no one has suggested that social scientists should learn to develop program ideas, write scripts, edit tape, or sell advertising time; but those would also be ways of bridging the disciplinary gap.

Because social scientists (and other television critics) find much on television to disparage, many of them have tended to regard those in broadcasting as lacking in positive personal and social values. Such a perception is accurate for some small percentage of people in the television community, just as it is accurate for some small percentage of social scientists. However, there is a growing recognition that organizational norms, structures, and processes—rather than individual values—substantially influence what is produced and broadcast (Cantor, 1980; Ettema, 1982; Hirsch, 1978; Stein, 1979). This is not to discount entirely the contributions that individuals—particularly producers and program executives—can make to the artistic and social elements of programming, not to deny that there are places where an individual may significantly influence content (Newcomb & Alley, 1982). However, one cannot simply look at a television program and infer the personal or social values of the individuals involved in its production and distribution.

AN ANTHROPOLOGICAL APPROACH

In the face of the complexity and novelty of the broadcasting environment, anthropology's perspectives and methods can be very helpful. Becoming a television consultant or applied researcher should be treated as a venture into a foreign culture—a culture the social scientists may know well at secondhand but must now understand firsthand. Previous assumptions about the culture should be put aside for the moment. Close observation, astute questioning, and calibrated participation should provide the evidence from which tentative understandings of the culture are formulated. One does not have to don khakis and a field hat, but the investigative spirit should be there.

Similarly, the anthropologist's simultaneous respect for other cultures and identification with his or her own culture should be brought into play. As already described, the values, language, roles, organizations, and interactional patterns in broadcasting differ from those in social science. These differences must be respected and treated as legitimate—at least within the confines of the culture of broadcasting. This does not mean that social scientists must agree with them or adopt them as their own. Instead, social scientists must walk the fine line that properly acknowledges and respects broadcasting's culture and simultaneously interjects elements of their own culture that can be helpful to broadcasting. If they can do that, then whatever advice they give is more likely to be considered useful by those in broadcasting.

THE LIMITS OF
SOCIAL SCIENCE KNOWLEDGE

One immediate problem for the consultant to broadcasting is that social science operates primarily in terms of abstractions, generalities, tendencies, and mean differences, whereas television operates in terms of specifics. We say "exposure to interpersonal physical aggression on television increases aggressive behavior in everyday life." Broadcasters say that some of their programs have to have some aggression, and they ask an amazing number of questions, many of which we cannot answer adequately based on existing research. This may seem an obvious point, but it is a serious stumbling block for social scientists cooperating with broadcasting. It is all too infrequently recognized by those who believe we have much to contribute to broadcasting.

To illustrate how difficult our task is, let me list 22 multipart questions I have actually been asked about the portrayal of aggression on television. I was tempted to give just a few sample questions, rather than this long (but not exhaustive) list; but only the longer list begins to convey the very real challenges faced by social scientists who wish to provide grounded advice to broadcasters. For each question, note how few unambiguous answers are provided by the enormous body of television and aggression research.

(1) Is it better if the aggression is shown explicitly or more implicitly? What do "explicitly" and "implicitly" mean in terms of what is shown on the screen, what is said, and what is suggested either visually or verbally?

(2) Does it matter whether a good person or a bad person is aggressive? Does it matter if the aggressor is a familiar or unfamiliar character in a series?

(3) What age, sex, ethnicity, nationality, social class, religion, occupation, physiognomy, and personality type should be assigned to those who aggress and those who receive aggression?

(4) Does it matter why characters aggress? What motives for aggression are good and bad to portray?

(5) Does it matter what happens to a character after he or she aggresses? Does this depend on his or her role (e.g., police officer vs. thug) or motive? If it ever matters, what consequences should be shown for whom, for what aggression, for what circumstances?

(6) Does it matter what happens to the victim? Does this depend on who the aggressor is, why he or she aggressed, who the victim is, why he or she was the victim, the severity of the consequences to the victim, or the realism of the show? If it ever matters, what should be shown?

(7) Do we need to show the consequences of aggression for every participant in aggression? Can the consequences just be described? If consequences need to be shown for only some participants, how does one decide which these participants are?

(8) Does it matter whether a weapon is used or not? Should the weapon be realistic or not? Should the weapon or the body be used in realistic ways in an aggressive encounter?

(9) Does it matter if the aggression occurs in some time other than the present? Does it matter is aggression is portrayed in a realistic or unrealistic past?

(10) What if the aggression is part of a comedy routine? What if it is part of a dream, a fantasy, a wish, or a recollection?

(11) Does it matter if the television program is puppetry, animation, or live action?

(12) Does it matter if the setting and story are presented as news, based on fact, realistic, or fantastic? What is the aggression is shown speeded up, slowed down, or in shades of blue?

(13) How long should an aggressive encounter last?

(14) How many aggressive encounters can safely be put into a half-hour or hour program? Does it matter where they occur during the half-hour or hour?

(15) In what sequence, with what clarity, and with what degree of contiguity and connection should the motives for aggression, the aggression itself, and the consequences for aggression be shown?

(16) For the average viewer, how many aggressive acts can safely be seen per viewing session or per week?

(17) Will it help if an advisory is put at the beginning or end of a program (or in *TV Guide*) saying it is all true, or all fantasy, or whatever? Will it help if the advisory suggests that children, aggressive persons, or other sensitive people should not watch the program?

(18) Will it help if all aggression is shown in programs airing after 9:00 p.m. or 10:00 p.m.?

(19) Will it matter if all shows containing aggression are shown back to back or if they are spread out over the week, or if they are preceded or followed by a lighthearted comedy or a warm family drama?

(20) If this show is put on the air, how many people are going to be hurt by it? What are these people like? Are they already aggressive?

(21) Since aggression adds excitement, drama, and intrigue to programs and helps to attract and keep an audience, what can replace aggression and still provide similar excitement and audience appeal?

(22) Since aggression is a fact of life for everyone in the United States, what harm can it do to show aggression (especially the fantasy aggression of crime drama series and cartoons) on television?

Similarly concrete and challenging questions arise for the creation and scheduling of commercial advertising, "prosocial" programming, educational programming, news, public affairs programming, movies, situation comedies, dramas, miniseries, docudramas, and all other forms of television content. The social scientist who wishes to use his or her professional expertise to advise broadcasting will have to work at this very concrete level—one quite different from our usual level of analysis and explication—if he or she is going to be at all useful.

All too often, however, our field fails to provide the clear, definitive evidence needed for authoritative advice (see Lindblom & Cohen, 1979, for an illuminating consideration of these issues). Consider again, for a moment, the 22 broadcaster questions. There is some research that can help answer nearly every question, but it is far from complete or conclusive. For example, some research shows that the consequences of aggressive actions affect recall of those actions and subsequent aggressive behavior. Actions followed by consequences are better remembered than actions followed by no consequences; positive consequences for aggressing (including negative consequences to the victim) encourage subsequent aggression, and negative consequences for aggressing (perhaps including injury, pain, and suffering for the victim and his or her family) discourage subsequent aggression. However, the studies supporting these generalizations are relatively small in number, do not include subjects who span the ages and other characteristics of most viewers, and usually employ artificial "television-like" stimuli, short-term exposure, and artificial measurement techniques. Moreover, they do not clarify how much difference the addition or omission of consequences makes to the negative effects of exposure to televised violence. Thus, social science research often does not provide a firm basis from which to derive a general recommendation about how to portray aggression on television.

It is also often difficult to use research as the basis from which to develop an accurate assessment or critique of a piece of existing or planned programming or scheduling. For instance, a network programming executive wants to know whether several scenes in a script will be frightening for children. The characters are mostly puppets, but life-size, compelling, and placed in an elaborate set (not on a puppet stage). There is some humor throughout. The potentially frightening parts cannot be portrayed extremely realistically (given the use of puppetry), but the script does not say enough about the visual details of the scenes to know what they will be like in any detail. The whole thing is presented as a fable, with the storyteller coming in and out of focus throughout, and set in a fantasy land. The program will be broadcast at a time when many children will view with other siblings and adults in the household. *Will these scenes be frightening or not, to a few children or many, to the intended audience of 6- to 12-year-olds viewing with their families or to others?* The social scientist consultant will be hard pressed to arrive at a definitive judgment, and it will be impossible to base it primarily on research findings. The script, like most situations the social scientists will encounter in working with broadcasting, contains far too many disparate, sometimes conflicting elements that our research does not tell us how to balance out, and it offers particularistic realizations of potentially frightening portrayals that are always different in some important ways from the materials used in our research.

The difficulties encountered in predicting audience reactions are legendary in broadcasting, where officials are always looking for the formula, pundit, seer, or program research that will let them identify the smash hits and the bombs before funding much production or settling on the broadcast schedule. Similar difficulties arise for anyone trying to predict people's responses to a particular situation. Two documented examples of problems in predicting people's responses to television content were published in the 1960s. In one study, the prize-winning children's shows from the biennial Prix Jeunesse (an international judging of television programs for children and youth) were tested in a cooperative project involving social scientists from five countries, including the country in which the program was produced. Although the programs were judged by highly qualified internationally known producers, writers, directors, and social scientists as best for children, children neither like them very much nor understood them very well (*Findings and Cognition,* 1969). In another study, adults were found to be highly inaccurate predictors of entertaining and boring segments of television programs intended for preschoolers, and better but not excellent predictors for preadolescents (Becker & Wolfe, 1960).

Social science itself, then, is at times an insubstantial base from which to provide advice to broadcasting. As a field it tends toward the general, while broadcasting deals in specifics. Research evidence itself is fragmentary and sometimes conflicting, and it rarely addresses the particular combination of elements in any specific instance of pro- gramming or scheduling. This is not to say that social science has nothing to contribute to broadcasting practice. I believe, along with most of my colleagues, that it has much to contribute. Rather, it is to emphasize that social science is a limited source of wisdom when it comes to broadcasting decisions.

BEING USEFUL

After the first hurdle of obtaining entry is passed, the challenge for the social scientist who wishes to cooperate with broadcasting is to be useful enough to be invited to stay or to return. There is no challenge, of course, if the social scientist is willing simply to be used as window dressing or as a "yes man," but nearly every social scientist who works with broadcasters has hopes of improving their programming and/or scheduling. To do so, he or she must learn enough about the culture of broadcasting to identify what social science knowledge can be used by those who create and schedule television content and to learn how to present that knowledge to them.

As discussed earlier, those who create and schedule television content must make innumerable decisions about the concrete details of programming and scheduling. The consultant who is going to base suggestions on social science theory and research needs a breadth of knowledge and a fine ability to apply that knowledge to very concrete problems. We cannot be very useful to broadcasters who must make exceedingly concrete choices (e.g., which photo to illustrate a news story, what age and ethnicity for the villainess, the order in which to broadcast three programs) if we are not prepared to talk concretely about their options.

The concrete suggestions we make must be ones that broadcasters could actually implement. Knowing the broadcasting culture helps enormously here. The suggestion that a male lead be changed to a female lead is fairly easy to implement while a series or program is being planned but quite costly to implement once a script has been written. The suggestion that an educational program or a preschool program be broadcast on a network Saturday morning is beyond the pale because it is widely believed (and probably true) that neither program would attract a large enough audience of children, teenagers, and adults to be competitive with the other networks. Both these suggestions may be reasonable from the social scientist's perspective, but there is no point in boring industry officials or, worse, losing credibility with them by offering suggestions they simply will not accept or at a time when they can no longer accept them.

Our implementable suggestions must also have some payoff for broadcasters if they choose to implement them. The kinds of payoffs will vary according to the situation. In some cases, it is enough that the broadcaster feels he or she has taken the advice of an expert so as to produce less harmful and/or more beneficial content or to schedule programs at better times. In other cases, the broadcaster needs to feel that he or she has avoided some critical or public protest or earned some acclaim because of the consultant's input. In still others, the broadcaster wants to see larger audiences, greater enjoyment or comprehension or knowledge in test audiences, more letters, greater sales, or some other concrete outcome. The one outcome the consultant to commercial broadcasting wants most to avoid is a smaller-than-anticipated audience for a show for which he or she gave advice on production or scheduling.

In selecting advice to give broadcasters, perhaps the major stumbling block for the consultant is ego (see Lindblom & Cohen, 1979). Most social scientists respect their field, believe it provides socially useful insights, and want broadcasters to regard them personally as knowledgeable and authoritative. When asked for advice, they want to give it. And they want their advice to come from social science theory and research, their special domain, not common sense, personal beliefs and values, or personal experiences—the domains of broadcasters and many other possible consultants as well. The pressures are strong to give authoritative advice, saying that it comes from our specialized training; but we need to be careful not to claim too much.

Every broadcaster I know ultimately acquires some sense of the debates among social scientists, of the shaky empirical foundations on which many theories and "facts" rest, and of the limits of social science research as a means of knowing. That broadcaster then finds any consultant who claims too much for himself, herself, or the field to be entirely lacking in credibility. Wise consultants will keep their ego in bounds and exercise modesty in their claims for expertness. In the long run that enhances credibility and usefulness.

Once one is able to identify advice that will be useful to broadcasters, the trick is to present it in an understandable, credible, and attractive manner. This is an art that has been the subject of some research (cf. Ettema, 1980; Johnston & Ettema, 1982; Lesser, 1974; Rothman, 1980). Research findings must be reduced to their essence (which means the findings and perhaps the barest bones of how they were obtained) and described in standard English. *All* details of the research must be at hand in case the broadcaster should want specifics, and these details must enhance the credibility of the findings (e.g., the sample was large, not small, and the stimuli were real television programs, not tapes the researcher made). The relevance of the findings to broadcasting decisions must be made clear without appearing to intrude on the prerogatives of broadcasters of to claim broadcasters' expertise for oneself. The so-called writers notebook was developed at the Children's Television Workshop as one means of doing this (Lesser, 1974). In the notebook, in-house researchers and out-of-house consultants enter suggestions for segments, scenes, characters, and the like based on social science theory and research and on ongoing program development research. Other means for translating research findings into practice include brief verbal sketches of sample applications of the research to the broadcaster's particular problem, brainstorming with creators and schedulers about how to put the research-based information into practice, and providing clips of previous programming that clearly embodies the advice (or clearly goes against it).

In summary, to make it worthwhile for broadcasters to work with social scientists, we must be able to choose our suggestions with broadcasting's realities firmly in mind, be concrete in the information we provide, offer implementable suggestions, make suggestions that will produce payoffs in the eyes of the broadcasters, be appropriately modest about what we have to offer, and present our advice in ways that will promote its acceptance and proper use by those who create and schedule television content.

NOT BEING CO-OPTED

Co-optation is an ever-present danger for the social scientist who succeeds in working with broadcasters. Understanding their culture, being able to operate effectively within it, and respecting it can all too easily lead to belonging to it. Social scientists can wake up one morning to find that they have implicitly, if not explicitly, bought into a value system that places very high priority on ratings or advertising revenue, or accepted the tenet that a prosocial children's series is impossible on network television. They may no longer exert even gentle pressure toward non-normative programming. Or consultants may find that it is suddenly too easy to give advice, because they have largely given up searching social science theory and research for the grounding from which to construct the advice.

Although social scientists sometimes unwittingly move too far toward joining broadcasters rather than advising them, broadcasters themselves will sometimes try to co-opt consultants. They occasionally want to use consultants to certify programming choices: A Saturday morning cartoon must be okay, they say, because child psychologists were paid to review every script; or a prime-time episode about racism must be praiseworthy because a social psychologist provided advice about stereotyping, racial attitudes, racism, and scapegoating. Broadcasters sometimes want to trot out their consultants for public relations purposes. They often want social scientists to adopt their values and provide advice consonant with these values (e.g., how to make programming more entertaining). And they certainly want social scientists to be pleased to work on any programming, no matter how unredeeming or banal.

There are no easy means to avoid co-optation, particularly if one wishes to continue to work with broadcasters. Some social scientists establish guidelines for themselves and periodically review their adherence to them (e.g., no work on programming with no redeeming social value, no public acknowledgment of their contributions, and regular polite assertions of broadcasting's responsibility to serve the public interest). Others maintain friendly relations with public interest groups or read their literature, so that they can compare what they have been doing with what public interest groups find troublesome in broadcasting. In other words, they look to public interest groups to identify problems, and then ask whether they have been part of the problem or part of the solution. Others simply trust that their good sense and firm grounding in social science will keep them on the straight and narrow or at least get them back rapidly when they stray.

OTHER RELATIONSHIPS
WITH BROADCASTING

The focus of this chapter has been on only one type of relationship between social scientists and broadcasters, the cooperative relationship in which the social scientist provides advice about the creation or scheduling of some television content. The goal has been to describe how the social scientist can create and sustain such a relationship and what can and cannot be achieved with such a relationship. However, such a relationship is neither the only possible nor the only desirable one between social science and broadcasting.

There are certain real costs associated with such a cooperative relationship. Many changes we might like to see in broadcasting will not come from such a relationship: for example, a weekday educational program for preschoolers, or quality children's programs until 9:00 each night, or an absence of action/adventure cartoons and crime drama programs on network stations. The contributions consultants can make will most often result in small changes with which it is often hard to be satisfied. Effecting those changes will require tact, vigilance, perspective taking, respect, and good humor in abundance. The effort involved in such cooperative endeavors will not ordinarily lead to scholarly publications that enhance one's reputation as a social scientist, and it will take time that might otherwise be given to such work.

In the face of these realities, many social scientists opt for other relationships with broadcasting. Some remain scholars who conduct and publish academic—and, more important, enlightening—research about television content and scheduling. Others set themselves up as television critics, using research to critique broadcasting, and keeping themselves always outside the system they seek to influence. Still others work with and through policymakers and citizens' action groups to influence broadcasting, often conducting critical or policy research that is useful in effecting changes that broadcasters do not themselves welcome. These roles are every bit as legitimate, desirable, useful, and productive in bringing social science knowledge to bear on broadcasting as is the role of consultant or researcher cooperating with those who create and schedule television content. Sometimes they are, in fact, the best ways to effect change.

When social scientists do succeed in cooperating with broadcasting, they will not radically alter television content or its scheduling. But if they are good, they will make some positive contribution to television and its viewers. Together with broadcasters they will have helped to create and broadcast television content that does more good and avoids more harm than it otherwise would. And this is a goal on which many people can agree.

REFERENCES

Baldwin, T. F., & Lewis, C. (1972). Violence in television: The industry looks at itself. In G. A. Comstock & E. A. Rubinstein (Eds.), *Television and social behavior: Vol. 1. Media content and control* (pp. 290-373). Washington, DC: Government Printing Office.

Barnouw, E. (1977). *Tube of plenty: The evolution of American television.* New York: Oxford University Press.

Barnouw, E. (1978). *The sponsor: Notes on a modern potentate.* New York: Oxford University Press.

Becker, S. L. & Wolfe, G. J. (1960). Can adults predict children's interest in a television program? In W. Schramm (Ed.), *The impact of educational television* (pp. 195-213). Urbana: University of Illinois Press.

Brown, L. (1971). *Television: The business behind the box.* New York: Harcourt Brace Jovanovich.

Cantor, M. G. (1971). *The Hollywood producer: His work and his audience.* New York: Basic Books.

Cantor, M. G. (1972). The role of the producer in choosing children's television content. In G. A. Comstock & E. A. Rubinstein (Eds.), *Television and social behavior: Vol. 1. Content and control* (pp. 259-289). Washington, DC: Government Printing Office.

Cantor, M. G. (1974). Producing television for children. In G. Tuchman (Ed.), *The TV establishment: Programming for power and profit* (pp. 103-118). Englewood Cliffs, NJ: Prentice-Hall.

Cantor, M. G. (1980). *Prime-time television: Content and control.* Newbury Park, CA: Sage.

Elliott, P. (1972). *The making of a television series: A cast study in the sociology of culture.* Newbury Park, CA: Sage

Ettema, J. S. (1980). The role of educators and researchers in the production of educational television. *Journal of Broadcasting, 24,* 487-498.

Ettema, J. S. (1982). The organizational context of creativity: A cast study from public television. In J. S. Ettema & D. C. Whitney (Eds.), *Individuals in mass media organizations: Creativity and constraint* (pp. 91-106). Newbury Park, CA: Sage

Findings and cognition on the television perception of children and young people based on the prize-winning programs of Prix Jeunesse 1966 Patrik and Putrik and Clown Ferdi. (1969).

Munich, Germany: Internationales Zentralinstitut fur das Jugend-und Bildungsfernsehen.

Gans, H. J. (1974). *Popular culture and high culture: An analysis and evaluation of taste*. New York: Basic Books.

Gitlin, T. (1983). *Inside prime time* New York: Pantheon.

Hirsch, P. (1978). Occupational, organizational, and institutional models in mass media research. In P. Hirsch, P. Miller, & F. Kline (Eds.), *Strategies for mass communication research* (pp. 13-42). Newbury Park, CA: Sage.

Johnston, J., & Ettema, J. S. (1982). *Positive images: Breaking stereotypes with children's television*. Newbury Park, CA: Sage.

Lesser, G. S. (1974). *Children and television: Lessons from Sesame Street*. New York: Random House.

Lindblom, C. E., & Cohen, D. K. (1979). *Usable knowledge: Social science and social problem solving*. New Haven, CT: Yale University Press.

Newcomb, H. M., & Alley, R. S. (1982). The producer as artist: Commercial television. In J. S. Ettema & D. C. Whitney (Eds.) *Individuals in mass media organizations: Creativity and constraint* (pp. 69-90). Newbury Park, CA: Sage.

Noble, G. (1975). *Children in front of the small screen*. Newbury Park, CA: Sage.

Rothman, J. (1980). *Using research in organizations: A guide to successful application*. Newbury Park, CA: Sage.

Siegel, A. E. (1980). Research findings and social policy. In E. L. Palmer & A. Dorr (Eds.), *Children and the faces of television—Teaching, violence, selling* (pp. 219-231). New York: Academic Press.

Stein, B. (1979). *The view from Sunset Boulevard: America as brought to you by the people who make television*. New York: Basic Books.

Turow, J. (1984). *Media industries: The production of news and entertainment*. New York: Longman.

25

SOCIAL SCIENCE RESEARCH
AND MEDIA POLICY ISSUES:
A Question of Fit

Television, virtually from the time of its arrival in the late 1940s, has been the focus of concerns as to its possible effects on the society at large, and particularly on society's youngest members. This newest of the mass media—in much the same way as radio and motion pictures before it—came to be seen as far more than simply a vehicle of mass entertainment and information For many observers, including media scholars, it assumed the status of a social issue.

It is highly desirable for media researchers to have an understanding of the configuration of the American system of television, of the dynamic interrelationships between the content of the medium—programming and advertising—and such other key factors as audience tastes and preferences, advertiser support, and government regulation. Understanding these realities, the non-industry researcher will be far better equipped to conceive meaningful research questions and, thereafter, to analyze and interpret the results of studies addressed to those questions. Among these television realities are what might be called the "mechanisms of social responsibility" that have evolved over a period of many years at the major television networks but are not widely recognized. One of them, the CBS Office of Social and Policy Research, has been my responsibility since 1984.

The Office of Social and Policy Research

Counterpart units have long been in place at ABC and NBC, and the history of the CBS Office of Social and Policy Research goes back to 1962, when it was formed due to the company's recognition of how little was really known about the social effects, positive and negative, that this relatively new mass medium of television might be having. Its first director was Dr. Joseph T. Klapper, one of this country's most distinguished social scientists and author of the classic text *The Effects of Mass Communication* (Klapper, 1960). From its beginning, the department's primary mission has been the conception and execution of major streams of research that would help to illuminate television's social functions and effects. The focus over the years has been on the relationship between television and its audiences, not only the antisocial influence its critics have attributed to the medium, but also the place television occupies in the lives of the American people, the uses they make of it, the satisfactions—and dissatisfactions—they derive from it.

Pursuit of the office's mission has always proceeded independently of CBS's day-to-day business concerns; in that sense, the unit's character has traditionally been more academic than commercial in nature. In addition, a good deal of the research that has come out of the department has been carried out collaboratively with members of the academic research community rather than being done entirely in-house.

An activity that the office does *not* conduct is the testing of audience responses to individual candidate programs for the network's schedule. This is handled at CBS through the Program Analysis unit, and the data it develops are one—but only one—factor in the ultimate decisions by programming people as to what appears (and remains) on the CBS Television Network. Obviously, each network wishes to present entertainment programs that will be as widely viewed and enjoyed as possible; that is true whether the programming is intended for children, adults, or general audiences. The Program Analysis findings, ratings, special studies of individual programs, the instincts and judgment of professional programming executives—all these go into the decision-making process that produces a network's schedule. So research on audience responses plays a key role in evaluating the popularity of what television is offering, and in recommending changes where they seem to be indicated.

The "Quality" Issue

As far back as the early days of radio, the goal of presenting programs that large numbers of people would enjoy led to the assumption by media critics that something called "quality" was being sacrificed, that there weren't enough (if any) "good" or "uplifting" programs available. However, these words are very subjective in their meanings. From long experience I've found that, with very rare exceptions, no two people define them in quite the same way.

The problem becomes even more acute when adults look at—and often recoil from—programs designed expressly for children. From the perspective of an adult critic of television, much of the Saturday morning children's schedule consists of the "wrong" kind of animation, the "wrong" kind of music, and "wrong" stories—ones that perhaps amuse their young viewers, but have no other redeeming feature. However, that objection misses the point: These shows weren't developed for the edification of television's critics or any other adult, but for the purpose of entertaining young children, whose cognitive and perceptual capabilities (to say nothing of tastes) are so very different from those of adults. If they succeed in that objective, do they not possess—from the *child's* perspective—quality? And if they did not possess it, wouldn't their audiences turn away from them in such numbers that their advertising sponsors would drop them and thus ensure the programs' disappearance from the air?

The Larger Issue:
Fitting the Answers to the Questions

Let me now turn to the question that is implicit in the title of this chapter. The media policy issues that I want to discuss are those springing from historical concerns about television's effects, referred to earlier. For example, *are* there measurable social harms that flow from television's depictions of violence or sexuality, from its portrayals of women or minorities, from its advertising or particular products— harms that would lead policymakers in the public sector, or the industry itself, to consider remedial changes? Just as important, would the consequences of the proposed changes be the ones intended, or would they simply constrict the traditional freedoms of expression so precious to our society?

Another word in the title needs clarification: "fit." What is meant by that is the degree of correspondence between the questions that policymakers and others have raised about television, and the answers research is able to provide. As researchers, we would agree that where research *can* contribute to the resolution of policy questions, it should be utilized. In recent years, the policymaking community has come increasingly to solicit the input of social science research for that purpose. But, having achieved a measure of acceptance in this regard, we research practitioners are now obliged to ensure the "tightness of fit" between the policy questions put to us and the answers we provide.

This question of fit has been largely ignored, perhaps on the theory that *any* empirically derived information is superior to the value judgments previously (and often even now) brought to bear on such issues. Still, it's not very helpful in seeking answers to media-policy questions when, for example, we turn to research that was actually carried out *before* those questions were ever formulated. This is not to deny the contributions afforded by prior research of a *basic* nature—for example, the work of Piaget and others in identifying the stages of children's cognitive development, which has been cited often and usefully in issues having to do with children and the media. But there have been cases where the data used were actually gathered for applications related indirectly, if at all, to the issue at hand. That represents an unfortunate reversal of the traditional research process, one in which studies originally conducted for other applied research purposes are "force-fit" to make them responsive to policymakers' immediate needs. Or alternatively, the policy questions themselves are sometimes adjusted to make them better correspond to the data available. Either way, it's a square-pegs-in-round-holes situation and not a proper use of science.

One classic example of this was the Federal Trade Commission's (1978) extensive inquiry into children's advertising. A number of the key studies drawn on for policy guidance in that proceeding had in fact been carried out some years earlier and, in terms of their conceptualization and application to the issues the Commission was raising, were clearly being interpreted post hoc. Another unfortunate example was observed in the 1982 revisiting by the National Institute of Mental Health of the research concerning the social consequences of television violence (NIMH, 1982, pp. 103-173). The verdict of that exercise—that television violence *is* implicated in aggressive behavior—was reached not through any demonstration of causation, but rather through the "convergence" of results from a number of studies, each one of which had designs that precluded demonstration of causality. Ironically, the one study included in the review that was expressly designed to detect causal relationships between the viewing of television violence and subsequent aggressive behavior in fact failed to find any (Milavsky, Stipp, Kessler, & Rubens, 1982).

These two examples, in somewhat different ways, illustrate failures of fit between policy questions and research-based answers. At a more basic level, it is disturbing that research often provides, and policymakers accept, simplistic responses to very complex issues. Implicit in many of the media policy issues discussed over the years is the idea that television is a contributing influence—perhaps the *major* influence—on unhappy social outcomes of one sort or another, such as criminal behavior, problem drinking, drug abuse, negative perceptions of minorities, and so on. The underlying model, whether it is articulated or not, is essentially a stimulus-response one, indicating that television acts *directly* on the viewer to produce these consequences. But, clearly, by now we know enough about the interaction between television and its viewers to question so simplistic a model. Television research is well past the point in its history when the viewer was assumed to be a passive and vulnerable creature who simply absorbed and responded to *whatever* content was transmitted. More recent and empirically grounded conceptions of the viewer/television relationship indicate that its character is highly interactive (Mendelsohn, 1986). The raw content of television is constantly being processed in the individual's consciousness—modulated, shaped, even changed outright—so that the correspondence between that content and perception is apt to be rather loose.

On this same point, concerning the influence of television, British social scientist Anthony Smith (1985) had this to say:

> The influences that are the objectives of research to capture and explain are deemed to occur at the point of connection between screen and mind; so much attention is concentrated on filling that tiny gap in the complex cycles of connections between medium and society that the cultural location of the influence, the self of the viewer, has been almost casually ignored, as if it were not relevant to the project of research.

Thus, in any discussion of television's "influences"—which are, of course, at the heart of many key policy questions—we have to recognize the mediating role of the viewer's self. The model should not be stimulus-response but rather stimulus-*organism*-response. This is the approach we should have been studying in depth all along, but for the most part we haven't.

Finally, I want to touch on the response component of the model—the outcome variable, be it a behavior, an attitude, or a perception, which is presumed to be linked to the television stimulus. Of course, such outcomes are determined by multiple influences, but far too often media research designs make no provision to measure the contributions of these other influences, and the focus is entirely or very largely on the television-viewing variable.

Here is one example: It has been seriously proposed that broadcast advertising for beer and wine should be banned on the grounds that such advertising fosters alcohol abuse among the young. Congressional hearings on the subject produced some modestly conceived research (Atkin & Block, 1981) that did little to support the alleged effects of advertising. Conspicuous by its absence, however, was any serious discussion of the *non*-media antecedents of alcohol abuse. Had anyone taken the trouble, as CBS did, to commission an impartial review of pertinent literature from the alcohol studies field (Braucht, 1985) it would have been clear that the roots of alcohol abuse among young people lie principally in the family context, and later as the child matures, in the influence of peer group behavior. In contrast to these vastly more direct and personal influences, television's portrayals of drinking—whether in advertising or programming—have yet to be causally implicated in problem-drinking by the young.

The moral is that if by omission we ignore other powerful determinants of the behavior in question and concentrate predominantly on its relationship to television, than our research findings cannot be adequately responsive to the policy questions that spawned them. Again, it comes back to that matter of *fit*.

Recommendations

In the interest of tightening that fit in future research, I would strongly urge both the policymaking and research communities that two preparatory steps *always* be taken before even beginning to design new studies addressed to a particular policy issue. The first step is systematically to search out, review, and synthesize all research on the policy issue wherein television was among the variables measured. In an age of on-line databases, this is less burdensome than it sounds; but, in any case, this kind of evaluative inventory of the evidence accumulated to date is absolutely essential as a means for setting the direction in which new research should go. The second crucial prerequisite is that we identify in advance the known *non*-media antecedents of the particular behaviors, attitudes, or perceptions whose influence by television we plan to study. To do so requires that we draw on the expertise of scholars who have studied the subject in question at length, but who may never have thought to explore its linkage to television. Then, using an interdisciplinary approach and having identified the key correlates and provided for their measurement in the study design, the research that emerges will be richer, more systematic, and better-grounded in the real world.

The crux of these recommendations is that matter of *fit*—being very sure that the questions we put to research are framed in such a way as to fit the underlying and often amorphous policy issue they are intended to address.

In one of his papers, George Comstock quoted a wonderful line from Thomas Pynchon's book *Gravity's Rainbow*: "If they can get you asking the wrong questions, they don't have to worry about the answer." In the area of policy-oriented research, I think we always have to remind ourselves of how easy it is to ask the wrong questions. When that happens, when the questions we're responding to aren't the ones that *should* have been asked, then our research necessarily loses much of its considerable power to aid in the resolution of important policy issues.

REFERENCES

Atkin, C., & Block, M. (1981). *Content and effects of alcohol advertising.* Springfield, VA: U.S. Department of Commerce. (NTIS No. 82-123142)

Braucht, G. N. (1985). *Problem drinking: A review of current scientific knowledge.* Denver and New York: Department of Psychology, University of Denver, and Office of Social and Policy Research, CBS/Broadcast Group.

Federal Trade Commission (1978). *FTC staff report on television advertising to children,* 43, Fed. Reg. 17967.

Klapper, J. T. (1960). *The effects of mass communication.* New York: Free Press.

Mendelsohn, H. (1986). *The limits of television's social influence.* Unpublished manuscript.

Milavsky, J. R., Stipp, H. H., Kessler, R. C., & Rubens, W. S. (1982). *Television and aggression: A panel study.* New York: Academic Press.

National Institute of Mental Health. (1982). *Television and behavior: Ten years of scientific progress and implications for the eighties: Vol. 2. Technical reviews.* Washington, DC: Government Printing Office.

Smith, A. (1985, Fall). The influence of television. *Daedalus, 114,* 1-14.

ELIHU KATZ **26**

THE RELATIONSHIP BETWEEN BROADCASTERS AND RESEARCHERS

People involved in broadcasting know that researchers sometimes get promoted to be bosses in the television system. The first point I wish to make is that that does not necessarily promise good research. I know from my own experience as the first director of Israel Television.

Israel Television was established late—not until 1968, in the wake of the Six Days' War, which pushed the government toward establishing television after years of hesitation. The reasons for founding it were somewhat roundabout. The Arab states all had television, and some had used it successfully for propaganda during the 1967 war, or so it was thought; as a result, Israel felt vulnerable. After that war, Israel hoped to establish some kind of dialogue with the million or so Arabs in the occupied territories; and the medium of television was thought by policymakers to be more humane somehow than the medium of radio, which was viewed as a more fighting medium. In this situation, where television was being introduced for the first time into a country, if I had still been wearing a research hat I could have tried to generate answers to two very big questions, which would have brought me a lot more immortality than being the first director of Israel Television.

One crucial question was about the effects of the introduction of television on a reasonably modern society. We could have laid the foundation for before- and-after work of the sort we all dream of, the sort we wish could have been done before and after Gutenberg— nothing less! There was such an opportunity, but it was missed. We did something, but nothing in any way like that. That was partly because I had arrived in Israel only relatively recently, so I didn't yet have a cadre of students who were working in the field, and also because I was occupied elsewhere—running television rather than studying it.

The other big question was whether the medium could be used effectively in establishing some kind of dialogue with the Arabs in the occupied territories. We did some reasonably interesting things, which still have not been followed up in the "after" phase; we established some base lines that I hope someone will go back to. For example, in the area of visual perception, we investigated whether people's image of the map of the Middle East was visually changed as a result of the introduction of television. But my experience illustrates that it isn't necessarily good for research when researchers get promoted out of research and into a managerial role.

My second points is that crisis helps. When the next war came in 1973, I was a researcher again and was asked to advise on the use of television in a war. What could television do for the home front? We studied very specific questions, to which very specific answers were required. The "fit" was clear both to the researchers and to the broadcasters. What were the uses of television in that crisis? Which medium served these needs best? What kind of content, what kind of genre, would serve what kinds of functions?

For example, what sort of program best served the felt need for the integration of society? We had a very specific answer to that: Among the possible programs available at that time, the sense of integration was most strengthened by live broadcasting of homemade—that is to say, Israeli—entertainment from army bases. By contrast, other kinds of entertainment, especially imported entertainment, were found rather annoying under such circumstances.

There were other questions that we could answer very directly. Did action-adventure programs exacerbate tension or reduce it? The answer was that they reduced it. Did advertising offend? The answer was yes. What about Arabic programs, which shared the one television channel with the Hebrew programs—did they offend? The answer was "a little, but never mind, they belong there." Did all-night radio (on the air around the clock for the first time) keep people from performing at work the next day? The answer was no, it rather helped them. So crisis helps in the relationship between broadcasters and researchers. The broadcasters need the researchers under such circumstances to advise and to validate their choices.

Like societal crisis, organizational crisis helps as well. England has royal commissions that repeatedly review the state and the prospects of broadcasting in that country. The British Broadcasting Corporation (BBC) was under observation on the eve of the establishment of the Annan Commission on the future of broadcasting in England. During these periods of siege, researchers are often recruited because the organization is in crisis and is interested in independent, professional, but friendly voices. So when I was asked to help in preparing a document on what the BBC might do in the area of social research, I found a lot of cooperation, a lot of interest in the sorts of questions that might be asked and answered by an alliance of social researchers and broadcasters. At that moment it was also very helpful that I *did* have experience as a broadcaster. It helped a lot to gain the confidence of the people I was working with in the BBC at the time.

But even then, the most cooperation and hope came from those departments that were less powerful within the organization: The adult education department, the children's department, and so on, looked to an alliance with researchers with more hope and more genuine willingness to cooperate than did more powerful departments such as the news. For example, children's television in England was then fighting against the importation of "Sesame Street," which was perceived to be frenetic and fast-paced, like American advertising. At least that was the argument of the BBC's children's department, which thought that its own television programs for children were more authentic and better suited to the longer attention span expected of British children. They hoped that research would be an ally in that debate. (In the end the BBC did not broadcast "Sesame Street." Even if the program's values are considered culturally acceptable, the production aspects of the program—for example, the pacing—are clearly not culture-free and have an American message, quite different from that of other cultures, which other cultures might not wish to convey to their children.)

Finally, let me point out that research often doesn't work when it is addressed to questions that are unasked or to departments that are very powerful. In the wake of my report to the BBC, a set of studies was undertaken, both in the United States and in England, on remembering and understanding the news. A lot of good work was done in both countries on that subject, showing the real difficulties in digesting the normal television news diet. However, such research is usually not attended to by decision makers because they make no room for such questions and don't wish to be told the answers.

What we're dealing with here is the great debate between so-called administrative and critical research—where administrative research is essentially defined from the point of view of the policy-related questions of the decision maker. There are very good examples of those often being the wrong questions. Here is a big example, a radical example, of the difference between administrative and critical research: If a researcher is asked, "How do people make up their minds between two presidential candidates, or two products, or whatever? " the question presumes that there is freedom of choice, which reflects the basic policy orientation of the decision maker or of the organization that asked the researcher to answer the question. But the researcher might prefer to ask larger questions: "Are these two choices serious? Is there an important difference between the choices? Is there genuine freedom to choose?"—quite different questions than the one presented to him or her. When taking such a critical stance, researchers may be conceived of as not having the *broadcaster* as their client, but having *society* as their client. And therefore they should not hope for much sympathy from the broadcaster, with whom they are at odds in the very asking of the question.

It is clear that there are some research questions that need to be asked that broadcasters don't want the answers to, or don't think to ask because they come from a different framework. However, there are public commissions that are open to critical viewpoints. Take the Annan Commission in England, for example, which was open to very critical questions about broadcasting financing as it then existed. The Peacock Commission in England was open to the question, "What harm will be done to the system of British broadcasting if *all* of it is commercially financed?" That is the sort of question that vested interests do not want to ask. However, the client for the answers is not the broadcaster, but the society.

When we consider the interaction between broadcasters and researchers who *do* wish to communicate with each other, the shared basis for such interaction is a collectivity orientation, to use sociological jargon. That is the sense of public service that defines the professions, and that both researchers and broadcasters presumably share. Several authors in this volume have addressed the complexity of that presumption, asking under what conditions the similarity of interests becomes most apparent—for example, in my case, during crises.

I think we should keep these complexities in mind when we call for maximizing the fit in media research between the questions asked and the answers proposed.

JOHN ABEL   **27**

MAKING RESEARCH USEFUL
TO POLICYMAKERS

This chapter discusses two topics: first, the relation of research and
public policy; and second, the marketplace theory as it relates to policy
formation, at least currently in Washington, D.C.

If you are like many academic researchers, I would guess that you
may have some frustration and disappointment about the use of
research by public policymakers, particularly in government. I think
there are several reasons for this:

First, there is a basic difference in training between social researchers, who are trained to be objective analysts, and lawyers, who are
trained as advocates. The conflict between an academic researcher and
a lawyer basically starts from the nature of their training.

Second, there is little understanding by researchers of the political
process that takes place in the development of policy. I think that most
researchers have a cynical view, perhaps an alienated view, of how that
political process works. But the political process of give and take, of
pressure and compromise, will be more important than the research
findings in determining the final policy.

The third reason is that research is almost always done in response
to a policy issue. In other words, research is almost always reactive and
not proactive, and therefore it is often too late to influence the policy
decision.

Fourth, another often-cited reason why policymakers rarely pay
much attention to research is that there's a communication breakdown
between the lawyers or policymakers and the researchers. In my view,
the researchers simply do not understand the language of the lawyer or
the policymaker, and certainly the lawyers and policymakers do not
understand the highly qualified and probabilistic statements of the
researcher. Of course, lawyers make their own kinds of qualified
statements—in fact, Harry Truman said he wanted to find a one-armed
lawyer because lawyers always say, "Well, on the one hand, it's this, and
on the other hand, it's that." However, researchers do not do a very
good job of making their research understandable and usable. Policy-

makers will definitely not use it if they do not understand it; and sometimes they will not use it if they *do* understand it, because it cuts against their own interests.

The last reason for problems in the use of research is the unknown biases of the academic or social researcher. To put that in perspective, consider what happens when I, as a representative of the National Association of Broadcasters, go in to talk to a member of Congress or an FCC (Federal Communications Commission) commissioner or an FCC staff member. They recognize where I come from, and they know what biases I have. Similarly, if someone from a large broadcasting company comes in, they know from which perspective that person is speaking. But when an academic walks in, they don't know his or her perspective, or what biases he or she has, or what interest he or she represents.

There are basically three ways in which social research can have a bearing on policy. First, as happens most often, a social scientist can synthesize a body of research and draw policy implications; but that is mostly reactive. A second option is to conduct a specific program of research in response to a proposed policy. This is also somewhat reactive, but at least it involves conducting original research. The third way, which is rarely attempted by academics and social researchers, is to synthesize and/or conduct original research for policies that you believe *should* be addressed. A possible result of that approach might be a proactive action such as filing petitions at the expert agencies—the FCC or the Federal Trade Commission—petitions for rule making or petitions for inquiries. In general that approach is less likely to be effective on Capitol Hill than it would be in an expert agency.

Marketplace Theory

The second topic I want to discuss is the nature of the marketplace theory. Social scientists need to understand this theory of deregulation because it is important to the kinds of research that they do. The marketplace theory is the theory that Mark Fowler, the past Chairman of the Federal Communications Commission, followed in his approach to regulation.

A central issue in the marketplace theory is how to define the relevant market. Traditionally markets have been defined in two ways. They've been defined by geographic boundaries; for instance, in various countries there are national, regional, or local markets in broadcast television. In U.S. broadcast television, the range of choices available to viewers depends on the number of outlets available in the local market. Thus we have a local system of broadcasting in this country. Markets have also been defined by products. The product in broadcast television is programming, but in advertiser-supported media the audience also becomes a product, or perhaps a byproduct. Advertisers purchase access to the audiences from broadcasters, who serve as distributors. Even national advertising is distributed in this country through local broadcasting outlets.

Let's examine the program product market more closely. Substitutions can occur in the consumption of the programming product by the audience. The audience can choose various firms' products to meet the same needs. Also over time, technological advances and changes can create new entrants into the market within the same industry; for instance, more TV stations may go on the air. There were about 70 independent television stations 10 years ago; today there are about 300. Or change can occur from outside the industry. For instance, there have been new entrants in the home video entertainment/information marketplace: cable, multipoint distribution service, subscription television, low power television, direct broadcast satellite, C-band direct satellite, and so forth. Particularly in the broadcasting and home entertainment/information programming market, there has been very rapid change and many new entrants; and this has created a wide menu of programming sources that are interchangeable in the eyes of the consumer. The programming itself, not the source of the programming, is relevant to the consumer. The consumer generally does not care whether the program comes from broadcast television, a cable system, a home VCR, or wherever. Though the programming on various media is somewhat different—for instance, comparing advertiser-supported media and subscription media such as the Public Broadcast System (PBS)—the evidence suggests that audiences accept most video programming as substitute goods regardless of the medium.

Thus the local marketplace has become increasingly competitive for broadcasters and for other providers of video material. The closest substitutes for broadcasting are cable, multipoint distribution service, satellite master antenna television, low power television, subscription television, direct broadcast satellite, and VCRs. Nonsubscription-supported media such as VCRs are a very easy substitute in our society at the current time. Consequently, the marketplace theory views broadcasters as participants in this larger marketplace.

The federal government's policies under this theory are directed toward maximizing the services the public desires. The government does not define public media demand and does not specify categories of programming to serve this demand. Significantly, the marketplace approach seeks an end to program content regulation. It holds that government oversight of content violates the First Amendment and interfaces with the proper functioning of the media market. Concerning ownership, the marketplace theory holds that the Federal Communications Commission should abolish rules that restrict growth by existing owners or that limit entry by new owners in the competitive video fields. The FCC's role under this theory is that it should examine each rule, each regulation, and each policy in light of whether the rule or policy undermines or fosters market forces.

Now you might ask, "Does the marketplace ever break down?" The answer is that it might. It certainly does in the area of technical regulation—we could not have broadcasters operating on all frequencies. There has to be some management of this spectrum, and that necessarily is government's role.

My key point is that social science research on the media should proceed with this marketplace theory as a backdrop, because researchers need to understand the basis from which the federal government is currently operating.

QUESTIONS AND ANSWERS

Guy Lometti, Director of ABC Social Research: Based on my own experience as an academic and as a network researcher, I agree with Aimée Dorr's points about cooperation between researchers and broadcasters. Also, I would suggest that researchers should regularly read the trade publications, such as *Broadcasting, Variety,* and *Advertising Age,* in order to learn what the important public policy issues are and what major concerns broadcasters have. Second, since Aimée suggested that researchers had to have an invitation in order to enter the broadcasting arena, I will initiate that invitation by informing you that at ABC we have a small social research grant program and we invite academic researchers to write, call, or introduce themselves to us. Tell us about the research that you're interested in or doing. It can be as theoretical as you like, but it has to be applied in an area in which we have an interest. It has to answer a question that we think is important.

Horst Stipp, Director of NBC Social Research: I also have a footnote to Aimée Dorr's paper. She made a point that the social researcher who wants to contribute and to be heard by program creators and programmers needs to know a lot about television. I have three examples of questions that were brought to our social research department and to a panel of consultants that we use.

One question was from the producers of a crime or action/adventure series, who wanted to know whether showing a violent act such as a shooting in slow motion will decrease or increase the impact. Is that format less dangerous? What does research have to say about that? The second question was, If we bring the live Punky Brewster to a Saturday morning cartoon show and give her a new pet, a pet that she does not have in the prime-time show, will kids perceive that as something wrong that doesn't belong in the story, or will they accept a new pet for Punky Brewster? Third, our programmers have decided that we should have more minorities in Saturday morning cartoons, and they want to introduce a Mexican character. If we try to be nonstereotypical about this character, and so do not give him a stereotypical Mexican accent, will kids even notice that this is a Mexican character, or will he just seem to them like a white character with a tan? If you have research answers to any of these questions, please contact me.

Q: I found Mr. Harding's points about asking the right question misleading. For example, wasn't something missing in the reasoning on the drinking issue? True, there are many causes for drinking other than television, but it's a fact that TV not only has advertising for drinking, but also drinking in most programs—in the soap operas all the glamorous people drink. So if we know there are nine other causes of drinking and television is the tenth cause, shouldn't it try to hold up a high prosocial standard anyway?

If the quality of TV—the aesthetics and values on the tube—is to go up, I think we somehow have to mitigate the pressure of profits, which say, "Titillate your audience, and you'll get big audiences and lots of advertisers." In order to mitigate the pressure of profits, we may have to pass more legislation.

Philip Harding: First, I think the work "quality" is an extremely subjective term. Your idea of quality on television may not correspond to mine or somebody else's. Relating that back to profit, of course you have to have profit. You've got to have revenues coming in, and they come from the advertisers; that's the way the system operates. To fund quality programs or nonquality programs, on the network schedule or on local stations, there has to be revenue coming in.

The other issue you raised is, as you put it, that having discovered television to be among the ten contributors to the alcohol abuse problem, why didn't we proceed to do something about that? However, my point is that television had not really been implicated at all—it was not among the ten factors. There were perhaps two studies looking at television and drinking. Charles Atkin did one, John Strickland did another, and there were no clear conclusions. But there was a rich literature of alcohol studies that looked at the biological, environmental, parental, familial, and sibling variables—all of which were much more determinitive. Since there are these kinds of variables, which are clearly related to alcohol abuse, and there isn't any evidence implicating television, why all the concentration on television as a causal agent?

Ellen Wartella: I'm a bit overwhelmed by the presumption that *all* social science research should be within the system of broadcasting or at the behest of broadcasters. Though such research is legitimate, I'd also like some attention to the role and efficacy of social science research that questions the assumptions of the broadcasting system, and to how that might bring desirable changes in media for our society.

Q: Concerning the current Washington regulatory climate, I want to emphasize that its whole underlying philosophy is not based on empirical fact; it's an assumption about what people think of pro-gramming. It is true that people will take programming from a number of alternate sources, but the philosophic assumption is that basically all programming content is of equal value to people, that viewers don't really care about the qualitative differences between different kinds of programming. I wonder, is that what media researchers are really finding, and can researchers do anything to improve the quality of network programming?

John Abel: There has been a substantial amount of research done on the value of programming. One major source of that research is the 1983 copyright royalty tribunal proceeding, in which several different interest groups—broadcasters, and programming interests such as the Motion Picture Association of America, and professional sports interests—did research on how cable subscribers and cable operators value different kinds of programming content. This research was aimed at a specific administrative question, and the several groups generally reported quite similar findings.

Q: There seems to be an underlying assumption that people watch television for entertainment, and they don't care what the entertainment is, so anything can be thrown at them. One unfortunate result is the overreliance on ratings, because the programmers don't have a good sense of what people really want to watch, and they assume that viewers will accept whatever is given to them.

Aimée Dorr: The work that I have done with children clearly indicates that they like things that are fun to watch and entertaining. Also, they clearly do have preferences; one program isn't just the same as any other to them. And it's also quite clear, judged by what they talk about and remember later, that things about *themselves* in relationship to the program are very important, so that they are not an undifferentiated mass audience. Girls care very much about seeing attractive, strong female characters—not physically attractive, but personally attractive. Black kids that I've talked to care very much about seeing attractive, strong, desirable black characters. So it is *not* the case that one program substitutes haphazardly for another and that all quality is the same.

Philip Harding: The networks are constantly testing programs that are on the air, as well as pilots of new programs. It's an ongoing process for all three networks to measure audience acceptance, popularity, and so on; and this is supplemental to the ratings. We often describe the ratings as the ultimate score keeper, but we have lots more information than that. In addition, the networks have done long streams of studies on the whole question of the relationship between the viewer and television: the uses and gratifications research that Charles Winick discusses in this volume. That's not oriented to specific programs, but rather to the satisfactions and the dissatisfactions that people derive from television in general. So there's an ongoing mix of research, both macrolevel research and also studies of individual programs.

Guy Lometti: Most people don't know that each of the networks spends millions of dollars for research above and beyond the ratings. We do research at times on a weekly basis, going out to national probability samples and interviewing people about programs. For example, in "Dynasty," we know that people were getting fed up with the story about Krystle tied up in the attic. People we interviewed told us that; as a result the story line was changed. There is a great interest in communication between programmers and researchers about such qualitative pieces of information, far beyond the numerical ratings.

Horst Stipp: Another example comes from the "Punky Brewster" show, which had an episode about the Challenger explosion only a few weeks after it happened. The astronaut Buzz Aldrin was on it, and the show was about Punky being devastated by what happened. Before the beginning of the season, when they started writing the script, the producers of the show expressed interest in getting social research input on the kind of serious, important issues that concern children and that would be appropriate to deal with. When the space shuttle exploded and there were stories about kids being affected, the producers immediately mobilized and did a segment on it with incredible speed. By the way, when they asked our advice, we suggested to them *not* to do stories on missing children because we thought that that problem of children had been overdone.

Seymour Feshbach: I want to raise a more general issue by beginning with a very concrete question. On Saturday morning, CBS has recently introduced a children's program that features wrestlers and rock music. I think that broadcasters, viewers, and all concerned would agree that this is a moronic program with no redeeming features whatsoever. I don't think anyone would try to defend its quality, yet here it is being introduced on Saturday morning after 30 years of conferences with parents and researchers. My question is, How does this come about, and how can research do anything to influence this process?

Philip Harding: I don't know. Those kinds of situations do occur at times. Those decisions are made by programming people.

Seymour Feshbach: But I don't think they're exceptional decisions; I think they're normative. The exceptional ones are the *good* kids' programs. But the normative, typical ones are the moronic things that we see so often. I'm depressed about this because the industry phrases the issue as "What harm are we doing? You social scientists, your job is to show us that we're doing harm or we're not doing harm." But they should be asking, "How can we make the product better? How can we fulfill our social mission within whatever economic constraints we have?" I don't hear the industry asking that.

Philip Harding: I don't have information on specific program decisions. These programs for young people presumably do entertain them. There probably was research done to show that the program had some measure of audience acceptance. Though you and I may think it is utter junk, it may be entertaining for young people, and after all there is nothing wrong with entertaining them. However, we have tried over time to maintain a mix of programming. There are these kinds of purely entertainment programs—"Daffy Duck" or "Bugs Bunny" or "Hulk Hogan"—that kids find entertaining. If they don't enjoy them, they won't watch, and the program will disappear like April snow. But at the same time we try to include some programming that is beneficial to children as well: prosocial programs like "Story Break," after-school specials, and so on.

There's another fact to keep in mind. If you take the percentage of children's total viewing that occurs on Saturday morning, it was 8.8% at last count. That means that the rest of the schedule is 91.2%. If you look at the rest of the schedule, I think you'll find a number of things that are of interest to children. You have to look at the whole broadcast day, because that's when kids are watching.

Seymour Feshbach: I look from 3:00 to 6:00, and I don't see much that is good for children.

Q: I think it's a mistake to put so much emphasis on having to *prove* harmful effects of television. We know that ads work, or the advertisers wouldn't keep using them. And we know that there are lots of TV segments that show bad behavior and outcomes, and that they must have an effect. For instance, on "General Hospital," Luke raped Laura, and later they got married. What do viewers learn from that? As another example, a child character in a TV program said that, if his mother and the television disagreed on something, he would follow the television's advice. Is that what we want our children to be learning?

Philip Harding: Any influence that television may have on sexual training pales in comparison with that of parents and close friends.

GEORGE COMSTOCK

28

TODAY'S AUDIENCES, TOMORROW'S MEDIA

Tomorrow's media will be shaped not only by technology but by their audiences, and much can be learned about the future of the media from what we know about today's audiences. There is no mass media topic that has been examined so assiduously and continuously if we take into account the enormous amount of proprietary data collected by financially interested parties, the media and their advertisers. However, there is also a substantial body of publicly available studies covering a wide range of public responses to the media. The proprietary findings that reach public view through the pages of *Advertising Age, Broadcasting* ("People's choice," 1976), *Editor and Publisher* ("Newspapers are," 1975), and other industry publications, do not suggest that the publicly available studies are in any way in conflict with the proprietary research or that the proprietary research would much alter the patterns discernible from the publicly available studies. Because the range of public responses examined has been so varied, these publicly available studies are not ordinarily thought of as composing a single literature. Yet, this is arguably so, and a major buttress of such an assertion is that the findings of this literature give us our most accurate vision of the mass media of the future.

The story told by these findings is fascinating, for it offers surprises, seeming (but resolvable) inconsistencies, and an occasional paradox. It can be summarized in 10 propositions.

(1) Public opinion and behavior in regard to the media are marked by incongruities.

Steiner (1963) reported that while education was correlated positively with being critical of commercial television entertainment and with the expressed desire for more informational and news programming, education was definitely *not* positively correlated with watching a greater proportion of informational and news programming. That is, persons with a college education were more likely to offer or endorse nasty statements about the medium, and more likely to declare or agree that they wanted more serious fare, but in fact they were not at all more likely to view more of the comparatively serious fare already available. These data, based on a representative national survey of about 2,000 American adults and a more intensive examination of the opinions and actual daily TV viewing of several hundred adults in a single city, are typical of the findings about public opinion and the media. Opinion data often set the stage for a surprise when respondents' behavior or other opinions are examined.

A similar incongruity is observed when the data from this survey are combined with two replications, one 10 years later (Bower, 1973) and the other 20 years later (Bower, 1985). For three decades, the A. C. Nielsen Company has recorded increasing use of television. Sets are in use more hours in any given 24-hour period today than they were a decade ago, and a decade ago they were in use more hours than two decades ago. As television has become increasingly accepted as an appliance of modern times, viewing too has increased. Seldom has a theoretical concept fared so poorly as the "novelty hypothesis"—the notion that after people got used to the medium of television they would spend less time with it. However, over the same period, these three national surveys recorded increasing dissatisfaction with the medium. It is perceived now as less exciting, less enjoyable, and less worthwhile. Such data prepare one to expect a decline in the consumption of television—not the actual increases recorded.

Frequently, public opinion about the media is inconsistent. Thus, survey data (Comstock, Chaffee, Katzman, McCombs, & Roberts, 1978) records that about three-fourths of the public subscribes to the view that there are too many commercials on broadcast television, while an almost equal three-fourths agree that commercials are a "fair price" for free entertainment. Similar contrary proportions occur when the focus is advertising on children's programming—a majority asserts that there are too many ads, that there shouldn't be any, and that they constitute a fair price for entertainment.

In sum, three decades of research about American public opinion and behavior in regard to the mass media encourage the conclusion that there is scant coherent or meaningful opinion on the topic.

(2) The mass media are accorded a place in social life very much on their own terms; liking them or disliking them has little to do with whether they are used, how they are used, or even how much they are used.

One of the most persistently pursued "big" questions about the mass media concerns their role in the organization and evolution of society. In their widely discussed chapter entitled "Mass Communication, Popular Taste, and Organized Social Action," Lazarsfeld and Merton (1948/1971) four decades ago proposed that the principal functions served by the media include conferral of status on depicted "issues, persons, organizations, and social movements"; enforcement of social norms by publicizing deviations and thereby precluding tolerant indifference to them; and a "narcoticizing dysfunction" of encouraging vicarious, passive review of public affairs instead of participation. Since then, the list of functions and dysfunctions has lengthened to include surveillance of the environment; interpretation and perception; transmission of culture; entertainment and diversion; the cultivation of fears, anxieties, and pessimistic beliefs; and the evocation of widespread dissatisfaction through an emphasis on consumer goods and consumption in both entertainment and advertising (Comstock, 1982; Gerbner, Gross, Morgan, & Signorielli, 1985; Gerbner, Gross, Signorielli, Morgan, & Jackson-Beeck, 1979; Hennigan et al., 1982; Mendelsohn, 1966; Wright, 1959). There is certainly some evidence in behalf of the media's cultivation of fears, anxieties, and pessimistic beliefs (Comstock, 1982; Gerbner et al., 1985; Heath, 1984; Heath & Petraitis, 1984). In addition, the assiduously documented rise in larceny—thefts without violence—that paralleled the introduction of television into the United States in the late 1940s and early 1950s (Hennigan et al., 1982) is certainly consistent with the evocation-of-dissatisfaction hypothesis.

However, there is much about the concept of functions (and dysfunctions) of the media that poses problems for empirical inquiry. For example, the narcoticizing dysfunction hypothesis is partially vitiated by the frequent finding (Comstock et al., 1978) that media exposure during political campaigns is positively correlated with expressions of support for candidates, including voting. However, such findings do not address possible effects (1) that might occur by means unrelated to direct exposure, or (2) for which correlations between media use and behavior are inadequate indices. Concerning effects that might occur by means unrelated to exposure, the issue is the way the media operate. The news values that govern the coverage of public affairs are pervasive and quite consistent among the media (Gans, 1979), and it is unlikely that degree of current exposure is a good index of the long-term influence of these values. It is certainly arguable that political participation of many kinds, including voting, is discouraged by the media's depiction of noteworthy political action as largely the domain of governments, institutions, and corporations instead of private citizens (Dahlgren, 1980), and of conflict with the law as the salient aspect of many social protests (Gitlin, 1980). Concerning possible media effects for which correlations between media use and behavior are inadequate indices, the issue is one fact possibly masking another. Media use and political participation of many kinds may be correlated because politically interested persons are motivated to use the media for political information, yet this does not rule out the possibility that for some persons or social strata the media discourage participation. The correlation in question may be the documentation and not the reproof of such effects; that is, the way the media operate conceivably could discourage both media use and political participation.

The major effects of the mass media are almost certainly associated with their presence or absence, rather than with variations in exposure to them; and in a modern society where the media are ubiquitous it is only variation in exposure that can be studied in regard to the roles and influence of the mass media. However, an ingenious research approach (Neuman, 1982) has employed survey data to weigh support for three major competing hypotheses about the social functions of the mass media:

(1) Cultural experience: The better educated a person, the more he or she will extract from a mass medium.
(2) Cultural polarization: The less educated a person, the more he or she will extract from a mass medium.
(3) Cultural homogenization: Education makes very little difference in what people extract from the mass media.

The cultural experience hypothesis expresses the often-documented fact that education enables people to make more elaborate or skillful use of further experience—the better educated get more from further education, comprehend the news better, can appreciate artistic departures because they know the conventions violated, and so on. The cultural polarization hypothesis expresses the opposite expectation—that because the mass media are specifically designed to attract the masses, and because they place few burdens on intellectual ability, education, or preparation, they should be better understood by and more meaningful to the less educated. For example, it is plausible that commercial television situation comedy and adventure dramas are the Sam Shepard, Neil Simon, and Arthur Miller of the hoi polloi. The cultural homogenization hypothesis holds that mass media are largely accepted in similar ways by all social strata.

Neuman's (1982) survey collected the reported thoughts of people while viewing a wide variety of television programs. Telephone interviews were conducted immediately after viewing, and began with a broad query: What thoughts had the respondents had while watching the program? The interview then proceeded to draw attention to various aspects of the program about which the respondent might have had a thought.

One-fourth of the almost 100 persons interviewed could not at first recall any thoughts at all. Typical of these replies are the following:

"Nothing, really . . . my mind was quite blank."

"A show like this gives me a chance to rest my mind and think about other things."

"What thoughts—nothing, nothing really. I was just waiting, you know, for the comedy to happen."

The totality of thoughts eventually recalled were categorized as either analytic or interpretive responses. *Analytic responses* were defined as ones concerning entertainment as entertainment—the general form of the program (plot organization, pace, character development), generic form (comparison with other programs or other media), and technical form (script, formula, symbols, production, editing). *Interpretive responses* were defined as applying the entertainment to the real world— the intent (ideas or feelings authors intended to arouse; motivations of producers or television executives), the impact (on own thinking or emotions, or speculations about the average viewer), and the implications (broader meanings or implications for society; relevance to current social problems; or political, moral, or religious ramifications).

The first striking outcome was that analytic responses outnumbered interpretive responses and that this held for the four levels of education into which the sample was divided—less than high school, high school, some college, and college degree. This implies that when people respond cognitively to television entertainment they do so primarily on its own terms.

This breakdown by education now permitted—at least for this small sample—a test of the three hypotheses: Cultural experience predicts a positive association between education and thoughtful activity while viewing television, cultural polarization predicts a negative association, and homogenization predicts no association at all. It was homogenization that was supported. Both total analytic and total interpretive responses were unrelated to viewer education.

When comparable data from a sample of 34 humanities professors were included, however, the picture changed. Associations between thoughtful activity and education now became statistically significant and positive for both analytic and interpretive responses. The professors on the average produced about one more interpretive thought than the 4.72 average for viewers with a college degree, but they produced more than twice as many analytic thoughts as interpretive ones and more than twice as many analytic thoughts (12.44 average) as did viewers with a college degree (5.03).

Except for the sample of professors, intellectual response to television entertainment was unrelated to education, and even among this elite category there were markedly more analytic than interpretive responses—the same directional finding as the smaller trend among those whose education ranged from a college degree downward. Bower (1973, 1985) and Steiner (1963) have documented that education is decidedly a predictor of being critical of and expressing dissatisfaction with television. Neuman's (1982) data suggest that in the actual viewing of television everybody reacts pretty much the same. This conclusion does not dispute that there are generational and cultural differences in the interpretation of television programs (as well as in much else), as Katz (this volume) suggests, or that differences related to age, culture, and personal variables may arise when people are asked in depth and persistently about what they have experienced in viewing television, and the meaning they attach to what they experience. It does mean that the basic mode of response to television does not appear to be much influenced by a variable (education) that ordinarily would be thought to govern such behavior, except when we look at respondents who are extremely highly educated and professionally engaged in interpretation and analysis activities. This is a surprise, and the larger implication of these television audience data is that the mass media are largely accorded the place in society to which they have assigned themselves— in the case of television, to be the grand entertainer.

(3) Evaluation of the mass media is aligned with other fundamental attitudes and dispositions, but behavior in regard to the media is to a large degree independent of such attitudes and dispositions.

In 1981, the Roper Organization interviewed a national probability sample of 2,440 adults concerning their complaints about 17 television programs (Roper, 1981a). One was "Little House on the Prairie." The other 16 were programs of types that had been singled out as objectionable and made the target of a campaign for their removal from the air by a coalition of fundamentalist religious groups calling itself "The Moral Majority." The 16 included "Dallas," "Dukes of Hazzard,"

"Hill Street Blues," "Love Boat," and "M*A*S*H." Roper's client was the National Broadcasting Company, which wished to document the degree to which the Moral Majority reflected public opinion.

The personal interviews sought from each respondent his or her volunteered objections and complaints of whatever sort about each of the programs. There was no hint that there was a covert interest in "sex and violence" responses. This techniques stands in contrast to the elicitation of an opinion about a program ("Do you think there is too much violence on 'Dukes of Hazzard'?") or a medium ("Do you think there is too much violence on television?"). Surveys indicate that between about one-half and two-thirds of the American public subscribe to the latter view when their opinion is so elicited, and that the scores are similar when sex is the topic (Comstock et al., 1978; Immerwahr, Johnson, & Doble, 1980; Roper, 1981a).

Another principal measure was agreement with eight statements representing a fundamentalist religious orientation:

- You went to church four or more times during the last month.
- You read the Bible four or more times during the last month outside of church.
- You were "born again"—a turning point in your life when you committed yourself to Christ.
- You were baptized as a teen or as an adult, either for the first or second time.
- Spreading the word of God to save souls is more important than leading a good, honest life and helping others.
- The Bible is the word of God and its writers recorded the Bible without any mistakes.
- The Devil is a real personal being as opposed to a "force."
- Christianity is the one true religion and everyone should be converted to it.

It was found that 25% of the public concurred with none of these, and were categorized as zero in fundamentalist disposition; 47% concurred with one, two, or three, and were categorized as low; 22% concurred with four, five, or six, and were categorized as high; and 5% concurred with seven or all eight, and were categorized as very high. Slightly more than one-fourth of the sample, then, expressed substantial accord with a fundamentalist orientation and thereby might be said to be the public represented by the Moral Majority.

The data make it forcefully clear that those with a fundamentalist orientation find some television entertainment much more objectionable than do others, and this is especially true for the tiny proportion who are very high in fundamentalist orientation. The response rates for objections to sex in "Dallas" display the typical pattern: zero and low, 6-7%; high, 14%; and very high, 25%. These views parallel a decidedly atypical perspective on many social and communications issues among those of a fundamentalist orientation. Respondents high or very high in fundamentalist outlook were pronouncedly more likely to oppose the women's Equal Rights Amendment; oppose abortion; favor regulation of the press; believe that values, idea, and life-styles of which they do not approve should not be dealt with on television; and believe that books dealing with topics of which they do not approve should not be permitted in libraries. Such views were most pronounced among those scoring very high in fundamentalism.

However, when the fundamentalists were combined with the rest of the public, the level of complaints about sex and violence in specific television programs was low. The 13% objecting to violence in "Dukes of Hazzard" and the 10% objecting to sex in "Dallas" were the maxima. For 14 of the programs, the objection figure was 3% or less for violence, and for 11 it was 5% or less for sex. When the options *and behavior* of the most extreme segment (those very high in fundamentalism) were examined, one-third had watched "Dallas" in the last month, and one-fourth rated it as their "favorite" or "very good," while one-fifth thought it was "unsuitable" for anyone. The comparable figures for that exemplar of secular humanism, "M*A*S*H," were 61% watched it within the month, 48% rated it "favorite" or "very good," and 6% said "unsuitable."

These data hold three lessons for students of mass communication and one for those who wish to defend the media, whether justly or unjustly attacked. The impression regarding public dissatisfaction with the media varies greatly as a function of whether opinion is volunteered or elicited, and opinions about the media are broadly consistent with basic beliefs and opinions on social issues; but behavior in regard to the media, as well as evaluation of their specific offerings, is not at all strongly predicted by basic beliefs of opinions on social issues. Thus those who defend the media will be more effective if they avoid the general and focus on the specific—this program, that newspaper, those stories.

(4) Opinions about the media, and particularly evaluation of them, have far less to do with media use than do the time available and the prevailing norms.

(1) The public's evaluation of television has become progressively less

favorable over the past 35 years (Bower, 1973, 1985), although in absolute terms the medium on the whole is still favorably evaluated by the public.

(2) Over the same period, public consumption of television has progressively risen (Comstock et al., 1978), although there have been oscillations from year to year.

(3) Much of the added viewing over these years has come from various demographic segments—older males, for example—viewing at time at which they previously did not view (Lyle, 1975).

(4) Data from several thousand East and West Coast viewers (Barwise, Ehrenberg, & Goodhardt, 1982) make it clear that whether or not a particular program is viewed regularly depends to a large degree on whether a person has something else to do. For programs scheduled at the same time four or five days a week, the likelihood that a person viewing on one day will be viewing the next day averages 50%. The figure is the same for programs scheduled weekly; that is, only about half of the persons who saw a particular program last Wednesday will be in the audience this Wednesday. Remarkably, these figures even apply to such specialized high-fan-appeal offerings as "Monday Night Football," and there is only a moderate amount of variation among types of programs (network evening news and some daytime soap operas are somewhat higher than average in repeat viewing, but even in the latter case a third of those viewing one day will be absent the next). However, if people are viewing television at all, they almost always will watch the program they watched previously in the same time slot. People drop out of the audience for a program not because they are viewing something else, but because they are not viewing television at all.

Findings 1 and 2 indicate that public evaluation of the mass media does not sensitively govern their consumption. Finding 3 exemplifies the importance of norms as an influence on media use—viewing has increased over the years because viewing (defined in audience research as being close to an operating television set) at various times and in various circumstances has become more acceptable. Finding 4 documents the extreme importance of available time as a determinant of media use—viewing a particular program is the reciprocal of other obligations and activities, and not the result of switching among available programs. As the investigators (Barwise et al., 1982) comment, the data support the view that "typically, television is consumed as a medium and the decision to view ordinarily takes precedence over the selection of what to view."

The applicability of these conclusions to the mass media in general is tempered by the fact that they reflect opinion and behavior in regard to television. Norms would surely play at least as strong a role with print media, for not only is there the question of the appropriateness of use of a medium at a given time, but also the perceived correctness of monetary expenditure for newspapers, magazines, and books. Available time, although a necessary condition for use, would be proportionately far less important for print media than for television.

(5) The performance of the mass media does not rank high among the concerns of the public.

There are innumerable instances in which public opinion polls have reported a large percentage and often a majority expressing dissatisfaction with the media. However, these are elicited responses to such queries as the following:

- Would you agree or disagree that national network television news is biased in a liberal direction?
- Would you agree or disagree that there is too much violence on television?
- Would you agree of disagree that there are too many commercials on television?

The evidence is unambiguous that such elicited criticism of the media exceeds volunteered criticism, sometimes by a factor of several times (Comstock et al., 1978; Immerwahr et al., 1980; LoSciuto, 1972; Roper, 1981a).

When people were asked in Gallup Polls between 1949 and 1972 what was the most important problem facing the country, the proportion mentioning the mass media in some way has never been large enough to record (Nie, Verba, & Petrocik, 1976). People named things such as war; communism at home or abroad; nuclear weapons; the economy (unemployment, taxes, cost-of-living, strikes); civil rights; the Vietnam War when it was in progress; social problems such as crime and delinquency; and drugs.

The media themselves are not salient to the public as issues. One reason is surely the diversity within and between the major media; to a large degree, people can selectively avoid what they consider objectionable or low in merit. Another reason is that the American public is largely satisfied with the broad contours of the mass media. When people are asked what they would change or what they would want from the ideal television network or ideal newspaper, the answers are not much different from what they have been getting (Bogart, 1981; Bower, 1973, 1985; LoSciuto, 1972).

(6) What the public says in regard to television news and what it does are

incongruent; television is the symbol but not the agent of regular news delivery.

There is no doubt that a large majority of Americans—about two-thirds in the mid-1980s—believe they get most of their national and world news from television (Bower, 1973, 1985; Comstock et al., 1978; Roper, 1981b, 1985). There is also no doubt that this reflects no innate or novel appeal of television, but rather the progressive preeminence in public thought of its news coverage. In the late 1950s and early 1960s, for example, when set ownership was approaching its present 98% of households, a majority said they got most of their news from newspapers.

The pattern is similar in regard to other evaluations of the news media. When comparing television, newspapers, radio, and magazines, a majority or plurality of the public cites television as the most comprehensive or complete, most credible, "quickest with the latest," fairest, as "presenting things most intelligently," and as giving the "closest understanding of candidates and issues in elections" (Bower, 1973, 1985; Roper, 1981b, 1985). As is true regarding TV as the claimed source of most news, these expressions of esteem represent the progressive displacement of other media—generally newspapers, but radio in the case of rapid dissemination.

These data imply that television is the nation's number-one source of news, but data on behavior give a very different impression. About three times as many people read a daily newspaper on any given day as are in the audience for the national network evening news programs, and half of the public will not see any portion of such a TV news program in a two-week period (Robinson, 1971). The average weekday audience for the three network evening newscasts is about 35 million, for the three major news magazines (*Newsweek, Time,* and *U.S. News and World Report*) about 50 million, and for daily newspapers more than 100 million (Gans, 1979). Fewer than one-third of the public watch either evening national or local news on a given day, and those who watch the same news program five nights in succession have been recorded as fewer than 1% (Lichty, 1982). Evidence on consecutive viewing in general (Barwise et al., 1982) suggests that certainly no more than 5% of the audience for a network evening news program on Monday will watch it for the succeeding four nights; and remember, almost none of those who are absent will be watching a competing news program. Further, within a few hours of viewing, the average number of stories that can be accurately recalled is only one out of four (Stauffer, Frost, & Rybolt, 1983); television is inferior to newspaper stories in recall (Patterson, 1980).

The television news audience certainly should not be confused with the audience for evening entertainment, for the average ratings for the three network newscasts are much lower than any of those for the various categories of prime-time entertainment. Also, TV news audiences markedly skewed toward those over 50 in age; 18- to 49-year-old adults watch news in startlingly modest proportions (Comstock et al., 1978). Those who do not ordinarily pay much attention to the news get most of the news they do receive from television. Socioeconomic status is negatively associated with use of television news and positively associated with use of newspapers. However, it would be an error to think of two distinct news audiences, with one attending largely to television and the other to newspapers. The fact is that there is a very large overlap in use of the two media (Levy, 1978; Patterson, 1980; Robinson, 1971). There are not two news audiences, but one audience for news drawing on both media, and on newspapers with greater regularity.

The disparity between public beliefs and behavior in regard to sources of news in no way diminishes the high regard in which the public holds television news. It is perceived to be the most credible and fair of the media (Comstock et al., 1978), but audience statistics also make plain that its preeminence in dissemination is symbolic and not real. Television apparently has become a synonym for news, probably because its vivid visual coverage is remembered and reminds people of events that themselves have become symbols of our times—assassinations, congressional inquiries, meetings between heads of state, men at war, moon landings, royal weddings, and shuttle disasters.

(7) There is no newly emerging public disenchantment with the news media.

The evidence suggesting public disaffection with the news media consists of shifts in public opinion in recent years toward greater criticism of the media and reduced confidence in the media (Dolan, 1984; Gergen, 1985; Lipset, 1985; Lipset & Schneider, 1983). Such changes in public opinion, however, do not demonstrate a malaise of any great seriousness in public attitudes toward the media. Interpretations of extensive public hostility toward the media or a crisis in public confidence in the media are not merited, for they ignore the historical and empirical context of the findings:

(1) There are many instances in which the media outrank other institutions

in public evaluation. For example, in the 1981 national survey sponsored by the *Los Angeles Times,* the media were ranked above three other institutions (business, government, and labor) for having "the highest standards of honesty and integrity" and for having "done the most to promote 'the public good,'" and they received the smallest percentage saying "their power should be cut back for the good of the country" (Gergen, 1985).

(2) There is evidence of substantial confidence in and satisfaction with the media regardless of people's political ideology. In national probability samples in both 1970 and 1980, similar majorities among persons accepting the labels "conservative," "middle of the road," and "liberal" (between 53% and 62%, depending on year and label) endorsed the statement that television news "gives it straight" (Bower, 1985). People in each category also displayed a remarkable ability to find a newscaster whom they perceived as compatible with their political persuasion, with a large majority within each group either perceiving such affinity or neutrality. In addition, over the past two decades of "a great deal" of confidence in the "persons running" the media have not so much fallen as oscillated, with shifts of +5% fluctuating around a mean of about 25% (Lipset, 1985).

(3) Trends in public opinion show that over the past few decades the media have fared as well or better than other institutions. Expressions of confidence in the leadership of other institutions on the whole have declined while evaluation of the media has displayed a different pattern. The standing of the media typically has edged downward during popular presidential administrations and upward when "bad news" (such as Watergate or a recession) tarnished an administration (Lipset, 1985).

The low salience of the media themselves as issues implies that elicited opinions about them will be unstable. There certainly has been variation from survey to survey (as a function of time and measures). Nevertheless, there remains a discernible pattern: much criticism and much praise, depending on how elicited, and scant evidence of a contemporary crisis in confidence.

(8) The news media cannot avoid audiences perceiving them as biased, and having an informed public will not eliminate the perception of bias.

There is little comfort for the news media in the recent research of Vallone, Ross, and Lepper (1985). They examined the reactions of viewers to six segments (totalling 36 minutes) of ABC, CBS, and NBC evening and late night news covering 10 days in Beirut beginning September 15, 1982, when the Israelis moved into West Beirut; the single most dramatic event was the civilian massacre in the Lebanon refugee camps. They found that perception of anti-Israel bias was far greater among pro-Israel viewers than among pro-Arab viewers; perception of anti-Arab bias was far greater among pro-Arab viewers than among pro-Israel viewers. This was true not only for the simple ascription of bias, but also for six less direct measures, such as the imputation of different standards ("excusing Israel when they would have blamed some other country" or "blaming Israel when they would have excused some other country"). The authors argue that their data depict these partisans as "seeing" different newscasts, with pro-Arab viewers perceiving almost three times as many favorable references to Israel as pro-Israel viewers, and pro-Arab and pro-Israel viewers both perceiving the newscasts as persuading unaligned viewers of the merits of the opposition case. In addition, when pro-Arab and pro-Israel viewers were divided into those with high and low degrees of factual knowledge about the situation, there was a result that will surprise some: The greater the degree of knowledge, the higher the degree of perceived bias in the network news coverage.

The credibility of these relationships is high because they represent the responses of sincerely partisan viewers to a substantial sample of actual news coverage by the three networks; nothing was simulated or duplicitous. The findings suggest that the news media cannot avoid the perception of bias when they cover events on which partisanship exists. They also suggest that expressions of faith in an "informed public" as the antidote to perceived bias are mistaken, for nothing here indicates that more extensive coverage would alter perceptions of bias. In fact, the data imply the opposite: More coverage will lead to greater amounts of knowledge held by partisans, and greater amounts of knowledge among partisans will produce greater degrees of perceived bias.

(9) The public understands poorly the First Amendment as the constitutional basis of mass media policy in the United States.

Given the centrality of the First Amendment to the character of American society and the American press, it might be expected that the public would have a good sense of the First Amendment's application as interpreted over the years by the courts. In fact, it does not. In 1979, a national probability sample of about 1,000 adults (Immerwahr & Doble, 1982) provided these elicited percentage responses:

	Agree	Disagree	Not Sure
• Major party candidates have a right to get as much coverage as their opponents get.	91%	6%	4%

	Agree	Disagree	Not Sure
• Television news has the right to give candidates of one of the major political parties more coverage than it gives to candidates of the other party.	13%	79%	7%
• Television news has the right to give less coverage to third parties such as George Wallace's American party than it gives to Republicans and Democrats.	22%	69%	9%
• A newspaper has the right to refuse to cover third parties such as George Wallace's American party, even though they give lots of coverage to the two major parties.	29%	59%	12%
• A newspaper has the right to give opponents of a controversial policy such as the SALT treaty less coverage than those in favor of the treaty get.	22%	65%	13%
• Opponents of a controversial policy such as the SALT treaty have a right to get as much coverage on television as those in favor of the treaty get.	86%	4%	10%

The public and the First Amendment have divergent perspectives. Under the First Amendment, no party has a "right" to coverage, nor do advocates or opponents of a position; the press is free to act as it chooses. Television is not obligated to give equal coverage to major party candidates or to third party candidates, although the Federal Communications Commission's (FCC) equal-time rule requires broadcasters to give equal opportunities of access to all candidates and parties, and its Fairness Doctrine requires broadcasters to give a reasonable amount of time to coverage of controversial public issues, and to do so fairly by giving exposure to opposing viewpoints. The broadcast media thus have a somewhat more restrained standing under the First Amendment, but it is not suspended in their case, and broadcast news has been explicitly divorced by the FCC from the implied equality of political coverage.

(10) The public assigns more importance to the responsibilities than to the rights of the mass media.

In regard to the right of freedom of expression, the same sample replied as follows:

	Agree	Disagree	Not Sure
• A person has the right to peacefully picket the construction of a nuclear power plant.	73%	18%	9%
• The government has a right to arrest a reporter who is constantly criticizing the president.	19%	72%	9%
• Members of the Nazi party have a right to publish their own newspaper.	59%	30%	11%
• A group of Nazis has a right to stage a march through a Jewish neighborhood.	26%	63%	11%
• A newspaper has the right to print a story about how to make an H-bomb, even when the government says this story might help other countries make such weapons.	14%	77%	9%
• A Communist has a right to say what he thinks on a television talk show.	61%	29%	11%
• A group of homosexuals has a right to get coverage in a newspaper to argue against laws they feel discriminate against them.	57%	31%	12%
• Members of the Nazi party have the right to get coverage in a newspaper.	49%	39%	11%
• The president has a right to close down a newspaper that prints stories he feels are biased or inaccurate.	22%	69%	10%

And in regard to legislation regulating the media, these were the sample's opinions:

	Favor	Oppose	Not Sure
• A law requiring television news to give major party candidates such as Democrats and Republicans the same amount of coverage.	81%	15%	5%

	Favor	Oppose	Not Sure
• A law requiring newspapers to give major party candidates such as Republicans and Democrats the same amount of coverage.	82%	12%	6%
• A law requiring newspapers to give coverage to third parties such as George Wallace's American party.	63%	24%	13%
• A law requiring newspapers to give opponents of a controversial policy as much coverage as those in favor of the policy get.	73%	17%	10%
• A law requiring television news to give opponents of a controversial policy as much coverage as those in favor of the policy get.	74%	18%	9%
• A law requiring newspapers to give coverage to groups such as homosexuals who feel that certain laws discriminate against them.	42%	43%	15%
• A law prohibiting newspaper stories that embarrass the president, the government or the country.	26%	67%	8%
• A law prohibiting television news stories that embarrass the president, the government or the country.	29%	62%	9%
• A law prohibiting newspaper stories that many people feel are biased or unfairly criticize a prominent person.	24%	60%	16%
• A law prohibiting television news stories that many people feel are biased or unfairly criticize a prominent person.	27%	56%	17%

These data imply considerable public support for freedom of expression; however, it must be remembered that the United States is in a period comparatively lacking in ideological tension, and that only three decades have passed since Joseph McCarthy. It is striking that one out of five people thinks the president has a right to shut down a newspaper he believes is biased or inaccurate, and that about one out of four favors laws prohibiting newspapers or television news that embarrasses the president, government, or country, or that many people feel is biased or unfairly criticizes a prominent person. A decided majority—between 73% and 82%—favors a law requiring both television and newspapers to give equal coverage to the two major party candidates and to opponents and advocates of a controversial policy, and about two-thirds favors such equality legislation for third parties.

Given the low salience of the mass media as a public issue in the United States, it would be wrong to view these data as reflecting a well-formed, coherent public opinion. What they represent is the opposite: ignorance of the legal basis of mass media policy in the United States, and a body of diverse impulses that impose on the media the responsibility of educating the public if they are to survive with their freedoms.

CONCLUSION

Examination of public opinion and behavior in regard to the mass media in the United States offers an exhilarating catalogue of paradoxes and seeming conflicts. It also offers a basis for expectations about the media of the future, for they will be the products of audience responses more than of technological feasibility.

The slower-than-anticipated adoption of cable, the failure of various specialized quality programming services, and the marginal financial health of many cable services were predictable. The bases for this statement are that television viewing is largely time-determined rather than program-determined; popular entertainment is what is expected of television; and the public has been on the whole satisfied with broadcast television, which is free once a receiver is purchased. New technology is a necessary and not a sufficient condition for change in the media, as is illustrated by the failure of videodisc players as entertainment devices and the public's indifference to videotext and teletext (Rice, 1984; Winett, 1986).

The adoption of new media and their displacement of old media rest on their meeting audience needs and interests. Theater movies survived after the introduction of television (although at about one-fifth of the earlier level of attendance) because there remained a substantial number of people—largely teenagers and young adults—who either wanted entertainment different from what was available on television or desired a social activity not provided by a TV set in the living room. Very often, media serve diverse functions, and new media may cater to one at the expense of another and thus fail to find widespread or quick acceptance. As one example, the electronic delivery of newspapers to the home, with information either displayed on a television screen, or reproduced by a printing device allowing the consumer interactively to select the content he or she wants, is technologically feasible. Such electronic newspapers serve the informational motive for newspaper reading superbly. However, they are not only far more expensive than conventional newspapers, but they are unlikely to serve the entertainment motive met by casual perusal of a newspaper's printed pages (Winett, 1986).

The networks can look forward to decades of health, and the cable business to slow growth. In terms of acceptance, cable, with its fees, has more in common with print media and especially books and magazines than with broadcast television. Cable apparently is now perceived by many people as adding little of importance to what broadcast television brings into the home; thus its penetration slows once cable-ready subscribers are enlisted. The decreases in the sales of comic books and in the public library circulation of fiction titles that are attributable to the introduction of television (Cook & Campbell, 1979; Parker, 1960, 1963) exemplify one process by which one medium affects another: functional displacement, or the providing of old satisfactions by superior means. For cable to displace network programming, there must be an increase in the proportion of the public who expect cable services from television; and this very likely must wait on new generations growing up in cable-subscribing households.

The videocassette recorder (VCR) stands in sharp contrast to cable. Its rate of adoption has proved more rapid than cable (Rogers, 1986); VCRs are currently present in about 40% of households, and there will soon be more VCR-equipped than cable-subscribing households. So far, however, VCRs appear to take only a negligible amount of time from broadcast television viewing (Nielsen Company, 1986). Playing of rented or purchased cassettes is apparently supplementary to viewing broadcast television; and use of VCRs to record broadcast material in order to view it at more convenient hours represents only a small fraction of time spent viewing television, and the VCR then complements the broadcast medium. If cable is more comparable in usage to certain print media than to broadcast television, VCRs are analogous to hi-fi or stereo. On one hand, they represent intriguing "gear" offering the promise of pride and pleasure in various features and technical supremacy; on the other hand, like stereo and hi-fi, they make possible private scheduling of a far richer as well as more personal program log. Given the success of its audio analogue, the triumph of the VCR should not have been a surprise.

Cable, Home Box Office (HBO), and other pay options will not within decades—if ever—offer a diversity of programming meriting the labels "high quality," "serious," or "cultural." Popular entertainment is what the public expects from television—broadcast or cable—and the audience that wants something different is not large enough to make such programming financially viable. Certain specialized kinds of vicarious experience will remain the province of other media and circumstances—the movies (which will reach cable), the stage, books, magazines, and recordings.

Network programming will change in response to competition from cable and related services. The fact that deciding *what* to view is largely secondary to the decision *to view*—that is, the predominance of available time over available programming—means that the broadcast audience will choose from whatever is available on the air, while the audience with cable available conceivably could choose broadcast television instead. Thus the tastes of the cable audience—more upscale economically and educationally, and younger—will have a sizable role in network programming decisions.

Pressure groups will never bring significant changes to television because boycotts or other anti-media campaigns have little chance of success. Self-selection has already divided the public into those who attend and those who do not attend to any specific offering of the media, and those who choose to attend presumably find more satisfaction than revulsion in doing so. In general, the low salience of the media as a public issues makes anti-media campaigns unlikely to succeed. In the specific case of television boycotts, available time is such a powerful determinant of viewing, and individuals so consistently choose the same program when they do view at a given time, that it is hard to imagine the exhortations of a political, religious, or social leader having much influence.

The media have little to fear from the public in regard to First Amendment issues in the present social and political climate. The public's criticism of the news media, though easily elicited, is undercut as a source of hostility by the low salience of the media themselves as public issues; most people are not particularly concerned about the behavior of the media. The media, however, are wise to be wary. They cannot escape being perceived as biased, and the First Amendment's rights of free speech are poorly understood.

The mass media will occupy an increasingly prominent place in everyday life. Time has proved elastic as regards the ability of people to fit increasing amounts of media into their lives (Caplow, Bahr, Chadwick, Hill, & Williamson, 1982), and the media themselves have increasingly become most cost-effective. In industrialized societies, most leisure time is devoted to the media, and most of that to television. In the United States, as elsewhere, average daily viewing has increased steadily since the early years of the medium (Comstock et al., 1978; Robinson, 1972; Szalai, 1972). Such developments as cable, pay-TV, in-home recording and playback, and satellite transmission can be expected to further these trends. Whatever our view of the media may be, we can expect that they will be with us and we with them increasingly.

REFERENCES

Barwise, T. P. , Ehrenberg, A.S.C., & Goodhardt, G. J. (1982). Glued to the box? Patterns of TV repeat-viewing. *Journal of Communication, 32*,(4), 22-29.

Bogart, L. (1981). *Press and public.* Hillsdale, NJ: Lawrence Erlbaum.

Bower, R. T. (1973). *Television and the public.* New York: Holt, Rinehart & Winston.

Bower, R. T. (1985). *The changing television audience in America.* New York: Columbia University Press.

Caplow, T., Bahr, H. M., Chadwick, B. A., Hill, R., & Williamson, M. M. (1982). *Middletown families.* Minneapolis: University of Minnesota Press.

Comstock, G. (1982). Violence in television content: An overview. In D. Pearl, L. Bouthilet, & J. Lazar (Eds.), *Television and behavior: Ten years of scientific progress and implications for the eighties: Vol. 2. Technical reviews* (pp. 108-125). Washington, DC: Government Printing Office.

Comstock, G., Chaffee, S., Katzman, N., McCombs, M., & Roberts, D. (1978). *Television and human behavior.* New York: Columbia University Press.

Cook, T. D., & Campbell, D. T (1979). *Quasi-experimentation.* New York: Rand McNally.

Dahlgren, P. (1980). TV news and the suppression of reflexivity. In E. Katz & T. Szecsko (Eds.), *Mass media and social change.* Newbury Park, CA: Sage.

Dolan, J. T. (1984, November). *A crisis of confidence in America's media.* Paper presented at the World Media Conference, Tokyo, Japan.

Gans, H. J. (1979). *Deciding what's news.* New York: Pantheon.

Gerbner, G., Gross, L., Morgan, M., & Signorielli, N. (1985). Living with television: The dynamics of the cultivation process. In J. Bryant & D. Zillmann (Eds.), *Perspectives on media effects.* Hillsdale, NJ: Lawrence Erlbaum.

Gerbner, G., Gross, L., Signorielli, N., Morgan, M., & Jackson-Beeck, M. (1979). The demonstration of power: Violence profile No. 10. *Journal of Communication 29,* (3), 177-196.

Gergen, D. R. (1985). The message to the media. In M. J. Robinson & A. Ranny (Eds.), *The mass media in campaign '84* (pp. 64-67). Washington, DC: American Enterprise Institute.

Gitlin, T. (1980). *The whole world is watching.* Berkeley: University of California Press.

Heath, L. (1984). Impact of newspaper crime reports on fear of crime: Multimethodological investigation. *Journal of Personality and Social Psychology, 47,* 263-276.

Heath, L., & Petraitis, J. (1984). *Television viewing and fear of crime: Where is the mean world?* Unpublished manuscript, University of Minnesota.

Hennigan, K. M., Heath, L., Wharton, J. D., Del Rosario, M. L., Cook, T. D., & Calder, B. J. (1982).

Impact of the introduction of television on crime in the United States: Empirical findings and theoretical implications. *Journal of Personality and Social Psychology,42*, 461-477.

Immerwahr, J., & Doble, J. (1982). Public attitudes toward freedom of the press. *Public Opinion Quarterly, 46*, 177-194.

Immerwahr, J., Johnson, J.,& Doble, J. (1980). *The speaker and the listener: A public perspective on freedom of expression.* New York: Public Agenda Foundation.

Lazarsfeld, P. F., & Merton, R. K. (1971). Mass communication, popular taste, and organized social action. In W. Schramm & D. F. Roberts (Eds.), *The process and effects of mass communication* (rev. ed., pp. 33-86). Urbana: University of Illinois Press.

Levy, M. R. (1978). The audience experience with television news. *Journalism Monographs, 55*, 1-29.

Lichty, L. W. (1982). Video versus print. *The Wilson Quarterly, 6*, (5), 48-57.

Lipset, S. M. (1985, April). *The confidence gap: Down but not out.* Paper presented at the Donald S. MacNaughton Symposium on Informing America: Who Is Responsible for What? New York.

Lipset, S. M., & Schneider, W. (1983). *The confidence gap.* New York: Free Press.

LoSciuto, L. A. (1972). A national inventory of television viewing behavior. In E. A. Rubinstein, G. A. Comstock, & J. P. Murray (Eds.), *Television and social behavior: Vol. 4. Television in day-to-day life: Patterns of use* (pp. 33-86). Washington, DC: Government Printing Office.

Lyle, J. (1975). *The people look at public television, 1974.* Washington, DC: Corporation for Public Broadcasting.

Mendelsohn, H. A. (1966). *Mass entertainment.* New Haven, CT: College and University Press.

Neuman, W. R. (1982). Television and American culture: The mass medium and the pluralist audience. *Public Opinion Quarterly, 46*, 471-487.

Newspapers are public's favorite ad medium. (1975). *Editor and Publisher*, March 29, p. 12.

Nie, N. H., Verba, S., & Petroccik, J. R. (1976). *The changing American voter.* Cambridge, MA: Harvard University Press.

Nielsen Company (1986). *1986 Nielsen report.* Northbrook, IL: Author.

Parker, E. B. (1960). *The functions of television for children.* Unpublished doctoral dissertation, Stanford University.

Parker, E. B. (1963). The effects of television on public library circulation. *Public Opinion Quarterly, 27*, 578-589.

Patterson, T. E. (1980). *The mass media election.* New York: Praeger.

The people's choice: TV is voted best advertising medium. (1976). *Broadcasting*, January 12, p. 29.

Rice, R. E. (1984). *The new media.* Newbury Park, CA: Sage.

Robinson, J. P. (1971). The audience for national TV news programs *Public Opinion Quarterly, 35*, 403-405.

Robinson, J. P. (1972). Television's impact on everyday life: Some cross-national evidence. In E. A. Rubinstein, G. A. Comstock, & J. P. Murray (Eds.), *Television and social behavior: Vol. 4. Television in day-to-day life: Patterns of use* (pp. 410-431). Washington, DC: Government Printing Office.

Rogers, E. M. (1986). *Communication technology.* New York: Free Press.

The Roper Organization, Inc. (1981a). *Sex, profanity and violence: An opinion survey about seventeen television programs.* New York: Television Information Office.

The Roper Organization, Inc. (1985) *Public attitudes toward television and other media in a time of change.* New York: Television Information Office.

Stauffer, J., Frost, R., & Rybolt, W. (1983) The attention factor in recalling network television news. *Journal of Communication, 33*, (1), 29-37.

Steiner, G. A. (1963). *The people look at television.* New York: Knopf.

Szalai, A. (Ed.). (1972). *The use of time: Daily activities of urban and suburban populations in twelve countries.* The Hague: Mouton.

Vallone, R. P., Ross, L., & Lepper, M. R. (1985). The hostile media phenomenon: Biased perception and perceptions of media bias in coverage of the Beirut massacre. *Journal of Personality and Social Psychology, 49*, 577-585.

Winett, R. A. (1986). *Information and behavior: Systems of influence.* Hillsdale, NJ: Lawrence Erlbaum.

Wright, C. R. (1959). *Mass communication: A sociological perspective.* New York: Random House.

29

PROGRAMMING DIVERSITY AND
THE FUTURE OF TELEVISION:
An Empty Cornucopia?

There has been an explosive growth over the last 10 years in the development of video delivery systems. They include VCRs, cable, new microwave and satellite video broadcast distribution systems, and disk storage technologies (Noam, 1985). Ultimately, perhaps, we will receive television from the phone company via optical fibers (Baer, 1985). As we enter the 1990s, we confront the technological potential for a veritable video cornucopia. But will this technical potential lead to real diversity and new forms of informational and educational programming? I would suggest the scenario that this may not happen at all. If so, it may prove to be one of the tremendous ironies of the media age.

Consider the following proposed law of mass communications: The more video programming that is available, the less diverse the viewing menu of the average audience member. Such a law is certainly counterintuitive, but nevertheless likely to be true. An appropriate analysis must consider the basic economics of the industry and the psychology of mass-audience leisure time use.

Cable TV, often used as a symbol of the video cornucopia, provides a case study. Cable can serve as a conduit for 35, 70, or in some cases 100 channels to the home. Cable entrepreneurs have experimented with a number of very interesting new programming ideas, including 24-hour news, which was to be offered on multiple and competing channels, new formats for cultural television, and a variety of specialized channels for religious, political, sports, and ethnically oriented programming. But due to the economics of the cable marketplace, all the cultural channels failed. Only one of the cable news entrepreneurs has survived. Most of the other services are struggling (*Channels of Communication*, 1986). The critical issue was not technology, but rather the costs of promotion and the basic fact that acceptable prime-time quality television costs approximately $1 million an hour to produce. The bottleneck for video diversity has moved from one of spectrum scarcity to one of production cost (Besen et al., 1984). This is a topic worthy of further research, both by the industry and by communications policy analysts.

Consider also the ratio of entertainment to news programs on cable television. Cable entrepreneurs proudly point to C-SPAN as providing very detailed, very interesting, and much appreciated coverage of the Congress. But in terms of the proportion of new programming available and viewed, news and information programming is a shrinking commodity. Ten years ago, when there were two to five broadcast outlets in most markets, all of them traditionally broadcast local and network news at the dinner hour. That solid block of programming led to rather large audiences exposed to news. With greater diversity now available, fewer viewers are exposed to news. For instance, generally something less than 1% of the cable viewing audience watches C-SPAN at any given point in time. Its availability may be much appreciated, but the competition with pay TV, variety and sports channels, and other entertainment-oriented programming tends to decrease news-and-information viewing and increase entertainment viewing, a curious result of the new technological potential.

The economic pressures on the television networks may have become more intense than ever. For example, in the early, struggling years of its existence, ABC remained far behind in the ratings. At that time ABC relied very heavily on cheaply produced game shows to fill its prime-time schedule rather than attempting to compete with the expensive programming formats of NBC and CBS. Now, it is interesting to note that ABC's new president has indicated in a highly publicized article that they are looking again at cutting production costs as a way of dealing with the current economic pressures (Abrams, 1985). The availability of new sources of video programming puts competitive economic pressures on programmers, and that may lead *away from* an increase in quality, diversity, or freedom to experiment with new educational and prosocial formats.

We are witnessing an unfortunate squeeze play that often works against diverse network programming. Although there are many citizens with strong interests in politics and informational programming, who revel in its availability and take advantage of the new forms of video programming, they present a small fraction of the total audience. This fragment of the audience is one that used to rely on print media, on libraries, books, and magazines—often on journals of opinion that might have total national circulations of only 5,000 or 10,000. But in the future, the video informational content that was shared in common between the smaller politically oriented and information-oriented audience and the mass audience may get squeezed out as more and more people are watching movies and entertainment programming.

Thus the smaller audience with particular interests in public affairs and cultural programming may have to shift to VCRs and seldom-watched cable channels to follow their interests (Neuman, 1986).

Another element that may be lost, and possibly the most important one, is the sense of public trusteeship, which was a central element of the 1934 Communications Act. Then it was clear, because of spectrum scarcity, that only a few broadcast voices would be heard, and therefore the radio and later the television networks had a very special public obligation not to misuse this scarce public resources. This led to the tradition of Edward R. Murrow and others, who rose to the challenge of bridging the gap between the mass and elite audiences. Now, with the theory that marketplace competition rather than government policy is the way to serve the public interest, the view of broadcasting as a public trustee is often submerged under the pressure of competition. What is needed in the modern media environment is a new model of public trusteeship, a new combination of entrepreneurship and experimentation that will build on new technological potentials to serve the full range of audience interests (Geller, 1986).

A relevant concept here comes from the often-cited article by George Miller (1956) "The Magic Number Seven, Plus or Minus Two." In early research investigating the number of factors a subject could consider simultaneously in making a decision, the number was found to be about seven in study after study. Similarly, the number of cable channels that are actually watched by the average individual is approximately seven or a little more (Lemieux, 1983). The limits in individuals' decision making are such that, when they sit down in front of the television set looking for the least objectionable program, they do not even consider viewing all of the channels available.

Ironically, the technique most often recommended to overcome the constraints of habitual media behavior is extensive, and usually expensive, promotion. For example, one of the very few times when public broadcasting had higher ratings than the commercial networks was for a widely acclaimed science program titled "The Body Human." But, in this case, the Atlantic-Richfield Company (ARCO) had invested millions of dollars in advertising and promotion for the program as a special experiment. The experiment worked, demonstrating that there is a window of opportunity; but one has to concentrate great advertising efforts in order to get substantial public attention for programming that might be regularly available but would otherwise be seen by only 1-2% of the population.

Future research on the new media ought to consider the interactive influence of technology, economics, and media psychology. New forms of public policy and private initiative will be necessary if the technological promise of the new media is not to become an empty cornucopia.

REFERENCES

Abrams, W. (1985, September 23). Cost reduction hit television business. *Wall Street Journal*, p.6.

Baer, W. S. (1985). Telephone and cable companies: Rivals or partners in video distribution. In E. Noam (Ed.), *Video media competition* (pp. 187-213). New York: Columbia University Press.

Besen, S. M., et al. (1984). *Misregulating television*. Chicago: University of Chicago Press.

Channels of Communication. (1986, March). In focus: Cable. 5 (6), 44-52.

Geller, H. (1986). *Sorting out the options for public policy*. New York: Aspen Institute, Wye Woods Television Policy Project.

Lemieux, P. (1983). *The multi-channel media environment*. Cambridge, MA: Massachusetts Institute of Technology, Future of the Mass Audience Project.

Miller, G. A. (1956). The magic number seven, plus or minus two. *Psychological Review, 63,* 81-97.

Neuman, W. (1986). *The paradox of mass politics*. Cambridge, MA: Harvard University Press.

Noam, E. M. (1985). *Video media competition*. New York: Columbia University Press.

JOHN P. BLESSINGTON

30

FUTURE VISIONS
OF TELEVISION

In discussing future visions of television, I will rely on personal experience as the foundation of my projections. My view of the future concerns the practical application of technology, and it comes from my experience as an educator for the 20 years prior to my joining CBS 7 years ago.

For many of those years as a teacher and a school head, I listened to how awful commercial television was and how it was to blame for so much of what is bad about youngsters today. It struck me as unlikely that even this extraordinary technology could alter so greatly the course of human evolution. My experience suggested that the formation of intellectual ability was mostly based on genetics and environment, and that television was merely a tool used well or badly by the individual. Also, I saw little of what became common plaints about addiction to television. When I ran a boarding school, I saw addiction to drugs and alcohol; but never did I meet, then or since, a child addicted to television.

If this theory of addiction to television were true, I would have offered to buy each student at the boarding school a color television set, because I could then have thrown a master switch and gotten them into their rooms at night (like drawing moths to a light). This would have saved us from chasing them around the mountains at night, trying to stop them from doing things that were clearly dangerous to their well-being.

My task when I came to CBS was to work with parents, educators, and institutions to make television a more friendly and useful experience. People are so worried about its bad effects (as they see them) that they don't have much skill or experience in using the technology to enrich or assist learning among youngsters. It is very interesting to stop asking "What does television do to children?" and ask "What do children do with television?" This reversal allows for more objective

AUTHOR'S NOTE: This chapter is a revised version of an informal oral presentation.

observation, and it doesn't tend to prejudge television effects or increase our sense of inadequacy about child rearing practices.

When you watch children watching television, you notice that they engage in a number of other activities at the same time; for instance, they may fight, talk, eat, and even sleep. They are very much like adults who iron, cook, read, balance checkbooks, and sleep, but still say, "I was watching television last night."

One program I worked with at CBS—the television script reading program—was designed to allow teachers, parents, and children to extend the value of a program beyond recreational use. Each year we have scripts for a few programs printed in a newspaper format, and our affiliates distribute them, with an instructional guide, free to teachers. (In the program's 10 years, over 33 million scripts have been printed.) Of course, it isn't wrong to use television for recreation, but people seem so fearful of it that CBS thought it would be useful to help people extend its uses and learn how television could be a resource for education.

When I first went to CBS, I could hardly concentrate on my job because everywhere I went in the company, people wanted to talk to me about their children. They wanted to discuss their reading problems, school life, college choices, and behavioral adjustment. It was not surprising to find that the people in this business were like everyone else: concerned about rearing the next generation with some wisdom and grace. We all feel responsible for our children—as we should—and working in television does not lessen our personal concerns and commitment.

The Future

What will the video resources of the future be, and what will be our future relationship to television? I suspect not very much different than the past and present. It is likely that people will continue to argue and disagree about television and its value, because many of our convictions have a religious or philosophic base rather than an empirical foundation. People differ in interpreting a glass as half full or half empty when they each see the same amount of fluid in the glass. It is unlikely, therefore, that in the near future we will agree about television as a social system of mass communication.

It is likely that in the future we will see more choice and sophistication in the use of television technology, and these will work their way into family life and into the schools. The networks and others will offer still more materials like the script program, but I would not claim that they will make any major difference in education. There will be a more direct educational effort made by television producers, and some of it will be in short forms such as the 60-second "An American Portrait," "The American Treasury," or "We the People" spots that you see on CBS. I suspect that these quick instructive presentations inform people in a useful way.

"Sunday Morning," the program with Charles Kuralt, is one of my personal favorites. It uses a long form, with some pieces as long as 20 minutes. The program has a second-cup-of-coffee style, which fits the leisurely pace of Sunday. In the future, I suspect, we will create some other good long-format programs like this one and, together with the short-form pieces, we will have more for the public to draw on as informational resources.

In the next decade or two, it is my hope that we will find ways to be a bit more civil and more able to laugh about our different views regarding commercial television. This is desirable since there is little to be gained by the intensity and, at times, implied moral superiority of some of the discussions in the past.

When I came into television from teaching, people asked whether it was a difficult transition. Actually, it was easy because I was accustomed to being defensive; people blame a lot on the schools and a lot on television. I never believed that educators and schools were so responsible for the bad things in American society—as if they were separate from society. Therefore, it is easy for me to exercise the same caution regarding the criticisms of television.

Our moral values come from the home, not from television; and the values found on television tend to be the same as the values of our culture. Criminals are bad guys, unfaithful spouses are sinners, and they pay for their sins by a life of guilt or diminished capacity. Children, despite the common complaint, are never just set down in front of a television set without their parents. Our parents are in our heads all the time—they do not have to be in the room. Even as a mature adult, I have the voice of my parents, my teachers, and my church in my head. Values are formed within our psychic boundaries and our conscience, and television cannot erase them any more than books can erase them.

Even after years of studying, observing, and questioning, I do not know what children get out of watching television. While I do have some suspicions, if not evidence, these lead me to suggest we ought to be slow in forming negative judgments about media effects. Even when we think we are seeing something clearly, we should be cautious about drawing negative conclusions. The other day, I saw a picture of the police arresting some protestors at the Library of Congress who were protesting because recent federal budget cuts had forced a reduction in the number of hours the library would be open to the public. It would be unwise, upon seeing this picture, for any of us to jump to the conclusion that those arrested were addicted to reading and that reading had distorted their sense of law and order and their respect for authority and made them violent.

My past experience also makes me cautious about not overestimating television's potential or what it will do for education and our children. I once petitioned my school board for money for electronic language labs with study carrels to instruct 20 students at a time. We were going to make our students all bilingual or trilingual. Years later, the carrels, with the addition of some wire, were used as hutches for our school rabbits. So much for the latest equipment and our innovative ideas!

The oral tradition is the oldest instructional form, and not even the invention of the printing press has changed our style of pedagogy very much. The future will bring us much new technology and many additional resources for learning—maybe even a TV set that will fit under one's eyelid. However, it is also likely that in the future people will be discussing the latest technological inventions, arguing and disagreeing about their effects and value. In the future, since human nature is so set, it is likely that teachers will stand up in front of classrooms and talk, because they will be more comfortable talking rather than using any new technology. They will be much more comfortable with the old, just as I am.

QUESTIONS AND ANSWERS

Q: I want to talk as a viewer about the use of time. I agree that time is probably the preeminent thing that determines how much we watch, and the advent of VCRs has been pretty revolutionary in that regard. I got a VCR 2 years ago, and as a result I watch a lot more television than I watched before—and I think I'm not atypical. I can watch David Letterman even though I don't stay up at night. I can watch soap operas even though I work during the day. At first I found it very disorienting to watch "Hill Street Blues" on a Saturday because I would see news clips for things that were already past, but that doesn't bother me any more. I'm now used to watching things irrespective of the night when they appear. And I can squeeze time: I fast-forward the title, and I zap through commercials. I think a lot of people do that, and as more homes get more VCRs, that will become more typical. I'm not used to sitting through an hour of television anymore without being able to go at my own pace. Is anybody studying that? I think that is significant, and is going to bring big changes.

W. Russell Neuman: There's a special issue of the *American Behavioral Scientist*, published in the summer of 1986, edited by Mark Levy at the University of Maryland, which has about half a dozen articles on VCRs and their social impact.

George Comstock: I agree with your perception of the VCR as a revolutionary device in terms of our media behavior. It is the sole thing that may change the public's relationship with television, because it teaches selectivity. VCRs may change the face of television.

Q: What is significant to me, and surprised me, is the satisfaction I get from having control. Now the TV is more like a magazine or a book where I control the pace. If I receive a phone call, I can watch the rest of a program the next day. And even though I love "The Cosby Show" and watch it every Thursday night when it airs, now I'm not used to getting through those commercials, and that's a new frustration for me which I didn't have before.

Q: It seems to me that one of the issues about whether television will be better in the future is whether people can distinguish what might be better or worse in programming. In local TV news, there are at least two styles that seem to try to take advantage of the viewer rather than to address any of the viewer's needs. One is the newscast that shows all the fires and murders that you can find, so that the viewer's emotions are aroused, and they don't seem to inform the viewer at all. The second style is one that omits all the reporters except the two anchors, and every story is 25 to 30 seconds long. By the end of a 30-minute newscast, the viewer almost needs an oxygen bottle because things have gone so fast and seemed so exciting, but in fact it wasn't all that exciting—it was just the same old news. There seems to be anecdotal evidence that, at least in the short term, those newscasts succeed and bring in viewers, and make a lot of money. Is there evidence that in the long term the viewers, or some subset of viewers, finally say, "I think I'm being taken advantage of here, and I'm going to switch the channel"?

George Comstock: Sadly enough, I don't know of any evidence to suggest that such exploitative techniques of television news in the long term turn viewers off. I think most of the evidence would suggest that people come to accept any media approach they are exposed to, and they unthinkingly accept that that's the "right" way to do it. So I don't think you can look toward falling ratings or audience dissatisfaction as the solution to such news techniques. Instead, you have to look to news people to stand up for the way they think things should be done, and to find ways to do them that will also pay off in acceptable ratings, because that's the nature of the medium.

Q: I think we need to keep working for social activism, even though all the wise heads tell us that we can't do anything about big social problems. I was told in graduate school, when I was going to do a dissertation on smoking, "Oh, you'll never do anything about smoking in this country." We were told that we couldn't do anything about drinking—remember prohibition? My question to the broadcast industry people is, All of you who are just regular fellows, who are interested in your kids' learning disabilities and so on, aren't you *embarrassed* by some of the stuff on TV? *Honestly?*

John Blessington: Honestly, I am embarrassed by a few things on television. I am also embarrassed by a few things about my church. But honestly, I am embarrassed also to think of my own behavior as a teacher, where I'm sure I caused more direct violence on the playground, both by being boring and not being very understanding. I can accept descriptions of television as "exploitative" and "greedy" because people wouldn't trust us if we didn't admit that such things sometimes happen. But I hope you realize that those who work in television *are* ordinary people, interested in the same values as the audience. Therefore, to continue our work, either we must be schizophrenic, or else our experience must lead us to see a different reality about television than our critics see.

I bring a lot of personal beliefs and wishes to my work. I did that in education and I do it now. But I also bring a respect for religious and political pluralism, and it alters my judgments, so that I accept differences in taste. Though I do find some television content unpleasant, when I mention those things before an audience, people tell me that they have a right to view such material in their homes, or to read it in the print media. I accept that, and I'm not worried about it. I think a certain tension of values is good, but I am concerned that we should retain civility and a sense of perspective. I certainly don't feel that I have to go to confession every night because I work in television.

Q: At a meeting of the Association for Media Psychology, with a group of network artists, producers, and directors, I raised the question of internal professional standards. Psychologists and other professionals have internal monitoring to prevent excess or improper behavior in the profession, and I think that the television industry and the people who work in it should adopt similar safeguards.

John Blessington: A lot of people in the television industry *are* responsible for internal standards, take them very seriously, and consider themselves to be doing a decent job. But that does not mean they satisfy you personally, nor do they always satisfy me or even themselves. We spend an awful lot of time getting criticized by producers for not letting them say and do things on television that they think are part of their prerogative as writers and presenters of the arts. But we look out at the audience and think, "People will be grossly insulted by this, even if there is a First Amendment, or even if there is a lot of this going on in our society." I find television rather conservative compared to other communication in the society, but I also find it upsetting to see certain scenes on the TV screen when I am viewing with my kids. But then, I also found going to "A Chorus Line" with my youngest sons somewhat embarrassing.

Q: How can those of us who care about television standards promote the kind of activism and responsibility that will improve the quality of television? What scares me is the number of hours of passive television viewing by people around the world. The average child viewer watches TV around 2½ hours a day, and adult viewers even more. What is this viewing replacing?

George Comstock: I don't honestly think that we can do a great deal to change the media. This may seem a radical view, but as a business, as an industry, broadcasting is about as responsible as major corporations and other institutions in our society. It is made up of educated, caring, concerned, responsible people, who continually strive—as the money wasted on unpopular programs sometimes proves—to be quite creative and constructive. I think there is a flaw in our society in that we are very far from achieving our human potential in terms of discrimination and judgment. As a result we don't distinguish between what's popular and what's socially valuable, what is successful and what is truly admirable. So we make folk heroes out of publishers of magazines such as *Hustler*. We think what's popular has to be good because it's popular. We think what's profitable must be meritorious because it's profitable. And we're confused in terms of where to give our respect. We need to learn that the fact that I laugh at something, the fact that I enjoy something, does not indicate that it's socially redeeming or valuable. It may be trash. However, I think we are evolving toward better discrimination.

The factors in the media that influence behavior can be summarized as efficacy, normativeness, pertinence, and susceptibility. The media manipulate those factors, but other aspects of society manipulate them to much stronger degrees. If one wants to protect people against the violence in the media, it needs to be done through teaching people— children and adults—other ways of coping with problems: teaching them that violence against someone of the opposite sex is not a proper way to behave; teaching them that violence is ugly and repugnant. In other words, we can manipulate through other means the reactions that the media may manipulate to a small degree. I think the improvements we make in the media can only come from improvements in the way we treat each other and in the way we raise our children and the values that we have. The media in the end are really reflective of those things in our society.

W. Russell Neuman: One suggestion I would make to the challenge of how activists might approach the media, especially the new media, is to take control over the media yourselves. One catch there is that you have been thinking about broadcast television with audiences of 30 to 40 million households, where the production costs are roughly a million dollars an hour. But in fact, you can buy a VHS video tape recorder and, if your local channel has a time-base corrector, you can broadcast or transmit over a cable system and thus explore and experiment with new formats of fiction and nonfiction. Of course, you would expect very small audiences. But if, after trying ten things, you discover one that tends to work well, the audience will grow. The first people to see it will be the people that are very interested in new formats in television. And to the extent that you've discovered something new that might even be commercially viable, it will start to stimulate experimentation in the professional broadcasting and film community. Thus you may be able, by example rather than simply by critique, to influence the way in which the broadcast television industry works.

John Blessington: I agree that an important issue is coming to know the technology so that it is not so mysterious. Bill Paley and David Sarnoff did not found this technology, they don't own it, and they ought not to. When we all learn to accept this technology as, for instance, we accept photography, we won't be afraid of it, and we won't worry so much about it—that's my expectation and hope. For example, I think we'll learn that network television news, and even the local news, is essentially a headline-paragraph-one system. That's all it's able to be under the mass formula. In entertainment, we all watch and enjoy some television programs that others find distasteful or boring. That's like the specialty magazines and journals, and as we come to understand this over the years ahead, I think we won't be so fearful of television. My children, and the students that I taught, are much more the generation of video and film than we are. After another generation, I think we will probably clear away most of our apprehension about television—but never our concern about the social problems of our society!

PART
VI

Epilogue and Overview

In this part, Professor Elihu Katz presents a final chapter that ties together many of the threads of earlier sections. In it he first mentions many of the issues that have arisen in media research—for instance, how should media content and the values inherent in media be studied? How important are program structure and pacing? How active or passive is the viewer? How much does television present reality, and how is television related to social change? Next, Katz gives a historical sketch of various conceptual ways of understanding mass media effects. These range form the conclusions of "no effects," through the use of key intervening variables to explain why media effects are limited, to several theories that posit differing kinds of powerful effects of the media.

Katz proposes that research should emphasize the concept of viewers' involvement, which is linked to their social roles, the social context in which the viewing occurs, and the emotional as well as cognitive effects of the media. He illustrates this approach with two studies of his own that attempt to focus on viewer involvement. One study is a cross-cultural comparison of how Israeli viewers understand and decode the meaning of a major U.S. entertainment program, "Dallas"; the other is a study of viewers' behavior as they watch live broadcasts of historic occasions. Though these are atypical viewing situations, both studies illustrate ways in which television can engage viewer involvement on a number of levels.

In his summary, Katz suggests several guidelines for future research on mass media effects: Television should be conceptualized and studied not just as a medium of social influence but as a medium of entertainment, much as cinema has been treated by students of literature and the humanities. We should pay attention to the social roles, the viewer involvement, and the emotion that are often important in viewing. And we should look for converging evidence from various different theories in order to attain a more rounded picture of the effects of mass media.

ELIHU KATZ

31

ON CONCEPTUALIZING MEDIA EFFECTS:
Another Look

This chapter is addressed to several different audiences: to broadcast media workers, to communication researchers, and to interested individuals who wish to appraise the findings of communication research. In it I first mention a number of themes or issues that have come up repeatedly in the preceding chapters. Then I describe some of the attempts by communication researchers to conceptualize the effects of mass communication, and finally I examine some of the problems of such conceptualization.

Issues in Media Research

One interesting issue that arose was how we should study media content. Should we study content quantitatively by counting or averaging, or are there critical moments that grab us and have an effect far beyond most of the regularly repeated stimuli, which we normally quantify and weight equally in our research? This is a famous issue in content analysis. It was expressed by Bradley S. Greenberg (this volume) as the difference between the "drip-drip" view of media effects and the "drench" view.

Another issue is, Where should we seek the communication's message or value? Where does it inhere: in the text, in the program, in the genre, in the medium? In the preceding chapters there are several references to the structure or the pacing of a program. Is that a message? Is that a value?

Indeed, how do we determine the values in a program? Barbara Lee (this volume) described the application of Rokeach's value scheme to television programs. But who does the reading or interpretation of those values—the researchers or the viewer?

Also, how should one characterize the viewer seated before the TV set? Is he or she in the role of a family member, or of an active consumer of a product, or of a passive recipient after coming home tired at night? Are there special roles that change people's responses to the media? The chapter by Ellen J. Langer and Alison Piper emphasizes mindfulness versus mindlessness as an important factor that influences the way people respond to the media.

Another issue discussed was, Does television represent reality? I submit that nobody really wants it to. It shouldn't, it doesn't, and it can't.

Likewise does television lead or follow social change? Does it retard social change? Should some portion of it try to advance desirable social changes?

Finally, what about television research? Are its methods adequate? How can it help us to answer some of the above questions? Those are some of the main issues that the preceding chapters have raised and that I will address at least briefly.

There are many conflicting views of media effects. We researchers get rewarded in various ways for saying the media are totally ineffective, and we get rewarded—sometimes even by the same people—for saying that the media are omnipotent, they're all-powerful, they're to blame for everything.

If you read the research reviews—the most recent is McGuire's (1986), in George Comstock's new series—you generally find conclusions of "no effect." McGuire has reviewed many different areas—not just violence—and he finds only trivial effects. If that's correct, which many researchers would dispute, you might conclude that the thing that keeps mass media researchers going is trying to reconcile our gut feeling that there are major effects of media with the fact that we can't find them.

This really is an interesting problem, and enough of a mystery to keep us working. Fortunately we're not alone in this, McGuire consoles us. Students of the effects of education and of the effects of psychotherapy haven't gotten any farther and yet, as McGuire says, that doesn't keep them from getting up early in the morning to go to their analyst, nor stop them from sending their children to school. If we followed McGuire's conclusions, all the ad agencies should close, politicians should stop buying television time, and so on.

Research on Media Effects

Here I will briefly sketch the history of efforts to conceptualize mass media effects.[1] We began mass media research with a study of publicity campaigns, that is, an assessment of short-run attempts to influence or to change opinions, attitudes, and actions. That research didn't show any dramatic results—nothing like the results that early students of mass communication had anticipated. As political scientists, as sociologists, as social psychologists, they were interested in the process of remote social control, but they didn't find very much of it in the study of campaigns.

What they did then was to open the black box and ask, "What's going on inside the person?" They identified a set of intervening variables, factors, that come between the message and the hoped-for response, to try to explain where the message is stopped or thwarted, and why it sometimes gets through and has an impact. The two intervening variables that seem to me most interesting, and to which I have devoted a lot of attention, are selectivity, which is central to much of social psychological research, and interpersonal communication, the fact that people talk to each other.

Selectivity is interesting because it suggests a more active audience than does the original mass-society theory from which communications research was derived. Whereas mass-society theory posited an atomized society made up of powerless and passive individuals, the idea of selectivity indicates that the audience is more active in negotiating with the message. Similarly, the idea of interpersonal relations opposes the image of the atomized, alienated, disconnected individual with the notion that people are (still) connected to others in their primary groups. Thus we began to reconceptualize the notion of media effects in terms of their interaction with interpersonal networks and interpersonal norms. There arose traditions of research, some bigger and some smaller, that have taken up questions different from the issues of how the media tell us *what* to think.

One example of such a research tradition is diffusion research, which in a sense conceptualizes the media as showing us *when* to think— when a particular view will be fashionable, so to speak, or when it is our turn to adopt it. Diffusion research posits that influence takes time and moves through mass media and interpersonal channels. Gratifications research, on the other hand, builds on the idea of selectivity. It doesn't really deal with media effects directly, but rather with the idea of choosing from a menu of media offerings those that can serve one's own needs. A third research tradition, knowledge-gap research, suggests that communication on a particular issue—trying to overcome the starting gap between two classes or two groups, one of which is more advantaged than the other—may result in the advantaged group becoming still *more* advantaged, even though both groups progress in their knowledge. That tradition of work seems to be asking the question *who* should think, not *what* to think and not *when* to think. Finally, socialization research is really asking the question of what to believe, which is close to the issue of what to think, but socialization research looks at a much longer time span in conceptualizing the effects of message and training. These research traditions are all studying limited effects, because they each invoke the intervening variables of selectivity and/or interpersonal relations in trying to explain the effects being investigated.

Theories of Powerful Media Effects

There have been three contenders in recent years positing *powerful* effects—that is, the idea that earlier research has been misleading and that media effects can be reconceptualized and shown to be powerful. One was the so-called agenda-setting tradition (e.g., Shaw & McCombs, 1981), which stresses that effects research should study, not the role of the media in *what* we think, but in what we think *about*. A second contender stressing the motion of powerful effects is what I call a media-effects or technological tradition. Consider McLuhan (1964), who proposed that the media tell us not what to think, not what to think about, not when to think, not who should think, but *how* to think. This viewpoint suggests that the different media differentially affect the functioning of our brains, and thus the effect of mass communications resides in the medium and not in the message. Third, perhaps the most interesting contending theory of powerful effects derives form an ideological tradition. It stems form the so-called critical school of Horkheimer and Adorno, the Frankfurt school, but it only recently has found some expression in empirical work. The two major examples, which I'll discuss shortly, are George Gerbner and Elisabeth Noelle-Neumann.

Appraising these three traditions that have proposed a revival of the idea of powerful effects, I will make a few brief comments about each. One can say that agenda-setting has retreated and become another tradition of limited effects; it has very quickly had to take account of selectivity and interpersonal relations in trying to explain how the mass media put an issue on the agenda of society. The media-effects viewpoint is still extant, but it is very unresearched since it's so difficult to operationalize McLuhan or Innis or Ing or Goody or Eisenstein for social-psychological research. It is very difficult to study the role of the mass media in affecting cognitive processes of the deepest kind— activating one hemisphere of the brain at the expense of the other, for example—particularly in the short run. Consequently this theory has been very little studied; but notice that it is the classic example of what I mean by a powerful effect, in that it doesn't require recourse to intervening variables such as selectivity or interpersonal relations to explain media effects.

Turning to studies from the ideological viewpoint, in recent years we've had attempts to operationalize some of the critical thinking of the Frankfurt school. George Gerbner's work is perhaps the best example (e.g., Gerbner, Gross, Morgan, & Signorielli, 1979, 1982). He says, in effect, that mass-society theory is more applicable today than before because television shuts people into their homes—he says they're afraid to go out anyway—and, disconnecting them from direct access to other people or to direct experience of their environment, it sends them a distorted message about reality, of which television itself is the only witness. Moreover, it has a monopoly, in that all of television is sending messages that are essentially the same, leaving little chance for individual selectivity. And television is talking to atomized people, connected to the TV set but not to each other.

Noelle-Neumann (1984) in her theory is slightly more sociological, but it's the same formula, except that the conspiracy she perceives is of the left. Noelle-Neumann thinks of the media not as a rightist mafia but as a leftist mafia, trying to promote unwanted change—and incidentally, preserve the myth of an opposition—whereas Gerbner sees them as supporting the status quo maintained by the established powers in society. Her theory suggests that journalists collude with each other monopolistically in order to distort reality, thus reducing the possibility of any kind of individual selectivity because they provide no variety from which to choose. By shutting people off from each other, the media become the sole reference group. People use the media to scan the distribution of opinion in society, and they find their own opinion to be either popular or unpopular. Since they are without recourse to other interactions or other reference groups, the scanning tells them whether to speak or not. The decision not to speak is thus a function of the extent to which they expect to be rejected by public opinion as reflected in the mass media. People may hold to a unpopular opinion, but if the media represent their opinion as unpopular, they won't *express* it, according to Noelle-Neumann. They won't speak out and won't recruit others to their position—thus creating a "spiral of silence."

According to the ideological effects viewpoint, the media do not tell us what to think, or how to think, or when to think, or who should think, but rather what *not to think*, or in the case of Noelle-Neumann, what *not to say*. This accords well with the Frankfurt school tradition, which suggests that the media influence us not to think about certain subjects that the elite would not like us to contemplate. For example, we should not have thought that women's place is anywhere but a home, as the mass media depicted it for so many years. How social change nevertheless takes place, such as the one we've seen in women's roles, is a question that troubles the critical tradition, because theories of hegemony don't provide for such changes.

In my previous article on this topic (Katz, 1980), I tried to show how the two variables, selectivity and interpersonal relations, not only help to define limited effects and powerful effects, but also provide threads that can tie these varied research traditions together. Thus the idea of selectivity, central as it is to the study of campaigns, takes us to the active audience of uses-and-gratifications research, and from there into knowledge-gap research, which posits a selectivity based on people's prior cognitive frameworks and differential capacities to absorb new information. Similarly, the idea of interpersonal communication leads form the study of campaigns to the study of diffusion, to study of the role of the media in socialization, and it continues into agenda-setting research, and so on.

Under the influence of mass-society theory, mass communication research seemed very different from other areas of communication. However, when tempered by the concepts of interpersonal relations and selectivity, study of mass media effects can be reconnected with some of the classical concerns of other humanistic and social science disciplines—for instance, how Christianity was spread in the first century, or how an archeological artifact or cultural pattern moves from one society to another, or how the folklore of children spreads around the world without benefit of mass media communication. The reintegration of these different disciplines is a healthy development.

Reconciling Media Research Findings with Our Gut Feelings

By and large, as McGuire (1986) has summarized, the research findings to date have not provided clear demonstrations of powerful media effects. So researchers must continue to struggle with the question of how to reconcile the research findings with our gut feeling that there are big effects—still the same question. The only answer seems to be to open the black box once more, to look at processes within the individual, and to accept the complexity that common sense and research tell us is there. A good formulation of television's complexity was presented by Aimée Dorr (this volume), who described an interaction among effects involving a complex viewer within a complex social situation. We simply must accept that complexity, however messy, however difficult it is to accept. At the same time we have to consider a lot of questions about how to think about communication. What is the text? Where do values inhere? Who is the viewer addressed by the text? Who is the viewer in fact? What role is he or she playing? What is the immediate viewing context? What is the nature of the society within which the viewer is decoding the message?

In an effort to conceptualize these last thoughts, I want to propose the concept of "involvement," which is related to the varieties of viewing experience and the roles assumed by viewers. This is not a clear-cut concept, since it obviously incorporates the concepts of selectivity and interpersonal relations, yet it is more than both of these. It contributes a social context to these abstract intervening variables. As examples, consider the findings that children viewing a television film at school will learn different things than viewing the same film at home (McCormack, 1984); that villagers in India's SITE experiment preferred developmental information to entertainment (UNESCO, 1981); and that Israeli children learn more from television than American children do (Salomon & Cohen, 1977). Each of these examples suggests that people's expectations of television, and the viewing experience implicit in the social roles and social contexts in which viewers find themselves, are important determinants of television effects.

Effects, of course, need not be limited to the cognitive effects discussed so far. Indeed, a badly neglected effect in research on mass communication is that the media may tell us how to *feel.* And they may situate us in certain *roles*—family members, consumers, students, farmers, or citizens. For historical reasons, mass communications research has mostly studied cognition. It is partly because of its roots in propaganda studies, in the interests of advertisers of politicians, and in the interests of researchers in cognitive opinion and attitude change, that we have largely neglected the idea of feeling, of emotion, of affect (whether as a prerequisite to cognitive change or as an impressive effect in itself); and of role. If television can make hundreds of millions of people feel something, that's a powerful effect—and one that's very neglected in our research. An example is the integrative effect of mass communication—the way in which the mass media can sometimes make the society feel as one. These points aren't original—I didn't invent them; but they are neglected conceptualizations of effect. They are both in Charles Wright's (1959) list of the functions of mass communication, but we simply haven't done very much about them.

ILLUSTRATIVE STUDIES OF
MEDIA INVOLVEMENT

I want to illustrate this notion of "involvement" or "role" by describing two studies on which I have been working over the last few years. I believe that both of these projects lead in the direction of more powerful effects, albeit via the intervening variables of viewer involvement, context, and role. They are not necessarily representative of everyday broadcasting; instead they involve deviant case analysis— that is, studying the exception in order to understand the rule. One of these is a cross-cultural study of "Dallas," and the other is a study of historic media events.

"Dallas"

Our study of "Dallas" (Katz & Liebes, 1985; Liebes & Katz, in press) was a poor man's cross-cultural study. We showed an episode of "Dallas" to focus groups containing 3 couples of homogeneous ethnicity, meeting in a home. We drew 10 groups from each of four ethnic communities in Israel—Arabs, Jews of Moroccan origin, new immigrants to Israel from Russia, and kibbutz members. Another 10 groups were drawn from second-generation Americans in Los Angeles. After the episode was shown, we asked them first to retell it in their own words as if they were telling it to somebody the next morning. Then we asked them what motivates the characters, and what does the episode say about America? We asked them, "Are they trying to tell us something, and if so what?" and so on. These are questions not about media effects but about understanding: What is the message? Who is the viewer? Does the message get decoded the same way in different cultural settings? Is it understood at all? (It is subtitled in Israel, by the way, in two languages, Hebrew and Arabic.) Or is the message only the pretty pictures and the pretty girls?

The answer, briefly, is that *a* story was understood, but not the same story. There were interesting differences among the ethnic groups. It seems that the decoding is a process of what has been rightly called negotiation between what the viewer brings to the story and what the story brings to the viewer. Also, there is a lot of mutual aid in decoding, with people relying on each other. In each of these 6-person groups there seemed to be an archivist, who reported where a particular character came from, or what happened in the previous episode. There was a lot of conversation about the program; this is true not only within our constructed groups, but also in everyday life, as we know from asking background questions about when and how and with whom the participants discussed the program. There was an active comparison of the viewers' own situations with what they see on the screen—a constant mental commuting between the fictional television and real life.

People in our study were *very* involved in the program, but there seemed to be two patterns of involvement. One pattern is an involvement with the reality of the program, and the other is an involvement with the program as a construction, as a work of art, as something that somebody planned and wrote and produced.[2] The more traditional groups saw the program as more real, but even critical groups related to the program as real to a large extent. However, the latter, more Westernized groups also tended to see the program as an artistic construction.

Thus if we asked viewers, "Why all the fuss about babies?" some people would say, "because those are very rich people, they need heirs, and what's the use of making all that money unless you have somebody to give it to," and so on. Other people—or sometimes the same people wearing a critical hat—would tell you, "Babies are very good for conflict between parents, and conflict is very good for a soap opera." Thus there are two wholly different ways of looking at the same thing. It is interesting from a cross-cultural point of view to see the ratio of those different kinds of statements within each of the groups, and also the ways in which the more critical viewers, the viewers who see it more as a construction, play with it "ludicly" (Stephenson, 1954)—that is to say, they take roles. "If my son were a bank robber, would I drive the getaway car?" asked a woman rhetorically in response to J. R.'s attempt to enlist Miss Ellie in his scheme to kidnap his baby back from the abductors.

I'm suggesting that we need to look at patterns of involvement. In reopening the black box, we need to look at the way in which viewers get involved in particular roles, with particular identities, with the text as they read it, and in particular social situations. Then we must raise the question of the relationship between involvement and effect, the answer to which is not obvious. Some researchers, Krugman (1971) for example, have suggested that people are most affected by mass communication when they are *least* involved, when the stimulus is mostly in the background rather than directly engaging their attention. On the other hand, one might argue that a playful, lucid kind of involvement, a poetic kind of involvement if you will, is in itself so engaging that it makes the involved person vulnerable, perhaps even more so than those who treat the program as real. However, the best bet, I feel, is that the people who treat a story as real are most affected by it.

This argument speaks to the hypothesis of cultural imperialism. At first glance it may seem ridiculous to posit that alien values can infiltrate even through media that are merely intended as entertainment. However, a case can be made that those most culturally remote from the locus of the program in Dallas, Texas, are more likely to think of the program as real. As a result, they may become involved in a kind of negotiation wherein they question themselves by comparison with the presumed reality of the program, and in the process allow the alien values—or at least the alien issues—to drip into their cultures. So our study of "Dallas" is one example of research on a potentially powerful media effect.

Broadcasts of Historic Events

The other example comes from our studies on the live broadcasting of historic occasions (Katz & Dyan, 1985). "The High Holidays of Mass Communication" is one of our subtitles. These media events include Sadat's coming to Jerusalem, the Pope's pilgrimage to Poland, the astronauts landing on the moon, the Kennedy funeral, the Olympics, the Watergate hearings, and other "historic ceremonies" in which the media interrupt the flow of our lives. They say, "Stop everything! We take you away from your regular schedule of living, away from our regular schedule of broadcasting, to something you can't afford to miss." People do stop and watch when these programs are on, and they expect others to do so. What's more, they dress up (rather than undress) for the occasion. They celebrate, they invite friends, they serve refreshments, they respond affectively. They do all of the things that some theorists would suggest are not typical of everyday television viewing. They're not tired, not boozy, not otherwise occupied, not just letting the programs flow onward. They're intent, they're concentrated, they are with others, they are discussing, they contemplate values that the event brings into focus. The Challenger explosion would be a recent example. In addition, viewers take a role as they participate: the role of citizen, the role of mourner at the Kennedy funeral, the role of fan for the World Cup or the Olympics, the role of loyal subject at the Royal Wedding, and so on. They are participating, not just as television viewers, not just as family members, not even as consumers, but in socially definable roles that have some of the quality of mindfulness that Langer and Piper's chapter in this volume described. At the very least they adopt the participant role of saying "amen." To Jews a blessing isn't complete unless somebody says "amen," and this role is also found in television viewing.

The three crucial partners in a ceremony—public opinion, broadcasters, and organizers—are equally involved in the making of a media event. In his book *Adventure, Mystery, Romance,* John Cawelti (1976) calls this process a "contract"—a contract among authors and audiences to make a particular genre move, be successful, have an effect.

Possible Implications

If you look at these two research programs as possibly dealing with deviant cases, you have to take a position as to what everyday television is like. Is the typical experience of viewing like that? If not, how are these experiences different? It's clear in these two cases that people are really *watching programs,* not just passively receiving a continuing media flow. They're concentrated, they are with others, they are playing roles, and they are participating in ways that are rather different, we think, from everyday television. It is possible that these conditions may obtain only rarely.

Here I would suggest that we should move closer to the humanities and try out a viewpoint that can augment the social science approach to mass communication. We can learn something from students of cinema and of literature.

God divided the world such that he gave cinema to the humanists and television to the social scientists. The humanists, students of cinema and of literature, are concerned with texts, whereas the empirical study of television only rarely looks at texts. We count acts of violence or role portrayals, or the use of bad language or whatever, as if these *were* the text. But the idea of the text as a narrative, as a story, is often neglected. And it's only because God divided the world this way that television is defined by social scientists as an agency of influence, involving cognitive effects, rather than as an agency of affect and involvement. If you go out on the street and ask anybody what television is about, they will *not* tell you that it's about changing opinions, attitudes, and actions. They *will* tell you that it's about entertainment, about pleasure. The psychoanalytic study of cinema— since cinema theory is informed by psychoanalytic theory, for better of for worse—is about pleasure, about regression, about positioning the viewer at some prior point in his psychogenetic development, which allows him to watch the film in a particular way. Whether you like that idea or not (and I suppose many of us social scientists might not like it), the idea of finding a role that is typical for audience members, and in which the text helps position you, is part of the heritage that we now have from cinema studies (e.g., Houston, 1985). Now that cinema researchers are moving into television, because mainline cinema has now moved into television, we may both get and give some new ideas about involvement, affect, role, and effects.

Summary

What can be learned from all this? First, we should study television not only as a medium of influence but also of entertainment. Second, we should study the interaction between viewers and texts as a complex process in which social roles are implicated. We should examine microscopically the types of readings of different texts that occur for viewers in different roles. Third, we should study patterns of involvement, study emotion, study the sense of attitudes, and actions—both in themselves and as elements in the process of media effects.

Fourth, we should be aware of the usefulness of converging evidence from different types of theory. I mentioned cinema theory, and I want to mention another hopeful reconciliation between different types of theory. We are, I think, witnessing an interesting convergence between the so-called dominant paradigm in mass communications theory and the critical paradigm. The dominant paradigm—let's use the gratifications expression of it—is that the viewer is so sovereign that there is virtually no text. The text is like a projective test, into which the viewer reads his or her needs and in which he or she finds gratifications. That extreme position is really ridiculous! For instance, it says that the *New York Times* is just as useful for pornography as for any other purpose. Such "vulgar gratificationism," I hope, is now expiring, and a more sophisticated awareness of the text and the interaction between the viewers' needs and the supply of messages is occupying gratification researchers (Blumler, Gurevitch, & Katz, 1985). For instance, Blumler (1983) points out that if you watch a political campaign as a spectator sport, you will learn something different that if you watch the same campaign in an attempt to reach a decision, or in an attempt to get ammunition for use in arguing against the other side.

On the other hand, critical research has been interested only in texts and not in audiences. This was not because they weren't interested in message effects on audiences, but because they thought they could *read* effects from the text itself and know what the effect would be just from their own content analysis. If the message was clear, they felt, why bother to study effects empirically? Hegemonic messages impose themselves relentlessly on defenseless viewers—that has been the view of critical research until just lately. But now some leading critical researchers—Stuart Hall (1980) and his colleagues in England (Morley, 1980) are a prominent example—are actually watching real viewers decode television news, and they're looking at readings that they call "dominant" versus readings that they call "oppositional."

The interesting thing is that there's a convergence: The gratificationists are becoming interested in texts and their influence, not only as messages but as ways to position viewers in roles, while at the same time the critical theorists are becoming interested in actual readings, in real viewers. Why critical theorists are changing in this way is itself an interesting question. One reason may be because you can't predict or explain any kind of social change using a hegemonic theory; so if indeed there has been a change in the image of women in the media, as researchers have told us, that is a reason to study how people decode hegemonic messages oppositionally, and how their opposition perhaps then feeds back to the program makers (Fajes, 1984). Similarly, you can't predict a revolution on the basis of critical theory, because it cannot explain how the leaders of the revolution could have seen through the dominant media texts and realized that they are a manipulation. However, if researchers can recognize manipulations, why can't some others in the audience recognize them also?

That brings me to my last point about conceptualizing media effects: Don't underestimate the viewer. Viewers in the "Dallas" study were very good at making critical statements, often not less sophisticated than those you can read in the press or hear in academia about the construction of the program and about its message. For example, the Russian Jews, coming straight from Russia to Israel (and learning that in order to be Israelis they have to watch "Dallas") were asked, "What is the message of the program? Are they trying to tell us something?" Together with the other groups, they say, "Yes, they're trying to tell us that the rich are unhappy." "But," they add, "don't believe it; it's a manipulation; it's what they want us to believe."

NOTES

1. I draw heavily in what follows on Katz (1980). For full bibliographical references, see that paper.

2. This distinction between "real" and "critical" follows Jakobson's (1980) distinction between "referential" and "metalinguistic." Neuman's (1982) terms "interpretive" versus "analytic" and Gross's (1985) "life" versus "art" are analogous. Clearly, it would be desirable to settle on some agreed nomenclature.

REFERENCES

Blumler, J. G. (1983). Communicating to voters. Newbury Park, CA: Sage,
Blumler, J. G., Gurevitch, M., & Katz, E. (1985). Reaching out: A future for gratifications research. In K. E. Rosengren et al. (Eds.), Media gratifications research: Current perspectives. Newbury Park, CA: Sage.
Cawelti, J. (1976). Adventure, mystery, romance. Chicago: University of Chicago Press.
Fajes, F. (1984). Critical mass communications research and media effects: The problem of the disappearing audience. Media, Culture and Society, 6, 219-232.
Gerbner, G., Gross, L., Morgan, M., & Signorielli, N. (1979). The demonstration of power: Violence profile No. 10. Journal of Communication, 29, (3), 177-196.
Gerbner, G., Gross, L., Morgan, M., & Signorielli, N. (1982). Charting the mainstream: Television's contributions to political orientations. Journal of Communication, 32, (2), 100-127.
Gross, L. (1985). Life vs. art: The interpretation of visual narratives. Studies in Visual Communication, 11, 2-11.
Hall, S. (1980). Encoding/decoding. In S. Hall, D. Hobson, A. Lowe, & P. Willis (Eds.), Culture, media, language (pp. 128-138). London: Hutchison.
Houston, B. (1985). Television: The metapsychology of endless consumption. Quarterly Review of Film Studies, 8, 183-195.
Jakobson, R. (1980). Linguistics and poetics. In R. deGeorge & F. deGeorge (Eds.), The structuralists: From Marx to Levi-Strauss. New York: Anchor/Doubleday.
Katz, E. (1980). On conceptualizing media effects. In T. McCormack (Ed.), Studies in communication (Vol. 1). Greenwich, CT: JAI Press.
Katz, E., & Dayan, D. (1985). Media events: On the experience of not being there. Religion, 15, 305-324.
Katz, E., & Liebes, T. (1985). Mutual aid in the decoding of "Dallas." In P. Drummond & R. Patterson (Eds.), Television in transition (pp. 187-198). London: British Film Institute.
Krugman, H. (1971). Brainwave measures of media involvement. Journal of Advertising Research, 5, 3-9.
Liebes, T., & Katz, E. (in press). Patterns of involvement in television fiction: A comparative analysis. European Journal of Communication, 1.
McCormack, T. (1984). Content analysis: The social history of a method. In T. McCormack (Eds.), Studies in communication: Vol. 2. Culture, code and content analysis. Greenwich, CT: JAI Press.
McGuire, W. J. (1986). The myth of massive media impact: Savagings and salvagings. In G. Comstock (Ed), Public communication and behavior (Vol. 1). New York: Academic Press.
McLuhan, M. (1964). Understanding media: The extensions of man. New York: McGraw-Hill.
Morley, D. (1980). The "nationwide" audience: Structure and decoding. London: British Film Institute.
Neuman, R. (1982). Television and American culture: The mass medium and the pluralist audience. Public Opinion Quarterly, 46, 471-487.
Noelle-Neumann, E. (1984). The spiral of silence: Public opinion—our social skin. Chicago: University of Chicago Press.
Salomon, G., & Cohen, A. A. (1977). Television formats, mastery of mental skills, and the acquisition of knowledge. Journal of Educational Psychology, 69, 612-619.
Shaw, D. L., & McCombs, M. E. (Eds.). (1981). The emergence of American political issues: The agenda-setting function of the press. St. Paul. MN: West.
Stephenson, W. (1954). A play theory of mass communication. Chicago: University of Chicago Press.
UNESCO. (1981). The S.I.T.E. experience (Reports and Papers on Mass Communication, No. 91). Paris: Author.
Wright, C. (1959). Mass communication: A sociological perspective. New York: Random House.

AUTHOR INDEX

SUBJECT INDEX

ABOUT THE AUTHORS

JOHN ABEL is Executive Vice-President for Operations of the National Association of Broadcasters. Formerly Professor and Chairman of the Department of Telecommunications at Michigan State University, he is the author of more than 50 articles and books and has served as a consultant for the Federal Communications Commission and numerous radio and television stations.

GORDON L. BERRY is Professor of Educational Psychology in the Graduate School of Education at University of California, Los Angeles. He received a B.S. degree from Central State University in Ohio, an M.A. from the University of Wisconsin, and an Ed.D. from Marquette University. His main research interests are in the areas of counseling psychology and media and social behavior. He has served as moderator of the TV show "Challenging Youth," and his latest books include *Television and the Socialization of the Minority Child* and *Strategies for Teaching in Urban Schools.*

JOHN P. BLESSINGTON is Vice-President for Broadcast Relations with the CBS/Broadcast Group. Formerly Headmaster of the Whitby School, and an educational and family life consultant, he has authored *Let My Children Work.*

GEORGE COMSTOCK is the S. I. Newhouse Professor of Public Communications at Syracuse University. He received his B.A. in journalism and economics from the University of Washington and his M.A. and Ph.D. in communications from Stanford University. He has worked as research director of a Peace Corps research project on an instructional television network in Bogota, Colombia, as Science Advisor and Senior Research Coordinator for the Surgeon General's Scientific Advisory Committee on Television and Social Behavior from 1970 to 1972, and later as a senior social psychologist for the RAND Corporation. Among his best-known volumes are *Television and Human Behavior, Television in America,* and a new annual series titled *Public Communication and Behavior.*

HELAINE DOKTORI is Director of Compliance and Administration in the Program Practices Department of the CBS/Broadcast Group.

AIMÉE DORR is a Professor in the Graduate School of Education at the University of California at Los Angeles. Trained in psychology at Stanford University, she previously held academic positions in communications and education at Stanford, the Annenberg School of Communications at the University of Southern California, and Harvard University. She is a media researcher and author of *Television and Children: A Special Medium for a Special Audience.* She has been a consultant for production groups, PBS action groups, industry self-regulatory groups, and the Federal Communications Commission.

HALFORD H. FAIRCHILD received his Ph.D. in social psychology from the University of Michigan. He has taught at the University of California, Los Angeles, and at the

California Institute of Technology. He is currently President of the Association of Black Psychologists in Washington, D.C.

NORMA DEITCH FESHBACH is Professor of Education and Psychology and Chair of the Department of Education at the University of California, Los Angeles. She earned her B.S. and M.S. degrees at City College of New York and her Ph.D. in clinical psychology at the University of Pennsylvania. Before coming to UCLA, she taught and conducted research at the University of Colorado, University of California, Berkeley, Stanford University, and the University of Pennsylvania. She has directed many research grants, written over 80 papers, and been elected President of the Western Psychological Association.

SEYMOUR FESHBACH is Professor of Psychology and former Chairman of the Psychology Department at the University of California, Los Angeles. He has written extensively on social policy issues and has a long-term interest in the effects of media violence. His early experimental field study was reported in the volume *Television and Aggression* (coauthored with Robert Singer). He has explored the influence of television aggression when viewed in a fantasy versus reality context, and has recently completed a longitudinal study of the relationship between television viewing and children's psychological adjustment. Currently President of the International Society for Research on Aggression, he has also served as a consultant to CBS and NBC on children's television programming and the effects of TV violence.

JONATHAN L. FREEDMAN received his B.A. from Harvard, and M.A. and Ph.D. from Yale. He has taught psychology at Stanford and Columbia, and is now Chairman of the Psychology Department at the University of Toronto. He has done research on attitude change, dissonance theory compliance, crowding, the effects of time pressure, and the relationship between viewing television violence and aggression. His continuing concern is with environmental stress, from crowding, time constraints, and over- and under-stimulation. He received the American Psychological Association's Media Award in 1975 for his book *Crowding and Behavior* and is the author or coauthor of several well-known texts and research volumes.

IRA GLASSER is Executive Director of the American Civil Liberties Union. He earned an M.A. in mathematics at Ohio State University and taught at Queens College and Sarah Lawrence College. Formerly Editor of *Current Magazine*, he is the author of many articles including "Making Constitutional Rights Work" and "The Coming Assault on Civil Liberties."

BRADLEY S. GREENBERG is Professor of Communication and Telecommunication at Michigan State University and Chair of the Department of Telecommunication. His research has centered on the social effects of the mass media, and he has three times served as researcher/consultant to different Surgeon General's committees on television and violence, television and social behavior, and most recently on pornography. He has authored *Mass Media and Mexican-Americans,* and recently spent a sabbatical in London as senior research fellow with the Independent Broadcasting Authority.

PHILIP A. HARDING is Vice-President for Social and Policy Research in the CBS/Broadcast Group. Prior to joining CBS in 1969, he earned an M.A. in social psychology from Rutgers University, held advertising and marketing research positions with Dancer-Fitzgerald-Sample, Inc., and worked in the research department of the National Association of Broadcasters. He has served for many years as a department editor of

Public Opinion Quarterly, and a trustee of the Marketing Science Institute, an independent center for research in marketing, and he is now Chairman of the Institute's Executive and Research Policy Committee.

ALICE M. HENDERSON is Vice-President for Sales Services and Development of CBS Broadcast International. She began her career at CBS in the Program Practices Department in 1969, and she was later Vice-President for Program Practices of the CBS/Broadcast Group from 1981 to 1986. She has also been a Trustee-at-Large for the American Women in Radio and Television Education Foundation and is a member of the National Academy of Television Arts and Sciences, International Radio and Television Society, and the American Film Institute.

ELIHU KATZ is simultaneously Professor of Sociology and Communication at the Hebrew University of Jerusalem and Professor at the Annenberg School of Communications of the University of Southern California. He earned a B.A., M.A., and Ph.D. in sociology from Columbia University and has taught at Columbia, the University of Chicago, and the University of Padua. He has authored more than 100 articles and books including *The Uses of Mass Communication* and *Mass Media and Social Change.* He served as the Founding Director of Israel Television from 1967 to 1969, has been a consultant on audience research for the British Broadcasting Corporation, and won a book award from National Association of Educational Broadcasters.

PHYLLIS A. KATZ is President of the Society for the Psychological Study of Social Issues (SPSSI) for 1986-1987 and organized its conference on "Television as a Social Issue," which brought together the authors represented in this volume. After earning a Ph.D in clinical and developmental psychology at Yale, she taught at New York University and City University of New York. She is currently Director of the Institute for Research on Social Problems in Boulder, Colorado, and an Adjunct Professor at the University of Colorado. She is the founder and editor of *Sex Roles: A Journal of Research* and has edited *Towards the Elimination of Racism* and *Eliminating Racism: Profiles in Controversy.*

ELLEN J. LANGER is Professor of Psychology and Chair of the Social Psychology Department at Harvard University. She received her Ph.D. from Yale University, taught at City University of New York and New York University, and has been a Guggenheim Fellow. Her research includes work on perceived control, decision making, aging, health, and mindlessness/mindfulness theory. She has written *The Psychology of Control,* and forthcoming volumes on *Mindlessness* and *Higher States of Human Development.*

BARBARA LEE is Director of Social Research in the Office of the Social and Policy Research of the CBS/Broadcast Group. Formerly she earned an M.A. in sociology at the University of Chicago, and directed studies at Yankelovich, Skelly & White, the Newspaper Advertising Bureau, and International Research Associates. She currently serves on the Executive Council of the American Association for Public Opinion Research, and is the coauthor of *Leading to Reading,* a guide for parents.

DIANA M. MEEHAN graduated from California State University, Fresno, took an M.S. in mass communication at San Diego State University, and a Ph.D. in communication from the University of Southern California. Her scholarly honors include the Western Speech Association Executive Board Award for Research, and a HEW Humanities Grant for feminist scholarship. She teaches in the Department of Media Communications at the University of California, Los Angeles, and has recently published *Ladies of the Evening: Women Characters of Prime-Time Television.*

J. RONALD MILAVSKY is Vice-President for News and Social Research at NBC. He earned a B.A. at Wesleyan University and a Ph.D. in sociology at Columbia University, and he has taught occasionally at Columbia and New York University. Before moving to NBC in 1969, he conducted social research for Columbia University's Bureau of Applied Social Research and for the Prudential Life Insurance Company. He has directed over 300 quantitative research projects, been senior author of *Television and Aggression: A Panel Study,* and is currently serving as President of the American Association for Public Opinion Research.

W. RUSSELL NEUMAN is Director of the Research Program on Communications Policy and Associate Professor of Political Science at the Massachusetts Institute of Technology, and has formerly taught and done research at Harvard, Yale, and the University of California, Los Angeles. He directs the Advanced Television Research Project's Audience Research Group in MIT's media laboratory, as well as the Future of the Mass Audience Project, and he conducts studies of public opinion trends and international communications system. He has authored *The Social Impact of Television* and *The Paradox of Mass Politics: Knowledge and Opinion in the American Electorate,* and he is currently writing a book titled *The Future of the Mass Audience.*

STUART OSKAMP is Professor of Psychology at Claremont Graduate School in California. He received his Ph.D. from Stanford University and has had visiting appointments at the University of Michigan, University of Bristol, London School of Economics and Political Science, and the University of New South Wales. His main research interests are in the areas of attitudes and attitude change, behavioral aspects of energy and resource conservation, and social issues and public policy. His books include *Attitudes and Opinions* and *Applied Social Psychology.* He is a past president of the American Psychological Association Division of Population and Environmental Psychology and the current editor of the Applied Social Psychology Annual series.

ALISON PIPER received her B.A. in psychology from Cornell University and is a doctoral candidate in the Social Psychology Program at Harvard University. She is also the Director of Career Planning Services and a lecturer in psychology at Curry College in Massachusetts. Her research deals with the application of mindfulness theory to televiewing.

THOMAS S. ROGERS is Senior Counsel of the U.S. House of Representatives Subcommittee on Telecommunications, Consumer Protection and Finance. He graduated from Wesleyan University, took his law degree at Columbia University, and worked for a time as an attorney for a Wall Street law firm. He has also served as Legislative Aide to Congressman Richard Ottinger of New York, coauthored "Telecommunications in Transition: The Status of Competition in the Telecommunications Industry," and drafted several recent laws governing broadcasting, cable TV, and communications policy.

FORREST SAWYER has been a CBS News correspondent and co-anchor of the "CBS Morning News," and formerly an anchor and news broadcaster for WAGA-TV in Atlanta. He has won many awards for interviewing and reporting, including an Emmy and a George Foster Peabody Award.

DOROTHY G. SINGER received a doctorate in school psychology from Columbia University, and is Professor of Psychology and former Director of the School Psychology Program at the University of Bridgport. She is also Co-Director of the Yale University Family Television Research and Consultation Center and a Research Affiliate at the Yale

Child Study Center. Her current research involves the effects of television on children, and she has authored numerous books and articles for scientific journals and popular magazines.

JEROME L. SINGER is Professor of Psychology, Director of the Clinical Psychology Training Program at Yale University, and Co-Director with Dorothy G. Singer of the Yale University Family Television Research and Consultation Center. He is the author of many books and technical articles on thought processes, imagery and fantasy in adults and children, and on the effects of television on child development. He has been President of the Eastern Psychological Association and of the American Psychological Association Division of Personality and Social Psychology, and Chair of the American Psychological Association Board of Scientific Affairs.

GLORIA STEINEM is co-founder, editor, and writer for *Ms.* magazine and widely known as a feminist lecturer and organizer. After graduating from Smith College, she lived in India for two years on a fellowship and wrote *The Thousand Indias.* More recently she has authored *Outrageous Acts and Everyday Rebellions* and a new book about Marilyn Monroe, *Marilyn: Norma Jean.* She has been a co-founder of *New York* magazine, the National Women's Political Caucus, the Coalition of Labor Union Women, Voters for Choice, and the Women's Action Alliance. Chosen nine times by *World Almanac* as one of the most influential women in America, she is a contributing correspondent for NBC's "Today" show, and she has received numerous honors and awards for journalism and public service.

CAROL TAVRIS received her Ph.D. in social psychology from the University of Michigan, taught at the New School for Social Research, and is currently a visiting lecturer in the Department of Psychology at the University of California, Los Angeles. With Carole Wade she has coauthored *Psychology* and *The Longest War: Sex Differences in Perspective,* and she has also written *Anger: The Misunderstood Emotion.* She has been an editor for *Psychology Today, Human Nature,* and *American Health,* and still contributes to numerous magazines.

ELLEN WARTELLA is Research Associate Professor in the Institute of Communications Research, University of Illinois at Urbana-Champaign. Recently a Fellow at the Gannett Center for Media Studies, Columbia University, she has also done postdoctoral research at the University of Kansas and taught in the School of Journalism at Ohio State University. She has published research on children's learning from television in a variety of sources, and is working on a book entitled *Electronic Childhood,* a history of public controversies about media and children. She served as a consultant to the Federal Communications Commission and the Federal Trade Commission during inquiries into children's television practices in the late 1970s.

DONALD D. WEAR, Jr., is Vice-President for Policy of the CBS/Broadcast Group and was formerly its Vice-President for Washington Affairs. An attorney, he has also worked for NBC as its European Counsel and as a Vice-President for NBC Sports, and served as Special Assistant to the Chairman of the Federal Communications Commission.

CHARLES WINICK is Professor of Sociology at the City College and Graduate Center, City University of New York. He previously taught at Columbia, the Massachusetts Institute of Technology, and the University of Rochester, and has been research director of the American Social Health Association and the Anti-Defamation League. Among his books are *Dictionary of Anthropology, Taste and the Censor on Television, For the Young Viewer, Trends in Human Relations Research, Children's Television Commer-*

cials, The Television Experience, Sociological Aspects of Drug Dependence, and *The Lively Commerce.*

TIMOTHY E. WIRTH was elected U.S. Senator from Colorado in 1986 and previously served six terms as congressman from Colorado's Second District, during which time he was Chairman of the House Subcommittee on Telecommunications, Consumer Protection and Finance. He earned his B.A. and M.A. at Harvard and a Ph.D. at Stanford University, later serving as Deputy Assistant Secretary of Education. Among his other legislative interests are science and technology, energy policy, and protection of the environment. In Congress, he has chaired Democratic Party task forces on Long-Term Economic Policy and on Promoting Economic Growth and Opportunity.